SKEPTICAL
ODYSSEYS

SKEPTICAL
ODYSSEYS

PERSONAL ACCOUNTS BY THE WORLD'S LEADING PARANORMAL INQUIRERS

EDITED BY
PAUL KURTZ

Prometheus Books
59 John Glenn Drive
Amherst, New York 14228-2197

Published 2001 by Prometheus Books

Inquiries should be addressed to
Prometheus Books
59 John Glenn Drive
Amherst, New York 14228–2197
VOICE: 716–691–0133, ext. 207
FAX: 716–564–2711
WWW.PROMETHEUSBOOKS.COM

05 04 03 02 01   5 4 3 2 1

Library of Congress Cataloging-in-Publication Data

Skeptical odysseys : personal accounts by the world's leading paranormal
    inquirers / James E. Alcock ... [et al.] ; edited by Paul Kurtz.
        p. cm.
    Includes bibliographical references and index.
    ISBN 1–57392–884–4 (hardcover : alk. paper)
    1. Parapsychology. I. Alcock, James E. II. Kurtz, Paul, 1925–

BF1042 .S54 2001
130—dc21   2001019038

Printed in the United States of America on acid-free paper

CONTENTS

5

II. PARAPSYCHOLOGY

III. UFOs

IV. ASTRONOMY AND THE SPACE AGE

V. ASTROLOGY

VI. POPULAR INVESTIGATIONS

VII. CREATIONISM

VIII. ALTERNATIVE MEDICINE

IX. SKEPTICISM AROUND THE WORLD

8   SKEPTICAL ODYSSEYS

X. SOME PERSONAL REFLECTIONS

XI. RELIGION

XII. FROM SKEPTICISM TO HUMANISM

THE FOUNDING OF THE SKEPTICAL MOVEMENT

PAUL KURTZ

I. THE RISING TIDE OF PARANORMAL BELIEFS

This book presents personal accounts of how many of the world's leading skeptical investigators have dealt with pseudoscientific and fringe claims on the borderlands of science. In particular, it examines the growth of paranormal perspectives and the methods that skeptical inquirers have used to evaluate them.

The "paranormal" is a term originally introduced by parapsychologists. It referred to phenomena which allegedly could not be explained by normal scientific means and existed alongside of or over and beyond normal science. Originally, this applied to extrasensory perception (ESP: telepathy, clairvoyance, precognition, and the supposedly related phenomenon psychokinesis), and questions of postmortem survival. J. B. Rhine (1895–1980) was instrumental in this use: though he maintained that normal science was unable to cope with these phenomena, he nonetheless thought that statistical and experimental methods could describe and explain them, and he set up a laboratory to test his theories. Many skeptical questions were raised within the scientific community about this research: If there were significant deviations from normal probabilistic expectations, of guessing runs in Zener (ESP) cards, for example, could they be given alternative naturalistic explanations? Did such anomalous phenomena exist? Were psi phenomena real?

The term "paranormal" was extended in the post–World War II world to still other anomalous events, which to many seemed mysterious and violated natural science and/or could not be explained in physicalist terms.

This referred to a wide range of "demonic forces," which had been popular in the Middle Ages and earlier and came back into vogue—such as possession by diabolical preternatural entities, exorcism, poltergeists, hauntings by discarnate spirits, vampires, werewolves, and other patently mythological entities, now given new reality in the public imagination. This fascination with the occult no doubt was enhanced by the new electronic media—films, radio, and television—which could use effective images, sound, music, and drama—from Boris Karloff and Béla Lugosi to the *X-Files*—and made these phenomena seem real. Thus the lines between fiction and reality were becoming blurred.

Another area in which the creative imagination soared was given impetus by the emergence of the space age, which began after World War II. Indeed, UFOlogy had its inception in 1947 when Kenneth Arnold reported seeing saucerlike objects skipping in the skies over Mt. Rainier in Washington State. As space probes by NASA and Russia accelerated, the popular mass media fantasized about the visitation of our planet by aliens from outer space and future human space travel. Gene Roddenberry's *Star Trek* enabled our imagination to soar. Today tens of millions of people in the United States and worldwide claim to have seen unidentified flying objects, which they attribute to extraterrestrial beings. Three decades ago Erich von Däniken in his popular book *Chariots of the Gods?*[1] postulated ancient visitations, which he claimed to see in the artifacts of ancient civilizations. A great number of UFO organizations and publications proliferated, spewing forth endless bombast and bunkum.

Dr. Edward Condon of the University of Colorado was commissioned by the U.S. Air Force in 1966 to study over twelve thousand cases of UFO sightings. The conclusion was that there was no hard evidence for the claim of extraterrestrial origin. Many disciples of ETI-visitations loudly proclaimed that there was a cover-up by the CIA and other intelligence agencies. Among the bizarre claims was that the space aliens had crash-landed in Roswell, New Mexico, in 1947, and that these creatures were hidden from the public by the U.S. Air Force. (This later was shown to be due to the top-secret Air Force Project Mogul whereby sonar balloons were sent up to detect nuclear testing by the Russians.) Immanuel Velikovsky in *Worlds in Collision*[2] maintained that the planet Venus had swiped Earth and this could account for the parting of the Red Sea and other biblical stories. When Harvard astronomer Harlow Shapley attempted to persuade Macmillan, a reputable publisher of science books, not to publish it, howls of censorship were heard emanating from the disciples of Velikovsky.

In recent years UFOlogy was confronted with many individuals who insisted that they had been abducted aboard these craft, that biogenetic experiments had been performed on them, and they returned to report their experiences. They claim that they were sexually assaulted or transplants were inserted in their bodies. At that time the Bermuda Triangle was also very popular. It was claimed that numerous ships and planes had inexplicably disappeared off the Florida coast and in the Caribbean, and some even attributed this to alien bases on the lost continent of Atlantis under the seas.

Added to this fascination with space, astrology came back into vogue with virtually every newspaper and magazine carrying astrological columns. To complicate matters, Michel and Françoise Gauquelin in France claimed to find new scientific evidence for astrobiology. Although they rejected classical astrology, they claimed that planetary configurations influenced an individual's personality, character, future profession, and destiny. The "Mars effect," postulated a correlation between the position of Mars in the heavens at the time and place of birth and becoming a famous sports champion. This claim was investigated by skeptical scientists in Europe and the United States. Critics of Gauquelin's Mars effect were skewered by his proponents.

The paranormal was extended to other areas: monsters of the deep, such as the Loch Ness monster, and reports of sightings of strange manlike creatures worldwide, such as Bigfoot and the Abominable Snowman. Indeed, anything bizarre or weird was considered to be grist for the paranormal mill—such as Charles Fort's report of frogs raining from the sky. Tabloid newspapers, pulp magazines, book publishers, sensational Hollywood movies, and television shows all fed the public a steady diet of "unsolved mysteries." And there were self-proclaimed psychics, such as Uri Geller, who claimed to have scientific support for his powers, and prophets, such as Jeane Dixon, who became a national figure. This tidal wave of paranormal tales led to wide sections of the public accepting them as the gospel truth and also to a steady erosion of scientific literacy.

Most scientists were horrified by these developments, which they encountered, not only in the mass media, but in the students in their classes and among members of their own families. An occasional scientist from time to time would provide criticisms of such claims—psychologists of parapsychology, astronomers of astrology and UFOlogy—but this was sporadic. There were occasional skeptical books, such as Martin Gardner's important *Fads and Fallacies in the Name of Science* (1952)[3] and Donald H. Menzel's *The World of Flying Saucers* (1953),[4] or *Time* magazine's exposure of Uri Geller; but there was no systematic coordinated scientific effort to examine these claims.

II. THE CREATION OF CSICOP

It is within this cultural milieu as background that I decided to convene a special conference to discuss "The New Irrationalisms: Antiscience and Pseudoscience." This was held on the newly built Amherst Campus of the

State University of New York at Buffalo on April 30–May 2, 1976. I drafted a call inviting a number of leading scholars to the inaugural session of the proposed new organization. This was endorsed by many leading philosophers, including W. V. Quine, Sidney Hook, Brand Blanshard, and Antony Flew. And I invited many of the leading skeptical critics to this opening session—Martin Gardner, Ray Hyman, Philip J. Klass, James Randi, L. Sprague de Camp, and Milbourne Christopher. There were other notable figures at this conference, including Jonas Salk (polio-vaccine discoverer), Ernest Nagel (philosopher of science), and James Farmer (black civil-rights leader). The new organization, which I cochaired with Marcello Truzzi, was to be called the Committee for the Scientific Investigation of Claims of the Paranormal (CSICOP). Out of this emerged the journal the *Zetetic*, which later was superseded by the *Skeptical Inquirer*. One of the reasons why I decided to organize CSICOP was that we had issued a statement, "Objections to Astrology," which was published in 1975 in the *Humanist* magazine which I edited, and which received widespread attention. And I surmised that surely what we did about astrology could apply to all these other unchallenged fields.

We recommended three strategies: (1) Scientists should devote some research effort to investigate these paranormal claims. We asked, "Could these alleged anomalies be given naturalistic causal explanations?" (2) Researchers should bring the results of their inquiries to the attention of the public. We were eager to encourage further research and to publish the findings. (3) Our long-range goal was public education of the aims of science, particularly an appreciation for scientific methods of inquiry and critical thinking.

Surprising to me was the fact that CSICOP and the *Skeptical Inquirer* took off from day one and became an instant success. News of CSICOP's inaugural meeting was extensively covered by the press, including the *New York Times* and the *Washington Post*. We had apparently crystallized a point of view that many, particularly in the science community, felt was long overdue. Many of the major science magazines and scientific bodies in the world welcomed our appearance and endorsed our programs. This included *Science News, Science, Scientific American*, the *New Scientist, Nature, Science & Vie*, etc. Moreover, the media found us so fascinating that they began to call us constantly for information and have not stopped since.

There had been other scientific efforts historically to investigate paranormal claims, such as the Society for Psychical Research founded in Great Britain in 1882 and in the United States in 1885 (by William James). And there had been many UFO groups which came into being in the post–World War II period, such as MUFON and the Center for UFO Studies. But most of these groups mainly attracted believers who were predisposed to accept the phenomena; the skeptics in their midst were few and far between. Thus

CSICOP was the first body made up predominantly of skeptics, who were willing to investigate the alleged paranormal phenomena. We have been attacked by believers for being "closed-minded" and by other skeptics who claimed that we were dignifying phenomena that did not deserve special attention. But we thought that we had an important task to fulfill.

III. WHAT IS SKEPTICAL INQUIRY?

How do present-day skeptical inquirers propose to deal with anomalous claims of the paranormal? Skepticism is surely one of the oldest intellectual traditions in history. It began with Greek philosophy in the fifth century B.C.E., and came to fruition in the Roman Empire when various schools of skepticism flourished. After a long hiatus during the Dark Ages it was rediscovered in the modern era, contributing to the growth of modern science, when scientists and philosophers began the quest for a new method of inquiry. Rejecting appeals to authority, tradition, faith, revelation, and emotion, they sought objective criteria for testing truth claims. Science could advance, they held, by questioning ancient unexamined premises and going directly to the Book of Nature.

Many mistakenly identified skepticism with universal doubt. The term *skeptic* derives from the Greek word *skeptikos*, which meant "thoughtful," "to consider," or "examine," and *skepsis*, which meant both "doubt" and "inquiry." Ancient skepticism was riddled with doubt about the nature of the world, or our ability to know it (for example, Pyrrho of Elis [360–270 B.C.E.]). Modern skepticism was unable to prove a person's own existence, the reality of external objects, the existence of God, or the foundations of ethical judgments (René Descartes [1596–1650], David Hume [1711–1776]). These forms of skepticism emphasized total doubt, which for some became equivalent to uncertainty, indecision, subjectivism, even nihilism.

Complete or universal skepticism took root in the ancient world before the growth of modern science. It was also influential at the beginnings of natural science and the Copernican revolution as skeptics questioned our ability to bridge the mind-body dualism or to know material substances. It became increasingly difficult, however, to defend this brand of skepticism in the face of the impressive strides of science. Both Descartes and Hume attempted to overcome unlimited doubt; and Kant sought to resolve the problems of skepticism and provide secure foundations for scientific knowledge. Since that time science has continued to progress. In the nineteenth century the Darwinian revolution marked daring new explanations for evolution, and in the early twentieth century nuclear physics, quantum mechanics, and relativity theory introduced important new explanatory concepts. In the mid to late twentieth century came the discoveries of DNA, the mapping of the human genome, new theories of consciousness, and the growth of the behavioral and computer sciences. This does not deny that some residual skepticism about the meaning of our scientific theories is relevant. We need always to ask: Do our scientific concepts and theories describe something in the real world, are they simply constructs, or are both interpretations most likely applicable?

The key point for contemporary skepticism today is that skeptical doubt is related to *inquiry*. I have labeled this *the new skepticism*, for it is positive, not negative; constructive, not deconstructive; contextual, not universal. The American philosopher Charles Peirce (1839–1914) pointed out that doubt is an integral part of the process of scientific discovery. We ask questions and seek to answer them, and the most effective way to do so is by using the methods of science, testing hypotheses by experimental verification and inferential logic.

Accordingly, some skepticism is essential in all scientific research. The lesson is clear: we ought to suspend judgment about a claim made until we have sufficient grounds for justifying it. Skepticism and inquiry are integral aspects of the same process; used together they have helped us to develop reliable knowledge. Any claims to knowledge, however, should be amenable to revision in the light of new discoveries of data or the introduction of more comprehensive theories. We need an open mind particularly on the frontiers of knowledge where unconventional or radical theories may be introduced. Recognizing our fallibility, we should be ever-willing to modify our beliefs that do not stand the tests of objective scrutiny—both in science and ordinary life.

Some influential twentieth-century philosophers, such as Heidegger and Derrida, reject science entirely. They consider it to be one mythological narrative among others. These latter-day critics, often not thought to be skeptics, go by the name of postmodernists. They deconstruct scientific concepts and consider them to be "social constructions," not literally true about the world but relative to the social conditions in which they originate. It is undoubtedly the case that scientific theories are related to their sociocultural contexts and perhaps can only be fully understood in the light of them (following Thomas S. Kuhn). But this surely cannot mean that there is no external world out there that we bump into and that enables us to ascertain the adequacy of one set of explanations rather than another, nor that these accounts cannot transcend the partial perspectives of a given sociocultural period. I remember full well debating a postmodernist philosopher at a Dutch university in Utrecht at a conference on the Enlightenment, and asking whether Mars was a social construct or whether it existed, independent of the paradigm imposed by our society. He became very vexed at my question, but conceded "of course Mars exists!" The point is, if all knowledge claims are only relative (to class, gender, society) as they maintain, then so is postmodernism itself, which would contradict its claim to authenticity or universality. In any case, it is difficult to see how this poetic, philosophical indictment can justify its nihilistic appraisal of science in the light of the considerable scientific and technological advances that have occurred. Postmodernist philosophy bakes no bread, nor understands how or why it is done. Science and technology do!

IV. THE AGENDA

There were four controversial issues that CSICOP had to address at its founding. These emerged in the first year and were debated heavily by the Executive Council, its policy-making body.

First, what would be our approach to such phenomena? Would we simply be debunkers out to show by ridicule the folly of the claims that were made, or would we be serious investigators concerned with research into claims; dispassionate, open-minded inquirers? The answer was clear: Our chief focus would be on *inquiry*, not doubt. Where we had investigated a claim and found it wanting, we would express our doubt and perhaps even debunk it, but this would be only after careful investigation.

Second, we asked what would be our relationship to pro-paranormal believers. We observed that there were by now hundreds, perhaps even thousands, of pro-paranormal magazines and publications in the world, and that we were virtually the lone dissenting voice in the wilderness, as it were. We would be glad to engage believers in debate, but it would be our agenda, not theirs. Accordingly, we decided that we wished by and large to pursue our own research strategy, namely to encourage exhaustive scientific and skeptical inquiry. Marcello Truzzi, professor of sociology at Eastern Michigan University, cochairman and editor of the *Zetetic* (founded by him but which we took over), insisted that we present *both* believers and nonbelievers in dialogue in the pages of the magazine, and this he proceeded to do. Although members of the CSICOP Executive Council found this interesting and perhaps useful, they demurred because they felt that there was already tremendous exposure of the pro-paranormalists' viewpoint, and that we really wished to focus on the neglected skeptical case. And so we dissented from Truzzi's wish to provide equal time—*none* of the pro-paranormal magazines provided equal time to skeptics. Truzzi resigned from the editorship of the magazine, and indeed from the Executive Council, and the *Skeptical Inquirer* came into being, edited by veteran science writer Kendrick Frazier, who had covered the first meeting of CSICOP for *Science News*.

Third, one of the most difficult problems that we faced was, What was the relationship of the paranormal to religion? Would CSICOP deal with religious questions? CSICOP was originally founded under the auspices of the *Humanist* magazine, sponsored by the American Humanist Association.

But the Executive Council decided immediately that it would separately incorporate and that it would pursue its own agenda. And so our position has been from the start that we would not investigate religious claims unless there were empirical or experimental means for evaluating them. We were not concerned with religious faith, theology, or morality, but only with scientific evidence adduced for the religious claims. Since the founding of CSICOP, the lines between religion and the paranormal have been fudged, particularly by believers; and in the last decade a whole number of topics formerly under the aegis of religion have been mixed in with the paranormal, such as communicating with the dead, ghosts, the Shroud of Turin, miracles, faith healing, prayer at a distance, intelligent design, etc. CSICOP has attempted to follow its mission—to deal only with those questions for which natural causal explanations could be found—and we have avoided philosophical debates about the existence of God, immortality of the soul, salvation, or biblical criticism. Many skeptics were fearful that we would be labeled as "secular humanists" or "atheists," whereas we wished to welcome anyone into the tent of inquiry, no matter what their religious proclivities. Thus, though many skeptics *are* atheists or agnostics, some, such as Martin Gardner, are skeptics about paranormal claims, yet believers in theism (see Gardner's article in this volume, chapter 31).

This question of whether CSICOP should deal with religious issues may likewise be asked of other fields of inquiry. Should we examine, for example, claims in political, economic, ethical, or social spheres? Obviously we cannot deal with them all, particularly because of the division of labor. We have expertise in the paranormal and we eschew other fields of inquiry, where there is adequate peer review or simply because we may lack trained researchers. I should add a personal note here: in my considered view skeptical inquiry, reason, and science should be applied wherever possible to *all* fields of human interest. (Meanwhile, we have left religion, ethics, and politics to our sister organization, the Council for Secular Humanism, publisher of *Free Inquiry* magazine at the Center for Inquiry.)

Fourth, a most interesting development occurred, and this was totally unexpected: immediately after forming CSICOP, many concerned scientists and skeptics said that they wanted to establish similar local groups in their areas in the United States. Similarly, researchers in other countries said that they wished to do the same. Thus skeptical organizations began forming throughout the world. What this meant was that CSICOP had become an international organization. Since science was international in scope, the critical examination of paranormal claims was also a matter for the international scientific community. This became all the more evident as the years went by, as the media became further globalized and paranormal programs produced, for example, in Hollywood, were exported virtually everywhere. Accordingly, if we were to really do a service to scientific inquiry and cultivate the public understanding of science, then our efforts should be global. Invitations to the staff at CSICOP poured in, asking us to assist in the formation of new groups. Today there are approximately one hundred skeptics organizations in thirty-eight countries and a great number of magazines and newsletters published worldwide, and they continue to grow.

V. ABOUT THIS VOLUME

Since 2001 marks the twenty-fifth anniversary of the founding of CSICOP, I decided to invite leading paranormal investigators from throughout the world to reflect on skeptical inquiry in the past twenty-five years. Interestingly, of the thirty-nine skeptics that I invited, thirty-six accepted—a very high rate of return! I sent out two letters of invitation. The first suggested that the contributors review a specific field (or fields) of investigation in which they were personally involved, and the second suggested that they perhaps give an autobiographical account of their own personal odyssey to skepticism.

It is clear from the responses in this volume that skepticism is not a dry, dull, abstract field; it is very meaningful in the innermost lives of individuals. Although it is a basic tool of all scientific inquiry, and critical thinking is essential to the educated mind, nonetheless it involves some passionate commitment. There is a kind of moral decision required of the skeptic to apply the agenda of skepticism to a field or fields of interest—a resolve not to accept a belief as true unless there is some rational or empirical support for it; and if that is lacking he or she should suspend judgment. Skeptical inquiry, to be effective, must be lived; it must motivate the person to pursue this quest. Often this resolve develops gradually. The scientific inquirer becomes committed to critical inquiry, at least in his field of expertise. There are a number of rules of the game that must be abided by: do not fudge or suppress any data, strive for conceptual clarity, be consistent, be honest about results, have integrity, be willing to modify or reject hypotheses in the light of the evidence, seek open peer review, etc. It is clear that ethical standards are implicit in all skeptical and scientific inquiry.

It is often difficult in society to adopt the life stance of the skeptic. The social principle seems to be against it. There are demands for conformity, acceptance of the sacred cows, and any effort by a skeptic to dig at the foundations of belief is often met with derision or opposition. To apply skeptical inquiry not only to a specific field, but throughout life, constitutes a moral judgment that often requires considerable courage—as is the determination to withstand the barbs of rejection by people offended by skeptical criticisms. This book represents a rather unique project. Heretofore skepticism was regarded primarily as an intellectual epistemological position; it was rarely viewed as an ethical way of life, but it is insofar as it motivates a person to persist. Clearly, for some of the great philosophers and scientists of the past the pursuit of skeptical inquiry was often met with scorn—this was the fate that Socrates, Spinoza, and Galileo suffered; they were martyrs to the cause of free inquiry. Descartes gave an eloquent autobiographical account of his own odyssey from unlimited doubt to reason. Even Hume showed how hard it was to live consistently as a skeptic.

Thus it seemed useful to gather together in one volume statements of how and why people became skeptics and the role that skepticism has played in their personal lives. There are two kinds of essays in this book; first, those that offer highly idiosyncratic quasi-autobiographical accounts of their paths to skepticism; and second, articles that apply skeptical investigations to specific fields—space-age astronomy, astrology, alternative medicine, creation/evolution, parapsychology, etc.

Many of these essays are written from the vantage point of the skeptical inquirers waging an uphill battle to be heard in various countries of the world besides the United States—Canada, Mexico, Spain, Russia, France, Italy, the Netherlands, and India. These highlight the common problems faced by skeptics everywhere as they are confronted with superstition, credulity, intransigence.

We hope that the reader of this book will embark with us upon these various skeptical odysseys. They are pluralistic and diverse, yet they enable the reader to explore the power of skeptical thinking and, I submit, to see its value to any civilized community. They also provide overviews of a significant skeptical movement that has emerged in the latter quarter of the twentieth century as it tries not only to grapple with pseudoscience and antiscience but to defend the integrity and significance of science and reason.

NOTES

1. Erich von Däniken, *Chariots of the Gods?* (London: Souvenir; New York: G. P. Putnam's Sons, 1969).

2. Immanuel Velikovsky, *Worlds in Collision* (New York: Macmillan, 1950).

3. Martin Gardner, *In the Name of Science: An Entertaining Survey of the High Priests and Cultists of Science, Past and Present* (New York: Putnam, 1952). Reprinted as *Fads and Fallacies in the Name of Science: The Curious Theories of Modern Pseudoscientists and the Strange, Amusing and Alarming Cults That Surround Them. A Study in Human Gullibility* (New York: Dover, 1957).

4. Donald H. Menzel, *The World of Flying Saucers* (New York: Doubleday & Co., 1963).

I

TWENTY-FIVE YEARS OF CSICOP

1

FROM THE EDITOR'S SEAT
Thoughts on Science and Skepticism at the Dawn of the Twenty-First Century

KENDRICK FRAZIER

My introduction to the modern skeptical movement came in a letter dated April 15, 1976. I still have it. I was then editor of *Science News*, the weekly newsmagazine of science, in Washington, D.C. The letter said the upcoming annual conference of the American Humanist Association, April 30–May 2, in Buffalo "is attracting international attention and will surely produce ongoing interest and controversy."

I could not have known then how true that statement was. Nor how much my going there would change my professional life forever. For the next quarter century and beyond (I hope), I would be happily caught up in a part of what—for lack of a better term—we might call the international skeptical movement. I prefer to call it scientific skepticism.

"Coincident with the Conference," the letter went on, "will be formal announcement of formation of a new international 'Committee to Scientifically Investigate Claims of Paranormal and Other Phenomena.' This committee is an outgrowth of 'Objections to Astrology,' which created worldwide attention when released in the *Humanist* magazine (September/October 1975). The primary thrust of the Committee will be to '. . . examine openly, completely, objectively, and carefully . . . ,' questionable claims concerning the paranormal and related phenomena, and to publish results of such research.

"We earnestly invite your consideration to covering this important series of dialectic discussions."

The letter said all the conference's Saturday sessions would center on

21

"The New Irrationalisms: Antiscience and Pseudoscience." It listed some of the participants and included a preprint of a formal announcement of the Committee and a copy of the "Objections to Astrology" statement, signed by 186 leading scientists, including eighteen Nobel laureates.

I was very familiar with that statement. The previous fall, we had published it verbatim, in small type, in *Science News* (vol. 108: 166), together with a short news article, "Science vs. Astrology: New Battle, Old War." The statement had immediately generated wide discussion and debate. Said our article, "Unlike many public utterances by large groups of distinguished scientists, the attack on astrology pulls no punches. The statement says the belief that the stars can be used to foretell the future has 'no scientific foundation' and bluntly labels astrologers 'charlatans.' " We spoke at the time with Bart J. Bok, a past president of the American Astronomical Society and lead author of the statement. He told *Science News* he had become disturbed at the increasing interest in astrology among his freshman students at the University of Arizona and confusion between it and astronomy.

The statement had ignited immediate worldwide controversy. Our news article at the time concluded:

"Reaction has been mixed. Astrologers understandably were upset, claiming they had been misunderstood. A *Washington Star* editorial called the statement 'the most futile verbal broadside of recent memory,' but concluded, 'we hope it made the scientists feel better.' Bok says most of his mail has been favorable. Whether any minds have been changed remains to be seen. If astrology could survive persecution by the Medieval Church, it is likely to outlive another scholarly blast."

My years at *Science News* had made me interested in what I called the flip side of science: pseudoscience. In more general terms I was interested in the widespread public interest in fringe-science ideas and the difficulties people have distinguishing what really is legitimate science, especially at its most speculative and fantastic, from equally speculative ideas not anchored in any kind of scientific knowledge or reality. All science editors get letters from readers with new theories of the universe, ideas for new inventions that seem to contradict the laws of physics, and full commentaries on any new speculative ideas reported in science. Some of these come from outright cranks and can be saved in the cranks file or tossed. But many others come from very intelligent people who have a lot of good ideas but don't quite know enough about how science works to connect them to real science, to research and write them up properly, and to get them tested and evaluated. In either case some evaluative function is needed.

The problem is compounded by whatever seems popular and faddish at the time. In response to readers' requests we had published three articles in *Science News* in the mid-1970s that tried to examine in a balanced way some popular claims of the time, such as Transcendental Meditation. But we weren't able to do a very good job at it, I'm afraid. I got a letter from Martin Gardner, gently complaining and wondering if we had changed our policy of covering only genuine science. I knew who Martin Gardner was. A decade earlier a physicist friend had given me a copy of Gardner's *Fads and Fallacies in the Name of Science*, and I had devoured it, fascinated with his keen and amusing insights into the underworld of pseudoscientists and crank scientists. And of course he was famous as *Scientific American*'s Mathematical Games columnist. After getting his letter, I wrote back. I said we hadn't changed our policies, we were only trying to respond to readers' interests in finding out what science knew about the topics in question. But I told him that was difficult. Editors like me badly needed a central resource to go to—a group of scientists and other experts interested in these issues but who, like him, had a critical bent and could help us evaluate fringe claims.

The invitation from Buffalo seemed to announce that very thing.

I flew up to Buffalo and covered this founding conference of what became the Committee for the Scientific Investigation of Claims of the Paranormal (CSICOP). It was one of the most exhilarating times of my life. It was held on the then brand-new Amherst campus of the State University of New York at Buffalo. It was there I first met and talked with Paul Kurtz (then a SUNY-Buffalo philosophy professor, editor of the *Humanist*, and cochairman with Marcello Truzzi of the fledgling committee), James Randi, Philip J. Klass, L. Sprague de Camp, Ray Hyman, Truzzi, philosopher Ernest Nagel, Larry Kusche, and several dozen other prominent participants. At *Science News* I had covered scientific meetings of many scientific organizations—the American Association for the Advancement of Science, American Geophysical Union, Geological Society of America, American Meteorological Society, and others. I had traveled all over and even visited Antarctica and the South Pole. But nothing dealt with people's deepest interests and emotional passions and intellectual misperceptions as the topics—the new irrationalisms—these scholars and experts were examining. I recently wrote about this founding conference again in some detail in my 8,000-word entry on "CSICOP" in the *Encyclopedia of the Paranormal* (Prometheus Books, 1996), edited by the late Gordon Stein, so I won't go into all the substance of it here.

I went back to Washington and eventually wrote a three-and-a-third-page *Science News* cover article, "Science and the Parascience Cults," subtitled, "How can the public separate fact from myth in the flood of occultism and pseudoscientific theories on the scene today? Help is on the way." We had an artist do a neat cover illustration of a knight on horseback spearing a multiheaded dragon. The dragon's heads had symbols for psychic spoon-bending, UFOs, astrology, and the Bermuda Triangle. The cover type read: "Challenging Pseudoscience." It was published May 29, 1976.

Some of the conference participants familiar with the passions these topics raise had warned me to expect a strong reaction to whatever I published, but I was not prepared for what happened. We received more letters to the editor than any previous *Science News* article in memory. Most of the writers commented thoughtfully about the issues of science and pseudoscience. But some were upset, and some considered the committee's effort an attempt by science to squelch mystery, imagination, intuition, and beauty (Paul Kurtz had addressed that very issue at the conference). Two demanded their subscriptions be canceled.

Other national publications also had been there and covered the conference.

So like the Objections to Astrology statement itself, the founding of CSICOP, although most of the scientific community was supportive, aroused controversy and debate, both thoughtful and heated, among the public and in the media. Much the same can be said about CSICOP's expanding activities ever since.

In August 1977, CSICOP held a news conference in New York City in conjunction with a meeting of its executive council, the first since the organizing conference. Here, too, a pattern was established. The committee called the NBC television network to task for credulous pseudodocumentaries on the Bermuda Triangle, Noah's Ark, and UFOs. It criticized the *Reader's Digest* for a number of articles on parapsychology that, said the committee, presented as fact a number of assertions and anecdotes for which there was little or no documentation. The *New York Times* gave the session a full-column article, "Panel Fears Vogue for the Paranormal" (August 8, 1977). It noted that the committee was appealing to the media of mass communications to provide more balanced and objective treatment of such subjects. It quoted an NBC spokesman about the programs criticized: "They are done as entertainment, not as news. We're not presenting them as fact." (This was a response that would become familiar over the years.) The *Reader's Digest* could not be reached by the *Times* science reporter for comment, but later when I wrote an invited feature article for *Smithsonian* magazine on CSICOP and its battle against pseudoscience ("UFOs, Horoscopes, Bigfoot, Psychics, and Other Nonsense," March 1978), the *Reader's Digest* quickly reprinted it in condensed form in all worldwide editions (July 1978).

That August 1977 meeting had been pivotal for me as well. At it I was formally asked to become editor of CSICOP's journal, then called the *Zetetic*, and subsequently the *Skeptical Inquirer*, succeeding Marcello Truzzi. In those first years it was published only twice a year, and I agreed. I have been editor ever since. Although the amount of material published annually and the workload have increased over the years—we went quarterly with the first issue of volume 3, fall 1978, and bimonthly (and to regular magazine format from the original digest size) with the January/February 1995 issue—it has been a pleasure. I feel it a privilege to be editor all these years of what has become the central international journal of scientific skepticism—the worldwide effort to promote scientific inquiry and critical thinking, to evaluate paranormal and fringe-science claims of all sorts from a scientific viewpoint, and to serve as a forum for informed discussion of all relevant issues.

Psychologists, physicists, philosophers (the three leading disciplines represented), academics in all other areas of university life, science teachers, scientific or investigative journalists and communicators, and informed citizens from many walks of life concerned about all these issues together have formed a strong worldwide community. They may have a wide variety of backgrounds and diverse views and approaches, but this is where they find a common bond, and an outlet for publication and discussion. From the small core group of Executive Council members and founding fellows who helped create the original committee, this effort has expanded multifold and worldwide over and over. In fact, the *Skeptical Inquirer* draws upon those with knowledge, insight, and expertise on these issues whatever their formal backgrounds, affiliations, memberships, and nationalities. It crosses disciplines, brings the physical and human-based sciences together, works both inside and outside of academia, draws upon investigative expertise wherever it may be found, and addresses issues of passionate concern to the public and of significance to science, education, and public policy. It is a truly democratic, merit-based movement. Its core unifying values are a respect for the creative and evaluative methods of science, reason, and rationality; critical thinking and judgment; and freedom of thought and inquiry, all applied to important issues that relate to scientific evidence or scientifically testable claims.

When CSICOP and the *Skeptical Inquirer* were founded twenty-five years ago here (in addition to the big-three perennials of psychics, UFOs, and astrology) were four of the hot fringe-science topics that captivated public and media attention: Velikovsky, and his fantastic planetary pinballs, worlds-in-collisions theories to try to explain catastrophic events in biblical times; Erich von Däniken, and his best-selling chariots-of-the-gods theories that ancient astronauts from other worlds had built many of the earth's ancient monuments; birthdate-based biorhythm theory; and the Bermuda Triangle. All these topics were touted in books that sold millions of copies. Notice something about all these latter issues. You don't hear much about them anymore. Is this a victory for reason and rationality? Did skepticism prevail? Not really.

Look at some of the hot topics of today: Several scholars in prominent academic positions claim that "intelligent design" instead of the creative processes of evolution is responsible for the intricacies of life. Therapeutic touch, a hands-waving therapy invoking invisible human energy fields unknown to science, is widely taught in nursing schools. Magnetic forces are assumed to influence health and human performance, so now "magnet therapy" has become a big business. Nineteenth-century spiritualism has been revived in best-selling books and TV programs as modern-day mediums contend they can help you communicate with your long-dead loved ones. Unproven medical remedies, under the attractive-sounding rubric of alternative medicine, have gained a proclaimed public respectability unheard of since the days of snake-oil salesmen. Modern-day numerologists profess to find hidden codes in computer analyses of biblical texts. And we may only now be emerging from a decade-long orgy of accusations and recriminations based on the dubious idea that accurate "repressed memories" of childhood sexual abuse or other horrible past events can through hypnosis and questionable kinds of therapy be revived.

And we still have the big three: psychics, UFOs, and astrology. With UFOs, for instance, we went through a credulity explosion in the 1980s and early 1990s. Claims of people being abducted by aliens—the hidden memories usually obtained through hypnosis conducted by UFO-abduction proponents—gained widespread popular acceptance. And we simultaneously went through an incredible period in which a series of books by UFO proponents and frequent credulous television programs all proclaimed a government cover-up of a crashed flying saucer near Roswell, New Mexico, in July 1947. Some even claimed alien bodies had been found. These reports gained increasing visibility and credence in the media and public—becoming essentially a modern folk myth. That is, until the past few years when clear evidence was produced that the recovered Roswell debris was actually from a lost assemblage of balloons and instruments launched from Alamogordo, New Mexico, June 4, 1947. These New York University atmospheric sciences experiments were to develop constant-level balloons. These unclassified experiments were in turn part of a top-secret project to detect round-the-world acoustic effects of future Soviet nuclear tests. Once these facts were disclosed and confirmed, the responsible media began to back off from the crashed-saucer claim. Nevertheless, the folk myth of a crashed saucer at Roswell will survive.

The point is that specific topics of pseudoscience, fringe-science, and the paranormal do come and go. This is especially the case with those who have a strong, charismatic figure associated with them. As long as that larger-than-life personage (Velikovsky was one example, with his silver hair and Old Testament demeanor) is still around writing and promoting his cause, the issue stays alive. Once he or she is gone, it may noticeably diminish, leaving only lesser disciples fighting rearguard actions for years to come to help keep the light alive. Other topics have their run in the press and among the public, until boredom sets in and some other fad belief emerges.

But while the specific topics come and go, the more general manifestations of fringe-science, pseudoscience, and the paranormal persevere. They arise, over and over again, in new guise, with new language, new clothing, and new proponents. And it is only rational for scientists and skeptics to realize that. Any hope scientists and skeptics may have to abolish from public consciousness nonsense and irrationalisms in the name of science is doomed to failure.

The positive appeal of such stories, the understandable human yearning for having the world the way we want it to be rather than the way it is, the lure of easy cure-all remedies, the appeal of comforting ideas, the search for significance and meaning, the desire for some all-powerful presence to guide our lives or reward good and keep the forces of evil at bay, the childlike attraction to New Age magical thinking, the quest for mystery and the "unknowable," the hope for everlasting life in some form—all these powerful psychological forces and human needs ensure that new manifestations of paranormal and fringe-science ideas will always have a welcome reception in people's hearts and minds.

So what can scientists and scientific-minded skeptics do? If I didn't think we were accomplishing something, I wouldn't be doing this. The first step, however, is to understand the human needs noted in the previous paragraph and have some compassion and understanding for the human condition. We are all in this together. It is self-defeating to put yourself above the fray, separate from the rest of humanity. Understanding these powerful needs is essential and should help shape how you frame your responses to others' arguments and claims.

Although the appeal of the paranormal and pseudoscience will always be with us, I think it should be the goal of scientists, scholars, and scientific-minded skeptics everywhere to combat and contain the most extreme and irresponsible elements of claimsmongering. Outright misrepresentations of science must be counteracted. Efforts to introduce bad science or pseudoscience into science curriculums or the political process must be opposed. The more irresponsible elements of the entertainment and communications media must be battled whenever they replace good science with unfounded speculations, pseudoscience, and lies. Responsible media must be encouraged and helped to gain accurate scientific information and be given well-informed scientific comment and perspective. The writers of excellent, scientifically responsible articles and producers of fine science-oriented documentaries must be encouraged and praised. Political leaders, lawyers, judges, and juries must be given accurate information about what is good science and what assertions have no scientific legitimacy.

I think the best way for most scientists, scholars, and teachers to do this is to emphasize the positive. Emphasize what you are *for*. We share important core values that should appeal to a good part of the public: honesty, integrity, and the value of good science, clear thinking, intelligence, scientific literacy, science education, and open scientific inquiry. Other important attributes include the error-correcting functions of science, the common-sense aspects of science, and the fact that in science the ultimate authority is not what any individuals may wish, believe, or say but what the evidence says. Authority just doesn't count in science, at least not in the long term. In that sense, science is highly democratic, even populist. Even those areas where science violates common sense and intuition, such as relativity or quantum mechanics, give us an opportunity. We can point out that these two highly successful areas of modern physics are examples where firm experimental evidence has ratified clearly bizarre aspects of nature, something that might appeal to many people.

Most scientists and scholars—except for the most incorrigible postmodernists—will agree that the methods of science are an extremely effective approach to getting knowledge about nature. Many scientists will go much further and say that the methods of science together represent one of the most successful, if not *the* most successful, ways humans have ever devised to expand our knowledge of the world.

"Skepticism" itself is a core value, but it can be a hard sell. We all know it is an essential part of science, vital and complementary to science's imaginative, no-holds-barred, go-after-the-facts-no-matter-where-they-lie, creative aspects. But to most people "skepticism" and "skeptic" sound negative. I try to point out that skepticism is just ordinary common sense. You kick the tires and get a mechanic to take a look before you buy a used car. Why not take a very close, skeptical look before buying someone else's opinion? From pyramid schemes to "pyramid power," skepticism can save you a lot of grief and money. It is an ultimate form of consumerism.

Science and scientific inquiry, however—despite some ever-present anti-science, and anti-intellectual trends in society—should really be an easy sell. Polls for the National Science Board's series of *Science Indicators* reports show that the public strongly supports science and has a fascination with new discoveries. They also show that the public doesn't know very much about science. This is especially true of the methods and processes of science. Some understanding of these processes is really necessary for getting a sense of what is good science and what is bad science (or worse). But the fact that the public has very positive attitudes toward science provides an opportunity. We can use that interest to good effect.

Here are just a few examples of what we can show:

- What we know (and more important how much we don't yet know) about how the human mind really works.
- How our brains still far outperform any computer yet built at pattern-recognition, yet usually fail us in accurately assessing statistical evidence.
- That these wonderful pattern-recognition functions evolved because they have immense survival value, yet at the same time they can mislead us when our brains overdo the connecting the dots and find patterns and meaning that may not really be there.

- That the study of consciousness is becoming a solidly experimental science. Using functional magnetic resonance imaging (fMRI) of the brain activity of volunteers when they became conscious of images gradually appearing before them, researchers can see visual signs of neuron activity as the volunteers press buttons indicating their perception. But the researchers viewing the images could see that the neuronal activity started *before* the volunteers pressed the buttons, essentially the emergence of a conscious thought. As one researcher says, "Consciousness is brain activity."
- How deep-time and the immensity of the universe dwarf our ability to comprehend them. The former provides ample time for the natural workings of evolution and the latter provides severe limitations to the possibility that we are being routinely visited by alien spacefarers.
- That although a succession of remarkable but unsettling discoveries over the centuries have seemingly downgraded our status in the universe, on a size-scale human beings are nevertheless at a centrist position—at about the exact midpoint from the smallest atomic particle to the largest cosmological distance.
- How while the evolution of life is solidly grounded in scientific evidence, the *origin* of life is still yet essentially a mystery.
- How not only does life evolve, the universe itself evolves. Astronomers can see areas of very young stars, newly born. Old stars, dying, collapsing, and exploding, provide some of the most stupendous explosions we can witness, and the explosions manufacture the heavy elements—the "star stuff"—out of which we are made.
- That while most scientists doubt we've ever been visited by extraterrestrial beings, the idea that the first molecular seeds of life may have come to Earth from elsewhere aboard comets or planetesimals at an early stage in the history of the Solar System is gaining some scientific respectability.
- That while many scientists feel that life must be widespread in the universe and we're monthly finding new planets around other star systems and also confirming the ability of organisms on Earth to thrive under extreme conditions such as boiling hot deep-sea vents and in rock deep underground, it doesn't necessarily follow that intelligent life is widespread in the universe. There is another, new view. These scientists agree that simple life may be very common in the universe but argue that Earth has a unique combination of circumstances (such things as an exceedingly large moon that helps keep Earth's axis stable and therefore long-term climate changes from being too extreme) that may nevertheless be very rare and special (the "Rare Earth" hypothesis). If that is so, the step from simple life

to advanced life is so difficult that it just may be likely that we are virtually the only civilization in our universe.

- That the science-fiction concepts of parallel universes and universes with more than three spatial dimensions are not entirely speculation. A recent theory seriously proposes that everything we see in our universe is confined to a three-dimensional membrane that lies within a higher-dimensional realm ("The Universe's Unseen Dimensions," *Scientific American*, August 2000). Remarkably, upcoming particle-physics experiments in Europe may actually be able to detect and verify the reality of the extra dimensions, if they exist. Such a discovery could explain some long-standing puzzles of physics and cosmology, such as why gravity is so much weaker than all the other forces.

You can see that I hope always to bring a scientific viewpoint—even an imaginative scientific viewpoint—to skepticism. I think to do so is important. I have tried to emphasize that whenever possible in the decisions that go into the *Skeptical Inquirer*.

Although probably the majority of claims and topics we examine lie outside the boundaries of mainstream science, keeping ourselves close to real science has essential advantages. Here are some of them:

- The daily advance of scientific discoveries is exciting and intellectually stimulating, and that excitement can carry over to skeptical investigation.
- The imaginative/creative and the skeptical/evaluative aspects of science intermingled in research on a continual basis, and it is important to keep both in mind.
- The methods of science are still the main tools used to evaluate claims outside of science (not the *only* tools, for we use everything from forensics to conjuring knowledge to historical analysis to investigative journalism, but the main ones).
- What helps separate science from nonscience (and worse) are not the specific topics under examination, but proponents' willingness to apply the various methods of science to their ideas and to frame propositions in a way that can be tested and proved wrong if they are wrong.
- Many of the institutional aspects of science such as peer review, open exchange of information and open publication, freedom of inquiry and discussion, the international aspects of science, reliance on observation and experimental evidence, and such things as double-blind studies are essential in scientific skepticism as well.

And a more subtle point: Just as good science uses skepticism, good skeptical inquiry uses both science and what philosophers call pragmatic or mitigated or moderate skepticism. In other words, there are limits to the degree of skepticism that is appropriate, and I think keeping close to science is very helpful in keeping on track in this regard. Dogmatic skepticism—doubt or denial unaccompanied by investigation—is sterile and unconstructive. Science uses pragmatic or mitigated skepticism. Science builds upon previous knowledge piece by piece and combines creative inquiry and criticism to the constructive end of gaining provisional new knowledge. It would never be healthy for "skeptics" to be more skeptical than the scientific community itself. Science deals successfully with absolutely bizarre claims all the time; the only difference is that the subjects involved have withstood previous evidentiary tests and have been defined as legitimate science by funding agencies, journals, and the like. Many new ideas in science, including bizarre ones, become repeatedly confirmed on the basis of strong experimental evidence. Other new hypotheses, perhaps more mundane, fail the tests of evidence and are eventually forgotten. It is the evidence that determines all this, not any preconceived opinion or ideological view.

If scientific institutions and the public funding agencies were to decide that it was in the public interest to do so, the same processes could be applied by mainstream science to the kinds of subjects the *Skeptical Inquirer* evaluates. Scientists are very pragmatic here too. They go where the funding is. They have no choice. And those funding decisions are not made arbitrarily. They also are a product of review panels and peer review. One of the key determinants is, essentially, *fruitfulness*. Is there a potential payoff? Is something here likely to advance our knowledge? Are there indications that an investment of scientific research in this area will open important new pathways of understanding? Is there an intellectual richness that has some value? These questions have been asked before about such things as UFOs, astrology, paranormal claims, and the like, and they have been answered (legitimately in my view) in the negative. So most scientists, especially in the early, most difficult parts of their careers, probably aren't going to spend much of their professional time thinking about these kinds of claims at all, let alone try to come up with ways to test and evaluate them. They have too many other priorities. But this then leaves a gap. The gap means there is a danger that high-level scientific competence may not be applied in examining paranormal and fringe-science claims.

This is where I think CSICOP, the *Skeptical Inquirer*, and the skeptical movement in general come in. We help fill that gap. We are in effect a surrogate in that area for institutional science. And we are most effective when we truly *represent* the views and values of the worldwide scientific community. We must essentially have the same values. In actual fact, in the majority of cases, the people who do our evaluations and articles are from the scientific and scholarly communities. This work may not noticeably advance their scientific or scholarly careers because it is unfortunately not often considered part of their regular scientific work. This despite repeated urgings from scientific organizations and others to encourage and reward scientists who devote a portion of their time to helping educate and inform the public. Rewards are still infrequent. Most do it to some degree on their own, drawing on all their scientific and intellectual backgrounds and making time available out of personal interest and because they realize that it is important. It is *terribly* important. I am so grateful to the many scientists, scholars, educators, and investigators who devote so much time and intellectual effort to preparing and writing articles, reviews, and columns for the *Skeptical Inquirer*. They are, in my view, scientific heroes.

The cross-fertilization between institutional science and scientific skepticism is extensive, and that is all to the good. Just as in science one cannot determine prior to rigorously examining the evidence whether a particular new idea or claim has validity, in scientific skepticism inquirers must be careful, especially if the topic or claim is new and unevaluated and presented as amenable to scientific examination, not to prejudge it and instead to let the evidence determine the outcome. In other words, a certain level of humility is required. The evidence is the arbiter, nothing else.

What I have said applies of course to *new, untested* claims and to theories that pose no obvious contradiction to scientific principles. What instead is frequently presented to scientific skeptics for judgment or approval are things that already have been scientifically tested and examined, over and over, countless times in countless ways, over years, decades, or (as with astrology) centuries, and found wanting, or things that violate repeatedly confirmed laws or principles of nature such as the second law of thermodynamics or the conservation of energy.

Here is when scientific experimentation can be put aside for a time and the even more difficult and frustrating task of public education begun. Explaining that someone's pet theory or idea is virtually identical to others that have been repeatedly tested and which failed those tests is not likely to be well received. Yet that is the position scientific skeptics are placed in over and over—both with proponents of the ideas and with the media. It is a bit thankless. But it must be done. And it can be made more palatable to both parties if you bring some patience and some of the compassion I spoke of earlier along with the necessary scientific knowledge and tough-mindedness when delivering the message. The message can be reinforced with a fundamental tenet of skepticism: the burden of proof is on those making the assertion. Even skeptics frequently forget this tenet and put themselves in a hole by trying to disprove some claim for which no reasonable evidence has been presented. Everyone must be reminded where the burden of proof rests. This is as true in science as in scientific skepticism.

Before concluding, I want to briefly mention two more topics. Both have been shaped by my determination to keep the *Skeptical Inquirer* close to science. The first is the fact that we have always been far broader in our interests than some might assume from the name of our parent committee: "for the scientific investigation of claims of the paranormal." *Scientific?* Yes, always. *Paranormal?* It doesn't have to be limited to that. Recall from my opening paragraphs, the initial announcement of the committee referred to "the paranormal *and related phenomena*" (my emphasis).

In my view, what relates all the topics we are concerned about is not whether they invoke the "paranormal" but whether they seem clearly to violate scientific principles or whether they have been handled in ways inimical to the spirit of scientific inquiry. Do they casually invoke "energy fields" science knows nothing about? Have they skirted all forms of peer review? Are there appeals directly to the public, without any form of prior expert review? Have any controlled tests been done? Are the hypotheses framed as scientific hypotheses, i.e., is the assertion posed in such a way that it can in principle be proved to be wrong if it is wrong? Or has just the opposite happened, has it been framed so that only positive evidence can be obtained? Are the proponents aware of previous scientific studies and examinations of similar claims and do they acknowledge and build on those? Have anecdote and eyewitness testimony been emphasized over scientific testing and confirmed evidence? Has authority been invoked, such as the word of a charismatic guru? Is the very spirit of science disparaged, such as the argument that if you don't believe (without evidence), you're just being close-minded. Are specious arguments used: "They laughed at Galileo too!" or "I know what I saw!"? These are all hallmarks that something's seriously wrong. And they are indications that we might want to get involved with some critical examination of our own.

And then, looked at from the other viewpoint, do the subjects raise issues for science education, science literacy, the public perception of science, or the philosophy of science? Do they raise consumer-protection issues? Is science invoked dishonestly to sell an idea or a product? Are national news organizations getting carried away treating something as real science that merits no such distinction? Or is there something here that is of special interest to science-oriented, philosophically minded readers. We are, after all, subtitled "The Magazine for Science and Reason."

So you can see there are many justifications for our interest in examining a topic beyond any "paranormal" connection. Many years ago I prepared a list of subjects we had written about in *SI* that had nothing to do with the paranormal. It took a full page.

Here are some new examples: Francis Bacon and the true ends of skepticism; mass delusions and hysterias of the past millennium; doomsday fears about a new particle accelerator; a skeptic's guide to the laws of nature; the pseudoscience of oxygen therapy; the quality of medical Web sites; "The Universe and Carl Sagan"; the physics behind four amazing demonstrations; how well do projective measures of personality work?; Carlos Castaneda and New

Age anthropology; NAGPRA, science, and the demon-haunted world; the myth that we use only 10 percent of our brain; organ-snatching urban legends; a claim of hidden messages in DNA; fears of the apocalypse; the failure of Munich dowsing experiments; a case study of gaps in the fossil record; the perils of posthoc reasoning; the Mead-Freeman controversy in anthropology; "science and the unknowable"; how to study weird things; open minds and the argument from ignorance; the compelling nature of extraordinary claims in the absence of alternative explanations; is cannibalism a myth?; hidden messages and the Bible code; alternative medicine in a scientific world. And so on.

Many readers would have us expand our reach even further, to encompass examination of organized religion. I am sympathetic to their appeal, up to a point. Once again, here we are guided by our connections to science. And one can strongly argue—and the arguments go on and on—that science and religion are separate domains, each treating different aspects of the human situation, the former the quest for knowledge of the natural world, the latter the search for personal meaning and significance. The hard fact is, although religion is a dominant cultural force in society, it is not a part of science, nor should it be. Science's always questioning attitudes and religion's appeal to unquestioning faith are anathema. And we are, essentially, a scientific organization and a science-oriented magazine. The very first issue of the *Skeptical Inquirer* (then the *Zetetic*) said this:

> [A] word might be said about our exclusive concern with *scientific* investigation and *empirical* claims. The Committee takes no position regarding nonempirical or mystical claims. We accept a scientific viewpoint and will not argue for it in these pages. Those concerned about metaphysics and supernatural claims are directed to those journals of philosophy and religion dedicated to such matters.

That was the original intention of our founding Executive Council members, and it has served us well. We have had abundant opportunity to deal with *empirical* claims related to religion. These have included the Shroud of Turin, the continuing abuses of science and evolution by the creationists and sympathetic politicians, claims of bleeding religious icons, the recent fad alleging spontaneously appearing crucifixion-like wounds or stigmata, religious cult groups such as Heaven's Gate whose members committed mass suicide in a belief they would ascend to join space people they thought were associated with Comet Hale-Bopp, and on and on. We have also dealt sociologically with the issues of religious belief, its extent, influence, and ramifications for society. So while we leave critical examination of religion itself to our sister publications, we nevertheless deal with certain aspects of it within the context of our role as both a science publication and a magazine of science and reason. In July/August 1999, we devoted an entire expanded issue of the *Skeptical*

Inquirer to "Science and Religion: Conflict or Conciliation?" I introduced it with an essay, "Science and Religion: Conflicting or Complementary? Some Introductory Thoughts About Boundaries." Twenty different authors including distinguished scientists and philosophers then wrote on different aspects of the matter. It was the most successful single issue of *SI* in our history: the greatest reader satisfaction as measured by the volume of letters to the editor (well over 140) and their overwhelmingly complimentary tone ("I greatly enjoyed the special issue," "I thoroughly enjoyed . . . ," "excellent articles," "thought provoking," "very welcome," "pleased," and a variety of other accolades). A few expressed disappointment that the articles didn't lambaste religion directly, but that wasn't our intention. My own feeling for why the issue was so well received focuses on two reasons: The first was that it was refreshing to many longtime readers because we had not ever devoted much space to the issues of religious belief. The more important reason, in my view, is that we did it in a very thoughtful and nonconfrontational way. Focusing specifically on the issue of science and religion allowed us to be respectful of sincere mainstream religious belief while clearly demarcating religion from everything science is all about. It was good to know that could be done in a way that most readers appreciated.

The modern skeptical movement has completed a resounding first twenty-five years since that inaugural conference on antiscience and pseudoscience that started it all in 1976. We have been a strong and resilient voice of scientific skepticism. Long an independent, international, nonprofit scientific and educational organization, CSICOP itself has steadily expanded its activities and reach. The tradition of stimulating conferences has continued and been internationalized. Our main publication, the *Skeptical Inquirer*, has expanded its audience, publication frequency, and page size. The subtitle added in fall 1994 describes the broader purpose: The Magazine for Science and Reason. We serve a vigorous community of scientists, scholars, educators, investigators, and others worldwide. Independent national, regional, and local groups with similar aims and intellectual ties to CSICOP have been founded nearly everywhere.

The influence of both CSICOP and *SI* has been significant. Both are widely referenced in scientific and scholarly publications as well as the popular media. CSICOP's media-outreach efforts serve news and entertainment media worldwide, providing authoritative, responsible scientific information and experts for comment and interviews. Workshops teach how to conduct investigations and how to examine various kinds of claims. A published quarterly newsletter, *Skeptical Briefs*, serves CSICOP associates. New electronic newsletters circulate timely announcements and critiques and relevant news. A Web site (www.csicop.org) provides broad information and access.

The controversy and media and public interest that accompanied our founding still surround almost everything we do. This is virtually inevitable given the inherent interest and fascination of the subjects we examine and the deep investment of belief many people have in them. But maintaining close ties to the values of science and scientific inquiry has helped guide us through and around all the worst thickets and pitfalls. In my view our reputation for commitment to scientific skepticism, rationalism, and scientific integrity is stronger than ever. And that serves us all well—the worldwide community of scientific skeptics and the broader public we serve—as we look forward to applying those attributes well into this new century and millennium.

KENDRICK FRAZIER is a science writer and the editor of the *Skeptical Inquirer*. He has served in that role since 1977, one year after its inception. Before that he was editor of *Science News*. He has written three books on planetary science and one on Southwestern archaeology, and is the editor of four *Skeptical Inquirer* multisubject anthologies (most recently *Encounters with the Paranormal: Science, Knowledge, and Belief*) and coeditor of a single-topic one (*The UFO Invasion*). He also is an editor and member of the staff at Sandia National Laboratories. He is a Fellow of CSICOP.

2

SCIENCE VS. PSEUDOSCIENCE, NONSCIENCE, AND NONSENSE

JAMES E. ALCOCK

As the nineteenth century turned into the twentieth, men and women of science were confident that in the century to come, universal education and the growth of science would slowly but surely eradicate ignorance, superstition, and irrational belief. How could they have foreseen that a century later, despite burgeoning enrollments in universities and almost unbelievable advances in science and technology, society would be awash in mysticism, psychic detectives, Creation Science, therapeutic touch, homeopathy, chiropractic, channelling, UFOs, and remote viewing? Had these people a century ago been given a glimpse of the world to come, our world of today, what sense could they have made of it? Indeed, what sense can we make of it?

Despite the central importance of science and technology in modern society, the public does not cry out for the testing of homeopathic remedies; instead, our trusted pharmaceutical chains promote them alongside the products of scientific research. The public is not concerned that the nursing profession—long characterized by devoted caregivers who were trained in the methods of data-based medicine—is embracing therapeutic touch, which involves no touching at all, but instead the supposed manipulation of magical energy fields. The public does not react with skepticism to the notion that refrigerator magnets, despite their extremely short range, can lessen pain and even heal the body. The public does not rise to challenge claims that psychics can and have solved crimes that baffled the police. The public does not wince when one celebrity after another talks of the importance of astrology or psychic readers or out-of-body experiences in his or her life.

Whither science? The public cannot get enough of the ultimate products of science. We rush to stuff our snouts firmly in the trough of technology, expecting each new season to bring us quicker, better, more exciting technotoys. We want faster computers, more pervasive Internet links, sooner-rather-than-later cures for the ailments that plague us. And yet, rather than honoring science, the public is generally disdainful of both science and scientist, while welcoming to their bosom the purveyors of magic, shamanism, and supernaturalism. And yet science thrives. It thrives in a culture of its own, to a considerable degree isolated from modern popular culture, the culture in which most people live. It is often perceived as too difficult, too arcane, too removed, to be of interest to most modern people.

Whither parapsychology? How has parapsychology fared over the past twenty-five years? Ironically, this age of magical thought and paranormal belief has given very little more succor to parapsychology than it has to science. Formal parapsychology and science are both being pushed aside by an undiscerning public eager to embrace uncritically the next spiritual or paranormal fad, the next "feels great—must be good" belief system. It is important to make a distinction between formal parapsychology and the psychic nonsense and superstition that often operates in its name. While we may "tut tut" the parapsychologists for their unending quest to put belief in the paranormal on a scientific basis, we need to recognize that we and they have much in common—a shared belief that the scientific method, with its insistence on the careful testing of theory against experience, hypothesis against data, is the best path toward the true understanding of the world around us. We may differ in our assumptions about the underlying nature of reality, but we generally share a common desire to employ appropriate methods to put our ideas to the test.

While CSICOP members may be galled by the seemingly insatiable public appetite for psychic nonsense, it must be even more galling to parapsychologists, who have labored long and hard for recognition of their field, to be ignored by a gullible public that pursues a beeline to the purveyors of psychic pap.

What is the state of parapsychological research? Eight years after CSICOP's founding, I reviewed what had happened in parapsychology during that interval:

> Despite the enthusiasm for the new "quantum mechanical" theories, nothing of substance has occurred in parapsychology in the past eight years. The same old reasons for skepticism—the lack of public replicability, the problems of defining just what it is that "paranormal" signifies, the circular reasoning inherent in explaining departures from chance in terms of a "psi effect," the unfalsifiability that enters the picture whenever it is suggested that the experimenter's own characteristics or even his/her own psi or lack

thereof may prevent him/her from ever observing psi, the failure of a century of research to improve the evidence—are as strong arguments against
the psi position today as they were in the past. A new reason for skepticism
is that, no matter how wild the hypothesis may seem, statistical evidence
can be adduced that supports the claim; this suggests that artifacts rather
than "psi" is the most probable explanation for the statistical deviations
reported in parapsychological research.[1]

Sad as the situation must be for the parapsychologists, nothing has really
changed in the intervening years that would lead me to revise this assessment.
Parapsychology is no closer to its goal of establishing a scientific basis for
paranormal phenomena than it was back then, or indeed, than it was even a
century ago. Oh yes—there are recurrent claims that new research is finally
demonstrating the reality of extrasensory perception or precognition or psychokinesis, but that is nothing new. Throughout its history, parapsychology
has been characterized by "breakthroughs" that subsequently prove to be
illusion, and fall into desuetude. Just as Rhine claimed in the 1930s and
1940s to have established the reality of ESP, so too at the time of CSICOP's
birth, Targ and Puthoff were laying claim to have proven the psychic powers
of Uri Geller, Charles Honorton was persuaded that his Ganzfeld studies had
finally provided the replicable and sound empirical evidence that had so long
been sought after, and Robert Jahn's extensive studies at Princeton University were supposedly on target to provide convincing evidence of the paranormal. A quarter century later, nothing has changed.

Wither parapsychology? Is parapsychology going to wither? Indeed, some
well-known parapsychology laboratories have closed, and one might expect
that the paucity of results yielded by parapsychological research might lead
parapsychologists to give up, to abandon the field. While this has not happened on a large scale, in recent years, parapsychology *has* lost many of its
senior scholars—to disillusionment in some cases, but more often to retirement, and to the shuffling off of this mortal coil. This is not unusual in any
field, of course, and this is not to say that there are not still a number of
bright, creative, and respectable scholars who are at the forefront—among
others, people such as Adrian Parker in Sweden, Jessica Utts and John Palmer
in the United States, and Robert Morris in Scotland—but the ranks are thin-
ning. Moreover, parapsychology has not been blessed, in my view, with
regard to replenishment of its key intellectual assets.There do not seem to be
many young John Beloffs, or Susan Blackmores, or Charles Honortons or
John Palmers or Robert Morrises or Adrian Parkers growing up in the ranks.

However, it is true that there are some signs of life in the field. For
example: after more than three decades, the *International Journal of Parapsychology* will resume publication (by the Parapsychology Foundation).
Some research laboratories—in particular that at the University of Edin-

burgh—are well established and active. Yet, to the outside observer, formal parapsychology appears moribund, although it is unlikely to die out any time soon. Its dedicated scholars seem no closer now than they were twenty-five years ago—or for that matter, a century ago—to establishing a scientific basis for their claimed phenomena.

Whither CSICOP? What have we accomplished and where are we going? Have we made a difference? Sometimes this question must give one pause, for surely the world is even more open to the paranormal and supernatural than it was when we began. CSICOP has in fact flourished as an institution. Having begun as little more than a shared idea, it now boasts a permanent headquarters with all the accoutrements, including an extensive library, as well as satellite offices in several cities. Moreover, CSICOP has spawned scores of like-minded organizations in many countries of the world. The *Skeptical Inquirer* continues to grow in popularity. Regional skeptic groups have been growing in number throughout North America and in other parts of the world. Other skeptics organizations with their associated publications have also come into being—the James Randi Educational Foundation and the Skeptics Society being the most notable. CSICOP created an environment that encouraged the establishment of other such organizations.

What has CSICOP accomplished? The world is quite a different place than it was twenty-five years ago when it comes to information about the paranormal. At that time, it was very difficult to find sources of information which provided critical analysis of parapsychological/psychic claims. Given the burgeoning recrudescence of paranormal belief which began in the 1960s, even many people immersed in science had difficulty in gainsaying the claims of psychic researchers. CSICOP was founded because there was no voice in opposition to the overwhelmingly pro-paranormal informational deluge presented by the media. Things were so bad in terms of one-sided information that I can recall some individual scientists telling me of the need for physics to develop a theoretical accommodation for psychic abilities that had apparently been verified by parapsychologists! CSICOP and the *Zetetic*, which was to evolve into the *Skeptical Inquirer*, began to change all that. For the first time in history, there was a publication and an organization dedicated to critical examination of claims of the paranormal.

CSICOP has provided a powerful magnet for people who are interested in strange and bizarre phenomena. Before CSICOP, the only avenue to pursue, if one was interested in such phenomena, was that offered by parapsychology. When I was nine or ten years old, having been fascinated in reading about psychic phenomena, I decided that I wanted to grow up to be a parapsychologist—not surprising, since the only people who took any interest in actually researching such phenomena were parapsychologists. Now, when people are drawn to the paranormal, there is an abundance of information written from a skeptical perspective that can serve to satisfy their curiosity while at the same time promoting an interest in mainstream science. I daresay that some contemporary young researchers—I will not name names, but the astute reader may have an idea about to whom I refer—who approach the testing of paranormal claims from a skeptical starting point may well have become mainstream parapsychologists had not CSICOP begun to provide a source of critical information.

So, I do believe that CSICOP has made an indelible mark on the world—a modest mark, perhaps, but one which serves as a beacon to those who really want to understand the weird and wacky experiences that so many people report, without jumping to a supernatural/paranormal conclusion.

Happy twenty-fifth, CSICOP.

Thank you for the memories.

And of course, what is the twenty-fifth anniversary without party favors and reminiscences? You'll have to go to Barry Karr for any party favors that CSICOP may have to give away, but I can offer you some reminiscences. For those of us who have been fortunate enough to be at or near the CSICOP front lines, there are many, many memories. Here are a few of mine.

The Joy of Finding People Who Share Your View. Before CSICOP was founded, I had already been involved in researching the growing belief in the paranormal. Such an interest was all but unheard of within psychology—the vast majority of psychologists took no interest in ESP and other such phenomena, and most simply did not believe that they existed. I sought the company of other researchers who might share this interest. Parapsychologists aside, there were very few of them. Reading the sparse critical literature on the subject of parapsychology brought me into correspondence with Professor Marcello Truzzi, a sociologist at Eastern Michigan University. It was a very positive experience to find someone who shared my fascination about the attraction that the paranormal has for so many people.

It was Professor Truzzi who invited me to a meeting at the University at Buffalo in 1976 that was to be held in conjunction with the annual meeting of the American Humanist Association. This meeting was to bring together a number of people who a shared a concern about the unbridled proliferation of belief in the paranormal, a proliferation fueled by one-sided media coverage. This event turned out to be the founding meeting of CSICOP. It was here that I first met the people who were to become the giants of CSICOP—Paul Kurtz, Ray Hyman, Phil Klass, James Randi, and my idol from my undergraduate days as a physics student, Martin Gardner. For someone like myself, who had felt—at least before coming into contact with Truzzi—quite isolated and alone with regard to my skeptical interest in the paranormal, it was a heady experience to meet so many powerful advocates of a viewpoint similar to my own.

Of course, Paul Kurtz provided the energy and foresight and determination that made CSICOP what it is today. One cannot help but be impressed by the man's ability to turn academic "wouldn't it be great" into reality. And almost as soon as I met him, I came to appreciate his almost legendary penchant for snap decisions—as I followed behind Kurtz and Truzzi and some others as they strode down a hallway, Paul turned to me and asked me where I was from. When I said "York University in Toronto," he replied, "Great, we need international representation—we'll make you a Fellow." And so a Fellow I became. Thus began my acquaintance with Paul Kurtz and with CSICOP.

From that first meeting in 1976, the Committee for the Scientific Investigation of Claims of the Paranormal emerged, its name a committee-produced appellation that has plagued us ever since. Worse, the name gave us the acronym CSICP, which was used officially for some time, but it was so hard to pronounce that the "O" of "of" was inserted to produce CSICOP. Unfortunately, this produced an unintentional homonym, "PSI-COP," and to this day, some of our opponents cannot be dissuaded from the belief that this was planned. Slowly, CSICP, or CSICOP, began its struggle to bring to the public a critical, science-based perspective on the paranormal. Through the *Zetetic*, edited by Marcello Truzzi, which became the *Skeptical Inquirer*, edited by Ken Frazier, CSICOP began to make its presence felt. And just as I had been overwhelmed to meet so many like-minded people at that founding meeting, so too were many of the early readers thrilled to realize that they were not alone in trying to bring rationality to the discussion of the paranormal.

Rationalization in the Defense of Paranormal Belief. At that same founding meeting, given my lifelong interest in conjuring, it was a thrill to watch a stage performance by James Randi. In those days, Uri Geller was in his heyday, and a good part of Randi's presentation was the duplication of Geller's tricks—showing that the same effects could be produced by conjuring, without revealing how. Surpassing my considerable appreciation of Randi's legerdemain was my astonishment at the intervention made by a professor from the University at Buffalo, who shouted at Randi after he had performed yet another Geller "miracle," and accused Randi of being a fraud. Randi shot back with "Yes indeed, I'm a trickster, I'm a cheat, I'm a charlatan, that's what I do for a living. Everything I've done here was by trickery." The interlocutor was not amused: he continued to shout at Randi, despite his wife's efforts to get him to sit down, and yelled, "That's not what I mean. You're a fraud because you're pretending to do these things through trickery, but you're actually using psychic powers and misleading us by not admitting it." This was my introduction to the powerful process of rationalization that traps even well-educated people who feel the need to defend a deeply held belief in the paranormal.

A Trip to China. Our trip to China in 1988 was one of my personal CSICOP highlights, of course. Along with Kurtz, Randi, Frazier, Klass, and

Karr, I had the privilege of participating in both a lecture tour of Beijing, Xian, and Shanghai, and in the testing of children who could supposedly read with their armpits and buttocks, as well in the testing of some qigong masters. This trip has already been well documented,[2] but there are many stories that did not make it into the article. Some of the memories that come to mind that were not recorded in that account include: (1) Being in a shop with Randi, who showed a group of young children how to make a pencil wiggle so that it appears to be rubbery, and then the next day, while taking a stroll with him, hearing "Landi, Landi"—and turning to see a couple of children smiling as each held up a pencil, wiggling it just as Randi had shown them the day before. Ah, how fame spreads. (2) Talking, through a translator, with a psychologist who had not only observed the same psychic girls who we were going to test, but who had employed a hidden videocamera that revealed their cheating. When I asked, "In that case, why do you need us to test them?" he asked, "Have you ever slopped pigs?" He had spent four years on a pig farm during Mao's Cultural Revolution, and wasn't going to risk anything that might put him at odds with the powers that be, and thereby risk being sent back to the farm. Indeed, these girls were held in high esteem by some very high officials in China, including the head of the Atomic Energy commission, a renowned scientist, who opined that China had given four great gifts to the world—paper, gunpowder, the compass, and movable type—and now they had a fifth gift to give—these psychic girls. Denying their powers might merit being sent back to the farm. (3) When we tested the girls in their hometown of Xian, they were brought to join us at a banquet that had been organized for us. Following the meal, we were all taken to something that was very surprising in 1988, a Xian discotheque. The scene that developed was almost surreal: Drinking beer in a discotheque in the midst of traditional Xian as these demure "psychic girls" transformed before our eyes into ordinary young adolescents, reveling in the loud Western music, while their decorous chaperones watched with apparent disdain.

The Power of Personal Experience. Since the history of CSICOP is inextricably tied to Paul Kurtz, those who wish to study and understand CSICOP need to some extent study and understand Kurtz. Although opponents have often viewed him otherwise, Paul Kurtz has not been rigid and close-minded about the paranormal. Indeed, in the early days of CSICOP, on more than one occasion he was heard to tell a radio interviewer that, while there is no evidence for the vast majority of paranormal claims, there was one exception—telepathy, and then he would relate how he and his wife often knew what each other was about to say, and that this might reflect ESP. Ray Hyman and I two or three times put on our psychology professor hats and explained to Paul how it is that normal psychological processes are likely, from time to time, to produce such experiences for all of us, without any involvement of ESP. Kurtz soon changed his expressed view, but this story is testimony both to the fact that he did not approach the paranormal with his mind rigidly made up a priori, and to the powerful impact of personal experience of seemingly paranormal events.

The Power of Experience that Violates Our Worldview. One day, during a CSICOP conference held in London in 1985, most of the members of the Executive Council were at lunch in a private dining room, and Randi was amusing us with some impromptu table magic. The waiter, a man with a heavy Portuguese accent, began to pay close attention to Randi's performance, and at one point remarked to Randi, "That is amazing." Randi beamed with pride at this commendation, and then the waiter added, "There's only one man I've ever seen do anything more impressive than that." Randi, who appeared slightly annoyed by this qualification of praise, asked, "And who might that be?" to which the waiter replied, "A Mr. Uri Geller, who stayed at this hotel last year." Oh boy! The gauntlet had been thrown down! Randi rolled up his sleeves, and magic enveloped us. Objects appeared from nowhere, minds were read, the hands of watches moved backward; the waiter was appropriately overwhelmed. However, that was not the end of the story. About an hour after lunch, I happened to pass through the lobby, when the hotel manager approached me and asked if I had been at the lunch where the magic was done. When I indicated that indeed I had been in attendance, he implored me to help him deal with one of his waiters. He led me to the kitchen, and there in a corner sat the Portuguese waiter, extremely distraught. The waiter told me that he had never seen such things happen, and that this must have involved tampering with spirits or even demons, and he was very, very frightened. Despite my training as a psychologist, I was unable to calm him down, or to dissuade him from his belief that he had witnessed supernatural dabblings. It was only when I began to praise Randi's virtues as a magician that he began to lighten up. But then, he wavered—he had seen magicians before, and magicians "can't do those things." Only when I heaped even more praise on Randi, telling him that Randi is no ordinary magician, but "one of the best magicians in the world," did he really start to soften. Finally, he said, "Well . . . maybe if he's one of the best magicians in the world, it could have just been trickery." He then calmed down, and the event was over. I had received a memorable lesson in the ability of inexplicable experience to produce powerful emotion.

Pockets of Irrationality. Another incident comes to mind that relates to our ability to sustain pockets of irrationality amongst our beliefs, while all the while persuading ourselves that we are rational people. This occurred during a CSICOP meeting in Mexico City in 1989. Professor Mario Bunge had just delivered an address in which he surveyed the subject of irrationality, moving from belief in the paranormal to such topics as psychoanalysis, which he argued is also pseudoscientific in its nature. He was not aware that a substantial part of this university audience was made up of psychoanalysts. After the talk was over, I recall listening to a heated discussion in English at the back of the hall—Professor Bunge was surrounded by a number of psychoanalysts—all happy to applaud any attack on parapsychology, but all quite offended by the criticism of psychoanalysis. It was fascinating to see so clearly something that is no doubt true of all of us—we can turn off our critical skepticism when dealing with some of our own favorite beliefs. The interchange ended on a humorous note. Professor Bunge asked them if they really believed that deep inside every man is an instinctive desire to murder his father. They did indeed agree, and then Professor Bunge turned to a young man at the edge of the circle, and asked, "So, do you want to murder me?" To which the man replied with a smile, "Yes indeed, sometimes!" Professor Bunge then identified the man, a professor of physics at the University of Mexico, as his own son.

I have many other happy memories of CSICOP:

- My first invitation to an Executive Council meeting at Phil Klass's apartment in Washington in 1978.
- Going for runs with Ray Hyman at just about every CSICOP meeting or conference—and especially at the conference in St. Vincent, Italy, where nuns—dressed in traditional habits with formidable headgear—laughed and laughed and pointed at us as we ran up the steep road past their convent, and they laughed just as hard when we came down again. Don't see many joggers in these parts!
- Sharing adjacent seats on a Chinese airliner with Phil Klass, at that time senior editor at *Aviation Week*, who explained that the airplane that we were on was a copy of a Boeing 737—except that the Chinese didn't bother with all the duplication that Boeing builds in for backup safety. No backup circuits, he said. Thrilled to learn this at 30,000 feet, I asked him why he was willing to fly on an airplane that had no backups if any system failed. He smiled that impish smile of his and said, "Well, this aircraft we're on has been flying for years, and it hasn't crashed yet, has it?"
- The long rides from Vancouver to Eugene, Oregon, with Barry Beyerstein, and once there, the wonderful times I have had as one of the team, along with Barry, Jerry Andrus, Loren Pankratz, Wally Sampson, and others at Ray Hyman's annual Skeptics' Toolbox workshop.
- Being at a private lunch during a CSICOP conference—not lunch really, but hamburger and lots of magic—with Hyman, Randi, Andrus, Penn and Teller . . . quite a thrill to watch magicians "jam."
- The list goes on. . . .

In fact, the greatest thing about having been fortunate enough to be deeply involved in CSICOP has been the wonderful people that it has brought into my life: Ray Hyman, Barry Beyerstein, Paul Kurtz, James Randi, Phil Klass, Ken Frazier, Lee Nisbet, Barry Karr, Amardeo Sarma, Sue Blackmore, Mario Mendez, the late George Abell, Jerry Andrus, Eugenie Scott, Joe Nickell, Bela Scheiber, and so many, many others.

So, thanks CSICOP, and happy birthday, and here's to the next twenty-five!

NOTES

1. J. E. Alcock, "Parapsychology's Past Eight Years: A Lack-of-progress Report," *Skeptical Inquirer* 8 (1984): 312–20.

2. P. Kurtz et al., "Testing Psi Claims in China: Visit of CSICOP Delegation," *Skeptical Inquirer* 12 (1988): 364–75.

JAMES E. ALCOCK is professor of psychology at Glendon College, York University, Toronto, Ontario. He is the author of *Parapsychology: Science or Magic?* (Pergamon, 1981) and *Science and Supernature: A Critical Appraisal of Parapsychology* (Prometheus Books, 1990). He is a Fellow of CSICOP and a member of its Executive Council.

3

NEVER A DULL MOMENT

BARRY KARR

I t is amazing really when you think about it: what the ramifications can be, at least for me, from an action that basically originated as an afterthought. You see, my sister was a senior at the State University of New York at Buffalo, and she had taken a part-time job with CSICOP, which her roommate had gotten for her. It seemed that they were still a bit short-staffed and needed some help with a large press mailing. After going through a couple of her friends she eventually thought of me, a sophomore at the university. She called me up and asked if I would like to work for a few hours a week between classes. I went into the office and did what they told me, which was, I believe, stuffing about 2,500 magazines into envelopes and helping to prepare them for mailing to members of the press around the country. Now how long it took to complete the task is uncertain. I like to think I must have made good time because by my third day there, and after a couple of other assignments, I was called into the office of Paul Kurtz for a job interview. I got the position by the way and have been involved with CSICOP ever since. Lucky for me my sister didn't have more friends.

Although at this point CSICOP as an organization was in its fifth year, and third office location, I still think of these as the very early days of the organization. There is a saying around the office these days: "Never a dull moment"—which is true. We used that expression back then too, but it meant a totally different thing. Whereas today it seems that there is always a new project that needs doing—some new television show or movie on the paranormal, or shameless promotion of some quack therapy that needs

47

looking into—back then it meant that "Today it is going to rain and we need to get the *Skeptical Inquirer* out the door before the leak in the ceiling destroys a thousand issues." Our offices were in a deteriorating office/apartment building in a deteriorating neighborhood in the city of Buffalo. Lunchtime generally meant going next door to the overpriced corner grocery store and trying to buy something with an expiration date roughly in the same year. We had basically no computer system; new subscriptions, renewals, and other in-house records were kept track of on index cards sorted by alphabetical order. The subscription data itself was handled by an out-of-house fulfillment agency that did the printing of the magazine and maintained our database. I can remember having to borrow a car to periodically head on down to the printer and load up with magazines and then take them over to the central post office. I can also clearly remember getting lost from time to time trying to find these places and in one exceptionally brilliant feat ending up on the bridge going into Canada.

There was, however, a definite feeling of camaraderie among the staff. We celebrated every birthday and major event in each other's lives. We held weekly and sometimes daily cookouts on the back patio—weather permitting. We even had a regular bowling night. It was certainly an interesting place to work while in college—a perpetual educational experience where I learned to think about things in a new way and not simply accept what I had been told. For example, while growing up I had been a notorious bad-movie junkie (truth be told, I still am), and was certainly a fan of all things paranormal. My favorite show has to have been *The Night Stalker*, and I can vividly remember running home from school to watch the vampire-themed soap opera *Dark Shadows*. I was a creature of my television generation. Never had I seen or read anything to suggest that some of these things were not somehow based in reality. Of course I wasn't naive enough to believe in vampires, but I must admit to having written a glowing wide-eyed book review on *Chariots of the Gods?*

By the time my senior year at the university rolled around I found myself working more and more hours at CSICOP each week and my status at the university trimmed to that of a part-time student. My plan had always been to go on to law school upon graduation, but a year with a first-year law student as a roommate soon cured me of that. When graduation rolled around I was very pleased to have Paul Kurtz offer me a full-time position as assistant public relations director. Although I thought I'd do this for a year and eventually go back to school I haven't quite made it back yet. I really don't regret it.

Over the years it has been my pleasure to take part in many adventures and investigations that, well—how should I say this?—not many of my friends, family, or neighbors have had the opportunity to experience. Probably my second-greatest thrill was the opportunity to travel to the People's

Republic of China in 1988 as part of a CSICOP team conducting investigations into qigong masters, amazing psychic children, and remote healers, along with other facets of traditional Chinese medicine. The results of these investigations have been well documented within the pages of the *Skeptical Inquirer*.[1] However, it is the personal moments that don't get discussed. I remember eating a spectacular dinner one evening with our hosts. To be honest I had no idea what some of what I was eating was. Sitting across from me and staring intently was James Randi. As I brought the chopsticks up to my mouth with a morsel of something, Randi burst out laughing at me. I never knew what it was I ate. It was good, but I never wanted to know.

Some of the other moments of the trip will live forever in my memory. I won't forget the way members of the CSICOP team played with and enjoyed entertaining the children. While a test was being conducted, everything was very serious, but the next moment at the conclusion of a test there would be Randi performing magic tricks. I remember how James Alcock, who is quite tall, would draw a crowd wherever he went, or Paul Kurtz telling jokes and laughing with them until he had tears in his eyes. He still keeps photographs of some of these children in his office today.

Also, what hasn't been mentioned is the absolute joy it was to meet with skeptics within China who requested the help of CSICOP to investigate these claims and bring in skepticism. Because of this trip an organization was established as part of the Chinese Association for Popularization of Science to promote skepticism within the country. Since then we have had a delegation from China attend several of our conferences over the years, and we were also able to send a second CSICOP delegation a few years later. This relationship continues. It illustrates in my view the powerful impact that CSICOP has been having worldwide in stimulating skeptical inquiry and crystallizing a scientific response to the great barrage of paranormal claims.

Such people as Phil Klass, Ray Hyman, James Randi, Joe Nickell, Richard Wiseman, Massimo Polidoro, and others wonderfully fill the role of paranormal investigator/researcher. Although there is a need for more people to do investigations, they must be done well. There have been several instances where I have been involved with investigations. Perhaps the most well known is the demon-haunting case of the Smurls in West Pittston, Pennsylvania. The case was made into a book, and later a television movie. And again, our investigation has been written up in the *Skeptical Inquirer*.[2] My fellow investigator (and former CSICOP staff member) Elizabeth Gehrman and I spent several days in West Pittston interviewing neighbors, visiting the Mining Office, the Street Commissioner, and the former owner of the house, and we briefly met with the Smurls, who would not let us in the house. However, I think my fondest memory of the trip to West Pittston was the hotel that Elizabeth and I booked. We arrived in town late after a long drive from Buffalo. We did not have a reservation confirmed at a hotel and decided to just pick the first one we saw. Little did we realize that the hotel we chose was right across the street from a porno drive-in movie theater. We were naturally suspicious when the man at the reception desk asked if we wanted the room for the night or if we wanted to pay by the hour! Being really tired we took a room with two double beds for the night. CSICOP is, after all, a nonprofit organization and we always have an eye on the bottom line. Sometime after we'd been in the room for a while Elizabeth began to complain that there was something crawling all over her legs in the bed. I went over to her side of the room and looked to find the bed and the room covered with bedbugs.

We went to the manager to complain. He was not too nice at that point but offered us another room. His mood turned even uglier when, for some reason or another, Elizabeth would not accept this offer. Here my recollection gets a little fuzzy and I am not sure whether we had paid in cash and had demanded our money back, or told him we would stop payment on the credit card. Either way he figured we had gotten our hour's worth and threatened to call the cops on us. I do remember leaving the parking lot quickly with Elizabeth screaming at the top of her lungs. I also remember thinking that a demon-haunted house would most likely be a more pleasant experience.

On another occasion members of CSICOP and the Western New York Skeptics were called upon to look into a haunted house in the Western New York area. Several skeptics went to the house and recorded interviews with the family that lived there. Most of the events centered upon the mother of the house. She would complain, for example, that while she was lying in bed unseen spirits would pull the covers over her legs. We asked her if we could observe this and she agreed to try the demonstration. As she was lying in bed she repeatedly said that the blankets were moving and asked if we could see them. Nobody else in the room could see anything happening. (We sent our report on the case, along with all of our audiotapes, to psychologist and noted haunted-house investigator Robert Baker for his analysis. Baker ended up writing about the case briefly in his book *Missing Pieces* where he attributed the woman's condition to a neurological disorder called "restless legs."[3]) Later, in the living room of the house, the woman claimed that every once in a while when she sat in a certain chair a spirit would flash across the room. A moment later she exclaimed that one had just done so. I too had noticed the flash and immediately suspected what was going on. I went to the window and looked out. The house was situated so that the front window looked out over an intersection and street. When a car would make a turn down the street from the intersection, the headlights would momentarily flash into the window between a gap in the curtains. She did seem to accept this when I was able to predict the next sighting.

Another event that was quite newsworthy a few years ago was the New

Age "harmonic convergence," basically an alleged mystical coming together of astrology and the Mayan calendar, when 144,000 people were needed to gather in "power points" around the world to mediate, welcome alien space-ships, and heal the earth. One of these "power points" was to be Terrapin Point overlooking Niagara Falls. At dawn of the appointed day several of us were positioned around the point to see what we would see. The day's activities consisted of alternating sessions of meditation, chanting, and prayer. It is probably needless to say that no aliens showed up and if a Harmonic Converged I must have missed it. At one point a number of the almost 500 to 750 people there became somewhat excited when a rainbow appeared over the falls. The excitement level seemed to dissipate somewhat when the skeptics started passing the word that rainbows are virtually an everyday occurrence at the falls. As I wrote in the *Western New York Skeptics Newsletter*, "When the chanting was finished and all the little crystals had been thrown over the falls, many people felt spiritually uplifted, enlightened, and full of a sense of accomplishment.[4] But, to quote from *Newsweek* magazine, 'Making yourself feel good about the world is not the same thing as improving the world. Want to think a good thought? Think about 144,000 people volunteering an hour a week to work in shelters for the homeless. That would be something to hum about.' "[5]

One of the investigations that skeptics around the world should be most proud of is the several-year-long investigation, led by James Randi, into the faith healers. During that time I had traveled around the Western New York area and into southern Ontario to attend the services of such faith healers as W. V. Grant, Peter Popoff, the Happy Hunters, and Willard Fuller. When James Randi went on the *Tonight* show and blew the lid off the Peter Popoff ministry, I know that skeptics everywhere felt a tremendous sense of accomplishment. When other national media news shows did much the same to W. V. Grant, we again felt rewarded for the many hours that a number of people put into the effort. I had two experiences that will forever leave a bad taste in my mouth. The first one occurred at a healing service by Peter Popoff held in Toronto, Canada. Several members of the Western New York Skeptics and the Ontario Skeptics met in advance and planned to distribute leaflets describing our objections to Popoff and explaining what it was he was doing and how he had been exposed. Other members, me included, would fake ailments and attempt to be healed. Popoff claimed to be directed by God as to whom to heal. Thus, our point was that, if one of us got called for healing, either God made a mistake or Popoff did not have the direct line to heaven that he claimed.

I walked into the arena with a fake limp, using a cane. Right away some of Popoff's people came up to me and asked me for the healing card I had filled out previously. I wrote that I had a ruptured disk in my back that caused severe pain in my leg when I walked. As the service started Popoff's people told everyone in the audience to crumple up the flyers they had received from the people outside because those people were unbelievers and worked for Satan. Things were not starting off well. Later on in the service, however, Popoff came down the row I was in and told me to stand up. I did. He then put his hand on my forehead and told me that God was going to heal me and took my cane and threw it up on the stage. He said that God was going to let me walk (which I could do anyway). He then told me to run around a bit, which I did. Either God or Popoff couldn't tell I was a fake.

If we had accomplished what we set out to do, then why did I feel so bad? Because sitting next to me was a father and mother with an obviously severely handicapped child in a baby stroller. It was clear that these people had come to the service hoping for a miracle for their child. Of course Popoff avoided them. But the way they looked at me will stay with me forever. The look said, "Why you? Why should you be healed and not my baby?" It was so clear that if anyone ever wanted to prove they could perform miracles and heal the sick then this child would be absolute proof. But their look showed they hated me and not Popoff. I pulled one of our flyers out of my pocket and handed it to them asking them to really read it over. I tried to explain to them that I wasn't sick to begin with and that no miracle had taken place. I think that only made it worse, as if some miracle had been wasted on someone who didn't even deserve it. I have no words strong enough in my vocabulary to describe my feelings toward Peter Popoff.

On another occasion the faith-healing husband and wife team, the Happy Hunters, came to Rochester, New York, for a "Healing Explosion." "Thousands will be healed!" promised the slick advertising supplement announcing the event. The first person on the podium that night was a member of the Rochester City Council, who gave the opening address and read a letter of welcome from Rochester's mayor. Traveling faith healers are not unlike a touring rock 'n' roll band, or the road show of a Broadway play in that they have a set program (or act) that they follow day in and day out in city after city. The Hunters were two of the more innovative. Not only did they themselves practice the art of laying on of hands, but they also ran a service that provided training for individuals who wished to become members of the healing teams. The Hunters did not charge for the training, but they would charge for the training materials.

The most striking aspect of the Hunter "healings" was the team's almost total reliance upon the lengthening of arms and legs to effect a cure. Although this trick was thoroughly exposed by James Randi in his book *The Faith Healers*,[6] a conservative estimate on my part was that 70 percent of all treatments offered by the healing teams were of this variety.

After the service I attempted to interview a number of people who were healed that evening. I had asked if I could follow up with them again in a few weeks and a number of them agreed. After a couple of weeks I began calling back the people I had spoken to at the service. One woman said that she felt better and that sometimes healings took time. When I asked her why God would only heal a little bit at a time she said, "God works in strange ways. If he sees fit he will do it." She then said two things that broke my heart: "Maybe I'm not entitled to it" and "Maybe I'm not trying hard enough to get out" (of the wheelchair). In these statements lie the reason for much of my resentment toward faith healers. If something that they promise does not work, it is not the fault of the healer. Mrs. Hunter said, "If you believe God is God, it is so easy to receive a healing."

The lady in the wheelchair was very devout in her faith, but she was not healed. Instead of calling into question the whole business of faith healing, or the Hunters' ability to either teach it or perform it, she blamed herself. Why weren't the Hunters able to heal her? Why wasn't she entitled to a healing?

I spoke to the Hunters two days before the Rochester event when they appeared on the local television program *AM Buffalo*. After the show I asked the Hunters about the people who are devout in their faith, yet who are not cured of their illnesses. I asked them what this might do to someone's faith, self-esteem, and belief. Charles Hunter looked at me and said simply, "I don't know." I wondered if he had ever thought about it before. I have no words strong enough in my vocabulary to describe my feelings toward the Hunters.

My take on the history of CSICOP probably wouldn't be complete without at least some mention of that formerly famous "psychic" Uri Geller. For a period of several years in the 1990s it seemed that a great deal of my time was spent dealing with lawsuits filed (Geller was suing CSICOP and James Randi for statements made by Randi which called into question Geller's alleged paranormal abilities), or lawsuits threatened, or numerous scare-tactic letters arriving from shopping-mall lawyers from around the world or some other form of puff and bluster which to me seemed like a desperate attempt to recapture faded glory, or at least to make himself feel important again. I always found this somewhat ironic because of my decision years earlier to avoid law as a career. I remember that the one time I met Geller was at our lawyer's office in Washington, D.C., where Paul Kurtz had been called for a deposition. We met Geller in the hallway where he was very personable and attempted to be charming. He stuck out his hand and said, "I'm Uri Geller and it is a pleasure to meet you." I refused to shake his hand and basically tried to ignore him. He became agitated and stated something to the effect that the difference between us was that he could still be a nice guy and did not take any of this personally. I responded that the difference between us was that he was suing us and we weren't suing him, which to me was personal. Eventually CSICOP won all of the lawsuits brought against us and managed to recover some of our legal costs as sanctions imposed upon Geller by the court. I often find myself wondering what he tells his children about his "powers." I have no words strong enough in my vocabulary to describe my feelings toward Uri Geller.

Through the course of this book I am sure that you will read articles describing the many, many contributions to rational thought and scientific inquiry that CSICOP has made. When you consider the body of knowledge that is the *Skeptical Inquirer* magazine and the Fellows and consultants who make up the committee, it is certainly impressive. Recently we conducted a rough tally of the number of events such as conferences, workshops, or seminars we had sponsored over the years and it was well into the hundreds. As public relations director for CSICOP for many years, and now executive director, I know that we would get between six hundred and eight hundred media calls each year from around the world. We try our best to supply journalists with the best experts on the subjects they are considering, or the best reference articles from the *Skeptical Inquirer* or another source. But it is also true that we receive probably several times as many calls and requests from members of the general public for information on a vast array of topics. From schoolchildren writing a paper on UFOs to people with a sincere belief that their houses are haunted, we run the gamut of topics and try to help whenever we can.

I say this often and I believe in it totally—I am amazed at the amount of information and effort that flows in and out of our little building each day. I have file cabinets and boxes filled with the by now tens of thousands of requests we receive for help and information. It is probably one of the most unappreciated roles that CSICOP plays in the world.

Perhaps I shouldn't actually say "little building" anymore. Because of the vision and hard work of many people we now have a much nicer headquarters (the Center for Inquiry) than in those early days and it seems we are doing more than ever before. It is still appalling to see how much more we have to do. Quite a bit of my time these days seems to be taken up by office mechanics, such things as publishing contracts, bids on new telecom systems, computer upgrades, legal issues, and the like. It is a sign, of course, of a maturing and permanent organization. It is very satisfying to realize that CSICOP will continue for a long time. Several years ago, I don't think I could have made that claim. We were always flying by the seat of our pants and really did survive on a day-to-day basis. On the other hand, I kind of long for the times when I personally could take time to ponder the latest UFO claim from Russia, or go out on a ghost hunt. Although I did get to take part in my first firewalk recently, these opportunities seem too few and far between.

As I travel around from city to city and country to country, it is always impressed upon me how belief in superstition, the paranormal, and fringe-science claims; untested alternative medical treatments; and antiscience and pseudoscience are part of a global phenomenon. The particular belief or the pseudoscience may be different in each country but the need for a skeptical response is vital. In 1980 in the back of the *Skeptical Inquirer* we listed a grand total of nine groups of skeptics from around the world with which we cooperated. Today we list well over a hundred with several others currently in various stages of formation. CSICOP constantly has someone on the road visiting groups, attending international events, sending out reader surveys, working the phones, and writing letters and e-mails. Over the years I have been to many localities across the United States, as well as visiting probably twenty other countries. It is generally fun, and always stimulating. It is also true that on many occasions the trip can be summarized as get on the plane, go to hotel, attend three days of lectures and workshops, go to the airport and get on the plane. In my experience the hotel I stayed at in Madrid, Spain, looks an awful lot like the one I stayed at in Tucson, Arizona. This has been hard work. But it is work that is important and necessary. We act as the international hub for a growing network of men and women who believe in science and the use of reason and critical thinking skills in examining claims. Think of the vast worldwide media companies whose only motivation is profit and market share. They have virtually no interest in telling things like they are, or presenting paranormal and fringe science from a skeptical perspective. The paranormal is entertainment and the paranormal sells. It does seem odd to think that as a twenty-five-year-old organization we've now got more work to do than at any other time in our history. Truly, and somewhat sadly, there never really is a dull moment.

Many of us are familiar with the names of the heroes of CSICOP. People like Paul Kurtz, Ray Hyman, Martin Gardner, Ken Frazier, Carl Sagan, Isaac Asimov, Stephen Jay Gould, Philip Klass, James Randi, Richard Dawkins, Joe Nickell, and others. I think there is a group of people who are unsung and deserve a world of thanks for the work they have done for the organization. These people include Mary Rose Hays, the first business manager of CSICOP who really kept it going during those lean, dark days. Doris Doyle, managing editor of the *Skeptical Inquirer* for so many years. The day for Doris must have had forty-eight hours in it. She seemed to work full-time for CSICOP even though her real job was at Prometheus Books. Doris was an absolutely delightful and totally wonderful person. One of the hardest-working people I ever saw was Alfreda Pidgeon. She would do whatever you asked of her and do it perfectly. She retired from our staff at the age of eighty-three. I used to tell her that I wished I could clone her and have several of her working for us at the same time. Vance Vigrass has been with CSICOP since almost the very beginning. He has literally kept some of our offices and machines working by duct tape and force of will alone. Paul Paulin is also a truly remarkable staff person as well. My hope is that we will be able to keep him on staff until he is eighty-three.

I also think Paul Kurtz is far too much an underappreciated and unsung hero as well. He is the founder of CSICOP and you know him by his writings, his speeches, and his media appearances. But so much of what he does is behind the scenes. You really cannot appreciate him until you see how much effort and dedication he puts into this organization. He works harder than anyone his age, half his age, a quarter of his age, etc. I can't keep up with him. I wish we could clone him as well. (I think we'll keep a bit of Paul Kurtz DNA locked up in the CSICOP archives just in case.)

Earlier in this article I mentioned that going along to China with the CSICOP team was probably the second-biggest thrill I have ever received from working at CSICOP. The biggest, by far and without question, is that I met my wife, Chris, when she was a graphic designer doing much of the production work on the *Skeptical Inquirer*. Chris and I were married on 9/9/99 (so I could remember the date) and we now have a beautiful baby daughter. I owe CSICOP quite a lot, but I do try to pay it back a little bit every day.

NOTES

1. James Alcock et al., "Preliminary Testing," *Skeptical Inquirer* 12 (summer 1988): 367–75.
2. Paul Kurtz, "A Case Study of the West Pittston 'Haunted House,'" *Skeptical Inquirer* 11 (winter 1986–1987): 137–46.
3. Robert Baker and Joe Nickell, *Missing Pieces: How to Investigate Ghosts, UFOs, Psychics, & Other Mysteries* (Amherst, N.Y.: Prometheus Books, 1992).
4. Barry Karr, "Message from the Chair," *Western New York Skeptics Newsletter* 2, no. 4 (September 1987): 1–2.
5. Bill Barol and Pamela Abramson, *Newsweek* (August 17, 1987): 70–71.
6. James Randi, *The Faith Healers* (Amherst, N.Y.: Prometheus Books, 1989).

BARRY KARR is executive director of the Committee for the Scientific Investigation of Claims of the Paranormal (CSICOP) and the Center for Inquiry (CFI) in Amherst, New York. He is coeditor of the *Skeptical Inquirer* anthologies *The UFO Invasion* and *The Outer Edge*.

THE ORIGINS AND EVOLUTION OF CSICOP
Science Is Too Important to Be Left to Scientists

LEE NISBET

T he founding of CSICOP was a fortuitous accident of time, place, and personalities. The founding of a CSICOP-like organization was a highly probable creative reaction of science-literate people to an immensely influential means of communication reflecting public ambivalence toward institutionalized science.

Any particular existence is contingent, not perfectly predictable. Randomness *is* a real trait of nature. But, when considering historical developments one might argue that a CSICOP-like organization was probable in the latter decades of the twentieth century. In this technically advanced world we had a intellectually undisciplined, economically driven means of communication serving a public highly ambivalent toward a way of knowing which had bestowed the gifts of increasing material and physical security. But why the public ambivalence toward a community of inquirers that had bestowed such considerable gifts? The answers to the ambivalence question explains the evolution of CSICOP from its primarily media-oriented origins to functions both more diversified and broad in scope.

Whatever creates, also destroys. Scientific inquiry carried on by an elite, specialized community has succeeded to an unprecedented degree in harnessing the processes of nature for human good. However, a logic of discovery, by nature and purpose threatens the intellectual and moral basis of traditional ideologies that materially depend on that logic (witness the threat that Darwinism poses to both contemporary theological creationists on the right and social creationists on the left). What all contemporary ideologies

57

demand of scientific inquiry is that it remain merely a means to secure ends established by tradition and biased thought. Unfortunately, a logic of discovery is difficult to keep in its place. Intellectual discovery requires continual correcting both political and moral. Therefore, the publics of universities, churches, as well as political and moral movements have good reason to feel ambivalent toward any community of inquirers, no matter how valuable the outcomes they produce. In short, both dispositions native to human nature and existing cultural institutions formed in prescientific ages are challenged by the very genie that sustains them.

However, beyond our reluctance to subject ideas with which we agree to the same degree of skepticism we subject disagreeable ideas lies another source of public ambivalence toward "science": the very process of "science education" itself. Ironically, formal science education with its narrow discipline, career-oriented focus has simultaneously created (especially in the United States) an enormously productive, successful enterprise *and* destroyed the very possibility of widespread, informed, public support. Worse, "science education" leaves many "well-educated" people feeling antagonistic toward institutionalized science. How so?

Formal science education as it operates now in the United States on the secondary/college/university levels is designed for not only those with superior intellectual gifts but also narrowed interests. It is narrow vocational education in the extreme. Generalists, if they exist, certainly don't prosper in the *vocation* of science. Specialists prosper. Young, intelligent, very focused, very intellectually narrowed people produce the cutting-edge research in today's scientific disciplines. Science people regard themselves as an elite group compared to the humanistically oriented. Their formal education receives by necessity of cost a much higher allocation of funds than those in nonscience or non-hard science disciplines, and rightfully so in their eyes. By conventional standards their intelligence and specialization produces highly valued and objective knowledge. It is not difficult then to understand given the success of the narrowed process called science education and the elitism it engenders how nonscientists might well feel excluded from, bored by, and even antagonistic toward science itself when it is identified exclusively with this process. Conceived in vocational terms, "science" becomes a specialized, arcane set of practices known only to a smug elite who serve the private and politically dominant interests of those who fund their research. Conceived in vocational terms scientific literacy becomes a thing both apart from and superior to cultural literacy. The irony of such a dualistic and elitist conception of scientific literacy in a culture simultaneously dependent on and battered by scientific discoveries is sobering.[1]

Science is obviously too important and potentially too destructive to be left to scientists. The methods of scientific inquiry adopted as active dispositions, active habits of mind need to be defined as a central part of what it means to be *both* scientifically *and* culturally literate. A basic knowledge of central scientific concepts and achievements and their impact, for better and worse, on the wider culture needs to be a central part of what it means to be both scientifically and culturally literate. Intellectually narrow, cultural ignoramuses who produce powerful knowledge are not desirable educational outcomes. Culturally literate people who are ignorant and disdainful both of scientific methods and discoveries and their social, moral, and political consequences are not desirable outcomes for a culture increasingly shaped by science and technology. But how does this analysis of factors that produce public ambivalence toward scientific inquiry, scientific literacy, and the scientific community itself bear upon an understanding of the origins and evolution of CSICOP?

CSICOP originated in the spring of 1976 to fight mass-media exploitation of supposedly "occult" and "paranormal" phenomena. The strategy was twofold: First, to strengthen the hand of skeptics in the media by providing information that "debunked" paranormal wonders. Second, to serve as a "media-watchdog" group which would direct public and media attention to egregious media exploitation of the supposed paranormal wonders. An underlying principle of action was to use the mainline media's thirst for public-attracting controversies to keep our activities in the media, hence public eye.

Who thought this strategy up? Well, Paul Kurtz, that's who. In 1975 as editor of the *Humanist* magazine this media-savvy philosophy professor published a statement entitled "Objections to Astrology" which ridiculed the purported "scientific" basis for astrology and condemned newspaper exploitation of "sun-sign" astrology columns. Newspapers picked up the article—many responded negatively. Other media sources picked up on what was a brewing controversy and before long the statement (which was signed by 186 scientists) had gained worldwide attention.

On the basis of the media response to "Objections," editor Kurtz decided to devote a major part of the forthcoming annual *Humanist* meeting to be held in late April 1976 in Buffalo to skeptical critiques of supposedly paranormal phenomenon. (I joined the magazine in November 1975 as an unemployed philosophy Ph.D. and promptly assumed duties of conference organizer and public relations man—hey, just do it!) These critiques, to be delivered by leading skeptics, would likely attract media attention and bring these individuals together for the first time.

The media coverage was unbelievable! Worldwide syndicated stories announced the formation of a new group dedicated to providing scientifically based information regarding widely publicized, supposedly paranormal phenomenon. We received front-page coverage in the *New York Times* and *Washington Post*. *Science News* sent its editor, Kendrick Frazier, who did an in-depth story concerning our mission complete with interviews of new committee members (e.g., Ray Hyman). The creation of our proposed new journal to publish skeptical critiques was highlighted in these stories.

Telegrams by the hundreds poured into the *Humanist* office. Some pledged financial support (Do you need money?). Within the year of the publication of the *Zetectic* we received a full-page story in *Time* magazine as well as continued coverage in the *New York Times* and other major newspapers. We were the recipients of welcomed attack after attack on the part of the paranormal press ("The New Inquisition," "The Return of the Dark Ages"), which gave us further media and public recognition.

Our publication, the *Zetetic*, (as advertised) featured skeptical critiques concerning media-hyped paranormal wonders. Our initial annual conferences had the same thematic emphases. Our conferences, like the journal (which became the *Skeptical Inquirer*), strived to attract media attention (successfully) by focusing on currently hot topics in pseudoscience. Again, the assumptions underlying these efforts were that the mass media were a major problem and both their attention and reform a primary remedy to public credulity concerning pseudoscience.

However, (I maintain) we discovered that although the way the media do business (an emphasis on the sensational to attract public attention) *is* an obstacle to accurate public assessment of issues, in a much more troubling, fundamental way the mass media *are* the public. The mass media simply share the widely held view, developed earlier in this essay, that "science" not only lies outside of popular culture but also has little to do with the ordinary thought processes of ordinary people relative to issues that interest them. The mass media, like politicians, dare not go past the limits imposed by the values and mental processes of its constituencies. Looked upon thus, mass-media credulity is more a consequence than a cause of public credulity.

Therefore, given this realization, it's no accident that as the decades of the 1980s and 1990s progressed there was an increasing variation of CSICOP conference topics (e.g., controversies in dinosaur extinction theories; ethical and scientific issues in animal experimentation; the teaching of critical thinking in secondary and higher education; cognitive, perceptual, physical, and motivational mechanisms underlying biased judgment; etc.). More telling yet, in the *Skeptical Inquirer*, we find essays redefining the nature of science literacy and science education which emphasize strategies that aim at making scientific thinking a widespread habit of mind and a subset of cultural literacy (e.g., Leon Lederman, "A Strategy for Saving Science" [November 1996]; E. A. Kral, "Reasoning and Achievement in a High School English Course" [May 1997]; Andrew Ede, "Has Science Education Become an Enemy of Scientific Rationality?" [July 2000]). One finds numerous articles, especially in the last decade, written by psychologists such as James Alcock, Barry Beyerstein, Susan Blackmore, Thomas Gilovich, and Ray Hyman, identifying the cognitive, perceptual, physiological, and motivational mechanisms involved in biased judgments together with strategies to overcome these predispositions. The investigative work of

Martin Gardner, Joe Nickell, and James Randi continually detailed the hubris that selective skepticism can bring to the lives of even distinguished scientists as well as more ordinary people. Also the *Skeptical Inquirer* in the 1990s increasingly featured a number of essays by scientifically literate philosophers and culturally literate scientists such as Arthur C. Clarke, Richard Dawkins, Stephen Jay Gould, Paul Kurtz, Steven Pinker, and the late Carl Sagan which explore the wider meaning of scientific inquiry for the personal as well as social dimensions of life.

Of course all these topics are interspersed with the traditional core of the *Skeptical Inquirer*—pieces debunking the media-hyped world of the "paranormal" and the latest pseudoscientific bunk (e.g., alternative medicine). But over time the *Skeptical Inquirer* (under science-writer Kendrick Frazier's astute editorship), CSICOP conferences, and the excellent courses and seminars offered through the Center for Inquiry have transformed CSICOP into a true science-education organization. Here science is conceived broadly as the cultivation of intellectual and personal dispositions that make for wise and sound judgment no matter what the subject matter. So defined scientific literacy and cultural literacy become integral, practical, and relevant to both public and personal life. So defined scientific literacy ceases to be vocationalized, elitist, arcane, archaic, and irrelevant to the lives we all lead.

NOTE

1. Two recent articles appearing in the journals *Skeptical Inquirer* (Adrew Ede, "Has Science Education Become an Enemy of Scientific Rationality?" [July/August 2000]) and *Academic Questions* (Vladimir N. Garkov, "Cultural *or* Scientific Literacy" [summer 2000]) provide valuable insights into the vocationalized, elitist nature of science education.

LEE NISBET, Ph.D., is professor of philosophy at Medaille College in Buffalo, New York. Dr. Nisbet holds degrees both in history and philosophy from the State University of New York at Buffalo. He is a cofounder, former executive director, and Fellow of CSICOP. He writes and lectures frequently on the application of logical and psychological critical-thinking techniques to controversial policy issues.

5

MY PERSONAL INVOLVEMENT
A Quarter Century of Skeptical Inquiry

PAUL KURTZ

I

In my introduction to this volume I detailed some of the special circumstances which surrounded the formation of the organized skeptics movement. In this essay I will focus only on one part of my personal skeptical odyssey. I wish to reflect primarily upon what happened in the twenty-five years since CSICOP's inception. As chairman of the committee, I can only highlight some aspects of this eventful odyssey. As I have said, we got off to a rousing start. The journey has been exhilarating ever since.

Personal Background

I should say by way of background that I have always been a skeptic, at least since my early teens. Like others in my generation, I questioned the regnant orthodoxy in religion and politics, and I flirted with Marxism as a young man, though I abandoned any illusions of Communism during the Second World War when I served in the U.S. Army on the western front. I saw that so many of the freed Soviet laborers in Germany—who had been forced into indentured servitude—refused to go back to Russia. I became an antitotalitarian early, though sympathetic to the social democratic agenda.

Although I flirted with mysticism and Catholicism for a brief period in my late teens, I was turned on to philosophy as a young GI after the war in the American army of occupation. I got a chance to go to a red-brick university in

Shrivenham, England, taught by both English and American professors. I took an introductory course in philosophy with Professor Charles W. Hendel of Yale University; the book that turned me on to skeptical inquiry was Plato's *Republic*, and in particular Socrates. I was intrigued by the arguments that Thrasymachus, a Sophist, laid down, and especially the effort by Socrates to respond to the challenge: "Why ought I to be moral?" Socrates was a gadfly, condemned to death by the Athenians for denying the gods, making the better appear the worse, and corrupting the youth of Athens. He took philosophy into the Agora, the public square, raising difficult questions and pursuing the life of reason. I resolved at that time to pursue a philosophical career, and after the war continued my studies on my return to the United States.

The most powerful intellectual influence on my life was Sidney Hook, who exemplified the Socratic method of inquiry. Hook was a student of John Dewey and was influenced by Karl Marx: knowledge for him was relative to praxis, truth claims can only be tested by the consequences of beliefs in experience and practice. I was impressed by Hook's course on "The Philosophy of Democracy," and enthralled by his ability to raise unsettling questions. He was the finest teacher that I had. He demonstrated the importance of the method of intelligence and the use of scientific inquiry, especially in dealing with social and political problems. Hook also disabused me of any lingering belief in Marxism, and I became a committed democrat. I had taken a triple major at NYU—in philosophy, political science, and economics. I accepted pragmatic naturalism in both epistemology and metaphysics. I had decided to go to Columbia University for my doctorate to study under other students of John Dewey, including Ernest Nagel, Herbert W. Schneider, and John Hermann Randall Jr.

I taught at a number of colleges, beginning with the conservative Episcopal school, Trinity College in Hartford, Connecticut (we called this the "Episcopal Party at Republican prayer"), Vassar, and Union College, and also for a period of time at the New School for Social Research (where I taught joint courses with Paul Edwards on atheism, agnosticism, and skepticism). Throughout my teaching career, I focused on the philosophy of the behavioral and social sciences, ethics, and value theory, but I had to teach a wide range of courses. At that time pragmatic naturalism involving a commitment to science and reason dominated American philosophy, but it went into eclipse for at least three decades as European imports began to dominate American faculties, especially analytic philosophy, but also phenomenology, existentialism, and even Marxism. For years I taught courses in the philosophy of religion and debated the existence of God—pro and con—and the immortality of the soul, and was a skeptic about both. One reason why I founded Prometheus Books in 1969 was that I thought that the country needed a dissenting press which would defend a thoroughgoing naturalistic and scientific-rationalist outlook.

My interest in the paranormal began especially in the early 1960s after meeting with and reading the works of Curt J. Ducasse of Brown University, and H. H. Price of Oxford, both of whom were involved in psychical research; and I was intrigued by the possibility of ESP and communication with the dead. Although I was doubtful of postmortem survival, the possibility of ESP seemed real. This was enhanced by my own personal experiences, because I thought that my wife, Claudine, whom I married in 1960, may have possessed telepathic powers (much like Upton Sinclair's wife). I was intrigued by the fact that she seemed to be able to read my mind. Perhaps I was causing certain perceptions or thoughts in her? I attempted some haphazard card-reading tests, and was surprised by the number that she guessed correctly. Although I did not myself investigate this phenomenon systematically, I was not unsympathetic to the claims of psychical research.

A development that disturbed me in the late 1960s and early 1970s was the emergence on American campuses in the wake of the New Left of a series of bizarre cults. I have in mind the Lyndon LaRouche U.S. Labor Party, which pursued me with a vengeance because of my commitment to democratic humanism; Hare Krishna; Reverend Moon's Church of Unification; and the Scientologists. This led me further into a concern with paranormal beliefs that were proliferating—from astrology and parapsychology to UFOlogy.

At that time, I was uncertain in my own mind about any number of issues. Although skeptical of astrology, I was not sure as to whether Michel Gauquelin's claims for a new science of astrobiology were true or not, and this inquiry occupied me for over twenty years. Similarly, like everyone else, I had been exposed to reports of UFOs and thought it most likely that they were extraterrestrial in origin. Indeed, I once devoted an entire issue of the *Humanist* magazine (May/June 1976), which I edited, to the question, "What should be our reaction to extraterrestrial beings should we ever encounter them on the planet Earth or in outer space?" My very first recognition that UFOlogy was mistaken was when I heard Philip J. Klass at the inaugural session of CSICOP. He provided alternative prosaic explanations of phenomena that seemed reasonable and led me to question my former beliefs in them.

Hence, at the inception of the skeptics movement, I had an open mind about the possibility of telepathy, the claims of Gauquelin, and the likelihood of UFOlogical visitations.

II

After launching CSICOP, we immediately became embroiled in controversy; claims and counterclaims were bandied about. Whatever we did as skeptics was intensely followed. Although we received a warm reception by mainline science magazines, we were bitterly attacked by believers. They accused us of being "the gatekeepers of science." They said that we blocked any consideration of new ideas and that we were suppressing new Galileos waiting in the wings to be discovered.

Astrology

This was particularly the case in regard to the Gauquelin affair. After issuing *Objections to Astrology* (in the *Humanist* in 1975), which detailed an attack on astrology, the Gauquelins threatened to sue the magazine for libel because of an article by Lawrence E. Jerome, who had criticized Gauquelin in one brief paragraph. I decided to invite Michel and Françoise Gauquelin to visit the campus of SUNY (even before the founding of CSICOP), and I asked my colleague, head of the Department of Statistics, Marvin Zelen (who later joined the Harvard faculty) to resolve the statistical issues; I also invited George O. Abell, noted astronomer at UCLA, to take part in the inquiry. We proposed, as CSICOP was being founded, to carefully examine Gauquelin's results.

The Gauquelins had claimed that they found an anomaly in the birth statistics of European, especially French and Belgian, athletes, such that Mars seemed to be in the first and fourth sectors as it traversed the twelve sectors of the heavenly sky at the time of birth, and that this was beyond chance. Since my wife was French, we visited the Gauquelins in Paris on several occasions, and we invited them to visit us in the United States.

Zelen had proposed an experiment, later called "the Zelen test," to check the hypothesis of the Comité Para in Belgium. This committee had investigated Gauquelin and disagreed with him because it differed about the baseline of probability of the birth of sports champions in relation to the path of Mars through space. Gauquelin was to go back to Paris and perform the Zelen test to see whether or not the Comité Para was correct. He was supposed to randomly select data and to determine what the normal path of Mars should be. The result of the test, according to Gauquelin, was that the Comité Para was wrong, and he concluded the Mars effect was real. Zelen, Abell, and I examined his work and found that he did not select the sample randomly; nor did he tell us, until we discovered it ourselves, that he had not included all the data from Paris. We thus thought that, before anything further should be said, we needed to try to get another replication of his thesis, and so we resolved mutually that we would attempt an independent sample of U.S. athletes. Gauquelin cooperated with us in this inquiry.

We attempted a careful compilation of data, and we ended up with 408 U.S. champions. The statistical calculations were done by Dennis Rawlins, a member of the Executive Council. Gauquelin disputed the results of the

American test, and he was able to arouse a sympathetic hearing from scattered scientists, who thought that his work had been carefully done. This was especially the case with Marcello Truzzi, who once having left CSICOP, made a career of attacking us for not being "fair-minded." The controversy was exacerbated when Rawlins split with the committee, primarily because George Abell was concerned about his academic qualifications and began to check his background. When Rawlins learned about this he resigned in a huff, but not before others believed that we had indeed used chicanery in the American sample. The results had been negative (Rawlins agreed here)—though Gauquelin sought to reinterpret the data post hoc and insisted they were positive. Hans Eysenck, a noted psychologist who was a friend and colleague whom I had worked with on other issues in the past, agreed with Gauquelin's critique, though he had never himself directly inspected Gauquelin's data.

Several articles on this research were published in the *Skeptical Inquirer* over the years, with responses by Gauquelin and Rawlins. The controversy became heated. Little did I know that this controversy would continue on both sides of the Atlantic for about two decades. We decided that we would need still another effort at replication, and thus we proceeded to work with a newly formed French committee of scientists. They were reluctant to take the time to perform the test, since they said that Gauquelin was not respected in France and that his work had little influence on French scientists. Nevertheless at our urging they decided to go ahead. Phillippe Cousin, the editor of *Science & Vie* (one of France's leading scientific magazines), said that he thought that such a test would be useful, and he called a meeting of Michel Rouzé, a veteran skeptic and editor of the journal *AFIS*, Gauquelin, and me, to lay out the protocol for such a test. This was a lengthy process: the French committee, working with an official scientific body, would send out for all the names in two French directories of sports figures, with an independent compilation of the data, not using Gauquelin's own data, which we suspected of some selective bias. This study took many, many years to complete. Led by Jean-Claude Pecker, Michel Rouzé, and other scientists, it was finally completed with the assistance of Jan Willem Nienhuys, a Dutch mathematician. The French committee concluded that the results were negative, and that there was no Mars effect, but that the statistical deviations that Gauquelin observed were attributed to selective bias (whether conscious or unconscious). Others, such as Geoffrey Dean, have since suggested still other explanations for Gauquelin's erroneous results (see chapter 15).

Shortly after the French completed their study Gauquelin committed suicide, with instructions that all of his data be destroyed. I should point out that we endeavored to maintain cordial relations with Gauquelin all during his life and indeed invited him to address CSICOP at Stanford University and on other occasions. There were other proponents of his hypothesis, however, such as Suitbert Ertel of Germany, who still defended the Gauquelin thesis; but we concluded after many years of hard inquiry that efforts at independent replications in the United States and France failed to sustain the hypothesis. The skeptics who performed these tests, namely Kurtz, Abell, and Zelen and the French committee, did not engage in debunking, but submitted the claims to a very laborious process of investigation.

I think that one of the chief contributions of CSICOP is that it led to demands that other claims of astrologers be tested. Indeed, perhaps more scientific effort has been devoted to testing astrology since the inception of CSICOP than ever in the history of the subject, and many of these papers were published in the *Skeptical Inquirer*. All of the results were negative.

We did at the same time conduct a public campaign in an effort to get newspapers to carry disclaimers to the effect that the daily astrological columns, which were based on sun signs, had no factual scientific support, but should be read for entertainment value only. Many professional astrologers agreed with this appraisal. We have managed to convince some sixty newspapers to carry such disclaimers. The conclusions of our efforts are first, that intensive scientific study has found no evidence for the claims of classical astrology or its horoscopes, and second, that the latter-day effort by Gauquelin to develop a new astrobiology has also failed to amass sufficient confirming evidence to support it.

Parapsychology

A good part of CSICOP's efforts were devoted to examining the claims of parapsychologists. We had an excellent parapsychological subcommittee, headed by Professor Ray Hyman of the University of Oregon, and including James Alcock, Barry Beyerstein, and others. This committee worked with other psychologists in the United Kingdom, including Susan Blackmore, Christopher French, Richard Wiseman, and David Marks.

The first alleged psychical claim that CSICOP agreed to investigate was that of Susie Cottrell, a young teenager who had appeared on Johnny Carson's *Tonight* show. Miss Cottrell was able to read cards in the hands of the players around a table, including Carson and Ed McMahon. Carson said that he was mystified. We received so many calls nationwide about her "powers" that we decided to challenge Miss Cottrell to a test in March 1978. Her own father said that he was puzzled about her abilities, and he agreed that she should be tested by an independent panel. The question was whether she possessed extraordinary abilities enabling her to read what was in other people's minds. The Cottrells sent an advance man to make arrangements. He arrived wearing a bowler hat, spats, and a nifty suit. Apparently there was some interest in developing a national show-biz career for Susie. He told me that he had had a sore on his nose that would not heal, and that after Susie touched it, the wound was cured instantly. I immediately became suspicious of what was afoot.

We used the facilities of the Department of Psychology laboratory at the State University of New York at Buffalo's Amherst Campus as a setting for the test, and we invited both Martin Gardner and James Randi to monitor the proceedings. There were several other observers present. ABC Television got wind of the experiment and sent a film crew. Martin Gardner was convinced that Miss Cottrell was using a standard card trick perfected by the Chicago card shark Matt Shulein; that is, in dealing the cards she was able to force a target card which she had peeked at to one of the assembled, and then later read the card in the recipient's hand.

Randi began by allowing her to display her feats. The controls at first were lax—she was allowed to deal the cards herself. Her performance was impressive. There was a TV camera on her at all times. Next it was announced that she would not be permitted to deal the cards. All of the subsequent results were negative. She failed every test run. Randi skillfully arranged a ten-minute break and told her that she could relax. There was immediate bedlam in the room. There was also a secret camera in the room hidden behind a screen. Unbeknownst to her, the camera recorded her peeking during the intermission at the top card. The next time she guessed correctly, but we knew why. We also invited Eddie Fechner, a well-known close-up magician, to duplicate her trick. He was able to palm five cards in his huge fist and call them out later, at which point Susie Cottrell broke into tears, crying, "That's not the way I did it." After Susie had been exposed little was heard from her again.

I should say that although I realized that there was intense trickery afoot in many of these cases or self-deception, I still was not certain whether psi phenomena existed. My skeptical colleagues insisted that such phenomena were unlikely, but I decided to investigate for myself, to satisfy my own curiosity. I did this by teaching a course, "Philosophy, Parapsychology, and the Paranormal," at the university. Most of the students who registered for the course were believers—I gave them a poll on the first day to determine their level of credulity. My plan was to work closely with students on various experiments in order to test psychic and other claims.

We did two things. First, we used the Zener cards to test for precognition, ESP, and telepathy, doing thousands of trials in class. Second, students would break down into teams of two to five investigators, conceive of a research project, and devote the rest of the term to performing tests. They would report on the design of the project, their progress, and the results. The students were extremely creative in what they proposed. Several well-known psychics were tested to see if they possessed any special abilities. There were also tests of Tarot-card readers and astrologers. The students investigated such things as whether psychics could influence the roll of dice (psychokinesis), reports of ghost hauntings, UFO sightings, and other phenomena. I repeated this course four times over eight years, and had over 250 students enroll. They conducted almost one hundred independent tests.

The most creative test was the Ganzfeld experiment conducted in the early eighties, which I designed with two top engineering students, using a Faraday cage in the Engineering Department. In this test we brought in at least a dozen well-known psychics from upstate New York and elsewhere.

The thing that absolutely stunned me was the fact that we never had positive results in *any* of the many tests conducted; they were always negative. I have never published these findings, for I did them basically to satisfy my desire (and my students') to ascertain whether anything paranormal could be uncovered. Betty Markwick did much to expose the Soal experiment in the British *Proceedings of the Society of Psychical Research*. After I told her about my testing experience, she remarked that chance dictates we should have had *some* positive results. Was the so-called goat effect suppressing the evidence? I doubt it. What I do know is that with rigorous protocol we invariably had negative results. Indeed, although 90 percent of the students began the course as believers, by the end 90 percent became extremely skeptical because of the failure to demonstrate the paranormal in their own experiments.

In any case, aside from my own involvement in this area, I think that parapsychologists have learned much from CSICOP's critiques, and they have attempted to tighten up their protocol, especially after the criticisms of Ray Hyman, Susan Blackmore, Jim Alcock, Barry Beyerstein, Richard Wiseman, and others.

In my view, if we are to accept any psi factor—and we should always be open to further inquiry—we need simply to insist upon three things: first, that any results be replicated in laboratories in which neutral and/or skeptical inquirers are involved; second, that tight protocol be used so that there can be no sensory leakage; and third, that careful and rigorous grading standards be adhered to, for what constitutes a hit is often questionable.

One of my most memorable experiences in the earlier years was my debate with J. B. Rhine on April 19, 1978, at the Smithsonian Institution in Washington, D.C. One amusing incident that occurred was that we were both wearing the same color and style of suit. I asked Mr. Rhine whether this was of paranormal significance or due to chance. I thought that he was a kindly gentleman but rather naïve. When I mentioned the chicanery of Walter Levy at his laboratory, who was caught cheating, he said that he was deeply hurt by the scandal, and was sorry that I brought it up.

Uri Geller

From the late 1980s till the mid-1990s CSICOP was confronted with legal suits brought by Uri Geller, who claimed that he had been libeled by James Randi and CSICOP. These legal battles took almost a decade to resolve. Geller was unable to prove his case, and CSICOP was awarded court costs. Geller also sued Prometheus Books for publishing books by James Randi (*The Truth about Uri Geller*) and Victor Stenger (*Physics and Psychics*), who had quoted Randi, and me for a passage I had published in *The Transcendental Temptation*, also drawing upon Randi's account. We agreed to modify these passages. At the present moment, suits still continue in Great Britain, and threats are constant from Geller, who has sued many others.

In any case, the courts refused to find in favor of Uri Geller, who claimed that he has special psychic powers, which he refused to have tested in a court of law. The amount of time and effort spent in defending ourselves against Uri Geller was exhausting. We were gratified that our readers rallied to the cause. They were deeply concerned about these harassing suits against a scientific body. Any time a new suit was leveled against us, contributions poured in, which enabled us to fight back.

One humorous incident stands out: I happened to be in London with my wife and daughter a few years ago, in an ice-cream parlor just off of Piccadilly Circus. The three of us were seated consuming our cones when I suddenly heard, "Paul Kurtz! Paul Kurtz!" A man approached me. He looked familiar. He said, "I'm Uri Geller! I'm Uri Geller! Paul Kurtz, how nice to see you!" I looked up and reciprocated the welcome. He introduced me to his wife, Hannah, and his son, who spoke French with my wife and daughter, and his colleague, Shipi Strang. Geller remarked, "I know that you don't believe in Jungian theories, particularly the theory of synchronicity; but the fact that Paul Kurtz should run into Uri Geller in London is too great an event beyond probability; therefore there must be something in the nature of things, something paranormal, to explain this." I smiled and said, "Well, most likely it was coincidental. I don't know that you can prove that there is a paranormal cause at work." Uri Geller invited me to visit him in his home outside of London the next day, but unfortunately we had to catch an early plane for the Continent. Throughout the legal proceedings with Geller over the years, I tried to remain friendly with him, though I must say it was trying. When I first met him in Maryland during a legal contest, I shook his hand. Of course, I remain convinced that he possesses no special powers.

It is important, however, that we distinguish the antics of psychics and gurus and the vast media hype about the paranormal from the serious work of parapsychologists. I have appeared on hundreds, perhaps thousands, of radio and TV shows over the years and have criticized the exaggerated claims made on behalf of the paranormal. But I have always insisted, and still do today, that any responsible claims made in parapsychology deserve a fair hearing, and I support the endeavor of serious parapsychologists to investigate anomalous phenomena.

UFOlogy

UFOlogy has proven to be especially fascinating. Philip J. Klass, a veteran UFO investigator, became chairman of a new UFO subcommittee which was made up of about nineteen skeptical investigators, including Robert Sheaffer, Gary Posner, and James Oberg. We each were numbered with a 00 before our name; by chance I happened to have the number 007, reminiscent of James Bond. There were so many claims proliferating in the public domain, and in the media, that the most this committee could do was selectively attempt to explain those which were most prominent. Philip J. Klass did a yeoman's job especially in seeking out alternative causal explanations. I myself was particularly intrigued by the ETI hypothesis, because as I said, I thought it was entirely possible that intelligent life existed elsewhere in the universe (even though it was sometimes difficult to find it on the planet Earth!). But whether we were being visited or had been visited by extraterrestrial beings manning advanced-state technological spacecraft was the issue. We needed to find some hard physical evidence to corroborate these claims. The one thing that perplexed me was that eyewitnesses were so often deceived. Given the cultural milieu and the prominence of such reports almost daily at that time, many people looking at the sky thought that they had seen UFOs. Obviously they had seen something in the sky, but whether it was a planet, entering rockets from Soviet or U.S. space probes, meteors, weather balloons, advertising planes, or something else was unclear. I had met many people who claimed to have seen UFOs and were intrigued by what I suspected to be the will-to-believe, or the transcendental temptation at work.

One case particularly stands out. It occurred in Voronezh in the former Soviet Union, a city about 200 miles from Moscow. We heard one morning on the radio and on television that a UFO sighting had occurred in the public square of Voronezh on October 9, 1989, and that creatures some eight to ten feet tall had descended, kidnapped two young lads, and taken off. The report said that the public square was contaminated with a substance where the landing pads had descended and was "unlike any substance seen on earth." They quoted a Russian geologist. The CSICOP office was besieged with many, many calls. Apparently the TASS news agency had sent out a press release about this. I remember well one reporter who asked me, "Now that the Russians have seen a UFO, do you accept it?" And my response was, "Well, this is a TASS report that we've not been able to confirm." "But TASS would not have lied," was the reply. And I asked, "Do you accept TASS reports about other matters?" The response was, "No, of course not." Then I said, "Why accept this at face value?" In any case, I began to work with a journalist for the *New York Times* and was able to place calls to Voronezh and to a nearby geology department to find out whether or not the scientist who said that the substance was unlike any seen on earth actually saw what was alleged. He denied the quotation attributed to him. It turned out after thorough investigation that the report was based upon hearsay and rumor spread by young children and that there was no objective evidence that such a UFO had landed. So much for the TASS report.

One area that really shocked us was the growth of reports of UFO abductions. Although Barney and Betty Hill in the famous New Hampshire case (in 1961) claimed that they had been abducted aboard a UFO, most UFOlogical investigators were dubious of this report. The psychiatrist on the case, Dr. Benjamin Simon, put Betty and Barney Hill under hypnosis. He said that he did not believe that such an event occurred, though the Hills themselves were convinced that they had seen something. Similarly for other popular abductee cases, a possible exception being that of Travis Walton, which many skeptics considered to be a complete fabrication.

Accordingly, it came as a complete surprise to us when about ten years ago reports of abductions not only began to proliferate, but were taken seriously. A number of popular books by Budd Hopkins,[1] Professor David Jacobs,[2] and John Mack,[3] a psychologist on the Harvard faculty, appeared. We were puzzled by the claims. I debated each of the proponents on television or radio. Carl Sagan wrote me to say that given the intense public interest, we really ought to look into this phenomenon carefully to see if anything is there. With this in mind we invited John Mack to our national convention in Seattle, Washington, in 1994, at a special session on UFO abductions. Mack said that he was convinced that these abductions were real, that he had a number of otherwise trustworthy people who reported such experiences under hypnosis, and he had to accept their claims as true. At an open meeting Phil Klass and John Mack tangled, but we allowed Mack every opportunity to present his point of view. What was at issue was whether or not psychiatrists should accept at face value the subjective reports of their patients. Would John Mack accept the hallucinations of schizophrenics who believe deeply in the worlds of fantasy that they concoct? If not, then why accept the uncorroborated reports of UFO abductees? Abductive reports were everywhere in the air, and indeed it was estimated by proponents that millions of people began to believe that they, too, were abducted.

An interesting sidelight: I headed a delegation of the CSICOP Executive Council to China in 1988. We spoke to several large audiences in Shanghai and Beijing. I invariably raised the open questions: "Has anyone in the audience ever been abducted aboard a UFO?" or "Does anyone know of anyone who has been abducted?" The response was always in the negative. What were we to conclude from this: that the ETs are prejudiced against Chinese and only kidnap Westerners, or a more likely explanation that the Western media hype at that time had not penetrated the Chinese mainland?!

There were many other famous cases that CSICOP investigated, most recently during the fifteenth anniversary of the Roswell incident, which allegedly occurred in 1947, and the Gulf Breeze case in Florida, which we exposed as a hoax. Where we stand at the moment is that there is insufficient evidence to corroborate the claim that UFOs are extraterrestrial in origin.

I must say that in my own empirical inquiry I was especially influenced by meeting and then reading a book published by Allen Hendry at the Center for UFO Studies.[4] Hendry was a colleague of Allen Hynek, a leading astronomer who accepted UFO reports as genuine. Hendry's book detailed over one thousand cases that came into Hynek's UFO Center during a year. The author, an astronomer, spent exhaustive efforts to investigate each case. He concluded that there was no hard corroborative evidence for the claims and as nearly as he could tell virtually all sightings for which there was sufficient data could be explained in perfectly prosaic and natural terms. I have yet to find a UFO case that withstood critical scrutiny. "What would it take for you to accept an ET visit as genuine?" I was often asked, and I replied: "I would like to see them flush a commode from outer space." At least that would give some corroboration of what otherwise seemed to be largely conjecture.

Hynek once said to me at a meeting at the Smithsonian that he agreed that there was no single case that withstood rigorous examination. However, he said that the great number of sightings worldwide were of sociological and psychological significance. I concurred with this fully, though the "sightings" in my view were not evidence for ET visitations; rather they were most likely in the "eyes of the beholders" and they told us something about ourselves. Isaac Asimov complained on a radio program that we jointly appeared on that when he wrote science-fiction novels he never imagined that people would believe in this bullshit!

III

Perhaps the most surprising thing that has occurred over the past few years is that as increasing waves of media sensationalism have inundated the public, what was formerly considered to be *unbelievable* is suddenly accepted as true by wide sectors of the public. Added to this is the "unsinkable rubber duck" phenomenon; namely, although skeptical investigators may thoroughly refute a claim in one generation, it may come back to haunt us in the next—as a Hydra-headed monster—with new intensity and attraction. I wish to briefly illustrate this by reference to other weird claims.

Communicating with the Dead

In the late nineteenth and early twentieth centuries spiritualism was very strong. Beginning with the Fox sisters in 1848, it was widely believed that some sensitives could communicate with discarnate spirits on the other side. Tens of thousands of spiritualists convened séances up and down the land, and many in the scientific community attempted to test these claims. They would put the mediums in darkened séance rooms and wait for some physical manifestation that could be observed by independent bystanders, such as rappings, table levitations, materializations, voices, and other such phenomena. The scientific community was very serious about evaluating these claims, and so a whole series of mediums, such as Eusapia Palladino, were carefully tested. In the end the preponderance of scientific judgment was that these mediums were fraudulent, that the so-called manifestations had no basis in empirical fact, and that efforts to communicate with the dead had failed. By and large, then, postmortem survival lacked intellectual respectability and had all but disappeared from the landscape.

In the decade of the 1980s, using such names as Ramtha, a latter-day form of spiritualism reemerged. The mediums were often called "channelers." These individuals claimed to have immediate contact with other dimensions from which they received messages of self-help, empowerment, and becoming one with the astral plane. Beginning in the 1990s a spate of best-selling books by a new generation of spirit mediums have appeared, and their authors were prominently interviewed on television. I have in mind especially John Edward (*One Last Time*), James Van Praagh (*Talking to Heaven* and *Reaching to Heaven*), Sylvia Browne (*The Other Side and Back*), and Rosemary Altea (*You Own the Power*). These mediums claim to have immediate communication with the dead in which they bring messages to bereaved relatives and friends. Unfortunately, there are virtually no efforts to corroborate what they have said by any kind of independent tests. Their subjective phenomenological readings are accepted at face value by publishers, popular television hosts, and the general public. This phenomenon is startling to skeptical inquirers who have been willing to investigate carefully the question of postmortem survival, but find this kind of "evidence" totally unreliable. Actually these so-called mediums are using familiar "cold-reading" techniques, by which they artfully fish for information while giving the impression it comes from a mystical source. What is so apparent is that gullibility and nincompoopery overtake critical common sense and all safeguards are abandoned in the face of guile, deception, and self-deception.

Lily Dale was the center of spiritualism at the turn of the nineteenth century. A decade ago it was considered to be of historical interest, a quaint remembrance of things past, a haven for white-shoe grandmothers engaged in psychic or spiritualist readings. At the end of the twentieth century Lily Dale has moved into vogue again as the fires of passion for an afterlife are fed with a new kind of frenzy—but with virtually all epistemological standards abandoned. Intense public fascination today with near-death experiences further illustrate this phenomenon. Phenomenological reports of out-of-body experiences by people who are near death can be given naturalistic, physiological, and psychological explanations without postulating a separable "soul leaving the body" and going to "the other side."

Miracles

Another phenomenon which is equally surprising is the return of miracles. Much of this has been fed by the implicit acquiescence of some within the Catholic Church. By the end of the eighteenth century the belief in miracles had been largely discredited by the powerful arguments of David Hume and other skeptical authors. By the nineteenth century it was believed that miracles were a substitute for our ignorance, and that if one examines long enough one can find natural causal explanations for otherwise inexplicable phenomena.

Within the last decade, however, miracle mongers have came to the fore. A good case is Medjugorje, in Bosnia-Herzegovina, which allegedly is a place where some young children were able to see the Virgin Mary and to transmit reports of her messages. Millions of pilgrims visited that site where it was claimed that miraculous events transpired, such as the changing of rosary beads into gold. (If you rub the silver plating, the brass underneath appears, which is mistaken for gold.) Interestingly, the children at Medjugorje never predicted the terrible wars of ethnic cleansing that ensued in Yugoslavia shortly thereafter. There was no forewarning from Mary. Skeptics were convinced, as were dissident Roman Catholics, that the best explanation for the miracles was that the children were fibbing. The willingness of young teenagers and children to deceive adults with preposterous paranormal claims is a common phenomenon that skeptics have encountered in psychical research and in "poltergeist" cases.

The outbreak of reports of miracles in the United States is especially disturbing, since America is supposed to be educationally advanced. There have been a great number of Jesus and Mary sightings, weeping icons and statues, even the return of stigmata. All of these claims, which were considered to be medieval superstitions by educated persons, have been moved to center stage by the media, and tens of thousands of devotees throng to places where miracles are proclaimed.

My colleague, the veteran skeptical investigator Joe Nickell, has spent years investigating alleged miracles. He has demonstrated, for example, that the Shroud of Turin was a forgery in the Middle Ages. Carbon-14 dating by three independent laboratories has confirmed that. Yet widespread belief that the Shroud of Turin is genuine is fueled by some prelates of the Church.

On the one hand, Church authorities claim that they employ rigorous standards in examining miracles; yet they encourage the disciples of the Shroud of Turin and other miraculous wonders to persist in their propaganda to the faithful. Scientific rationalists thought that the days of miracle-mongering were long gone. Now they have returned with a vengeance. According to a recent poll, some 86 percent of Americans believe that miracles are occurring and that the hand of God intervenes in the course of nature.[5]

Intelligent Design

The case for intelligent design, long thought to have been discredited in the sciences, has been brought to new prominence. The United States is perhaps the only major democracy in which the theory of evolution is hotly contested and in which a significant percentage of the population still believes in biblical creationism. This battle has been going on in the public schools for many years. What is surprising is the sudden emergence again of the intelligent-design argument, such as defended by Michael Behe in his book, *Darwin's Black Box.*[6] Arguments for intelligent design are also encountered in physics and astronomy. We are beginning to hear statements that the only way the universe can be explained is by postulating a Grand Designer. How else account for the "fine tuning" that has occurred? they ask, supposing that life could not have existed unless the proper conditions were present, and only an intelligent being could have arranged that. The arguments against intelligent design go back in the history of science; to wit, there is no evidence for a Designer. To read into nature the mind of God in analogy with the mind of Man is a vast postulation, a speculative thesis not based upon scientific evidence. Here we are dealing with a leap of faith, not fact.

Alternative Medicine

One other recent and startling development is the rapid growth of "alternative" or "complementary" medicine. A wide range of alternative therapies have become popular, most of them ancient, many of them imported from India and China. The list of these therapies is extensive. It includes acupuncture, qigong, therapeutic touch, magnetic therapy, iridology, naturopathy, reflexology, homeopathy, the extensive use of herbal medicines, esoteric cancer cures, crash diets, and the like.

One has to have an open mind about such therapies. They cannot be rejected a priori. Skeptical inquirers have insisted that proposed alternative therapies need to be submitted to double-blind randomized testing. Unfortunately, much of the support for alternative medicine is based on anecdotal hearsay or testimonials by self-proclaimed gurus and healers—such as Andrew Weil and Deepak Chopra—and much of this is spiritual in character.

The reason why skeptical inquirers are dismayed by this development is that scientific evidence-based medicine has made enormous strides in the past century combating illnesses, extending human life, and mitigating suffering—including the discovery of anesthesia, antibiotics, and modern surgery. Of course, not all diseases have been cured by the medical profession, and so out of desperation many patients turn to alternative therapies. In some cases, if you leave an illness alone, the body will restore itself to health. In others, the placebo effect can have powerful therapeutic value. In any case, the failure of large sectors of the public to appreciate how the scientific method works in medicine is one reason why alternative therapies seem to be gaining ground.

There have been so many other fascinating inquiries that I have been involved in as chairman of CSICOP over the years, that I could not possibly hope to describe them all. Among these are our examination of the claims of Indian gurus (such as fire-walkers), demonic possession, and exorcism (such as the Smurl family in Wilkes Barre, Pennsylvania), poltergeist manifestations (Tina Resch of Columbus, Ohio), faith healers (in cooperation with James Randi), the ongoing creation/evolution controversy, and so much more. All bear striking similarities as a psychosocial phenomenon.

IV

I wish to conclude by offering some personal reflections on the development of the skeptics movement in the last quarter of a century. This movement I submit is a very significant event in the history of science, for it helped to galvanize for the first time scientific inquirers who are willing to take part in systematic critical evaluations of paranormal claims.

The basic question that we need to ask is, Why do paranormal beliefs persist? At the end of the nineteenth century it was widely expected that irrationality and superstitions would decline as education was extended to more people and affluence increased. This has surely not happened, for paranormal and pseudoscience claims continue to proliferate. Although the fruits of science and technology are widely appreciated by the public, unreason still has wide appeal.

May I suggest some possible reasons for this: One explanation is because the claims of religions—old and new—are largely unexamined within present-day American culture. It is considered to be in bad taste to question anyone's religion. Granted, we ought to be tolerant of other points of view. On the other hand, should claims that are patently false be immune to criticism? There are a plethora of religious denominations in the United States and hundreds of bizarre sects and cults. Religious miracles like paranormal claims postulate a nonnatural transcendental realm that allegedly cannot be evaluated by evidence or reason. The universe is bifurcated into a natural world, which science deals with, and a transcendent spiritual realm, which allegedly lies beyond our ability to comprehend it. Concomitant with these two realms, their proponents insist, are two truths. This dualism is also said to apply to human personality where we confront a "separate soul."

This classical religious outlook had been eroded by the Copernican and Darwinian revolutions and by steady advances in the behavioral and neurological sciences. In spite of this, the spiritual realm is very rarely questioned. In my view it is impossible to isolate paranormal claims from religious claims. Most skeptical inquirers have said that they wished to deal only with those questions that have some empirical grounding. Interestingly, believers in the paranormal/spiritual worldview have blurred the borderlines between the paranormal and the religious. Religious conservatives and fundamentalists have, of course, been highly critical of New Age astrology, UFOlogy, and psychic phenomena, which they consider to be in competition with traditional religion. Nonetheless, paranormal phenomena, which allegedly exist over and beyond or beside normal science, are similar to religious miracles. I have labeled religious miracles as "paranatural," for they lie midway between the supernatural and the natural and are amenable to some evidential examination. In this sense, communication with the dead, the sighting of ghosts, exorcisms, faith healing, prophecies, and prayer at a distance are not unlike UFO abductions, out-of-body experiences, or precognitive predictions—they *all* are capable of being investigated scientifically.

Unlike many European and Latin American countries, the United States has never had a strong anticlerical tradition. The truths of the Bible, the Koran, or the Book of Mormon are promulgated daily from pulpit, radio, and television, and they are accepted on the basis of faith alone. They are institutionalized and become part of the historical traditions and structures of society. As such, they go largely unchallenged. There are few, if any, objective examinations widely available to the public of the so-called sacred literature. Why should reports of miracles in holy books—faith healing, exorcism, the virgin birth and Resurrection, the ascension of Mohammed to Heaven, or the visitation of Joseph Smith by the Angel Moroni—be any less amenable to critical scrutiny than any other extraordinary paranormal reports? The fact that these claims appeared in the past is no justification for nontreatment. If similar claims were made by anyone today, we would surely attempt to investigate them. Given the current cultural phobia against the investigation of religion, however, I submit that irrationality will most likely continue strong—unless skeptical inquirers are willing to use the best standards of science, including archæology, linguistics, history, biology, psychology, and sociology to uncover naturalistic explanations.

Another explanation for the persistence of the paranormal, I submit, is due to "the transcendental temptation." In my book by that name,[7] I present the thesis that paranormal and religious phenomena have similar functions in human experience; they are expressions of a tendency to accept magical thinking. This temptation has such profound roots within human experience and culture that it constantly reasserts itself. Given this, the most outrageous claims are often accepted as gospel truth. If this is the case, then there will always be new forms of transcendental mythology to entice us. And as quickly as one faith system is refuted or dies out (for example, the religion of Isis and Osiris, the Homeric myths, etc.), new forms of irrationality are likely to replace it.

Is there a genetic disposition for this powerful temptation? There are most likely a variety of complex biological, psychological, and sociological causes at work. Transcendental myths offer consolation to bereaved souls who cannot face their own mortality or those of loved ones. They provide psychological succor and social support, enabling them to endure the tragic elements of the human condition and to overcome the fragility of human life in the scheme of things. We need to ask how and in what sense the transcendental temptation can be modified and whether naturalistic moral and poetic equivalents can be found to satisfy it. I am convinced that belief in the paranormal is a religious or quasi-religious phenomenon: Astrology postulates that our destiny lies in the stars. Psychics maintain that there are untapped extrasensory powers that can probe other dimensions of reality. UFOs transport semidivine ETs from other worlds. All of these are efforts to transcend the normal world.

Still another factor in the recent growth of the paranormal is the introduction of new electronic media of communication that are radically altering the way that we view the world. Symbols and concepts are being replaced by signs and images: the abstractions of logic by contrived virtual realities. The culture of books is supplemented by the visual and auditory arts. These media express imagery and sound, form and color. Cinematography transforms intellectual content. Science fiction becomes the Sacred Church of the Paranormal. Soaring flights of imagination distort what is true or false. Instead of explicating a thesis, the immediacy of photography in motion seizes us and renders products of fancy as real.

The special problem that we face today is that the dramatization of spiritual-paranormal claims without adequate criticism now dominates the mass media, which are all too often more interested in box-office appeal than accurate information. The general public is exposed to a steady diet of sensationalized claims and is apt to accept them as authentic without sufficient skeptical dissent. Huge media conglomerates find that selling the paranormal by means of books, magazines, TV, and movies is extremely profitable.

Computers are also rapidly transforming the way information is imparted. The Internet is a vast repository of data bytes that presents a huge quantity of unfiltered claims that can be scrolled without critical analysis. By undermining standards of objectivity, any sentence or utterance is as true as any other, and in this process the methods of logic and science are deemed irrelevant.

I believe that the skeptical and scientific community has a special responsibility to help redress the current state of misinformation. This becomes difficult, however, for science has become overspecialized. Surely, a division of labor is essential if we are to advance the frontiers of knowledge; we need technical experts focused on specific fields of investigation. Yet one reason why the scientific outlook is continuously undermined by antiscience and pseudoscience is because specialists in one field may not necessarily be competent to judge claims in others, nor do they always understand that science primarily is a *method* of inquiry. Likewise there is insufficient understanding of the broader implications of scientific discoveries to our conception of the universe and our place within it. We need to state forthrightly the scientific case against intelligent design, the survival of the self after death, or the dearth of evidence for personal salvation. I submit that it is incumbent on us to defend the naturalistic interpretation of reality, a materialistic not a spiritual-paranormal account. We need generalists of science who can sum up what science tells us about the human condition in a universe without purpose or design, yet who have the ability to awaken wonder and excitement about the scientific quest itself. Philosophers have performed this task in the past; scientists need to do so in the future.

Given the massive cultural fixation on the spiritual-paranormal outlook, perhaps the most that skeptical inquirers can hope for is that we can lessen the excessive follies of its proponents. Perhaps our most effective course is to moderate untested overbeliefs and encourage critical thinking as far as we can. In my view, all human beings need to use some degree of cognition in ordinary life if they are to cope and function in the world. Our agenda should be to encourage the extension of critical thinking to all areas of life— including religion, politics, ethics, and society.

Looking ahead, I think that we can expect, unfortunately, that spiritual-paranormal beliefs will continue to lure large sectors of humanity. Although the content of their beliefs may change in the light of criticism, some forms of the paranormal will most likely persist in the future. Skeptical inquirers thus will have an ongoing role to play in civilization. Our mission is to light candles in the dark, as Carl Sagan so eloquently stated, and to become Socratic gadflies questioning the sacred cows of society and cultivating an appreciation for reason.

NOTES

1. Budd Hopkins, *Intruders: The Incredible Visitations at Copley Woods* (New York: Random House, 1987).

2. David Jacobs, *Secret Life: Firsthand Accounts of UFO Abductions* (New York, Simon & Schuster, 1992).

3. John Mack, *Abduction: Human Encounters with Aliens* (New York: Scribners, 1994).

4. Allan Hendry, *The UFO Handbook: A Guide to Investigating, Evaluating and Reporting UFO Sightings* (Garden City, N.Y.: Doubleday, 1979).

5. Reuters *Newsweek* poll, conducted in April 2000.

6. Michael J. Behe, *Darwin's Black Box: The Biochemical Challenge to Evolution* (New York: Simon & Schuster, 1996).

7. Paul Kurtz, *The Transcendental Temptation: A Critique of Religion and the Paranormal* (Amherst, N.Y.: Prometheus Books, 1986).

**PAUL KURTZ** is professor emeritus of philosophy at the State University of New York at Buffalo, and founder of CSICOP. He is the author of over five hundred articles and reviews and thirty-five books, including *The New Skepticism* (Prometheus Books), *Skepticism and Humanism: The New Paradigm* (Transaction), *A Skeptic's Handbook of Parapsychology* (Prometheus Books), and *The Transcendental Temptation: A Critique of Religion and the Paranormal* (Prometheus Books). He is also founder and president of Prometheus Books, the Council for Secular Humanism, and the International Academy of Humanism. He took his B.A. (1948) at New York University and his M.A. (1949) and Ph.D. (1952) at Columbia University. He is a Fellow of the American Association for the Advancement of Science.

II

PARAPSYCHOLOGY

6

WHY I HAVE GIVEN UP

SUSAN BLACKMORE

Imagine this . . . Imagine a world in which if you love someone enough, or need them enough, your minds will communicate across the world wherever you are, regardless of space and time. Imagine a world in which, if only you can think a thought clearly and powerfully enough it can take on a life of its own, moving objects and influencing the outcome of events far away. Imagine a world in which each of us has a special inner core—a "real self "— that makes us who we are, that can think and move independently of our coarse physical body, and that ultimately survives death, giving meaning to our otherwise short and pointless lives. This is (roughly speaking) how most people think the world is. It is how I used to think—and even hope—that the world is. I devoted twenty-five years of my life to trying to find out whether it is. Now I have given up.

If any one of these three possibilities turned out to be true then the world is a fundamentally different place from the one we think we know, and much of our science would have to be overthrown. Any scientist who discovered the truth of any of these propositions—or, even better, was able to provide a theory to explain them—would surely go down in the history of science as a hero; as the woman who changed the face of science forever. As Richard Dawkins puts it, "The discoverer of the new energy field that links mind to mind in telepathy, or of the new fundamental force that moves objects without trickery around a tabletop, deserves a Nobel Prize, and would probably get one" (Dawkins 1998, p. 128).

This is something that many critics of skepticism just don't see. I am

85

often accosted by people who seem to think that I think as follows (Note—I don't!): "I am a scientist. I know the truth about the universe from reading my science books. I know that telepathy, clairvoyance, psychokinesis, and life after death are impossible. I don't want to see any evidence that they exist. I am terrified that I might be wrong." The way I really think is more like this: "I am a scientist. I think the way to the truth is by investigation. I suspect that telepathy, clairvoyance, psychokinesis, and life after death do not exist because I have been looking in vain for them for twenty-five years. I have been wrong lots of times before and am not afraid of it." Indeed I might add that finding out that you are wrong, and throwing out your previous theories, can be the best way to new knowledge and a deeper understanding.

I long ago threw out my own previous beliefs in a soul, telepathy, and an astral world, but even then I kept on searching for evidence that my new skepticism was misplaced, and for new theories that might explain the paranormal if it existed (Blackmore 1996). I kept doing experiments and investigating claims of psychic powers. Finally I have given up that too.

One of the reasons I have given up is probably a trivial and selfish one—that I have simply had enough of fighting the same old battles, of endlessly being accused of being scared of the truth or even of trying to suppress the truth; of being told that if I don't come and investigate x (my near-death experience, my psychic twin, Edgar Cayce, the miracle of Lourdes, D. D. Hume, or the haunted pub round the corner) that proves I have a closed mind. It doesn't. It only proves that after years of searching for paranormal phenomena and not finding them, I am no longer prepared to spend my precious time and limited energy in documenting yet another NDE; setting up more carefully designed experiments to test telepathy in twins; going over all the reams of published argument about Cayce, Lourdes, or Hume; or sitting up all night waiting for the ghost that (because I am a psi-inhibitory experimenter) will never come.

I am sick of being told that I do not have an open mind. Long ago I wrote about the difficulty of having a truly open mind—or even knowing what this means. I called it "the elusive open mind" (Blackmore 1987) because I know, after years and years of struggling with competing beliefs, searching for evidence, and looking deep into my own motivations and fears, that having an open mind is not easy. To me an open mind means this: that you are prepared to change your mind if the evidence suggests you should. This sounds simple, but is not. It is a balancing act between having a mind so open that it changes every time the wind blows, and so closed that impossible standards of evidence are required to change it. It is a world away from the kind of "open mind" that critics love to flaunt; the kind that really means "If you agree with me you have an open mind—if you agree with scientists you don't."

Recently I was on the stage with three other "skeptics" for a TV chat show about mediumship and clairvoyance. We had been explaining various ways in which mediums can appear convincing without any spirits, how Tarot cards work without paranormal powers, and how the evidence refutes the claims of astrology, when a woman in the front row jumped up and said, "The trouble with you is you don't have an open mind!" I surprised even myself by jumping right back at her with an impassioned speech, concluding "and would you be prepared to change your mind if you found out you were wrong?" Maybe she would have, but in my research I have learned how hard that is.

A few years ago a young student called James Basil came to interview me for his media project. He asked me lots of interesting questions about alien abductions and sleep paralysis and then shocked me by proclaiming that he knew I was wrong—he had experienced both and knew they were not the same thing at all. I then started asking the questions, and learned about the aliens who landed in the fields outside his house, their visits to his bedroom, and the operations they performed on him inside their spaceship, starting when he was only five years old. Finally he showed me a tiny metallic object that the alien creatures had implanted in the roof of his mouth and which he had removed after two weeks of discomfort. Would I, with my "closed mind" on UFOs, be prepared to analyze it scientifically?

I think he was surprised when I jumped at the chance. He seemed to think I wouldn't want to know—that I would be afraid to learn the truth. Yet my own skeptical view of abductions was open to test by just this kind of object. Indeed, if he had found a piece of alien technology in his mouth every scientist worthy of the name would want to know about it.

But I had no equipment to analyze it with. I put round an e-mail call to everyone in our Faculty of Applied Sciences asking for help. Another myth was incidentally exploded—that hard-nosed physical scientists are eager to suppress the truth about the aliens among us. I had not one negative response to my plea—not a single scientist telling me I was wasting my time or theirs. Instead I received several extremely helpful ones—from simple suggestions about what to do, to offers of time and technical help on the scanning electron microscope and X-ray Microanalysis system.

James and I spent a morning in the lab, first looking at the object under a light microscope and then in the electron microscope. He pointed out the similarities with previous published implants, and got increasingly excited as we saw telltale hairs and other features that he compared with John Mack's famous implants. Then came the crunch. The mysterious object, though it looked very much like other "implants" under the electron microscope, turned out to be made of dental amalgam (Blackmore 1997).

I was concerned about how he would react, and over a cup of coffee he struggled to tell me. He did not, as I guessed some people in his situation might, claim that the object had been switched or the machine was not working or the technician in error. He tried to understand how the machines worked and to accept the conclusion. In fact he almost seemed relieved. He likened his feelings to those after having had a brain scan and learning he was not seriously ill. He had clearly been frightened of the aliens implanting more objects in his body and now he knew that this was unlikely. I do not think he stopped believing in the aliens or his abductions, but his views did change in important ways. He also showed me—yet again—how difficult and emotionally taxing it can be to shift your beliefs in the face of the evidence.

People are not always so willing to grapple with evidence. In 1998 I was reading the only newspaper available on a holiday flight when I saw a photograph of Cherie Blair, the prime minister's wife, wearing something called a bioelectric shield. Apparently this attractive pendant hanging round her neck reduced her stress and protected her from harmful radiation. Hillary Clinton was said to own one too. I was angry. I assumed the pendant had no effect. How could intelligent and high-profile people like this possibly believe in, much less promote, such lies? Then I noticed the price—£119 (US $139) for the cheapest, and £749 (US $995) for the gold version, and was sufficiently angry to want to do something about it.

First, I realized I was jumping to conclusions. What if the shields really did work? If they did then some extraordinary new principle must be involved and I would learn something very exciting indeed. If they did not then the facts should be made known. I decided to do some experiments to find out.

The bioelectric shield Web site (http://www.bioelectricshield.com) and leaflets make several claims, among them that "The shield utilises principles of physics to help you cope with the energy overload/stress of your daily life." Each shield "contains a composition of a matrix of precision-cut quartz and other crystals designed to balance and strengthen your natural energy field." My own favorite is this: "Not only does this crystal force field deflect harmful electromagnetic energies coming from your Computer Screens, Cell Phones, Microwaves, Hair Dryers and other electronic equipment but it deflects any personal energy that is incompatible with you. The shield resonates at your personal frequency after wearing it for 24 hours, it will act as a 'Gatekeeper' letting in only energies that are compatible with you and deflecting those not compatible with you."

These were the claims I had to test, and test fairly. On the positive side the effects were mostly measurable, such as increasing muscular strength, reducing stress, and improving well-being. Among the problems of testing it was that the shield takes some time to balance itself to a person's personal energy and that it cannot be shared with anyone else. This meant doing a long-term study with one shield per person.

I tracked down the British distributor, David Chambers, and through him the American manufacturer, Virginia Brown, and after many discussions they supplied us with six real and six fake shields. Nick Rose and I asked twelve women to wear these for several weeks and measured their hand strength, mood, and stress levels at regular intervals, without either them or us knowing which shields were which (Blackmore and Rose 2000). We tried to arrange the double-blind precautions to be fair to both the manufacturers and to us. We did not want to find either that we had negative results and they thought we could have cheated, or positive results and we thought they could have cheated. Arranging this was not easy, partly because they did not seem to understand what was required. Eventually, however, we all agreed that Nick and I would prepare results for each subject coded by letter and a list of who had worn which numbered shield, and that David and Virginia would come to our lab with a list of which of the numbered shields was fake and which real. We would exchange these in front of an independent witness so that neither side could cheat.

Up until the moment they arrived I had been obsessed with the precautions, but as soon as they arrived I knew there was no need. They were genuine, eager to find out the results, and trying to give us their code list even before we got into the lab. We stopped them from doing so and laid out the results for them. This way they could see, out of twelve subjects, who had become stronger, more relaxed, or calmer, and we gave them the chance to choose, from these twelve people, which six they thought had worn the real shields. By chance they should get three right; with the probability of getting four right 0.24, five 0.04, and six 0.001. In other words, if they correctly chose five or six of the subjects we would have a significant result. We could analyze the complete results later. David and Virginia studied the graphs carefully, made their choice, and then handed over the code list.

It was a genuinely exciting moment. We believed no one could have cheated and we had no idea which shield was which. If they got five or six right we would know we had some strange and incomprehensible effect on our hands. If not we would know we had more false and potentially damaging claims to deal with. We took their list and marked up the graphs. They had gotten four right.

What happened next was the most informative event of all. They began to explain what had happened. This person had obviously been blocking the shield's energy. This person may have needed longer with the shield—shields can spend at least four weeks rebalancing some people. This person had become more relaxed even with a fake shield. Over lunch we talked more—they seemed disappointed, but only slightly so. They were sure there was some explanation, and they never seemed to entertain the possibility that the shields do nothing at all.

Later we did the full analysis and sent them the results. Virginia wrote that she had initially thought the results were a disaster but finally came to see them as a "blessing in disguise." Apparently her consultant told her that the placebo shields should not be made by the same person as the real shields because the makers "have been making shields with such clear intent that they will strengthen and balance people, that this 'energy' goes into the shield with or without the actual crystals." She seemed surprised by this strange claim but also willing to accept it, and she recommended that we use shields made a different way for our next experiments. Indeed, she kindly had a new set of three real and three fake shields made especially. Using these we carried out two further experiments to find out whether the shields protect people from the weakening effects of holding a mobile phone (cell phone). The results suggest they do not (Blackmore and Rose 2000).

I had started this study with the opinion that someone somewhere was maliciously and greedily making false claims to take money from vulnerable people. I ended up with quite a different view—that well-meaning people were selling a product they genuinely believed in to people who also believed in it and felt better, even though the specific claims are false. You might argue that as long as people feel better no harm is done, but the harm is that the effects of a powerful placebo can lead people to adopt a demonstrably false, and even antiscientific, view of the world.

One final example concerns a psychic claimant, David Spark, a soft-spoken man in his late thirties who just turned up one day in our lab. David claims to be able to predict the outcome of horse races, not by knowing the form or juggling the odds (though he is very good at that) but by using his psychic powers. He spends three or four hours a day in the "bookies" practicing, and finally decided that he wanted to be properly tested. Nick Rose and I agreed and asked him what he could do. He said he could tell the suit of playing cards, so for six weeks I hid a playing card in a filing cabinet and he rang in with his guess. He was quite successful with this task, getting three out of six guesses right, but said he preferred the horses where you have a list of names to look at. So we devised a new test using lists of names chosen by him.

He made fourteen guesses and got none right. Yet he was sure that if he could get more relaxed, or improve his sleep and diet, or find a task more like horse racing, the results would improve. Nick then wrote a program which displayed a simple horse race on the computer screen, and between April and May 1999 David made ten guesses from home. Again the results were below chance and again David came up with numerous reasons why he had failed. Finally we invited him to come to the lab for properly controlled tests, and after each experiment I recorded an interview with him.

In the lab David could work in his own time, predicting the outcome and then running the race when he was ready, as often as he liked up to a preset number of trials. In the first experiment we decided on one hundred trials (several weeks' work with anything between five and fifteen trials per session) and David predicted he would get about half the winners right. In fact he got just six—fewer than the ten predicted by chance. Afterward I asked him about these results.

"Well, I was very happy with the results that I got. I was totally pleased with them because one of the things I said was sort of linking some of the numbers up . . . like one, two, and ten together; three, four, and nine together, and five, six, seven, and eight together. . . . You can look at them in lots of different ways, but looking at them that way, one, two, and ten, come up with thirty-nine answers out of a hundred. . . . So I was totally happy when I saw the results. The second last session I did, there was still ten more to do and at the end of that I added all the results and come up with a graph and everything and I looked at that and I saw a few things there, and I thought, I'm really pleased with that."

He did indeed make a graph, and a chart of results, and numerous calculations. His understanding of probability was far sharper than mine, and yet he seemed always to conclude that he had succeeded, when I thought he had not. The problem, as so often in psychic claims, is looking for patterns after the fact. If you study the results of any such experiment you can always find interesting patterns, and we did. The question is—are they chance or real? The answer is—if they are different every time, and only visible in retrospect, then they are probably chance. As we explained, if he could predict in advance that he would get, say, more hits on positions seven and eight—or indeed any pattern he cared to predict, then we could test that.

We eventually carried out five experiments of this kind. In the later ones we gave him toy money with which he could bet a different amount on each race. The results of these experiments were fascinating. None of the individual results was significant for first-place hits. Overall David completed 210 trials with ten horse races, and obtained exactly twenty-one hits. In other words, it appears as though there is nothing but chance guessing operating. Nonetheless, he came out with a small profit on his winnings, a sum of ranks significantly below chance (which suggests something other than chance going on), and a conviction that his powers were real. After each experiment he explained why he had failed, and maintained great optimism about his achievements.

In our final interview I was quite straight with him. I knew him fairly well by now and really wanted to understand what was going on in his mind. I suggested that "it's all chance, and all these ideas you have are actually completely irrelevant." To my surprise he agreed this was possible, but added, "I'm totally convinced that I do have an ability—what the first hundred experiments show is that I can't just do anything I want to, I just can't consciously decide. I have to have my mind in a certain status, a certain way, and it's something I've got to be relaxed about, and I've got to be confident about what I'm doing. . . . I'm still learning." I told him that skeptics would not yet be convinced and he replied, "But I'm so certain, so positive that I definitely can do it that it's only a matter of time—that it will be there."

In all these cases the people involved stuck to their own familiar paradigms—and here the much overused word "paradigm" is quite apposite (Kuhn 1962). When the results were not as they expected they did not consider the possibility that their whole paradigm was false, but instead preferred to patch it up with ad hoc explanations for every failure. Although

James did change his mind in important ways, he did not abandon the idea that aliens were abducting him. But then imagine how hard it would have been for him, or any of them. In all cases they were deeply committed to their worldviews and to some extent their whole lives were bound up with their beliefs. James was involved with various UFO organizations and with magazines about aliens. David and Virginia made their living out of selling bioelectric shields and other similar products, and David Spark once told me, referring to his work with us, "It is the actual focus of my life."

Skepticism is the focus of many skeptics' lives. Some have committed their careers to promoting skepticism and to debunking paranormal claims. Would they find it easy to change their minds if good evidence for the paranormal came along? I think not. The problem in making this comparison is that there is, as far as I can tell, no good evidence for the paranormal. Nevertheless, some skeptics display just the same reluctance to change, and tendency to biased interpretations, as the most ardent believers do. In skeptical books and magazines we can read again and again authors who prefer to accept even the feeblest and least well founded skeptical explanation of a claim, rather than consider the possibility that the claim might be true. Yet if we are going to study psychic claims at all, we must always consider the possibility that they are true. Unlikely as it is, ESP and PK might exist. There could be forces as yet undiscovered. We should accept the best explanation we can find—not the one that we like the most. The lesson we should learn from James, David, Virginia, and David Spark is not that believers find it hard to be open-minded but that we all do.

Not only is it emotionally taxing to consider our least favorite theories, but it is hard work too. It takes a lot of time and effort to make a reasonably fair and unbiased assessment of any paranormal claim. I knew I was no longer prepared to do it properly when one day a huge pile of papers arrived in the post. The Stargate affair had just broken. The evidence coming out of all the Stanford Research Institute remote-viewing work was published and various people were arguing about whether it did, or did not, provide evidence for psi. Several people asked for my opinion and a friend sent me a huge packet containing all the information. I balked. I was not prepared to be an ignorant parapsychologist/skeptic and give opinions on experiments I had not studied. I knew that I would be prepared to give an opinion—whether publicly or privately—only if I had read all that material. And I knew that I did not want to read it.

I knew then that I had to give up. In the fall of 1998 I gave a lecture to the Society for Psychical Research entitled "Why I Must Give Up Psychical Research."

The more serious reason why I have given up is that I no longer believe in the world I outlined at the start. Indeed, I no longer believe that the search for paranormal phenomena will provide insight into the "big questions" of life—though when I started out on my career in parapsychology I was sure it would. I really believed that studying the paranormal would help me with such mysteries as "What kind of world is this? What am I? and How should I live my life?"

As the founders of psychical research perceived, questions about ESP, PK, and survival of death strike right to the heart of these big questions. If ESP and PK exist, our minds have the power to reach beyond the body with its ordinary senses and physical limitations. Much of psychology and neuro-science must be wrong because they are entirely founded on the assumption that physical transfer of energy and information is required to produce behavior, understanding, and awareness. If there is personal survival of death then we humans must have some kind of soul or inner self that can survive independent of the body. Some form of dualism must be true, however inconceivable that seems to our present-day science and philosophy. The implications are immense.

So, too, are the implications for how we should live our lives. If telepathy or PK are real then we might be able to help others with their use. Perhaps we should cultivate them, or learn to protect ourselves against their misuse. If survival is real then we must live our lives in the knowledge that there is some realm beyond—where our earthly deeds may have conse-quences, and which gives some new meaning to our lives here on earth.

But what if they don't exist? Then each of us is a biological creature, designed by natural selection for the survival of our genes and memes; here for no reason at all other than the dictates of chance and necessity, and unable to contact or influence anyone else except through the normal senses and physical processes. Our consciousness, and the perceived world around us, emerge from the complex interactions between brains and their envi-ronment, and when those brains decay then our awareness stops.

Living in a world like this is truly scary. There is nothing to hang onto. It seems to me now that free will is an illusion, and even our precious selves are not solid persisting entities but ephemeral constructions that change all the time. There is no continuous self who lives our lives, let alone one that could survive our deaths. There is no point in behaving well so as to have our reward in the afterlife, for there is no afterlife. There is only this world now, and our actions must reflect that knowledge. I say this is genuinely scary, though I think it gets easier with practice. And to those who accuse me of being scared of the paranormal, I can only say, "Try this instead." But asking which you find most scary really is not the point. Fear is never a good reason for choosing one's view of the world.

How then can we answer the big questions? I would say in two ways. One is by personal experience and disciplined observation; trying to see clearly the truth about oneself and the world. That is why I meditate and practice mindfulness. So throwing out the paranormal does not mean aban-doning spirituality or spiritual practice. The other is by doing science, and for me the interesting questions now concern evolutionary processes, memes, and the origins of consciousness (Blackmore 1999).

What then of parapsychology? The world still might be as I imagined it at the start and because the implications would be so profound I am glad that others are carrying on. The recent resurgence of funding for parapsychology means there are several new labs and many new researchers at work. If psi does exist then one day one of them will find a way to demonstrate it and a theory to explain it. If that happens I shall be back like a shot, but until then, happily, I have given up.

REFERENCES

Blackmore, S. J. 1987. "The Elusive Open Mind: Ten Years of Negative Research in Parapsychology." *Skeptical Inquirer* 11: 244–55.

———. 1996. *In Search of the Light: The Adventures of a Parapsychologist.* Amherst, N.Y.: Prometheus Books.

———. 1997. "Scientific Analysis of an 'Alien Implant.'" *UFO Magazine* (November/December): 9–11.

———. 1999. *The Meme Machine.* Oxford University Press.

Blackmore, S. J., and N. Rose. "Testing the Bio-Electric Shield." Submitted for publication.

Dawkins, R. 1998. *Unweaving the Rainbow: Science, Delusion and the Appetite for Wonder.* London: Penguin.

Kuhn, T. S. 1962. *The Structure of Scientific Revolutions.* Chicago: University of Chicago Press.

SUSAN BLACKMORE is Reader in Psychology at the University of the West of England, Bristol, where she teaches the psychology of consciousness. She has a degree in psychology and physiology from Oxford, an Msc from Surrey University, and received one of the first Ph.D.s in parapsychology in the country. Her research interests include consciousness, evolutionary psychology, and the theory of memetics. She is a Fellow of CSICOP, and has been awarded prizes by both the Society for Psychical Research and CSICOP. She is author of more than fifty scientific articles. Her books include *Beyond the Body* (1982), *Dying to Live: Science and the Near-Death Experience* (1993), (with Adam Hart-Davis) *Test Your Psychic Powers* (1995), and an autobiography, *In Search of the Light* (1996). She has been training in Zen for many years. She writes for several magazines and newspapers, and is a frequent contributor and presenter on radio and television. Her most recent book, *The Meme Machine*, was published by Oxford University Press in March 1999, and has been translated into eight languages.

7

THE MAGICIAN AND THE THINK TANK

LEON JAROFF

always knew that I had a skeptical gene, but it didn't fully express itself until one day in January 1973 when I received a teletype from correspondent John Wilhelm,[1] then stationed in *Time* magazine's Los Angeles bureau. Wilhelm had visited the prestigious Stanford Research Institute, in Menlo Park, California, which was testing a twenty-five-year-old Israeli man named Uri Geller who, according to Wilhelm's story suggestion, had uncanny powers. He could communicate by telepathy, detect and describe objects completely hidden from view, and by sheer "psychic" energy cause metal to deform, electronic equipment to malfunction, watches to stop, and compass needles to deflect!

In my capacity as a *Time* senior editor of the magazine's science, medicine, environment, and behavior sections, it was my responsibility to evaluate the suggestion and recommend either accepting or rejecting it. My degrees from the University of Michigan were in electrical engineering and math, I had taken several physics courses, and I was all too aware how tiny the brain's electrical currents and corresponding magnetic fields were. Certainly they were far too weak to have produced any of Geller's claimed feats.

My immediate reaction, one of disbelief, was followed quickly by a sense of alarm. *Time*'s managing editor, Henry Grunwald, also received copies of suggestions and, like Wilhelm, had a weakness for paranormal claims.

There was no time to lose. Suggestion in hand, I raced up the stairs, stood at Grunwald's office doorway, waited until I caught his attention, and blurted, "If one claim in this suggestion by Wilhelm is true, I'll resign, book passage to Tibet, and become a monk."

95

Grunwald had already read the suggestion, and looked annoyed. "How can you be so sure?" he asked grumpily. I had no doubts. "Let me prove that this is a lot of nonsense," I pleaded. Looking even more irritated, Grunwald threw up his hands and waved me away dismissively. "Okay," he said resignedly, "let's see what you can find."

Back in my office, I assigned Wilhelm to file a detailed report of his observations at the Stanford Research Institute (now called SRI International), queried our Jerusalem correspondent to get the lowdown on Geller's activities in Israel, and placed a call to a personal friend employed at SRI.

The institute was one of America's largest and best-known think tanks. Its staff of 2,600 specialists did research for government agencies and private industry, worked on counterinsurgency programs in Southeast Asia, explosives technology, chemical and bacteriological warfare, and antiballistic missile systems. Its reputation was impeccable. Then why had it undertaken the Geller project?

Word among staff members was that President Charles Anderson, who had first opposed the project, changed his mind after viewing demonstrations by Geller. Indeed, an SRI physicist named Russell Targ had sent a letter to several science journals proposing a report on the psychic research that he, SRI physicist Harold Puthoff, former astronaut Ed Mitchell, and Kent State physics professor William Franklin were conducting. I found it most significant that none of the four, including Puthoff, was apparently put off— so to speak—by Geller's claims that the source of his powers was some extraterrestrial "intelligence."[2]

Interviewed by Wilhelm, Mitchell insisted that "from Anderson down, SRI views Geller as legitimate." Anderson would not go that far. "Mr. Geller was provided to us as a subject for experimentation," he hedged. "Measurements were made in our laboratories and the work will stand on its own merits."

That work soon caught the attention of the Department of Defense (DOD), which at that time was naively taking paranormal reports seriously, fearful that the Soviet Union might soon be using psychics to get a leg up on the Pentagon. Concerned, the DOD promptly sent a team to Menlo Park to investigate the strange goings-on. One team member, frequently used by DOD as a consultant, was Ray Hyman, a University of Oregon psychology professor. He was accompanied by George Lawrence, a project manager for DOD's Advanced Research Projects Agency, and Robert Van de Castle, a University of Virginia parapsychology researcher.

After a day of observing Geller as he demonstrated ESP and psychokinesis in action at SRI, Van de Castle, as might be expected, thought that Geller might be "an interesting subject for further study." But Hyman and Lawrence were not impressed. Hyman, especially, was disdainful, having spotted "loopholes and inconsistencies" in each of Geller's performances. In fact, he charged Geller with outright deception.[3]

Geller, for example, asked Lawrence to think of a number between one and ten and to write it down in large letters on a pad. While Lawrence wrote, Geller covered his eyes and appeared to be concentrating. But Hyman, his gaze fixed steadily on Geller, saw that his eyes, visible through spaces between his fingers, were wide open. That was enough for Hyman. Geller, he knew, was able to see the motion of Lawrence's arm as he wrote and was able to call out the number (which turned out to be ten) that Lawrence had written. And, of course, Hyman knew that most able magicians have learned to read arm movements involved in writing.

While Geller was causing a compass needle to turn about five degrees, Lawrence noticed that the Israeli was wiggling his body and vibrating the floor. The DOD man immediately did the same, causing the needle to deflect even more, startling Geller and Targ, who immediately accused Lawrence of using trickery and insisted on searching him for hidden magnets—which, of course they didn't find. Strangely enough, Targ never felt it was necessary to conduct a similar search of Geller. Indeed, both he and Puthoff time and again demonstrated a strong, and definitely unscientific, compulsion to believe in the Israeli.

Hyman's conclusion: the SRI tests were performed with "incredible sloppiness" and produced "the most uncontrolled and poorly recorded data I have ever encountered."[4]

The obvious skepticism of Lawrence and Hyman hardly deterred SRI (which was simultaneously testing a psychic named Ingo Swann, supposedly blessed with the ability to do "remote viewing"). It continued testing Geller, filming him and awarding him with a $100-a-day honorarium, a car, and all expenses for a total of six weeks.

After departing from Menlo Park, and leaving the awestruck Targ and Puthoff behind to write their report, Geller traveled to Ossining, New York, and the home of his sponsor in the United States, the late Andrija Puharich, an eccentric medical doctor who had set up his own laboratory to study psychic phenomena. Wilhelm, whom I had now assigned to report the story, followed him there, witnessed some of Geller's demonstrations, and was impressed. Indeed, according to a weird book later published by Puharich,[5] Wilhelm seemed convinced that Geller was legitimate. He had also informed Puharich and Geller disapprovingly that I, his editor, was convinced that Geller was a fraud.

Meanwhile, as we made preparations for a story, we phoned Puharich and asked that he bring Geller to our offices to perform his feats in front of the *Time* science staff.[6] Puharich agreed, and when he and Geller arrived at the Time and Life Building in Manhattan the next week, they were escorted to a conference room where my staff—writers, researchers, and secretaries— was assembled. While Puharich waited outside, Geller began to perform. Keys and spoons bent, watches stopped, and minds were read, phenomena that often occurred immediately after Geller distracted his audience by asking a secretary to get him some water, for example, or a writer to adjust the room lights.

Yes, and each time that Geller made a request, most of the *Time* staffers looked toward the person Geller was addressing. But two of the people in our group kept their eyes fastened on Geller. Though they were dressed informally—some might say shabbily—to resemble editorial types, they were not *Time* staff members. In fact, unknown to Geller and Puharich, they were magicians, invited by *Time*'s talented picture editor, John Durniak. One was Durniak's friend, Charles Reynolds, editor of *Popular Photography*, the other a professional magician with whom I was about to begin a long and collaborative friendship—James (The Amazing) Randi. Their rapt attention paid off. For they observed Geller bending a key manually, for example, during one of his planned distractions.[7]

After Geller had departed, leaving behind some genuinely puzzled *Time* staffers, Randi stood up, introduced himself, and proceeded to duplicate virtually every one of Geller's feats. In fact, Randi's performance was more polished than Geller's, as well as being interlaced with humorous asides. None of the wondrous happenings depended on any paranormal ability, Randi assured us, just on skill and deception.

Evidence against Geller continued to mount.[8] From Jerusalem, our Middle East correspondent reported that Geller had been investigated by a team of scientists from Hebrew University, who followed him on one of his "psychic" tours and observed him using a variety of magicians' techniques to deceive his audiences. Before a performance, he peeked though a hole at the audience assembling in a theater lobby, noting, for example, that one woman had opened her shopping bag and displayed to a companion her new light blue scarf. Later, during his performance, he picked the woman out of the audience, asked if they had ever met, feigned concentration, and then declared that he sensed something blue and diaphanous in her bag. Astounded, the woman pulled the scarf from the bag and displayed it to the audience.

On another occasion, Geller provided a local newspaper with a photograph of himself with Sophia Loren, claiming that he had used psychic ability to help her with some problem. The photograph turned out to be faked, a skillfully assembled composite of two separate pictures. Exposed, Geller left Israel in disgrace.[9]

Using material from all of our sources, including Wilhelm (but ignoring his naïve conclusions), I assembled a story that caused some controversy at the magazine. The Los Angeles bureau chief protested that I had not followed the tenor and conclusions of Wilhelm's report. Ralph Davidson, *Time*'s publisher, happened to be a trustee at Stanford University, which at that time administered the institute, and expressed his dismay to me. But to his credit, and Grunwald's, they trusted me enough to publish the story, which ran under the headline, "The Magician and the Think Tank," and concluded rather bluntly that Geller had not shown himself to be a psychic. My only regret was that the top editors, while leaving most of the story intact, substituted a rather lame paragraph for my original ending, which had read, "At week's end, it appeared that the prestigious Stanford Research Institute had been hoodwinked by a discredited Israeli nightclub magician."

Even without that zinger, the story had repercussions. Geller, according to Puharich's book, first raged and then went into deep depression.[10] The *New York Times, New York* magazine, and *Newsweek* published follow-up stories on Geller, the latter two taking a particularly credulous approach. And the producer of the *Tonight* show, after inviting Geller to appear, called me to ask what precautions Johnny Carson might take to prevent cheating. I suggested consulting with Randi, who recommended, among other safeguards, that a guard be posted near the props Geller had requested and that no one, including Geller, be allowed to go near them prior to the show.

True to form, Geller appeared at the NBC studios early, approached the prop area, and despite his protests, was prevented from coming any closer. One of the props, for example, was a card table, on which several capped, metal 35 millimeter film cannisters had been placed, all empty but one, which was filled with water. During the show, Geller was to move his hands above the cannisters, concentrate, and then point out the can that was water filled. Well aware of that trick, Randi knew that Geller, before the show, would "accidentally" bump into the table, note which cannister (weighted with water) did not jiggle, and later identify it as the one that contained water.

As a result of those precautions, Geller's appearance on the *Tonight* show was a total disaster, so bad that it even embarrassed me. Nothing that Geller tried worked, and his excuses were sad and unconvincing. Carson, himself a skeptic and amateur magician, stared heavenward after each failure, not even trying to keep a straight face.

A week after that show, Martin Gardner, Ray Hyman, Randi, and I had lunch in a Manhattan restaurant, lamenting the fact that, despite rational explanations, commentators like Barbara Walters, many publications, and the public at large were still buying Geller's act, as well as other paranormal claims and demonstrations. Some sort of organization was needed, we agreed, to counter the wave of irrationality, and three of us suggested that Randi set about putting one together. But he begged off, citing a full schedule of appearances.

That idea languished for two years until Paul Kurtz stepped forward, a quarter century ago, to launch CSICOP and provide a platform for what has become a worldwide skeptical movement.

One afternote: Mary Cronin, a *Time* correspondent in London, was flying back to New York several years ago, and struck up a conversation with a seatmate, who turned out to be Uri Geller. When Mary mentioned her affiliation with *Time*, Geller was momentarily stunned, then turned to Mary with a question: "Why does Leon Jaroff hate me so much?"[11] Geller obviously had mistaken an attitude of amused contempt for one of hatred.

Indeed, in a small way, we should all be grateful to Geller. After all, he was the lightning rod who focused the energy of skeptics and led to a more unified and effective movement to counter the growing tide of irrationality.

NOTES

1. Correspondent Wilhelm's behavior and observations at Puharich's house in Ossining, New York, and elsewhere are described in detail in Andrija Puharich, *Uri: A Journal of the Mystery of Uri Geller* (Garden City, N.Y.: Anchor Press/Doubleday, 1974), chap. 9.

2. The passages about Geller's extraterrestrial intelligence sources come from chapter 8 of Puharich, *Uri*.

3. Ray Hyman's characterization of Geller's performance at SRI as outright deception was confirmed to me personally and was documented in detail in my story "The Magician and the Think Tank," *Time* (March 12, 1973).

4. Ibid.

5. Puharich, *Uri*.

6. The details about Uri's performance in front of my assembled science staff can be confirmed by at least a dozen witnesses, including James Randi, John Durniak, and me.

7. Ibid.

8. The characterization of Geller's activities in Israel was reported and filed upon by *Time* Jerusalem Correspondent Marlin Levin, and detailed by me in "The Magician and the Think Tank," *Time* (March 12, 1973).

9. Ibid.

10. Puharich, *Uri*.

11. Mary Cronin related to me the story of her trans-Atlantic flight with Geller.

LEON JAROFF is currently a contributor to *Time* magazine. He was a reporter at *Life* magazine, and a correspondent, associate editor, and then senior editor at *Time*, specializing in science, medicine, and environment stories. He founded and was the first managing editor of *Discover* magazine. A large asteroid (7829) bears his name. He is a Fellow of CSICOP.

8

FROM FATE TO SKEPTICAL INQUIRER

BARRY L. BEYERSTEIN

As I was growing up, for as long as I can remember, our family had subscriptions to both *Fate* magazine and *Popular Science*. Nothing could have seemed more natural to my father because, as far as he was concerned, psychic phenomena were merely things the rapidly advancing fields of psychology and physics had yet to overtake and explain. In the 1950s, he and I used to watch with fascination the weekly TV show *One Step Beyond*, hosted by the urbane and understated John Newlands—with its litany of ghostly appearances, astonishing coincidences, and tales of mind over matter, gleaned from the files of the British Society for Psychical research. This enchantment we shared almost certainly inclined me toward an eventual career in the study of consciousness. Although I came to reject my father's optimism about parapsychology, and I'm sure this caused him some disappointment, this sort of filial rebellion was in keeping with his own fiercely independent turn of mind. Often an outsider himself, he always encouraged my brother, Dale, and me to think for ourselves, especially when the herd accepts something as given. Ultimately, this led to our disagreeing with our father on politics and religion, as well as the paranormal, though we never ceased to love and admire him for his integrity, humanity, breadth of knowledge, and his unstinting devotion to our mother and to his sons and their goals. About our differences of opinion, we agreed to disagree and remained close until his death. In his later years, it must have been bittersweet for him to watch Dale and me on television attacking some of his cherished beliefs—surely, he would have been disappointed at the tack we were

101

taking, but still, he never left us in any doubt about the pride he felt that his boys' opinions would be of interest to national and international media. If we have prospered in our academic pursuits and our contributions to the skeptics' movement, Dale as a philosopher and I as a psychobiologist, it is in no small part because our father piqued our interest in all things mental and instilled in us a "That's nice; prove it" attitude.

Throughout high school, I managed to retain this parallel interest in science and the occult. Conventional religion had already lost its appeal for me, but not the paranormal. The group of high-achieving oddballs with whom I hung out in my teens embraced these interests as well. When we were not making music or tinkering with cantankerous British sports cars, we spent hours in philosophical discussions that often spilled over into debates about the reality of psychic phenomena. With one member of the group (now a biochemistry professor in California) we conducted scientific experiments in his well-equipped basement lab, somehow managing to come away with all digits still attached (I never did learn whether his mother ever found out what really happened to her concrete birdbath). All the while, we were staging séances at another friend's house that seemed compellingly believable at the time—the mother of one of the group was convinced that mediumship had run in her family for generations.

Thanks to the local library, my interests had expanded to include hypnosis and handwriting analysis as well. With the aid of the former, we were sure that we had enhanced the performance of another friend who was a champion discus thrower (obviously, the concept of a control group was not yet one of my mental reflexes). My girlfriend at the time remains convinced to this day that posthypnotic suggestions contributed to the phenomenal recall that let her ace her provincial government scholarship exams (the idea of an experimental confound wasn't second nature to me yet, either—she was extremely bright and motivated to begin with). Meanwhile, the handwriting analyses I churned out for my classmates with the aid of Dorothy Sara's weighty tome were accepted by one and all as amazingly accurate and revealing (familiarity with the Barnum effect [Hyman 1977; Dickson and Kelly 1985] was still a way down the road for me as well).

Another strong influence at this time was my best friend's grandfather, a crusty old Brit with a sardonic sense of humor and an inexhaustible supply of gripping stories. A true iconoclast and the black sheep of a "good English family," he had run away to the colonies as a young man. He'd been an adventurer who'd fought in several wars and made it around the world before settling down in a beachfront paradise on Vancouver Island. Along the way, "old granddad" had become a harsh critic of the hypocrisy of conventional religion and an exponent of the writings of Madame Blavatsky and the Theosophists. He used to regale us with these ideas as we chopped wood or rowed his dinghy around the bay in front of his retirement home. With his exotic past, endless practical knowledge, and keen suspicion of anyone who happened to be in authority at the moment, it was impossible not to be swept along with some of his views on the occult forces that underlie mundane reality.

By the time I reached Vancouver's Simon Fraser University, as a freshman in the fall of 1965 (the year the university opened), I was torn between philosophy and psychology as a major. In those heady days of the rebellious 1960s, the new university—by billing itself as experimental and nontraditional—had attracted an intriguing array of unorthodox scholars from around the world, both as faculty and as students. Some (with the benefit of hindsight) were offbeat in truly brilliant ways, others were just, . . . well . . . offbeat. Ultimately, I settled into psychology as a major with philosophy as a minor. But as I delved deeper into those subjects, I began to doubt the inevitability of an eventual happy marriage between science and the paranormal. Although I don't think he even mentioned the word "parapsychology" in my first course in the philosophy of science, Professor Lee Forstrum, a medical doctor turned philosopher, left no doubt that the fundamental assumptions and modus operandi of science were seriously at odds with most of what I knew of psychical research. These apprehensions were nurtured in later philosophy of science seminars I took with Professor Norman Swartz who is now a friend and valued colleague at SFU.

In keeping with the 1960s *Zeitgeist*, the love of all things weird and wonderful permeated much of the bustling new campus, along with the political unrest of those tumultuous times. Nonetheless, the psychology department at Simon Fraser University, thanks to the efforts of its founder, the late Professor Lorne Kendall, was an extremely hard-nosed collection of experimentalists. They drove home to us the need for strict operational definitions, tight experimental controls, and a ruthless search for confounds and artifacts that could make research seem to be telling us something it really wasn't. I remain grateful for the strong grounding in experimental design and statistics I received from a brilliant young statistician in the department, Raymond Koopman, himself barely out of graduate school at the time. Still a close friend, and now a colleague, Raymond regularly extricates me from statistical jams, cheerfully sacrificing much of his own precious time in the process. Needless to say, the no-nonsense crew of which he was a part had little good to say to undergraduates about parapsychology; some even combed the parapsychological literature for examples of how subtle artifacts can lead to flawed conclusions.

In my third undergraduate year, two encounters nudged me onto the path that led to what I do today. One was an honors seminar in history of psychology with Professor Jane Ingling that hooked me on the mind-body problem, the ancient debate over whether mind is a spiritual entity that occupies an ethereal realm beyond the reach of materialist science, or a physical one, somehow generated by the electrochemical activities of the brain (and thus subject, ultimately, to the same laws that govern matter and energy elsewhere in the universe). Jane's seminar reinforced my interest in the philosophy of science and my belief that it is essential for researchers to have a good historical perspective on their field of inquiry.

About the same time, there arrived at SFU an exceptionally talented new assistant professor named Harold Weinberg. Hal Weinberg promptly set about building what evolved into SFU's highly regarded Brain Behavior Laboratory, where, thanks to Hal's efforts, I was to find a happy home after graduate school. Since there were, as yet, relatively few graduate students at the new university, we senior undergraduates enjoyed unparalleled opportunities to work alongside faculty in their research. Hal has always preferred to teach in his lab rather than in a lecture hall, and his infectious enthusiasm and penetrating insights kindled my enduring fascination with the brain. Once the hook was in, I had a lot of catching up to do because, up to this time, I had acquired virtually no biological background at all—that branch of science simply hadn't interested me before. Tagging along with the first graduate students admitted to the biopsychology program at SFU, I learned to do electrode implants in monkey brains and how to record signals from them. We did numerous brain histologies and learned how to record and analyze human brain waves as well. The first lab computers were just becoming available and we toyed with them endlessly. For my graduating thesis, done in Hal's lab, I did an electroencephalographic study of dream deprivation, losing much of my own sleep in the process. Thanks to Hal Weinberg's tutelage and encouragement, I decided to pursue graduate studies in biological psychology. Imbued with his views on the brain-mind relationship, I also became more firmly skeptical about psychic powers.

Although none of us was sure how a degree from a brand-new university would be viewed by more established institutions, I was pleased (and relieved) to find that I had won several of the graduate scholarships I had applied for and had been offered admission at a number of graduate schools known for their excellent biopsychology programs. It was an embarrassment of riches, but the choice eventually narrowed down to Montreal's McGill University and the University of California at Berkeley. Although the National Research Council of Canada fellowship I had won, but could not take out of the country, paid more and offered more perks than the Woodrow Wilson fellowship that I could use in either Canada or the United States, the lure of the San Francisco Bay area in the fall of 1968 proved too strong. Fortunately, the issue of academic quality was moot, for although McGill was home to giants in biopsychology such as Donald Hebb, Wilder Penfield, Dalbir Bindra, Robert Malmo, and Peter and Brenda Milner, Berkeley offered the chance to learn from the likes of David Krech, Frank Beach, Mark Rosenzweig, Marion Diamond, Horace Barlow, and Russell DeValois.

From DeValois, Barlow, and my ultimate dissertation supervisor, Ralph Freeman, I learned about the structure, development, and function of the brain, especially the intricacies of its visual system. It was Krech, Rosenzweig, and especially the late Arnold Leiman, however, who encouraged my desire to stop occasionally and look at "the big picture." Experts in their own areas of brain research, these scholars maintained throughout their careers an interest in the philosophical underpinnings of their craft. When I was his graduate teaching assistant, Arnie Leiman used to begin his physiological psychology course with a detailed discussion of the reasons why biopsychologists, and indeed most contemporary philosophers, believe the brain is the organ of consciousness. Most biopsychologists take this to be so self-evident that it hardly bears mentioning in their courses—they jump right into the job of explaining which neurons do what when any given psychological function revs up.

Leiman, Krech, and Rosenzweig, however—though they never doubted that mind equaled brain function—thought it worthwhile to discuss *why* a biopsychologist should find this more believable than the dualist alternatives on the mind-body question. Indeed, as they pointed out, it would make little sense for a psychologist to study the brain at all unless there were a lawful and inextricable link between thoughts, perceptions, motivation, and the like, and specific states of the brain that could be measured in the lab. Although they left the implication for the brighter students to arrive at themselves, it should have been apparent to them that the exquisite relationships between electrochemical states of the brain and psychological phenomena that were emerging from the neuroscience lab left little room for disembodied consciousness or a brain that could simply "know something" (by telepathy or clairvoyance, for instance) without having had it encoded first by the intricate neural mechanisms of vision, hearing, or one of the other conventional senses. Of course, the implications for reincarnation or an immortal soul were less than encouraging as well (Beyerstein 1987).

Needless to say, materialist leanings of this sort were not the vogue among most young Berkeley residents of the time. On the contrary, most were quite convinced that meditation and LSD trips had propelled their minds into higher dimensions of being and that everyone, including their pets, possessed psychic powers. The books of Carlos Castaneda were not yet known to be blatant frauds and the Beatles were singing the praises of the Maharishi and Transcendental Meditation to disenchanted sons and daughters of privileged families eager to supplant their parents' metaphysical worldview with a blend of pop psychology and Eastern mysticism. Shortly after I arrived, Timothy Leary (who had received his Ph.D. from Berkeley in the 1950s and had recently been kicked out of the Harvard psychology department for his psychedelic indiscretions) returned to give a seminar at his alma mater. In his talk, he announced that LSD had given him spiritual enlightenment, part of which was the realization that astrology contained far more valid insights into human character than all he learned from academic psychology. Many students in the psychology department were duly impressed. Across campus, the philosopher Paul Feyerabend had been telling his classes on a regular basis that science really had no greater status than voodoo as a way of understanding the world.

This was the era of which the sociologist Theodore Roszak (1969) wrote approvingly in his book, *The Making of a Counter-Culture*, and the philosopher Charles Frankel wrote equally disparagingly in his article, "The Nature and Sources of Irrationalism" (Frankel 1973). Berkeley considered itself the vanguard of the new consciousness, from which Marilyn Ferguson's (1980) "Aquarian revolution" was supposed to envelop the world. As they said at the time, "The 'New Age' was a-bornin'." With its commitment to intuition over reason, the counterculture embraced mysticism, the psychedelic revolution, "holistic" medicine, the human potential movement, and experimentation with "alternative" lifestyles. Politically, this centered on opposition to the Vietnam War and rejection of consumerism and the corporate culture, while fueling an entirely laudable push for appropriate use of technology and for social, racial, and gender equality. As these trends were coalescing in the pressure-cooker environment of the San Francisco Bay area in the latter half of the 1960s, not everyone in the great state of California was entirely pleased. The governor of the day, a former B-movie actor by the name of Ronald Reagan, had campaigned (successfully) on a platform of "cleaning up the mess in Berkeley."

Amid the Vietnam protests, the Black Panther rallies, the People's Park riots, the Cambodia riots, and the National Guard patrolling the streets of Berkeley, it was often difficult to concentrate on mere academic matters like the causes of orientation-specific amblyopia, the subject of my dissertation research. The more politically obsessed among us considered such "irrelevant" pursuits bourgeois luxuries, or as they called it, a "cop-out." Be-ins, sit-ins, and "consciousness expansion" were the order of the day and soul-baring "encounter groups" were all the rage as neurotic amateurs tried to help each other rid themselves of the "hang-ups" caused by growing up the most wealthy and secure generation in history. When party chitchat could accept a guest's description of his latest out-of-body experience or the need to have her chakras realigned as casually as one might receive the morning's weather forecast or an opinion on the latest hit movie, it was often difficult for a would-be rationalist to keep his cosmological bearings. I frequently found myself the odd man out in discussions with friends and neighbors whom I really liked. They tended to come away thinking I was a nice guy, but hopelessly "linear" and "left-brained," despite my de rigueur shoulder-length hair, tie-dyed T-shirt, bell-bottoms, and cowboy boots. I often found myself after such discussions wondering if the rest of them were nuts or I was really the obtuse one who "just didn't get it."

After these jarring interludes, it was often long, far-reaching conversations with David Krech and Arnie Leiman that quelled any wavering I might have felt in my conviction that empiricism was still the most reliable route to knowledge. Though my resolve was challenged occasionally, usually by extremely articulate spokespersons for the other side, I remained convinced that the accumulating data of neuroscience make the likelihood of psychic phenomena quite remote. Moreover, these discoveries were already bolstering my hunch that brain research might also suggest naturalistic explanations for odd subjective experiences that many, throughout the ages, have assumed to be supernatural.

In this regard, Arnie Leiman nurtured the interest in epilepsy I had developed back in Hal Weinberg's lab. Arnie introduced me to a trove of underappreciated literature on the sometimes bizarre subjective sequelae of certain kinds of seizures that may well have fomented many supernatural beliefs over the course of history. He and Mark Rosenzweig both had an insatiable appetite for unusual facts about the brain which they delighted in discussing. Both being occasional migraine sufferers, they cued me into some of the more out-of-the-way literature on this neurological condition that also seemed capable of explaining certain ostensibly paranormal experiences. It was also from them that I first learned about some of the quirks of the brain's limbic system that could cause feelings that look awfully like religious ecstasy or spiritual possession (Beyerstein 1988). They also alerted me to some peculiarities of the brain's arousal mechanisms that could produce what are essentially waking dreams that can have immense emotional impact and seem stunningly real (Beyerstein 1996b, 1996c).

Some of my happiest recollections of graduate school are many long conversations with David Krech, or "Krech," as he used to like to be called. Krech was the guy for whom the term "irascible old fart" must have been coined. By then well into his seventies, this Grand Old Man of psychology was one of the last of the old school who thought it perfectly reasonable that one researcher could make useful contributions to subdisciplines as disparate as social psychology, learning theory, and physiological psychology. The senior, and arguably most famous member of the Berkeley department, he still taught introductory psychology on a regular basis, because he thought it important to nurture young minds and keep abreast of the newest ideas. He also felt passionately that whatever we learned from scientific research should be put to use to make a better society. And if that entailed stepping on a few toes and exposing sloppy thinking along the way, so much the better.

Until his death, Krech remained fascinated by how it ALL fit together—in an age of increasing specialization, he maintained there was a need for someone to take the broader view. It was from this lofty perch that he urged me to delve deeper into the voguish findings of parapsychology that seemed to fly in the face of the very foundations of our field of behavioral neuroscience. Psychical research didn't hang together, in Krech's opinion, with the rest of psychology, let alone the rest of science, a view I have long shared. Even if we don't know exactly where the artifacts in an ESP study lie, he used to say, it seems more likely that someone made a subtle error somewhere than that so much of what is easy to replicate in physics, psychology, and neuroscience should be so grossly wrongheaded. What I have since learned, from mentors such as Ray Hyman, James Alcock, Susan Blackmore, Richard Wiseman, and Mark Hansel, is that when the long and tedious work finally reveals where the subtle "leakage" to the conventional senses might lie in some experimental paradigm, the answer is invariably more interesting than the "spooky" explanation that it was ESP.

It was in discussions with Arnie Leiman about the same time that I began to become interested in psychopharmacology, which eventually became more my main research interest than the electrophysiology and vision research I was doing at the time. Berkeley in the 1960s was a natural laboratory for the study of how chemicals can alter consciousness. I tried a few myself, and though I found the experiences engrossing and I could see how my neighbors could interpret them as mystical revelations, I remained convinced that psychedelics tell us more about who we already are than what we might become. It seemed to me that the fact that a molecule produced by a plant could affect consciousness by altering physical processes in the brain (and that one can't stop this from unfolding by a mere act of will) stands as the most dramatic evidence I can think of that mind equals brain function. And by extension, it makes the possibility of disembodied consciousness extremely remote, despite what it feels like at the time.

Since finishing graduate school, the glue that has bound together whatever I have done in my somewhat randomly dispersed career, has been this obsession I developed at Berkeley, having to do with how brain function could produce consciousness, normal and sometimes stunningly bizarre. It is the quirky, seemingly supernatural, warps of brain processes and consciousness in otherwise normal people that have intrigued me ever since (Beyerstein 1987, 1988, 1996b, 1996c, 1996d).

Given the prevalent New Age worldview shared by much of the cognoscenti of the industrialized world back in my Berkeley days, there were bound to be moments of friction between what I was learning in the neuroscience graduate program and what was generally believed off campus, and even by some of my fellow graduate students. The materialistic view of my neuroscientist colleagues seemed to have virtually no impact once one hit Sproul Plaza and ventured down Telegraph Avenue. Among Southside denizens, there was hardly the slightest doubt that mind was a spiritual entity that could travel outside the body, influence physical objects at a distance, and communicate with other minds telepathically. While few of my fellow graduate students in behavioral neuroscience shared these views, a surprising number of grad students in other areas of the psychology department did, at least to some degree. The validity of astrology was widely accepted and the likelihood of psychic phenomena was by no means ruled out by many of these elite young scholars.

What struck me most forcefully about this state of affairs was that there seemed to be no correlation between intelligence or educational attainment and belief in "things that go bump in the night." Some of the brightest of my generation of grad students were the most ardent believers in astrology and one of the smartest of us all actually quit the program altogether in order to pursue a full-time career in Scientology. Another dropped out to become a Tai Chi master. The latter did this after confirming his subjective experiences by running an experiment (a poorly controlled one, in my opinion) in which rats seemed to spend more time between his vertically outstretched palms when he was beaming his Chi energy at them. Trying to understand the motives of our classmate who defected to Scientology, which even then I thought of as a quack theory pushed by avaricious pests, we spent some time talking over her decision with her. She said that, despite her privileged upbringing and prodigious academic achievements, she had always felt some kind of gnawing, indefinable lack at the core of her life. She had long ago abandoned her traditional (though not strict) Christian upbringing, but until she encountered Scientology, she could find nothing that could relieve that emptiness. We lost touch soon after she quit grad school and I do not know whether L. Ron Hubbard and his minions could provide a permanent answer for her or not.

As I encountered, first at SFU and then at Berkeley, more and more highly intelligent people who were drawn to occult beliefs, it gradually dawned on me that these leanings stemmed from emotional needs rather than intellectual ones. It struck me that if I had escaped these tendencies it was through no brilliance or effort of my own. My interest in occult topics had always been intellectually motivated and when the evidence tipped in the opposite direction, I had not the slightest difficulty in changing my beliefs (I like to think that, if the evidence warranted it, I would be able to switch back again). The brilliant novelist and chemist Primo Levi summed it up nicely when he said, "Science has an essential virtue. It respects what is."

For whatever reason, I seem to be able to live with the ambiguity of not knowing the answer to the "big-ticket" questions of existence. For many, however, the need to have THE answer, any answer, is just too strong—so much so that it causes them, probably without realizing it, to override what they already know in other, carefully sequestered sectors of memory. It was not until years later, when I met and became friends with James Alcock, that I found someone who had devoted much of his professional life to understanding how this kind of self-delusion works. The dynamics of wishful thinking are part of us all and they serve important enough functions that they seem to have been favored by natural selection. This kind of self-serving, quick-and-dirty reasoning works tolerably well in many situations, but it can lead to comforting but egregiously wrong beliefs in many others (Gilovich 1991; Schick and Vaughn 1995). These mental habits can easily make people accept things in one avenue of life that they would dismiss as absurd in another.

Jim Alcock, who had shared a similar background and come to much the same conclusions about psychic phenomena as I had, has thought this out in detail from the perspectives of social and cognitive psychology (Alcock 1981, 1987). Jim is justly noted for his work in the psychology of belief (Alcock 1995) and he has always been quick to remind his fellow skeptics that they often take too much personal credit for having escaped the superstitions and occult beliefs they disparage. Many who are just as bright and had all the same training and exposure we skeptics have had still find the secular, naturalistic worldview lacking in some essential way. At an emotional level, they long for a human-centered universe driven by moral rather than impersonal, mechanistic laws. They want humans to be above, not part of, the natural world. I think the literary critic George Steiner put it well when he described this need as "nostalgia for the absolute" (Steiner 1974).

It was obvious that it wasn't a "smart-us-versus-dumb-them" kind of split that I was experiencing on the streets of Berkeley and during arguments with colleagues while I was teaching one night a week at nearby John F. Kennedy University (I was the token experimental psychologist in what was on its way to becoming a hotbed of humanistic and transpersonal psychology and parapsychology). Thus, some part of me had to harbor at least a shred of doubt that "they" might be right and I was wrong. At JFK, I realized that there were some smart parapsychologists out there who were attempting to use the same tools I was to prove the reality of psychic phenomena. If their claims could be taken at face value, then the materialist view of mind upon which all of physiological psychology is predicated would be on shaky ground, to put it mildly. If minds can leave their bodies and still think, perceive, and remember, or if they can survive death to roam as ghosts or inhabit new bodies as reincarnated souls, than my chosen line of work would be a colossal fool's errand. Behavioral neuroscience would be at best sadly incomplete, if not a total waste of time. The exquisite correlations between neural events and psychological phenomena that modern neuroscience was accumulating made it hard to believe that mind could be anything more than brain function, but nonetheless, some obviously competent parapsychologists, who seemed to be following the accepted rules of scientific investigation, were insisting that there was believable evidence that a powerful nonmaterial mind exists. They were claiming that mind is capable of influencing material events in ways that would kick the props out from under biological psychology once and for all. As a twenty-two-year-old training for a career in biopsychology, I felt it might be prudent to see whether these people knew something that should prompt a reevaluation of my career plans. This was, after all, about the time the American Association for the Advancement of Science voted, at the urging of Margaret Mead, to admit the American Parapsychological Association to its ranks.

When I mentioned these disturbing thoughts to Krech, he encouraged me to read the papers of some of the best of the parapsychologists carefully, even to try to replicate them. He predicted that I wouldn't get the same results and he suggested some methodological slips to avoid, ones he suspected might have generated many of the positive results reported in the parapsychology journals. After we had been talking for a while, he paused and a broad grin opened between his carefully trimmed moustache and goatee. "Why don't you," he said, "go tell Geoff Keppel [then chair of the department] that you want to hold a symposium on parapsychology? I'll back you up." To his credit, Keppel, author of a best-selling experimental design and statistics text, who didn't believe the results of the parapsychologists for a minute, agreed and found us the money. In retrospect, I wish we had invited some critics as well as supporters of parapsychology to speak, but it seemed at the time that the department was already stacked with doubters.

Our miniconference on parapsychology was well attended and it further added to my discomfort because the supporting data presented from the stage seemed solid. Could it really be, as speakers such as Charles Tart claimed, that it was nothing more than prejudice on the part of a dying old guard that was keeping these results out of mainstream psychology texts? I wanted to remain a committed materialist, but here were the likes of Tart, a tenured professor of psychology at the University of California at Davis and Thelma Moss, from UCLA, presenting empirical evidence that mental powers could indeed project themselves beyond individual brains. Other speakers, whose names I can no longer remember, introduced me for first time to the name Uri Geller. One of these presenters projected electron micrographs on the big screen that purportedly showed that metal bars Geller had broken with his psychic powers had fractured in microscopic patterns that were previously unknown to metallurgists. Someone else on the program extolled the feats of the Russian-born psychic and healer Nina Karagula, and on it went late into the evening. I vividly recall Tart describing one of his electroencephalographic studies that showed odd EEG signals when an (unobserved) subject had supposedly left his body to float up and retrieve a random number placed on a shelf, above eye level. It all seemed quite impressive, not exactly the effect Krech had hoped for.

Unfortunately, for those of us who came away more impressed than we had expected to be, the one person most knowledgeable about such matters, and who could have revealed where some of the sticky points had been glossed over, had recently left the department. Barry Singer, one of Al

Riley's recently completed Ph.D. students, had graduated and taken a faculty position in Los Angeles. Singer subsequently produced several important contributions to the critical literature on parapsychology—too late to ease our qualms in 1972, however. One was a book he edited with one of the founders of CSICOP, the late UCLA astronomer George Abell (Abell and Singer 1981); another was an influential piece he cowrote for the *American Scientist* (Singer and Benassi 1981).

Searching in the aftermath for the responsible critique we should have included on our parapsychology program, I came across the work of Ray Hyman. I already knew of him in other contexts because of the famous Hick-Hyman Law (Response-time is proportional to stimulus uncertainty) and from his excellent primer on experimental methodology (Hyman 1964). I was relieved to see that there was someone with impeccable methodological and statistical skills (not to mention impressive conjuring skills) who was willing to look into the parapsychological literature in detail—and who had not come away as impressed as we naifs had been at first glance (Hyman 1991).

Soon, however, I was about to graduate, and to my satisfaction a job opened up at my alma mater, Simon Fraser University. With my third-generation San Franciscan wife, Suzi, I headed back to Vancouver in the fall of 1973. I pitched into assembling a lab and a busy schedule teaching biopsychology, experimental methods, and sensory psychophysiology. Along the way, I sort of inherited a course that was a holdover from the hippy-dippy sixties, "The Psychology of Consciousness." I came to call this my "Trojan Horse" class, because it was the perfect vehicle for attracting students who were scared stiff by my other courses that featured neurons and (gasp!) numbers. Attracted by a promise (which I kept) to discuss meditation, hypnosis, dreams, out-of body and near-death experiences, altered states of consciousness, ESP, and the like, they heard my take on these inherently fascinating topics, which wasn't exactly the one most were hoping for. In the process, I tried to teach them a bit about the brain, experimental psychology, and critical thinking. Jim Alcock had introduced me to two important works, by Graham Reed (1972/1988) and Andrew Neher (1980/1990), that set much of the theme for my course: i.e., that anomalous experiences such as these can seem subjectively very real, though they are not exactly what they feel like at the time. They are, in my opinion, the result of interesting twists in the way the brain produces our normal subjective stream of experience (Beyerstein 1996b, 1996c, 1996d). As exercises in this course, I have set the students the task of replicating some of the classic studies of parapsychology. As far as I can see, after more than twenty-five years of trying, PSI remains as elusive as ever.

Inevitably, my consciousness course stirred up strong feelings and a certain rivalry sprang up between my students and those of a colleague in another department, Robert Harper, an educational psychologist and professor of communication studies at the time. I had known and liked Bob Harper in my undergraduate days at SFU. He had always leaned toward an antimaterialist view of mind and we'd had many animated but friendly discussions about psychic research, both when I was an undergraduate and after I returned to SFU as a new faculty member. This remained an amicable disagreement until the tragic death of his son added a more personal dimension to our differences of opinion. After this sad loss, Bob embraced spiritualism as a means of communicating with his son and began to invite various mediums to address his classes. At that point, I believe Bob's academic objectivity on such matters had diminished and doubters such as me came to be seen as the enemy rather than congenial dissenters. It still saddens me because I retain a personal liking for him that I fear he has lost for me.

Though he lacked the discipline to get his ideas published throughout most of his career, Bob Harper was a formidable debater and a very popular teacher. Over the years, he had made the acquaintance of Robert Jahn and his colleagues at the Princeton Engineering Anomalies Research Lab, who supported him in various ways. Under the rubrics of transpersonal psychology and "unconventional modes of communication," Bob had been teaching courses in parapsychology as "special topics" (but credit-bearing) courses in the communications department at SFU. There, he used to delight in savaging me and my hopelessly outmoded confederates. Things would probably have continued in this fashion indefinitely had Bob not decided that he would prefer to present his views in courses in the regular curriculum with the specific course title "Parapsychology." Unlike the special topics courses he had been teaching up to then, the contents of these new courses would, like all new course proposals, need to be approved by the academic senate. Needless to say, there was strong opposition in some quarters to the university offering such courses and a battle broke out at the senate meeting when the proposal was tabled. It was decided that the matter needed further study before a vote could be taken and the academic vice president suggested that someone outside of the senate should be asked to assemble the pros and cons and report back. My name came up. It was as a result of gathering the materials for this report that I got to know, personally, for the first time, some of the leading figures in the nascent skeptics alliance that Paul Kurtz was in the process of forging. Little did I know at the time that these contacts were about to affect the future direction of my academic career. As I assembled the writings of Kurtz, Hyman, Alcock, Gardner, Randi, Frazier, Klass, Hansel, Hilgard, and others for my report to the senate, I became aware of aspects of CSICOP's work that I hadn't known before—and got hooked on it.

In the end, I recommended to the senate that they should approve Bob Harper's new courses, providing he would consent to certain changes in his syllabus. I suggested that the courses be moved up to the third or fourth year (by which time, I thought, students might have a bit more perspective) and that there be added as prerequisites a course in statistics and one in experimental design. I also recommended that the required reading list (which was originally entirely comprised of pro-paranormal items) be amended to include a number of readings from the skeptical side. In retrospect, it seems I was somewhat naive to think that this would ensure a balanced presentation, but I was, and remain, a strong advocate of academic freedom—I thought this would be a reasonable compromise. In my report I pulled no punches in stating my doubts about parapsychology, but I still felt that Bob Harper should be able to teach his courses as long as a more balanced treatment was introduced. When word of my impending recommendations got out, my brother, Dale, who was then in the philosophy department at Malaspina College on Vancouver Island; Ron Apland, a Malaspina psychologist; and CSICOP consultant Gary Bauslaugh, then dean of the college, fired off a scathing letter to the SFU senate, denouncing courses such as Harper had proposed. Likewise, my good friend Hal Weinberg, who was on the senate at the time, wanted nothing of my weak-kneed approach. Along with several senators from the physics department, Hal came out swinging. The Harper proposal was solidly voted down. He went back to teach, until his retirement, what he had been teaching all along in his special topics courses.

Far from appreciating what I thought had been an evenhanded approach, Bob Harper immediately accused me of duplicity, a position he maintains to this day. In his opinion, I didn't have the courage to oppose him outright, so I produced a lukewarm report and then connived behind the scenes to get my brother and my best friend on the faculty to do my dirty work for me. No amount of assurance on my part has convinced Bob that Dale and his colleagues, and Hal Weinberg, had acted entirely on their own—in fact, they had been rather chagrined that I had not taken a more strident anti-parapsychology stance. Over twenty years later, Bob Harper still maintains that I set him up and, though he has long since retired, he still phones me occasionally, out of the blue, at home, to reiterate his denunciations of my unprincipled behavior.

Recently Harper enlisted the help of Douglas Todd, the religion and ethics reporter of the *Vancouver Sun*, to reopen these old wounds. I talked on the phone with Todd for at least half an hour before he wrote his piece and offered to send him a copy of my senate report to substantiate my version of events. I also explained in detail to him what was wrong with the supposedly airtight ESP studies Harper had insisted were being ignored by mainstream psychologists—again I offered to send him the relevant papers. Todd assured me that this would be unnecessary and then proceeded to write one of the most ferocious attacks on me I've ever been subjected to in the media. He implied that I had sabotaged Bob Harper's courses and that I am such a narrow-minded scientific fundamentalist that I give students bad grades merely for disagreeing with my old-fashioned materialist philosophy. In an ensuing exchange, Todd accused me of impugning his journalistic ethics but simply didn't seem to understand how serious a charge he had leveled at me. Short of plagiarism, or exploitation of one's students, I can think of no more damning allegation of academic misconduct. If true, such grading practices would, and should be, grounds for strong disciplinary action against a faculty member. In fact, I encourage my students to disagree with me, and probably err on the side of leniency when they have the pluck to take me on. Todd's attack on my integrity stands as a sad reminder of how personal these metaphysical differences can become.

I should note, however, that out of *l'affaire Harper*, some very good things have emerged as well. It was out of this dispute that I first came to know Jim Alcock, Ray Hyman, Paul Kurtz, and other principals at CSICOP. Eventually, I invited them to speak at SFU and in the process they became valued friends as well as admired collaborators. They encouraged me to write for the *Skeptical Inquirer*, my first such effort being a critique of "brain tuners" and so-called alpha consciousness (Beyerstein 1985). This was followed by a two-part article on why brain science should make one dubious about various PSI phenomena (Beyerstein 1987, 1988). These forays led to my eventual election as a scientific consultant and later a fellow and member of the executive council of CSICOP.

My interest in the brain nicely complemented some of the other expertise on the executive council. It was in that vein that, with two of my students, we published a critique of a famous near-death experience that, if it had happened as generally recounted, would have created virtually insurmountable problems for the materialist view of mind, as outlined above (Ebbern, Mulligan, and Beyerstein 1996). In the realm of "near-death studies," I have debated supporters of the other side, e.g., Raymond Moody, Maurice Rawlings, and Melvin Morse, in venues such as the *Oprah Winfrey* show, the *Dean Edell* show, and *Unsolved Mysteries.*

It was also my interest in the brain, particularly in how it stores memories, that first led me to doubt the assertions of the "recovery movement" that memories of abuse could be repressed and then revealed by special therapeutic probing techniques. With colleagues, I ended up organizing two international symposia on the topic of false memory syndrome and advising many people I came to accept had been falsely accused (Beyerstein and Ogloff 1998).

At Paul Kurtz's urging, with the help of my brother, Dale, Lee Moller, Jim and Bill Henry, Gary Bauslaugh, and others, we also formed, more than a decade ago, our local skeptics group, the British Columbia Skeptics, with its newsletter, the *Rational Inquirer*, ably edited by Lee Moller. It was through the notoriety achieved by the BC Skeptics that I came to revisit my long-abandoned adolescent infatuation with handwriting analysis. As chair of the BC Skeptics, I was approached by a local reporter who had discovered that some employees in the personnel department of the Vancouver School Board had been collaborating with a local graphologist on a secret project to identify the actual *and potential* child molesters in the teaching ranks. This they expected to do from surreptitiously obtained samples of their handwriting! The reporter asked me if there was any validity to handwriting analysis. By now, I knew that there wasn't, but the reporter asked for some evidence to support this blanket dismissal. It became apparent that there was a need for a book that compiled all the data on graphology, pro and con. With Paul Kurtz's support, Dale and I edited a volume, *The Write Stuff*, in which three famous graphologists had their say, head-to-head, with critics from several relevant disciplines, including ourselves (Beyerstein and Beyerstein 1992; Beyerstein 1996). We subsequently recreated some of the crucial tests of graphology for Alan Alda's PBS program, *Scientific American Frontiers*. Although there are strong empirical grounds for doubting graphology, based on evaluation of graphologists' performance, my doubts also stemmed from my knowledge of neuroscience. What we know about brain mechanisms for skilled movements and for personality make the connection of handwriting and other psychological traits extremely doubtful (Beyerstein 1992). The same is true for a variety of vigorously marketed self-help devices and training courses that supposedly work by "tuning up" the brain (Beyerstein 1985, 1990, 1999a, 1999b).

With my mix of training in physiology, pharmacology, and psychology, and my skeptic's background, it was perhaps inevitable that I would be drawn into the controversy over alternative medicine. I had maintained an interest in both psychological and medical quackery over the years, and in 1995 Paul Kurtz asked me to join a delegation to China along with Dr. Wallace Sampson from Stanford and Andrew Skolnick, then associate news editor of the *Journal of the American Medical Association*. Wally Sampson, a CSICOP fellow and a founder of the National Council Against Health Fraud, was at the time laying plans for his new journal, the *Scientific Review of Alternative Medicine*, and, somewhere in China, he asked me if I would become an associate editor. Wally, Andy Skolnick, and I spent a delightful time as guests of the China Association for Science and Technology, touring the principal centers of traditional Chinese medicine (TCM) in the People's Republic. We reported our less than enthusiastic findings on TCM in the *Skeptical Inquirer* (Beyerstein and Sampson 1996; Sampson and Beyerstein 1996). Since that time, fighting the pseudoscience of alternative medicine has occupied an increasing amount of my time (Beyerstein 1997, 1999; Beyerstein and Downie 1998). With Drs. Lloyd Oppel and Bessie Borwein, and, as always, my brother, Dale, I helped form a new group devoted to supporting scientific medicine, the Canadians for Rational Health Policy (www.crhp.net). It cooperates with the American body, the Council for Scientific Medicine, on whose board I also sit.

In closing, I'd like to say that I've always considered the difference between academics' salaries and what they might earn by flogging their talents on the open market to be a tax we pay for looking forward to going to work in the morning. Academia is a delightful place for the terminally curious and I am grateful to a sucession of department chairs and deans who have tolerated, even encouraged my diverse meanderings. I've long been aware that the path to rapid advancement in universities is to garner big grants to study increasingly narrow specialties. This is a good thing, of course, for what would generalists have to ponder if the specialists were not constantly adding these individual bricks to the wall of knowledge? So far, though, I have managed to do fairly well bucking this trend toward ultra-specialization. There is a need, I think, for those of us who are more fascinated by what David Krech called "the big picture," and I've been privileged to have the freedom to follow this route in my career. Finding new connections between existing branches of knowledge has always intrigued me.

One of the many reasons I have enjoyed my association with CSICOP so thoroughly is the opportunity it has afforded me to meet so many world-class scholars, both in and outside my own field. They are a fascinating as well as a genuinely friendly and generous group of people. I think the work that they do in the skeptical arena is often underappreciated in academic circles because many specialists fail to grasp the potential consequences of the strong antirational and antiscientific trends in modern society. They see no pressing need to oppose something publicly that they see as transparently ridiculous. They fail to grasp the strong emotional appeal of the paranormal for the public, a majority of whom, if the polls are accurate, believe in creationism, ESP, and that a government conspiracy is afoot to cover up UFO landings and alien abductions. I am convinced that there can be serious costs involved in letting pseudoscience flourish, economic and otherwise (Beyerstein 1998). Fortunately, I enjoy teaching as well as research and I like the rough-and-tumble of public debate. It is unacceptable, I think, merely to decry the paranormal pollution of the airwaves if one is not willing to cooperate with the media when they do call on us for comment. Consequently, I average over a hundred media interviews and appearances per year, in addition to my extensive lecturing schedule. If we want the public to pay taxes to support research, we owe them understandable explanations of what we do and the significance it has for them. If we expect them to urge government agencies to support scientific medicine rather than waste scarce funds on alternative therapies, we need to come out of our labs and lecture halls occasionally and tell them why this is in their own interest. With so much misinformation glutting the popular media, this watchdog function is one of the most important contributions of the skeptics' movement and the *Skeptical Inquirer* is the jewel in its crown. When I need a sound bite to convey what CSICOP is all about, I say, "It's a sort of *Consumer Reports* of the mind," which sums it up quite neatly, I think.

One of the many enjoyable tasks I undertake for CSICOP is to lecture in Ray Hyman's annual summer workshop at the University of Oregon. Not only is it the towering presence of Ray himself, and the joy of observing the the sheer brainpower of my fellow faculty at work, it is also the people, literally from around the world, who enroll in this and other CSICOP functions that keep me from suffering that occupational hazard "skeptic's burnout." They are a remarkable lot, genuinely nice people committed to critical thinking and leaving the place a bit better than they found it. They make me very pleased that my fate was to become a skeptical inquirer.

REFERENCES

Abell, G., and B. Singer. 1981. *Science and the Paranormal.* New York: Charles Scribner's Sons.

Alcock, J. E. 1981. *Parapsychology: Science or Magic?* Oxford: Pergamon Press.

———. 1987. "Parapsychology: Science or Search for the Soul?" *Behavioral and Brain Sciences* 10, no. 4: 553–65.

———. 1995. "The Belief Engine." *Skeptical Inquirer* 19, no. 3: 255–63.

Beyerstein, B. L. 1985. "The Myth of Alpha Consciousness." *Skeptical Inquirer* 10, no. 1: 42–59.

———. 1987. "The Brain and Consciousness: Implications for Psi Phenomena." *Skeptical Inquirer* 12: 163–73.

———. 1988. "Neuropathology and the Legacy of Spiritual Possession." *Skeptical Inquirer* 12: 248–62.

———. 1990. "Brainscams: Neuromythologies of the New Age." *International Journal of Mental Health* 19, no. 3: 27–36.

———. 1992. "Handwriting Is Brainwriting. So What?" In *The Write Stuff*, ed. B. Beyerstein and D. Beyerstein, pp. 397–419. Amherst, N.Y.: Prometheus Books.

———. 1996a. "Graphology." In *Encyclopedia of the Paranormal*, ed. G. Stein, pp. 309–24. Amherst, N.Y.: Prometheus Books.

———. 1996b. "Visions and Hallucinations." In *Encyclopedia of the Paranormal*, ed. G. Stein, pp. 789–97. Amherst, N.Y.: Prometheus Books.

———. 1996c. "Altered States of Consciousness." In *Encyclopedia of the Paranormal*, ed. G. Stein. Amherst, N.Y.: Prometheus Books. pp. 8–16.

———. 1996d. "Dissociation, Possession, and Exorcism." In *Encyclopedia of the Paranormal*, ed. G. Stein, pp. 544–52. Amherst, N.Y.: Prometheus Books.

———. 1997. "Why Bogus Therapies Seem to Work." *Skeptical Inquirer* 21, no. 5: 29–34.

———. 1998. "The Sorry State of Scientific Literacy in the Industrialized Democracies." *Learning Quarterly* 2, no. 2: 5–11.

———. 1999. "Social and Judgmental Biases That Make Inert Treatments Seem to Work." *Scientific Review of Alternative Medicine* 3, no. 2: 16–29.

———. 1999a. "Pseudoscience and the Brain: Tuners and Tonics for Aspiring Superhumans." In *Mind Myths: Exploring Everyday Mysteries of the Mind and Brain*, ed. S. Della Sala, pp. 59–82. Chichester, U.K.: John Wiley and Sons.

———. 1999b. "Whence Cometh the Myth That We Only Use Ten Percent of Our Brains?" In *Mind Myths: Exploring Everyday Mysteries of the Mind and Brain*, ed. S. Della Sala, pp. 1–24. Chichester, U.K.: John Wiley and Sons.

———. 1999c. "A Cogent Consideration of the Case for Karma and Reincarnation." *Skeptical Inquirer* 23, no. 1: 51–53.

Beyerstein, B., and D. Beyerstein, eds. 1992. *The Write Stuff.* Amherst, N.Y.: Prometheus Books.

Beyerstein, B. L., and S. Downie. 1998. "Naturopathy." *Scientific Review of Alternative Medicine* 1, no. 2: 20–28.

Beyerstein, B. L., and J. R. P. Ogloff. 1998. "Hidden Memories: Fact or Fantasy?" In *Child Sexual Abuse and False Memory Syndrome*, ed. R. A. Baker, pp. 15–28. Amherst, N.Y.: Prometheus Books.

Beyerstein, B. L., and W. Sampson. 1996. "Traditional Medicine and Pseudoscience in China (Part 1)." *Skeptical Inquirer* 20, no. 4: 18–26.

BARRY BEYERSTEIN is associate professor of psychology and a member of the Brain Behaviour Laboratory at Simon Fraser University. A native of Edmonton, Alberta, he received his bachelor's degree from Simon Fraser University and a Ph.D. in experimental and biological psychology from the University of California at Berkeley. He serves as chair of the Society of B.C. Skeptics and he is a Fellow and a member of the Executive Council of CSICOP. Beyerstein is on the editorial board of the *Skeptical Inquirer*. He is also an elected member of the Council for Scientific Medicine, a U.S. organization that provides critiques of unscientific and fraudulent health products, and a founding board member of the group supporting evidence-based medicine, Canadians for Rational Health Policy. He is associate editor of the journal *Scientific Review of Alternative Medicine* and is on the editorial board of a new journal, *Scientific Evaluation of Clinical Psychology and Psychiatry*. Dr. Beyerstein has published in these areas himself and was an invited presenter on the topic of false memory syndrome before the Canadian parliamentary committee investigating the laws concerning child custody and access.

Beyerstein's teaching interests include courses on brain research, drugs, sensory psychophysiology, and consciousness, and the history and philosophy of psychological research. His awards include a Woodrow Wilson Fellowship, the gold medal of the B.C. Psychological Association, and the Donald K. Sampson Award of the B.C. College of Psychologists. He has also held a visiting professorship at Jilin University in the People's Republic of China where he had the opportunity to interact with various practitioners of traditional Chinese medicine.

Dickson, D. and Kelly, I. 1985. "The 'Barnum Effect' in Personality Assessment: A Review of the Literature." *Psychological Reports* 57: 367–82.

Ebbern, H., S. Mulligan, and B. Beyerstein. 1996. "Maria's Near-Death Experience: Waiting for the Other Shoe to Drop." *Skeptical Inquirer* 20, no. 4: 27–33.

Ferguson, M. 1980. *The Aquarian Conspiracy: Personal and Social Transformation in the 1980s*. Los Angeles: J. P. Tarcher.

Frankel, C. 1973. "The Nature and Sources of Irrationalism." *Science*, 180: 927–31.

Gilovich, T. 1991. *How We Know What Isn't So: The Fallibility of Human Reason in Everyday Life*. New York: Free Press.

Hyman, R. 1964. *The Nature of Psychological Inquiry*. Englewood Cliffs, N.J.: Prentice-Hall.

———. 1977. " 'Cold reading': How to Convince Strangers You Know All About Them." *Zetetic* (spring/summer): 18–37.

———. 1991. *The Elusive Quarry: A Scientific Appraisal of Psychical Research*. Amherst, N.Y.: Prometheus Books.

Neher, A. 1990. *The Psychology of Transcendence*. 2d ed. New York: Dover Publications.

Reed, G. 1988. *The Psychology of Anomalous Experience*. 2d ed. Amherst, N.Y.: Prometheus Books.

Roszak, T. 1969. *The Making of a Counter-Culture*. New York: Doubleday.

Sampson, W., and B. Beyerstein. 1996. "Traditional Medicine and Pseudoscience in China (Part 2)." *Skeptical Inquirer* 20, no. 5: 27–34.

Schick, T., and L. Vaughn. 1995. *How to Think About Weird Things*. Mountain View, Calif.: Mayfield Publishing.

Singer, B., and V. Benassi. 1981. "Occult Beliefs." *American Scientist* 69 (January/February): 49–55.

Steiner, G. 1974. *Nostalgia for the Absolute*. The 1974 CBC Massey Lectures. Toronto: Canadian Broadcasting Corporation Publications.

UFOs

9

UFOs
An Innocent Myth Turned Evil

PHILIP J. KLASS

Until a few years ago, if someone told me that they "believed in UFOs" because they had seen one, I would typically respond that if they wanted to believe that they had seen an extraterrestrial craft such belief was harmless—if erroneous. I would usually add that if they would go outside on a clear night and spend several hours looking at the sky, I could almost guarantee that they would see another UFO, i.e., something unfamiliar and seemingly inexplicable—unless they were an amateur astronomer.

The significant changes in UFOlogy that have occurred since I entered the field in mid-1966 were brought home to me when I attended the annual conference of the world's largest pro-UFO organization—the Mutual UFO Network (MUFON)—in mid-1996. Its stated theme was: "UFOlogy: A Scientific Enigma." But most of the featured presentations, dealing with claims of UFO abductions and "alien implants" removed from the bodies of (alleged) abductees, impressed me as ultra pseudoscience.

What a contrast with the situation when I first entered the field thirty years earlier. At that time UFO researchers focused their attention on reports from airline and military pilots, some of which were seemingly confirmed by radar. My interest was sparked by my training as an electrical engineer and my experience as the senior avionics editor for *Aviation Week & Space Technology* magazine. The foregoing provided insights into the limitations of radar and eyewitness testimony.

In 1966, the nation's largest and most prominent pro-UFO organization was NICAP (National Investigations Committee on Aerial Phenomena). NICAP would question the veracity of anyone who reported

123

seeing "creatures" in or near a UFO. Anyone reporting a UFO sighting to NICAP would be asked if they had had any previous UFO sightings. If the person claimed several, they were characterized as "repeaters" and scant credence was given to their report. When the first "UFO-abduction" case (involving Betty and Barney Hill) achieved international prominence in the fall of 1966, NICAP director Donald Keyhoe publicly expressed doubts about whether an abduction had really occurred.

Three decades later, at the MUFON conference, some of the featured speakers claimed that thousands of persons had been abducted by UFOs, and that some of them had been abducted many times, beginning in their early childhood. At least one woman claims to have been abducted more than one hundred times—and she may not be the top claimant. During a subsequent question-and-answer period at the 1996 MUFON conference, none of these claims was challenged.

One paper by Dr. Roger K. Leir, a California podiatrist, reported on the surgical removal of small objects from the toe of one "abductee" and the hand of another, supposedly implanted by ETs without leaving any surgical scars. (ETs reportedly insert their "alien implants" in a wide variety of locations, including the brain, the nose, the chest, and even in the penis.)

Another of the 1996 MUFON conference papers dealt with the question of the authenticity of a movie, earlier broadcast several times on the Fox TV network, purporting to show the autopsy of an ET recovered from a flying saucer that (allegedly) had crashed near Roswell, New Mexico. The speaker, Philip Mantle, admitted the *Alien Autopsy* movie might be bogus but concluded that "no one, and I repeat no one, has yet conclusively proven it a hoax." (Barely two years later, Robert Kiviat, who had earlier produced the several Fox TV shows on the *Alien Autopsy* movie, produced another Fox TV show which exposed the ET autopsy film as a hoax.)

Other photographic evidence discussed at the MUFON conference included a paper dealing with the (alleged) "Face on Mars" and other "structures" in the Cydonia region, supposedly created by ETs and photographed in 1976 by the Viking orbiter. (Subsequent photos taken by the more recent Mars Global Surveyor, show the "face" to be a creation of natural forces which does not really resemble a human face.)

For some members of the MUFON conference audience, the most impressive "hard evidence" was presented by Dr. Bruce S. Maccabee, an optical physicist employed by the U.S. Navy. Maccabee showed several videos of UFOs, taken by Ed Walters of Gulf Breeze, Florida. One, shot through a large picture window from Walters's home office on the morning of July 21, 1995, seems to show a dark, oval-shaped object zoom from left to right at a speed that Maccabee calculated to be about 500 mph. On the video, the object stopped and *instantaneously reversed direction*, zooming back at a similar speed until it disappeared behind the wall of Walters's office.

Maccabee dismissed the possibility that the video might be a hoax because of what he perceived to be a very faint shadow from the UFO moving along treetop foliage in the distance. Detailed analysis of the video by UFO researcher Jeff Sainio indicated that while the (apparent) faint shadow on treetop foliage stopped moving when the UFO stopped moving, the shadow's location deviated from its expected position if it really was a shadow from the UFO.

Maccabee offered a very profound hypothesis to explain this discrepancy: "We are left with the video evidence which seems to imply that the light rays were somehow bent around the UFO!" If true, Maccabee's discovery would qualify him for a Nobel Prize. But so far as is known, he has not since tried to verify his theory using other UFO videos or still-photos.

Maccabee concluded his presentation as follows: "Recent videos show UFOs accelerating and even 'disappearing.' *These videos provide, for the first time, quantitative evidence that UFOs are capable of extreme acceleration and speed. . . . Now, with some 'hard' data to go on, it appears that we must confront the ridiculous (by our standards) evidence that phenomenal acceleration, without the usual action-reaction, is possible*" (emphasis added).

If the Ed Walters videos provide such impressive evidence, one should expect that navy physicist Maccabee would have shown them to top Pentagon scientists and officials. They would be eager to explore technology that could enable military aircraft to accelerate to high speed and reverse direction almost instantaneously—or disappear. If Maccabee has provided top Pentagon scientists and officials with copies of the Walters videos, they were not sufficiently impressed to fund Maccabee's research into UFOs.

If NICAP still existed, surely Ed Walters would head its list of "repeaters." Within a few months in the late 1980s, Walters made public about two dozen UFO photos, most of them taken at night which seemed to show a giant circular craft with illuminated windows hovering over his back or front yard. These were taken with an old model Polaroid camera which can easily make double-exposure UFO pictures by first photographing a small model hanging in the dark then taking the camera outside for the second exposure. The resulting photos seem to show a giant UFO hovering over the back/front yard.

Later, when Walters was challenged to photograph the UFO with a 35 mm camera which had been sealed to prevent any "hanky panky" and which could not make double exposures, the resulting photos showed only faint lights in the night sky. Walters claimed the ETs communicated with him telepathically, and even transmitted images of beautiful, buxom women. On May 1, 1988, Walters claimed he was briefly abducted by a UFO.

Not surprisingly, Walters soon was offered a contract to write a book about his UFO experiences, and received a $200,000 cash advance. Shortly, Walters signed an option for a TV show about his UFO experiences. With

Walters's new riches, he decided to build a new house and sold his old home to Mr. and Mrs. Robert Menzer who recently had moved to Gulf Breeze.

In the spring of 1989, Mr. Menzer made an interesting discovery while searching for the master water valve in the attic of the former Walters house. He discovered a small model UFO constructed from plastic picnic plates which resembled the UFO in Walters's photos. The center section of the UFO model had been fabricated from a drawing that Walters himself had made for a house he hoped to build. (Walters was then in the house construction business.) When a Pensacola journalist interviewed the Menzers, they mentioneded the chance discovery of the small model UFO which they showed him, which resulted in a feature story in the June 10, 1990, *Pensacola News Journal.*

When the story broke, Walters had a ready explanation: UFO skeptics had stolen his house-plan drawing from his garbage can and used it to construct the small model UFO. Then, they had broken into his old house and hidden the model under the insulation in its attic—where it would not have been found if Mr. Menzer had not needed to find the master water valve so he could install a new ice-making refrigerator.

The discovery of the small UFO model, plus the public disclosure by a youthful friend of Walters's son that he had witnessed Walters making bogus UFO pictures using a small model, prompted MUFON director Walter Andrus to appoint UFOlogist Rex Salisberry and his wife to conduct an independent assessment of the Walters UFO photos. Two months later, the Salisberrys submitted a written report offering newly discovered evidence that the Walters UFO photos were bogus.

Later, one of Walters's most impressive photos, which seemingly showed a UFO hovering over a deserted highway, was analyzed by a famous photo analyst who declared it a double-exposure hoax. The photo was later replicated by a Pensacola TV station reporter using a small UFO model and a Polaroid camera like the one Walters had used.

Despite the foregoing—and additional evidence that the Walters UFO photos were bogus—Dr. Maccabee declared that his investigation showed that *ALL of the Walters UFO photos were authentic.* Later it was learned that Walters paid Maccabee $20,000 to write a single chapter for the Walters's book which endorsed the authenticity of his UFO photos. (Maccabee's payment for writing a single chapter exceeds the royalties I've earned on my last three UFO books.) Subsequently, Maccabee and Walters coauthored the book *UFOs Are Real: Here's the Proof.*

Three decades ago when I entered the UFO field, it was not surprising to meet intelligent people, including engineers and scientists, who suspected that a few UFOs might indeed be extraterrestrial visitors. Initially, I hoped that my own research might find credible evidence of a few ET visits so I could rush to my (then) typewriter to write the greatest story of my career for *Aviation Week & Space Technology* magazine. This would probably win me a Pulitzer Prize, and certainly a giant bonus.

As the years passed and I found prosaic, down-to-earth explanations for famous, seemingly mysterious UFO cases, I naturally became increasingly skeptical. But until the late 1980s, I felt that UFOs were a harmless myth. That view began to change with the publication of Whitley Strieber's "best-seller" *Communion* and Budd Hopkins's book *Intruders* with their claims of UFO abductions. Although this prompted me to write a book which traced the history of such claims (*UFO Abductions: A Dangerous Game*, Prometheus Books, 1989), I never imagined how many persons would become victims of this dangerous cult.

The danger stems from the dogma that is espoused by the cult leaders: that if a person is abducted by a UFO, they will be abducted frequently throughout their lifetime. (One attractive young woman who appeared on the *Larry King Live* show claimed she had been abducted more than a hundred times.) Further, that when a parent is abducted, the ETs will return later to abduct their children, and even grandchildren.

The cult dogma promotes belief that ETs extract ova from female "abductees" to create hybrid creatures which their Earthling parents are allowed to see only briefly—during a subsequent abduction. The dogma is spread via books, TV talk shows, and the use of hypnosis by cult leaders, and also via cult leaders' "support groups" where "abductees" relate their experiences to attendees who suspect they might also be victims.

Several years ago I received a call from a psychotherapist in a mid-Atlantic state who told me of a female patient, a divorcee with an eight-year-old son, who had been referred to him by the woman's physician. The physician had discovered a small tumor in her brain, and he thought the tumor should be removed via surgery. But the woman, who had joined a UFO-abduction support group, was convinced that the tumor was an "alien implant" which should remain until the ETs decided to remove it. That had prompted her physician to recommend that she visit the psychotherapist, which in turn had prompted the therapist to buy my book on UFO abductions.

The psychotherapist said he had given my book to the woman to read and asked if I would be willing to talk with her via telephone. I agreed. He added that the woman's young son had become afraid to be alone or go outside at night lest he also be abducted by a UFO. I had hoped that my book would at least raise some skepticism in the woman's mind.

But when the woman called a few days later, she harshly criticized me for questioning that she had been chosen by members of an advanced civilization to participate in their experiments. Their implant in her brain, she explained, undoubtedly would make her much more intelligent. After listening to her harsh criticism for about fifteen minutes, I said that the decision was hers to make and we ended our conversation. Since that time, I've heard nothing further from the woman or her psychotherapist. But her son will bear the scars of fear of UFO abduction for many years—perhaps a lifetime. Perhaps also, his children will be needlessly instilled with similar fears.

But perhaps the most significant evil consequence of the current path of UFOlogy is its adverse effect on the confidence of many citizens in our government. Beginning in the late 1980s, many network TV shows featured the claim that the U.S. government had covertly recovered a "crashed saucer" near Roswell, New Mexico, in 1947—as well as recovery of several *live* ETs—which had been kept secret from the public for many decades.

As a leading UFO skeptic, I participated in the prebroadcast taping of many of these shows. On numerous occasions, prior to the taping, I provided the producer with photocopies of once "Secret" and "Top Secret" Central Intelligence Agency and U.S. Air Force documents which proved that the Roswell crashed-saucer/government cover-up tale was *not* true. And I informed the show's producer that these documents had never before been shown on TV. *Yet these documents were never used.*

In one incident, while being interviewed in Roswell by CBS News for its show *48 Hours*, I whipped out one of these "Top Secret" documents from my pocket and held it up in front of the camera, saying it had never before been shown to TV audiences. When the show aired several months later, the *entire* interview with me ended up "on the cutting room floor." (A more detailed account of such experiences can be found in my article "That's Entertainment! TV's UFO Coverup," published in the November/December 1996 issue of *Skeptical Inquirer*.)

In view of this very biased treatment by TV-show producers, the results of a poll conducted in 1995 by Ohio University/Scripps Howard News Service are not surprising. When asked if they believed that the U.S. government "is hiding the truth" about UFOs, *50 percent chose "very likely" or "somewhat likely."* In 1996, *Newsweek* magazine conducted a survey which asked: "Do you think the government is concealing UFO information?" Of those surveyed, *49 percent answered "Yes."*

The results of a survey published in the July 7, 1997, edition of *USA Today* indicated that *66 percent* of the respondents believed that a UFO crashed near Roswell in 1947—despite strong government denials. Also, that *80 percent* of those surveyed believe "the government is hiding evidence of intelligent life in space."

These and other recent polls indicate that at least half of our population believes that the U.S. government has been "withholding the truth about UFOs" for more than half a century. This belief incriminates ten American presidents from both major parties since Harry Truman. It includes such highly respected presidents as Truman, Eisenhower, and Reagan.

On September 19, 1949, President Truman was advised by a panel of experts that recently acquired evidence indicated that the Soviet Union had successfully tested its first atomic bomb. *Within four days,* after notifying congressional and British officials, the Truman White House publicly announced this secret. Although this meant that the United States would soon be vulnerable to atomic devastation, there was no public panic.

Even if ET craft were *only* visiting U.S. airspace, it is most unlikely that any administration would be so foolish as to try to keep this secret for more than a few days or weeks. (As President Clinton would later learn, even intimate Oval Office incidents known to only two people are difficult to keep secret for long.) Because UFO sightings were being reported around the globe, it would be ridiculous for any U.S. government to hope that Communist Bloc and other unfriendly governments would agree to a U.S. UFO-cover-up policy.

The truthfulness of individual government officials on specific issues must always remain open to challenge. But it would be tragic if the time should ever come when a once innocent myth turned evil—promoted by TV-show producers—prompts U.S. citizens to consider abandoning our democratic form of government.

PHILIP J. KLASS, a graduate electrical engineer turned technical journalist for *Aviation Week & Space Technology,* has spent more than thirty-four years investigating famous UFO incidents as a hobby. Initially he hoped he might find credible evidence of extraterrestrial visitations, so he could write the greatest article of his career. But he invariably found more prosaic explanations for the incidents he investigated—utilizing his technical training and journalistic skills. Today, Klass is acknowledged to be one of the leading skeptical UFO investigators. He has published five books on the subject, the most recent being *The REAL Roswell Crashed-Saucer Coverup* (Prometheus Books, 1997). Klass publishes a bimonthly newsletter, *Skeptics UFO Newsletter* (*SUN*), which has subscribers in more than a dozen countries. He is a Fellow of CSICOP.

10

THE ODYSSEY OF A UFO SKEPTIC

ROBERT SHEAFFER

When I was a youngster growing up in Norridge, Illinois, just outside Chicago, I was intensely interested in astronomy and the space program. I had several telescopes that were always in various states of repair and disrepair. I wrote fan letters to the astronauts, resulting in a large collection of autographed photos, especially the original *Mercury 7*. This interest led me invariably to the question of UFOs, which were then as now inseparable in the public mind from the question of space travel and astronomy.

When I first thought about these questions when I was about ten years old, I was a believer in UFOs. I had read some of the sensationalist books and articles on the subject, and not having seen or heard anything to the contrary, I believed that they were probably true. Of course, in those days, UFO cases consisted of "sightings," and nothing more. You saw something unusual in the sky, and that was that. There were no claims about sightings of "aliens," or of "contact," let alone "crashes" or "abductions." Just funny stuff up in the sky. And it was an article of faith among UFO buffs that the government—especially the air force—knew more about these funny objects than it was telling.

When I was about eleven (probably 1960) I had my telescope in my yard when my friend and I saw a bright satellite go across the sky—possibly the echo balloon, or a large Russian satellite. We knew that it was a satellite—at least, that is what it was *supposed* to be. But look—it's changing its path! First it was moving toward the left, then it turned and moved toward the right. Then it zigged and zagged again! One's eyes can so easily play

130

tricks, especially if one is halfway expecting to see something weird. Of course, we made no serious attempt to record its motion against the background stars, which would surely have shown the object to be following a straight curve across the globe of the sky. We were convinced we had seen one of those things that the air force didn't want to talk about. They could fool the public, but they couldn't fool us!

Even more impressive to me was a sight I saw when I was probably twelve. It was a summer evening during twilight, around the last week in August. I was standing in the driveway of my house and leaning against the car, talking with a different friend. Suddenly I looked up and called out—we both saw them. Moving overhead noiselessly at a high angular rate, from north to south, was a small formation of apparently luminescent objects. About six objects—no time to take an exact count—were in a formation that was slanted about 45 degrees to the direction of travel, with the lead object on the right. In a few seconds they glided from the zenith to a position about ten or twenty degrees above the horizon in the south, when they suddenly went off like a light—or so it appeared. (Or else, they were no longer illuminated so that we could see them.) We had no idea what we'd just seen—genuine saucers, it seemed for sure. I ran into the house to tell my dad what we'd seen. He thought it was a lot of silliness. (He still does!)

For years I puzzled myself over what I had seen. In retrospect, I was never cut out to be a good UFOlogist because I was too keen on science. I understood and respected the scientific method. I held great hopes for what science would do for humanity's future. While on one hand, I understood the problems associated with believing UFOs to be interplanetary spacecraft, on the other hand I could not deny what I had seen. From the library I got a copy of *The World of Flying Saucers* by the Harvard astrophysicist Donald H. Menzel and science journalist Lyle G. Boyd, practically the only skeptical UFO book in print at that time (1963). I learned about the problems with eyewitness reports and memories, and the unreliability of the UFO information in the popular culture that surrounded us. However, until I could personally explain what I had seen, I could not consider myself fully a skeptic.

I now am quite convinced that my brief-but-impressive UFO sighting was a flight of birds migrating south at the end of summer. All the pieces of the puzzle fit into place. On several subsequent occasion, I have seen flocks of birds capture that same effect of noiseless, effortless gliding across the sky. I learned that my sighting was very similar to the classic incidents known as the "Lubbock Lights" in Texas during the last week of August 1951. These turned out to be migrating plover headed south.[1]

In 1967 I finished high school with good grades and some scholarships. My head was filled with ideas of math and science, and I headed off to Northwestern University in Evanston, Illinois. One of the thoughts in my mind was the desire to meet and to talk with J. Allen Hynek, who was then chairman of the Department of Astronomy at Northwestern. Hynek (1910–1986) was the astronomical consultant to the U.S. Air Force for Project Bluebook, its UFO investigation project, and his name was in the news a lot whenever UFOs were mentioned. *Newsweek* magazine proclaimed him to be "Mr. UFO." In the 1950s and early 1960s, Hynek had the reputation, along with Menzel, as being a hardheaded, scientific UFO skeptic. Hynck was quoted in the 1960 book *Flying Saucers and the U.S. Air Force* calling UFO proponents "wishful thinkers." He asked, "What evidence? As a consultant on these matters to the Air Force for many years, I have seen this evidence; and as a scientist it leaves me quite frustrated. There is nothing here that any scientist would truly call scientific evidence."[2] (In later years, Hynek would attempt to portray himself as always having been a quasi-believer in UFOs, but the facts simply do not bear this out.) UFOs had been fairly quiet during the early 1960s, but by 1965 the country was once again in the throes of wild UFO excitement. UFOlogist and computer scientist Jacques Vallee had been a graduate student at Northwestern several years before I arrived, and was largely responsible for persuading Hynek that UFOs were a genuine scientific mystery.

As I was to discover firsthand at Northwestern, Hynek was anything but a hardheaded scientist.

While quite well-known to the public at large because of his association with UFOs, Hynek was not terribly well respected within the astronomical community.[3] Whatever astronomical publications and other accomplishments were associated with his career had occurred years earlier; by the 1960s Hynek was primarily an administrator and fund-raiser who was trotted out before the public, and taught only elementary astronomy to undergraduates. Hynek apparently realized that if he were to be remembered it would more likely be as "the Galileo of UFO Studies" rather than any work he did in astronomy.

Nonetheless, Hynek undeniably had a charming personality and was a persuasive public speaker. His elementary astronomy course (in which only a single lecture was devoted to UFOs) was one of the most popular on campus, a favorite course for nonscience majors seeking to fulfill a science requirement. His explanations of complex astronomical concepts in simple terms were among the very best I have ever heard, even to this day. Had Hynek stuck to "straight" science education, he could have been among the very best, a true media celebrity. Indeed, to a limited extent Hynek did fulfill this role, but his credibility was fatally compromised by his uncritical embrace of wild UFO claims.

Each year in the fall, Hynek invited over to his home those undergraduates who were current or prospective astronomy majors, for informal and informative chats. While I ended up majoring in math, not astronomy, I participated in several of these gatherings.[4] The atmosphere was friendly and informal, and the discussions were wide-ranging. Of course the subject of

UFOs came up. Hynek argued that UFOs were a genuine scientific anomaly, and that they hinted at some great realm of undiscovered knowledge promising a scientific revolution as significant as those of Copernicus or Galileo. Discussing such claims with him, it was obvious that he was totally naïve about the problem of the unreliability of human eyewitness testimony. He staunchly maintained that it was possible to separate individuals into categories of "credible" and "noncredible." Whenever "credible" persons reported "incredible" things, it was something that science had to take seriously, and indeed even to modify its laws to encompass these reports.

While I was at Northwestern, Hynek was in the process of organizing his Center for UFO Studies (CUFOS), which was supposed to put the study of UFOs on a solid scientific footing. Hynek and Vallee were fond of pointing out that the scientific revolution firmly established itself when a small, informal group of scholars calling themselves the Invisible College became interested in new discoveries, and ultimately founded the Royal Society and other scientific groups. They immodestly imagined themselves now poised to make the same breakthrough with the study of UFOs. Hynek wrote, "(The College) remained invisible until the scientists of that day gained respectability when the Royal Society was chartered by Charles II in the early 1660s. Similarly, the creation of the Center for UFO Studies from the UFO Invisible College represents a step toward recognition."[5] Hynek clearly did not understand that the great scientific revolution of the seventeenth century took place precisely because unverifiable anecdotal testimony was, for the first time, deliberately disregarded. Indeed, the Royal Society of London in 1660 adopted as its motto Nullius in Verba, "nothing in words," signifying that experiment, not anecdote or authority, was to be the foundation of scientific knowledge. Stories of miracles abounded in the seventeenth century as they do today, and the great wisdom of the original Invisible College was its decision to ignore them, relying entirely on quantitative observation and on experiment. Hynek would not take seriously my suggestion that he was attempting to stand the history of science on its head, by once again embracing anecdotes as a legitimate cornerstone of knowledge.

I had offered to Hynek to serve as their "resident skeptic," as this was a role that seemed to me to be sorely needed. Hynek did consult me on a few cases, although I wasn't able to make any dramatic new findings on them. At this time he was working on the manuscript of his first UFO book *The UFO Experience*, whose publication was a major event in UFOlogy. He gave me the proofs of one of the main chapters to get my comments, insisting that I tell *not a soul* about having seen it. Not long afterward I returned to him a detailed commentary, making the argument that the presence of any degree of "noise within the channel" of human perception and communication ensures that there will be a residue of seemingly "unexplained" UFO cases, *even if there were nothing unusual flying around.* This argument seemed to annoy him when I raised it verbally, and he chose to largely ignore it when presented in written form. The unnumbered footnote added to chapter 4, beginning "Many critics maintain that all UFO reports are garbage," is an obvious although unattributed response to my critique. Hynek obviously didn't want his pro-UFO colleagues to know that he had allowed his long-awaited and much-touted manuscript to be reviewed by one of those closed-minded skeptics.

In the 1960s, the numbers of skeptical books about UFOs were extremely small. When Philip J. Klass's *UFOs Identified* (1968) was published, I was very interested in it not so much because of the "plasma theory" of UFOs that it promoted, but because of the hardheaded skepticism directed toward many UFO claims. I began corresponding with Klass in 1968. He was very interested to hear about Hynek's goings-on at Northwestern. Our correspondence became extensive, and he began jokingly referring to us as "Plasmarians" 0.00001 and 0.00002 (usually abbreviated as "01" and "02"). Not long afterward we met. He became my mentor in UFO matters. It was not long before Klass came to realize that there were problems with the "plasma theory" of UFOs, especially after I convinced him that the "classic" UFO photos of the Lucci brothers that he suggested in *UFOs Identified* [6] might be genuine "plasma UFOs" were much better explained as hoaxes. Klass soon came to appreciate how the fallibility of human testimony provided a much more solid explanation for UFO claims. With the publication of his second UFO book, *UFOs Explained* (1974), "plasma UFOs" were largely forgotten, and human error and knavery shown to provide the best accounting for many reported UFOs.

In 1972 I finished at Northwestern and took a job in the Washington, D.C., area, but still kept in contact with Hynek and CUFOS. In the fall of 1973 the country was in the midst of a UFO "sightings frenzy," and news stories about Hynek and his center were everywhere, especially in the tabloid press. People who wrote to the Center for UFO Studies requesting information were sent a paper stating that "much of the material being developed is too complex for general discussion," and were given a list of recommended books. One book on the list stated flatly at the beginning, "We predict that by 1975 the government will release definite proof that extraterrestrials are watching us."[7] In May of 1974 I wrote Hynek suggesting that he was squandering his scientific reputation by endorsing such highly dubious UFO books. I wrote, "Permit me in my role as the Center's resident skeptic to point out what appears to be a significant deviation from the Center's professed role as a sober and respectable investigative group." I then gave him my objections to the sensationalist paperback. Hynek replied that while he "tend[ed] to agree somewhat" in the matter of the book, "Still, it is not as bad as all that." He went on, "As far as you being resident skeptic of the Center, I have to inform you that 'membership' in the

Center is limited to scientists established in their own field. . . . So I guess you will have to be skeptical on your own time." His claim about "membership" in the Center was of course untrue. One of CUFOS's most prolific and prized investigators worked as a county employee in a blue-collar job. Hynek's message was clear: constructive criticism from skeptics was entirely unwelcome. Later, Hynek collaborated with UFOlogist Raymond Fowler on a highly uncritical book claiming to be a "documented investigation" of how a woman was abducted literally "through the looking glass" and onto a UFO.[8] For the rest of his life Hynek remained something of a laughing-stock among astronomers, vainly seeking scientific respectability for the study of UFOs. He had no one but himself to blame.

The last time I saw Hynek was at the CSICOP Conference at Stanford University in Palo Alto, California, in November of 1984, which I helped organize. He attended as the "worthy opponent" we invited to balance our panel of skeptical UFO presentations by Philip J. Klass, Andrew Fraknoi, and Roger Culver. I had had no direct contact with Hynek for several years, but when he saw me at the reception on the evening before the panel he greeted me warmly, apparently harboring no personal animosity over our long-standing disagreements. The conference's UFO panel discussion, of which I was moderator, went smoothly but probably didn't change anyone's mind. It was ironic that Hynek nonetheless managed to capture much of the publicity for the CSICOP conference! Newspapers paid more attention to Hynek's talk than to the conference itself. For example, the *San Jose Mercury News* reported on November 11, 1984, "Researcher charts UFO sightings"—a story about Hynek. The casual reader would have thought that the event was an homage to Hynek the UFOlogist, rather than a group of skeptics who organized a major event, invited Hynek, and listened to his arguments in polite disagreement. But the longer one is active in the field of skepticism, the less surprised one is at such results.

One day in April of 1976, some enigmatic handwritten signs suddenly began appearing around the University of Maryland in College Park, which I was fortunate to spot. The signs proclaimed a lecture on the evening of April 19 "to explain the UFO Two." I suspected that this mysterious meeting may involve "Bo and Peep"—Marshall Herff Applewhite and Bonnie Lu Nettles (also known as "The Two," "Him and Her," and many other names), who had recently been in the headlines as the "Pied Pipers" of UFOlogy. In numerous cities they had appeared without advance notice to give lectures about a type of "salvation" involving UFOs. They had somehow lured dozens of people away from their homes and normal lives into a UFO cult. I made plans to attend.

It indeed did turn out to be one of the cult's recruiting meetings. Arriving early, I recognized Applewhite and Nettles standing around and chatting with the cult members. I said nothing. During the meeting, Applewhite and Nettles sat incognito among the audience while the cult members at the speakers' table talked glowingly about the coming "harvest." Those who were ready to be "harvested" would be taken up to the "next level" by the UFOs, where they would live a better life. Bo and Peep were the only two people on earth representing that higher level. The cultists on the panel obviously believed every word of this nonsense. When asked the whereabouts of their leaders, the cultists claimed to not know where they were: "We believe they are in the Midwest somewhere." They were lying. The Two were seated in the audience, although amazingly nobody seemed to realize this. Some of the audience members were quite angry, presumably having had friends or relatives disappear into the cult—probably this is why Bo and Peep chose to remain incognito. When I had a chance to ask a question, I raised the issue of The Two's previous brushes with the law—news reports had mentioned several—and I asked if these were the kind of persons whose word they would trust so completely. As I was speaking, Applewhite rose up from his chair on the other side of the aisle, stood full up and glared at me, from about fifteen feet away. He was a large man, and he had an air of being dangerous. It would have been easy to blow apart the charade by confronting him right there, but I did not. I have always regretted my failure to act in that moment, most especially in light of what ultimately happened.

Bo and Peep gradually faded from sight, their cult largely forgotten, until the astonishing news burst upon the world in March of 1997. Believing reports from an unreliable source that the brilliant comet Hale-Bopp was being followed by a mysterious "UFO companion," Applewhite proclaimed to his followers that the sign had at last come for them to move on to the "next level" and join Nettles, who had died several years earlier. In Rancho Santa Fe, California, thirty-nine members of Applewhite's cult, now calling itself "Heaven's Gate," put on their sneakers, took fatal doses of drugs and alcohol, then lay down with plastic bags over their heads expecting to "rise up" to the "next level" and join Nettles on the comet.

I was not involved in the founding meeting of CSICOP in May of 1976, although Phil Klass was. In fact, I did not even hear about the founding meeting until afterward, when it appeared in the papers. I immediately informed Phil of my eagerness to participate in the new organization. He assured me that there would be plenty of opportunity to do so, and that he had already recommended me as someone having a lot to contribute. Soon I was sending off material for publication in the *Zetetic* (the original name given to CSICOP's publication, now the *Skeptical Inquirer*). My review of two books by Hynek and Vallee appeared in the second issue of the *Zetetic* (spring/summer 1977), and I have had material appearing in most issues of CSICOP's magazine since them.

In 1976 when Jimmy Carter was running for president, stories began to circulate in UFO circles to the effect that "Jimmy Carter had seen a UFO."

However, nobody seemed to have any definite information about it to determine what it was. Several stories purporting to give details about the incident appeared in UFO publications and in the tabloid press, but upon investigation turned out to be totally inaccurate. Finally, I was able to obtain from Hayden Hewes's International UFO Bureau in Oklahoma a copy of a 1973 sighting report in Carter's own handwriting that he had sent them. It contained the location of the incident, but even Carter himself did not recall the exact date. Fortunately, it tied the Carter sighting to a specific event, which after a great deal of digging and many blind alleys I was able to tie to an exact date and time. The brilliant planet Venus turned out to have been exactly where Carter reported his UFO to have been. In 1977 Paul Kurtz was editor of the *Humanist* magazine, and he eagerly published my findings on the case.[9] The mainstream press, however, was far more eager to present the Carter UFO as supposed "enigma" than publish its solution. Even the "venerable" *Washington Post* gave far more coverage to the story that "Carter had seen a UFO" than to the *explanation* of that incident that I provided them—which was news, and had never been published before.[10]

My first in-person contact with CSICOP was on August 9, 1977. The group was holding a meeting and press conference at the Biltmore Hotel in New York. I remember my excitement as I got up early that morning to take the shuttle flight from Washington Airport to La Guardia and rode the bus into Manhattan to meet these amazing people. It was a new experience for me, listening to these accomplished and polished skeptics make their presentations and take questions from the major national press like the *New York Times* and *Time* magazine.[11] I was excited to see the skeptical perspective finally getting some serious media attention.

Paul Kurtz was running the show, along with Marcello Truzzi who was then the codirector of CSICOP. I met Randi, of whom I had been in awe since reading his brilliant exposés of Uri Geller. He immediately put me at ease, saying he'd heard so much about me and he greeted *me* as if *I* were the celebrity! The magician Milbourne Christopher was there, looking pleased but rather haggard. I felt honored to meet him, and told him how much I had enjoyed reading his biography of Houdini. He died a year or so later.

Perhaps what impressed me most of all that day was meeting Martin Gardner, who at that time was still living in the New York area and writing the "Mathematical Recreations" column for *Scientific American*. He, too, greeted me as if I were a celebrity, and his modest, self-effacing mannerisms immediately put me at ease. I had the great privilege to have lunch with him that day in the hotel coffee shop. He told me of his background and his studies at the University of Chicago, at that time a famous bastion of the Liberal Arts. I had expected that he would be a great mathematical whiz, wrapped up in clever mathematical conundrums. He dismissed that as just one small facet of his interests, and we went on to discuss many other things.

In the afternoon the press conference was over, and CSICOP held a general meeting for its fellows and others. At the meeting Truzzi resigned as editor of the *Zetetic*. Several people attempted to dissuade him from resigning, but his mind was set. I soon realized that it was best for Truzzi and CSICOP to go their separate ways. Truzzi's outlook on the "paranormal" was quite different from the rest of CSICOP. It was at this meeting that Paul Kurtz presented a young science journalist who already had a splendid reputation and who had volunteered to take on the job as editor— Kendrick Frazier. He seemed capable and eager, and over the years he has abundantly proven that that first impression was more than justified.

One of the first things I did after becoming affiliated with CSICOP was to make, on my own behalf, a formal complaint to the National News Council concerning an outrageous pseudo-documentary program shown on NBC-TV in 1977 called "In Search of the Bermuda Triangle." This program made wild assertions about "mysteries" that had already been solved, and took no pains whatsoever to attempt to determine the facts. The National News Council was a group to promote fairness and accuracy in news reporting. While they had no legal authority, their findings were regularly published in the *Columbia Journalism Review*. Their moral authority was such that a finding against a journalist or news organization was widely perceived as a black mark. At first, the council dismissed my complaint on the grounds that the program I objected to was not produced by the news department, and hence fell outside their purview. However, soon thereafter I was delighted to receive a reply that they had reconsidered their policy of refusing to review material that was not produced by the news department. This was a wise move. Obviously, a network might use a pseudo-documentary to promote false and misleading claims on any subject, then disavow all responsibility for the irresponsible act on the grounds that the program was "entertainment," not "news." My complaint was ultimately upheld: "The Council believes that NBC was lax in its oversight of this program."[12] Unfortunately, the National News Council ceased operation in 1984. Since then, there has been no comparably effective media watchdog organization.

Another small success of mine was when in 1977 I wrote to David Sendler, the managing editor of *TV Guide*, complaining that outrageously unreliable pseudo-documentaries such as the *In Search Of* programs were invariably listed as "documentaries." I objected that there was little or no factual content to such shows, and that to call them "documentaries" was misleading. I suggested that they be called instead "science fiction." I was delighted to receive a reply soon afterward from Mr. Sendler, saying that the editors agreed with my objection. They decided to label them "speculation"—a most appropriate term—and for quite some time all such shows were so designated by *TV Guide*.

While I was living in suburban Maryland I had the opportunity to see

Klass often. Sometimes we went sailing on the Potomac on his sailboat. Through Klass I met James E. Oberg and his wife, Cookie. At that time Jim was a captain in the U.S. Air Force and stationed in Washington, D.C. Jim is about six foot seven, feisty, and amazingly energetic. There are very few people like him! About two years later he was transferred to Houston, Texas, to work on the space program, where he has been ever since. Klass also introduced me to skeptics Gary Posner and Michael Dennett, who were both in Maryland at that time. Gary is now running the Tampa Bay Skeptics in Florida, while Michael is active in skeptical activities in Washington State.

I also made the acquaintance of Dr. Bruce Maccabee, one of the few UFO proponents who also has good scientific training—in his case, a Ph.D. in physics. We began discussing the Trent photos, the famous "classic UFO" photos taken in 1950 and left unresolved by the Condon Report in 1969. Maccabee was somehow able to locate the original negatives, and we jointly investigated them—reaching, of course, different conclusions.[13] Unlike most pro-UFOlogists, Maccabee is not intolerant of differing opinions, and hence did not become angry when discussing with skeptics. We shared an interest in astronomy as well as music, and we often took our telescopes and went out observing together. He wrote highly technical papers purporting to show why certain famous UFO photos were authentic, and not hoaxes. It would be difficult for someone who does not have a professional background in optics, as does Maccabee, to determine how solid are his arguments. However, Maccabee later went on to "authenticate" one of the most bogus series of UFO photos ever taken: the Gulf Breeze UFO photos of Ed Walters. These are known to be hoaxes for reasons quite independent of any information that may be contained in the photos themselves.[14] Therefore, Maccabee's "scientific" analysis of UFO photos is known to be flawed, even if we do not know where the flaw lies. Maccabee's photo analysis is like a computer program that is known to have given incorrect answers to easy questions. We cannot so easily determine if a program is correct when it is dealing with complicated operations on exponents of hyperbolic cosines, but if it tells us that "two times two" is something other than "four," we know its calculations cannot be relied on.

On September 6, 1980, I had the opportunity to participate in an all-day UFO Symposium sponsored by the Smithsonian Institution in Washington, D.C. It was held in the large lecture hall of the Museum of Natural History. Six top UFOlogists, pro and con, were invited to participate. It is unusual for UFO symposia to be so evenly balanced, although from the Smithsonian one should expect nothing less. On the "pro" side were Allen Hynek, Allan Hendry (who at that time was CUFOS's chief investigator), and Bruce Maccabee. On the skeptical side were Philip J. Klass, James E. Oberg, and myself. We each gave our presentations, and took questions in writing from the audience. One member of the audience who was furious at not having been selected as a panelist was Stanton T. Friedman, a professional UFO lecturer who bills himself as the "Flying Saucer Physicist" even though he has not worked in physics since the 1960s. Throughout the presentations Friedman could be heard, muttering and loudly declaiming comments, whenever any speaker said something with which he disagreed. Apparently this made him a panelist in his own mind.

In October of 1980 I moved to San Jose to work in California's Silicon Valley. At this time, the Bay Area was still very much renowned as the center of supposedly serious "parapsychological research." Russell Targ and Hal Puthoff were still conducting their celebrated if ill-controlled experiments of Uri Geller and other "parapsychological" subjects at SRI International in Menlo Park. Soon after arriving, I made the acquaintance of magician and skeptic Bob Steiner, who is now a CSICOP Fellow. Because of his natural gregariousness and extroverted behavior, combined with a high intelligence, he had already attracted an interesting circle of friends, many of whom had a skeptical bent. After attending a few parties at his place, it occurred to me that here was the nucleus to create something unique and remarkable: a local skeptics' group, a "hands-on" skeptical organization. To read articles from CSICOP in far-off Buffalo was all well and good, but it offered no opportunity for personal interaction. However, a local skeptical organization would offer the opportunity to discuss issues, to present lectures, to make friends and participate in social activities, as well as to offer a local presence for media appearance, to counter the usual pro-paranormal misrepresentations.

Bob Steiner heartily agreed with my idea. I felt that his gregariousness, combined with my methodical, analytical nature, could forge a splendid organization (which it did). On April 12, 1982, I wrote to Paul Kurtz suggesting that we form a "local chapter" of CSICOP in the Bay Area. I had in mind the "local chapters" of some UFO groups—we would beat them at their own game! Kurtz encouraged us to proceed, although CSICOP's legal counsel insisted that local groups must be autonomous organizations, rather than "chapters" of CSICOP. And so it was.

Like any new organization, there was a great deal of disagreement and confusion over how to proceed. We spent hours arguing over bylaws, dues, memberships, and so forth for the Bay Area Skeptics (BAS). Eventually we reached a consensus that satisfied nearly everyone, and with much fanfare we launched the organization. (Not everyone was satisfied, of course, and in those disagreements was the birth of the East Bay Skeptics Society, with the usual personal animosities on both sides playing a major role. Even we skeptics sometimes act like the primates we are.) BAS was launched during the summer of 1982.[15] One of our first actions was to issue a "Challenge to All Psychics" to back up their claims, and it created quite a buzz when we distributed it widely within the hotbeds of parapsychology such as SRI. Among those who played a role in the early years of Bay Area Skeptics were astronomers Andrew Fraknoi and Donald Goldsmith, physician and educator Wallace Sampson, author Lawrence Jerome, science educator Eugenie Scott, and psychiatrist Francis Rigney.

In 1987 I was invited to participate on a TV show in San Francisco with the far-out writer who claims frequent contact with "the visitors," Whitley Strieber. When he arrived in the Green Room, he was furious to learn that there would be an "opposing voice" to his bizarre claims about the supposed antics of mysterious creatures. He threw a world-class temper tantrum, refusing to go on unless I were removed from the show. The show's hosts worked out a last-minute deal (out of my earshot) that satisfied Strieber—almost. I would be on the set, but almost totally excluded from participation. However, Strieber was *still* not satisfied, and even though he was on a book promotion tour, he persisted in refusing to allow the hosts to mention his book![16]

In June of 1992 I was fortunate to have an opportunity to participate in another historic UFO event, the "Abduction Study Conference" at MIT in Cambridge, Massachusetts. This was a "by invitation only" conference organized by psychiatrist John Mack of Harvard, physicist David Pritchard of MIT, historian David Jacobs of Temple, and artist/UFOlogist Budd Hopkins. The conference was "emphatically closed to the press," which of course generated a great deal of speculation and interest. But instead of the conference containing great revelations, it was a circus of astonishing folly. The proceedings from the conference make for bizarre and entertaining reading.[17]

In April of 1996 I took a "UFO tour" of Mexico, organized by a pro-paranormal group that takes people to "mysterious" places worldwide.[18] Wild and fabulous claims have been made about supposedly commonplace UFO sightings occurring since 1991 in certain areas of Mexico. We visited the very hottest of the UFO hotspots, and talked with people who claimed to be seeing UFOs on a regular basis. While their stories sounded impressive, in spite of an abundance of still and video cameras, nobody had any clear and convincing evidence of anything out of the ordinary. If solid UFO evidence had existed anywhere in Mexico, we would have seen it.

As one of the few skeptical UFOlogists I have been to many other conferences, talks, and strange goings-on that space does not permit me to mention. At the present time I'm involved in preparing for a historic "stealth UFO conference" that I'm not now at liberty to discuss. When I finally am at liberty to "tell all," it will be a most entertaining story!

NOTES

1. For the story of the Lubbock Lights, see Donald H. Menzel and Lyle G. Boyd, *The World of Flying Saucers* (New York: Doubleday and Company, 1963), pp. 123–29.

2. Lt. Col. Lawrence J. Tacker, *Flying Saucers and the U.S. Air Force* (Princeton, N.J.: D. Van Nostrand, 1960), p. 78.

3. Hynek made an amazingly candid self-assessment in an interview in *New Scientist* (May 17, 1973): "When I look back on my career, I've done damn little that was original. I seem to have had the ability of seeing the value of an idea and bringing other people together to do something about it. I've never launched any new theories; I've never made any outstanding discoveries. I guess I am not very innovative."

4. I took enough astronomy courses to qualify as an astronomy major, but I did not take all the physics courses required of astronomy majors. My major was in mathematics.

5. J. Allen Hynek, "The UFO Mystery," *FBI Law Enforcement Bulletin* (February 1975).

6. See Philip J. Klass, *UFOs Identified* (New York: Random House, 1968), pp. 70–71, and plate 1; contrast this with Klass's *UFOs Explained* (New York: Random House, 1974), p. 151.

7. Ralph Blum and Judy Blum, *Beyond Earth*.

8. Raymond E. Fowler, *The Andreasson Affair* (1978).

9. *Humanist* (July–August 1977): 46. A complete account of my investigation of the Carter UFO case is in chapter 2 of my book *UFO Sightings* (Amherst, N.Y.: Prometheus Books, 1998).

10. The *Washington Post* story belatedly telling of Carter's UFO sighting (after

ROBERT SHEAFFER is a writer with a lifelong interest in astronomy and the question of life on other worlds. He is one of the leading skeptical investigators of UFOs, and a founding member of the UFO Subcommittee of CSICOP. He is a Fellow of CSICOP. He is also a founding director and past chairman of the Bay Area Skeptics, a local skeptics group in the San Francisco Bay area pursuing aims similar to those of CSICOP.

Mr. Sheaffer is the author of *UFO Sightings* (Prometheus Books, 1998), and has appeared on many radio and TV programs. His writings and reviews have appeared in such diverse publications as *OMNI*, *Scientific American*, *Spaceflight*, *Astronomy*, the *Humanist*, *Free Inquiry*, *Reason*, and others. He is a regular columnist for the *Skeptical Inquirer*. He is a contributor to the book *Extraterrestrials—Where Are They?* (Pergamon Press; Hart and Zuckerman, editors), which *Science* magazine called "one of the most interesting and important of the decade." He has written the article on UFOs for Prometheus Books's *Encyclopedia of the Paranormal*, as well as for the *Funk and Wagnalls Encyclopedia*. He has been an invited speaker at the Smithsonian UFO Symposium in Washington, D.C., at the National UFO Conferences held in New York City and in Phoenix, as well as the First World Skeptics' Congress in Buffalo, New York.

Mr. Sheaffer lives in California's "Silicon Valley," where he is a data communications engineer, and sings in professional opera productions.

countless magazine and tabloid articles had already appeared) was given sixteen column-inches on April 30, 1977, p. 1A. I was interviewed for that story, but was still waiting for additional information from Georgia to complete my investigation. When I was able to provide the solution a week later, it received two column-inches on May 9, p. A3, and was largely ignored.

11. For some media coverage of that press conference, see the *New York Times*, August 10, 1977, p. A11; *Washington Post*, August 11, 1977, p. A8.

12. See the *Skeptical Inquirer* (spring/summer 1978): 9.

13. There is a lot of information about the Trent photos on my Web site, www.debunker.com. Search for "Trent."

14. Gulf Breeze: *Skeptical Inquirer* 13, no. 2 (winter 1989): 130; vol. 15, no. 2 (winter 1991): 135; vol. 15, no. 4 (summer 1991): 359.

15. The *San Francisco Chronicle* featured a big article about the new organization on July 22, 1982. See also the *Skeptical Inquirer* 7, no. 1 (fall 1982): 15.

16. The full story of my Strieber encounter is on my Web site http://www.debunker.com. Search for "Strieber."

17. Andrea Pritchard et al., eds., *Alien Discussions* (Cambridge, Mass.: North Cambridge Press, 1994). The book by C. D. B. Bryan, *Close Encounters of the Fourth Kind* (New York: Knopf, 1995), also deals with this conference, but it is a version "authorized" by the conference organizers and does not present a balanced picture. See my review in *Scientific American* (November 1995): 84.

18. A detailed account of my UFO tour of Mexico is in chapter 21 of my book *UFO Sightings*.

ROSWELL ALIEN DESCENDANTS COME OF AGE

BILL NYE

Recently during World Space Week at the United Nations, a young man asked about the predictions of the Mayans. According to him, the Mayans had successfully predicted many things in history. He wanted my opinion about the Mayan prediction that the Moon would fall into the Earth and our planet would explode . . . soon, in 2012. That would be barely enough time for a trip to the wholesale store for a pallet of Ritz crackers and a drum of cheese spread. I responded that the Mayans were good at the astronomy of agriculture, but maybe not so good at the long-term prospects of the Moon. Although rocks tossed in the air run out of energy and fall to the Earth's surface, the Moon's orbit is growing. Tidal forces are conspiring with centripetal forces to gently let our Moon go, strangely the opposite of the prediction.

He was at first puzzled. Near as I can tell, this eventuality hadn't occurred to this New York City middle-school student. It wasn't the Moon's ascending motion that bothered him. It was that the heroic Mayans might be mistaken. It hadn't quite occurred to this inquirer, or many of his classmates, that the rumored ancient truth might not be true, just false. Why is that?

Well, it's our fault as a society. Fundamentally, the crazy claim struck the kids as more interesting than the real science, or if you will, the truth. To me, what could be more interesting than the actual motion of the Moon? In a few dozen hundred million centuries, the Moon will not be in the Earth's sky. It will have moved on to more influential gravity fields. How extraordinary a claim is that? Nevertheless, these kids were, and I suspect still are to an extent, captivated by the notion of this ancient assertion. The inevitable descent of the Moon and our annihilation. It is up to us, my fellow skeptics, to change the way young people think.

For me, there are three kinds of people we need to include or address in a skeptical argument: ghosts, aliens, and tricksters (con artists). If you can hit examples of belief in these three areas, in my opinion, you'll be a long way to convincing people to think critically. Belief in astrology is, on the other hand, so deeply rooted that I find that I cannot convince people to let go of it after just one demonstration or talk. That takes time.

The outlandish attribution of mystic insights to the Mayans is just an example of the fringe claims being more compelling than science. In my view, we as skeptics need to show people, especially kids, that being skeptical is good for you. It makes you feel virtually unafraid of the unknown. It's a point of view that many young people never get exposed to. I look forward to CSICOP's "Young Skeptics" programs (www.csicop.org/youngskeptics).

When producing the *Bill Nye the Science Guy* show (a television show for kids about science), I came across studies that pointed out that ten years old is about as old as you can be to get excited about science. And, based on my experience with the show, I wouldn't be surprised if it isn't as old as you can be to get excited about anything. Ask your accountant, when did he or she want to account? That person will probably report that he or she loved numbers from early in elementary school. Ask your physician when did he or she want to be a doctor. Almost everyone recalls an incident with a living thing, a dissection, a pet, or a plant that changed the way he or she looks at life and human bodies. Very few physicians first dreamed of medical school in their thirties, except perhaps in nightmares. The dream starts in your single-digit years. The same could be true for critical thinking.

It's an opportunity for us. If we can influence young people to be skeptical, they'll carry their critical thinking skills through their lives and perhaps make the world a better place through rational thought.

When you're talking with a young person, let the strength of your skeptical conviction come through. Kids are often afraid of ghosts. I was. Seldom do kids meet people who have thought their feelings on the paranormal through. If you can say, "There are no ghosts. But I sure understand why people are afraid of the dark. If ghosts were real, they would be scary. The ones we come across in stories are angry about being dead and having to walk around in muddy clothes or in chains," your conviction will go a long way toward encouraging kids to have their own convictions. Show that being afraid of the dark or afraid of being in the woods is quite reasonable, and that you don't need ghosts to be reasonably afraid or aware of the possible dangers. There may be ancestral programming for this. Our ancestors, who were not aware of nocturnal predators, became food, and their genes disappeared. But fundamentally, what's scarier: a big hungry animal like a bear, or a human enemy, like a marauding axe murderer? The human bad guy is scarier; that's all there is to it. Humans are dangerous, especially when they're armed; they're irrational; and you can't see them coming. So we can be on guard without the ghosts. Most kids hardly ever hear it put in those terms.

I want all of us skeptics to work not only to debunk charlatans and con artists, but also to take time and show our skeptical arguments to young people, the critical thinkers of the future. Adults, as you may have concluded yourself, are often unreachable on skeptical points of view.

Of course, it would be great if we all could take the time to visit schools and present compelling debunking demonstrations. But if you're not a professional educator, you'll find it soaks up your whole day, or life. Instead, talk to kids and parents about skeptical thinking. Have some prepared answers, and practice delivering them. In my opinion you want to somehow show your audience a skeptical train of thought rather than just tell them that they are misguided or nuts.

Extraterrestrial alien visitations are in the visual media as strongly as ever. If you watch television, and I'll bet you do, you can see a Warner Brothers show called *Roswell*. It is, like many TV shows, a coming-of-age story. It's about some teenagers who aren't just anxious about being teenagers. It turns out that they are the half-bred sons and daughters of aliens! They even emerged from pods. What a hassle . . . there I go, making what I regard as our biggest mistake as skeptics—scoffing at believers in debunked myths.

I ask my listeners or viewers to decide how reasonable it is that aliens came here and had kids. In general it's not. When my audience asks, "Well, what *did* happen?" I tell them the government was building a secret weapon, and it crashed. It wasn't from outer space. That's usually not enough.

I visited a private school in Vancouver, British Columbia. Many of the kids there are convinced that something happened in Roswell, New Mexico, in 1947 that the U.S. government is covering up. Something did happen. It was a secret, more ominous yet, a *government* secret. But the secret had nothing to do with extraterrestrial aliens, just high-stakes cold war spying.

In the case of Roswell, it's easy to be cynical and critical of believers. But when they're kids—smart kids—it's just frustrating. You could take issue with the creators and promoters of a show that ignores the facts of history so aggressively. And it's easy to denigrate the viewers, who at first glance just don't seem to know any better.

Keeping things classified as secret is one of the things that governments have to do. My mom and her friends were classified for forty-one years after they were discharged from the navy. Nevertheless, the kids in Vancouver would have none of it. They believe in some Roswell spooky events because we haven't provided them with a good way to evaluate the evidence.

I spoke with some of the writers on *Roswell*. They pointed out that they have to do things each week on the show that maintain their "mythology." They have all manner of books about Roswell conspiracies on their shelves. They read them and do what they have to do to work around the facts that come up. They were unfamiliar with the Skyhook Balloon Project and so on. They don't ignore what happened so much as avoid it.

The creators of *Roswell* have set it up so that everyone has a secret. The alien descendents, the FBI (or a secret arm of the FBI), the young woman who was healed with alien powers, and others who come across these kids all have something to hide. It makes a puzzle for viewers to parse. Not having explanations fills the future with possibilities. Viewers want to see what happens to the stranded strangers.

This is fine. It's a TV show, for cryin' out loud. It is based on myth, and people enjoy it. How do we know people like it? Well, it was renewed, and is in its second season. But it is up to us, not the producers of the successful TV episodes to help the public keep the show and the history in perspective.

Recently, discussing *Roswell* with some kids, I tried this one. Suppose I had a scale that said I weighed a ton. Right there on the dial it said 1,000 kilograms or 2,000 pounds. Would that be enough to convince you that I weighed a ton? The kids got it right away. Somehow that example was accessible. They saw that the quality of the evidence wouldn't cut it. We need to work to come up with more examples like this to show young people the way of a critical thinker.

When it comes to thinking about astrology and the influence of the stars, things get much tougher. The best demonstration I've found so far is to just juggle the horoscopes for different days or overall characteristics of someone supposed to be born under a given sign. Then, see if people can guess which sign belongs to which person. This is usually not quite enough. The step needed next seems to be to encourage kids to write a horoscope prediction of their own. Once they do, they see how little information is

WILLIAM S. NYE is the host of the popular public television program, *Bill Nye the Science Guy.* He hosts a Web page at http://nyelabs.kcts.org/openNye Labs.html. He is a Fellow of CSICOP.

needed to generate one. Supposed characteristics of a sign are plenty vague for everyone to have a success. Even with this though, it takes time for the real meaning, or lack of meaning, of the demonstration to soak in.

Now, I may have convinced a few viewers of my show that skeptical thinking is empowering. It makes life a lot easier. But, each time I do it, I know that I have reached a small fraction of the audience. All of us working together have hardly made a dent. Astrology flourishes, Roswell aliens march on, and there are magnets in products from head to toe, from insoles to headbands. But as has often been said, "The longest journey starts with but a single step." Although we have a long way to go, the alternative is unpalatable. Let's all keep on trying to change the world. It's a big job. It is very difficult for a society to teach critical thinking to every student and future citizen. If it were easy to learn critical thinking skills, deceiving people would be hard. So far, it has not been so. Press on!

12

METAMORPHOSIS
A Life's Journey
from "Believer" to "Skeptic"

GARY P. POSNER

Turn on Channel 2! Turn on Channel 2! That's what I saw!

I was a high school sophomore or junior when she phoned excitedly that Saturday afternoon. Although I had been a science-fiction buff ever since I can remember, and had probably seen the film a half-dozen times before, my grandmother never was and never had. I got up from the sofa and, as I tuned into the station, I immediately recognized one of my favorite movies as a kid: *Earth vs. The Flying Saucers.* Within minutes, a classic saucer-shaped craft would slice the Washington Monument in two. I ate it up.

It's not that I looked forward to the prospect of interplanetary war. But for years I had yearned for a real saucer to land in Washington or New York, so that what I knew to be the hidden truth would finally come out. I was a firm believer in UFOs and alien visitations. And in large part I can thank my strait-arrow grandmother for that.

I was probably ten years old or so when she first told me about what she, my grandfather, and uncle had seen around 1950—the year I was born—at a time when UFOs were in the news on a fairly regular basis. Driving home one Sunday afternoon from Frederick to Baltimore, Maryland, my uncle, who was sitting in the back seat, noticed something odd in the sky. My grandfather, upon seeing it himself, pulled the car over to the side of the road. As all three sat watching the noiseless object flutter about, within a minute or so it would disappear from their field of view. They also noticed that a couple of other cars had pulled over to watch as well.

149

Although my uncle has described its shape as that of a "stovepipe," and assumes that the object was an experimental aircraft of some sort, my grandmother recalled the shape quite differently (I don't remember my grandfather ever adding anything to her version). And I was sufficiently impressed by her story that, by the time she called me that day in 1966 or 1967, not only was I a dues-paying member of the largest pro-UFO organization in the country, I was its Youth Council representative for the state of Maryland.

The group was known as NICAP—the National Investigations Committee on Aerial Phenomena—based in Washington, D.C. The *News American* (Baltimore's now-defunct secondary newspaper) even ran a brief story about my appointment, "Student Helps Trace UFOs," accompanied by my photo. And a friend wrote an article, "Student Seeks Saucer Sighting Truth," for our high school newspaper. I can even remember my first college English composition being about UFOs.

It wasn't for another decade—when I took some time off in 1977 between my internship and my first year of internal medicine residency to read, travel, etc.—that my metamorphosis from UFO believer to semiprofessional skeptic began in earnest. I had already dropped out of NICAP five years earlier, when its newsletter veered embarrassingly toward sensationalism. But one day I happened to see an article on UFOs in the *Baltimore Sun*, in which Philip Klass was quoted. Klass had helped to found the Committee for the Scientific Investigation of Claims of the Paranormal (CSICOP) the year before.

I had purchased Klass's book *UFOs: Identified* during my years of UFO activism, just so I could have a "skeptical" book among my collection of UFO paraphernalia. I decided that it was time to reread it. And this time around, I found it to be quite persuasive. But the book concentrated on only a small subset of UFO reports—those involving glowing objects that Klass thought might be explainable as something in the "plasma" family, a rare electrical atmospheric phenomenon related to ball lightning. Thus, I was motivated to write to him with questions about several classic cases which, if genuine, seemed explainable to me only as extraterrestrial spacecraft.

That same week, I decided to buy *The Hynek UFO Report*, and sent a three-page letter to Dr. J. Allen Hynek, the country's premier UFO proponent and founder of the Center for UFO Studies. I told Hynek that his new book "left me as perplexed as ever about what, other than hoaxes or [ET] spacecraft, could possibly account for some of [his] better cases." I zeroed in with pointed questions about several classic UFO photographs. And I went on at some length about Klass's book, mentioning that although it concentrated on plasma-type reports, "each time I arrived at a passage which I found particularly weak, or which evoked a specific question in my mind, the following paragraph would either admit the weakness of that particular statement, or contain clarifying material to answer my question."

I soon received in the mail a paperback edition of Klass's newer book covering many of the most famous "unexplained" cases, *UFOs Explained*, which I never even knew about. In it, Klass inserted a note inviting me to write back if the book didn't answer all my questions, adding that I could reimburse him the book's $2.45 cost if I found it worthy. At about the same time, I received from Hynek a two-page letter whose first paragraph read: "Thank you for your most excellent letter of December 27th. Because you have taken the time to write in considerable detail, I am putting your letter ahead of the stack to acknowledge it."

But, as they say, the Devil is in the details. Despite their comparable degree of graciousness in replying to my inquiries, the contrast between the substance of their responses helped spur the completion of my metamorphosis from a now-somewhat-skeptical believer to a full-blooded skeptic.

Though he prioritized my letter because of its "considerable detail," Hynek's reply failed to address any of my questions about the specific cases endorsed in his book. "As it stands now," Hynek told me, "I continue to have questions, not answers." His lengthiest paragraph dealt with my favorable comments about the work of Philip Klass. From that discussion:

> I wonder if you are aware that in his second book, UFOs EXPLAINED, [Klass] refers not at all to his first book, UFOs IDENTIFIED, in which the plasma theory was put forth, and now resorts almost entirely to considering UFO reports as hoaxes, hallucinations, etc. . . . The plasma theory was so effectively shot down that . . . he appears embarrassed [by] UFOs IDENTIFIED. . . . I urge you to read UFOs EXPLAINED and to note in particular [how] when he can't find serious evidence, he resorts to character smearing. This is hardly the scientific method.

I devoured *UFOs Explained* in a single day. And in my four-page reply to Hynek, I rebutted his letter point by point. For example, regarding his assertion that Klass's second book "refers not at all to his first":

> This is simply not so. On pp. 111–112 (paperback, 1976) he mentions the name of the book, lists the publication information, and summarizes the plasma-family theory. On p. 119 he again mentions the book by name, while discussing a plasma-like case (which was probably a hoax). Page 121 also contains the name of the book, and chapter 17 deals with the possibility that the tail of a meteor, under certain conditions, might generate plasmas. In addition, the Socorro and Hill chapters both contain footnoted references to his first book, which he mentions by name, and to which he refers the reader for additional details.

And as for Hynek's charge that Klass "now resorts almost entirely to considering UFO reports as hoaxes, hallucinations, etc.":

After carefully reading the book, I cannot cite a single example in which a hallucination was alleged. As for hoaxes, he does indeed invoke this explanation for a number of cases, including the Trent photo case, to which you neglected to address yourself in your letter, despite my specific questions to you about it. . . . [But] his book is [also] replete with examples of the following:

1. Misidentification of such things as:
    a. meteor/tail
    b. rocket boosters reentering the atmosphere
    c. unusual airplane maneuvers
    d. celestial bodies
    e. balloons
    f. aircraft under unusual atmospheric conditions
2. Interception of ground radar signal, with subsequent misinterpretation of its origin (RB-47 case)
3. Radar anomalies due to inherent defects in design, as well as atmospheric conditions
4. Subconscious dreams entering the conscious mind (Betty Hill), with subsequent acceptance as reality by husband also
5. Rare natural atmospheric phenomena such as plasmas

. . . It seems to me that when Klass offers "answers," they are simply unwelcomed by you, despite the persuasiveness of his arguments. . . . Since, at least to this reader, you discard the possible answers, it is not surprising that, as you are forced to admit, you have none.

Yes, the Devil is indeed in the details. Phil Klass is considered the Devil incarnate by many in the pro-UFO community. And he has been consumed by the details ever since getting caught in the UFO quagmire more than thirty years ago. When I sent him a copy of my correspondence with Hynek, he replied in part:

It was 7 P.M. before I left the office, exhausted from a hard day probing a very controversial international aviation issue, and by a cold and hacking cough that should have sent me to bed but for the press of *Aviation Week* business.

But your letter [to Hynek] has moved me almost to tears and so I must respond tonight and express my thanks.

Soon after I entered the "Strange Land of UFOria," I realized that I had undertaken a largely thankless task. That for most people, who think the whole issue is nonsense, I was on a fool's errand, while for those who are interested and who generally are "believers," my efforts would evoke only harsh criticism. . . .

But your letter of Jan. 23 [to Hynek] is ample reward for all my efforts—truly.

> What you have *dared* to say to the "Galileo of UFOlogy" [as Hynek had been dubbed in a recent issue of *Newsweek*] has long needed to be said. ... You are the first, to my knowledge, to brazenly comment that the Emperor is NAKED!

It turned out that Klass was scheduled to deliver a lecture on UFOs at the University of Delaware in several months. Living in D.C., and with me in Baltimore, Klass suggested that he pick me up on his way, so that we could talk UFOs at length. That we did, and we became lifelong friends in the process. It was during that trip that Klass formally introduced me to the concept of "critical thinking," which had previously occupied a black hole in my education, despite a Phi Beta Kappa key and medical degree.

In 1976 Klass had been selected as one of the first Fellows of CSICOP. During our trip he told me about their journal, *Skeptical Inquirer* (originally named the *Zetetic*), and I soon began subscribing and attending CSICOP's national conferences. Thanks to Klass and CSICOP, by late 1978 I would find myself becoming inexorably drawn into the "paranormal" quagmire.

On October 19 of that year, an article in the *Baltimore Evening Sun* (and picked up by the Associated Press) was headlined, "World Series Results Foreseen by Stone." It began: "Mark Stone, a [Baltimore] stockbroker and self-styled psychic who has appeared on national television, apparently predicted correctly the outcome of each game of the 1978 World Series, including key plays like Reggie Jackson's full-count strikeout and Davey Lopes' two-homerun performance."

Stone's performance took place on WJZ-TV 13, Baltimore's ABC affiliate. As the article explained, "Stone wrote his predictions on a single sheet of paper on Oct. 8, two days before the first game. ... The paper was placed in a matchbox which was bound with a rubber band and sealed in an envelope. That, in turn, was locked in a metal box that was wrapped in brown paper and taped shut, then given to [sportscaster Klaus] Wagner on the air. Wagner held it until last night, when it was opened during the station's evening newscast." Wagner was then quoted: "I couldn't believe it, honestly. He couldn't have gotten to it beforehand. No way he could have faked it—no way."

Aside from doing a few card tricks, the one and only piece of magic apparatus I can remember having, as a young child, involved getting a coin into an empty cloth pouch, which was contained within a closed matchbox, which in turn was enclosed within a larger cardboard box. The trick involved surreptitiously slipping the coin through a hidden slot in the side of the box, with the help of a little shoehorn-type device. (My sincere apologies to David Copperfield if this revelation derails his career.)

Could Stone have merely performed a slightly more sophisticated version of this child's play? That was my immediate suspicion, not only because of my evolving skepticism of all things paranormal, but because I knew more about Stone than the article had revealed. Although I hadn't realized that he was a "psychic" stockbroker, I knew that he was a magician, having seen his classified ads in the *Baltimore Jewish Times*, such as this one I later saved from February 16, 1979: "HAVING a party? Call Mark A. Stone, mentalist, for an evening of unique entertainment! [Phone number]."

And I had also seen both of his "national television" appearances on the *Tonight* show several years earlier. During the first, Johnny Carson, an amateur magician himself, was very polite as he observed Stone's card machinations. But he then invited Stone to return several weeks later at which time Carson would control the conditions himself. I remember Carson telling Stone that, if he was indeed a genuine "psychic" as opposed to simply a magician, he should be able to succeed just as easily under such conditions.

Fool that he was, Stone took Carson up on his offer. But, for this test, Carson had Stone move across the stage, so that he couldn't observe the order of the symbol cards as Carson shuffled the deck. Stone's performance this time was again 100 percent—a 100 percent disaster. I didn't remember ever having been as embarrassed for a *Tonight* show guest, other than the night Carson had devoted his entire ninety-minute program to New Orleans District Attorney Jim Garrison and his incoherent Kennedy assassination conspiracy theories.

A few days after the World Series miracle, I wrote to WJZ station manager William Baker to make him aware of what I knew about Stone. I included the 1976 *Time* magazine article about the founding of CSICOP and its philosophy with regard to claims such as Stone's. And I received a prompt reply from Baker thanking me, and informing me that, "I have asked my news department and program department to contact you regarding appearances on our air to explain what might have occurred." But I heard from neither, and eventually assumed that the entire fiasco had simply blown over. Not quite.

Rather than taking heed of my warnings, the powers that be at WJZ soon invited Stone back for a command performance—to predict the results of the upcoming Super Bowl! At that point I brought James "The Amazing" Randi in on the case, and he sent the station manager and news director a few simple tips as to how to keep Stone "honest." Randi added, "I urge you, if not only for the protection of your viewers, then for the dignity and integrity of WJZ-TV, to control the tricks of Mark Stone."

Although neither Randi nor I heard further from the station, apparently we were somewhat successful in getting our message across. During the January 5 evening sportscast, when Stone (purportedly) sealed away his "predictions" for disclosure later in the month following the big game, this bit of byplay took place:

STONE: I make no claims to having any psychic abilities. I am here as an entertainer. This will be a fun part of the news. . . .

WAGNER: Are you saying this is a trick?

STONE: No. I'm saying I'm an entertainer. . . . I set it up to show.

And here's what happened on January 22, 1979, the day after Super Sunday. During the sports segment of the 6 P.M. news, Stone's locked box, which had been stored off the premises by Purolator Security, was ceremoniously carried back into the studio by one of the company's armed guards and handed to sportscaster Klaus Wagner. He then unlocked the outer box with a key given to him by Stone, who was seated immediately beside him. Inside was a well-taped cardboard box, which Wagner proceeded to tear open, revealing another locked metal box. But this time, when handed its key, Wagner could not jimmy the lock open. The news anchorman then tried himself, but the key simply wouldn't work. Then Stone said, "I know I can get it open if you just give me the key for a few seconds" (a close paraphrase if not an exact quote).

And within a few seconds, Stone did indeed manage to unlock the inner box. But while doing so, he had placed the box on his lap, hidden from camera view by the news desk. The box was partially open when he handed it back for Wagner to retrieve the hidden "predictions." Wagner then tore open the innermost cardboard box, which—hold onto your hat!—contained astonishingly accurate "predictions" about the Super Bowl's score and key plays.

As a medical resident, I happened to be on call at the hospital that night, and watched the spectacle from our lounge. I think the staff at WJZ was still applauding when I sprang up and telephoned the station. I was able to reach news director Scott Goodfellow, whose secretary had assured me earlier in the day that, during his appearance, Stone would issue a clear statement as to "what he is and what he isn't." No such disclaimer was made, however. And I also pointed out to Goodfellow how, by hiding the box for several seconds, magician Stone had ample opportunity to slip his list of "predictions" into a trick box.

Only the next afternoon did I find out what had been revealed on the previous night's 11:00 newscast! Right after the 6:00 news had concluded, and perhaps as a result of my call (and a few others), Wagner took a closer look at the innermost cardboard box and found a covert slot. With the cameras still taping, he then confronted Stone, who said, "Well, I told you all along I was an entertainer" (per a newspaper article). The station led the 11:00 news by showing that tape, accompanied by lame apologies from Wagner ("We were had") and news anchor Jerry Turner, who solemnly proclaimed that the station's news personnel had not been a part of what he termed a "publicity stunt."

The local press had a field day. The *Baltimore Sun*'s TV critic titled his article, "Why the *Gong Show* News at Channel 13?" The *News American*'s counterpart called his, "Step Right Up, Folks, for the Television Circus at Ch. 13." Funny how both had remained mum following the World Series.

Most unfunny to me was news director Scott Goodfellow's disingenuous "spin" to the *Sun*. In an article ("Super Bowl 'Mentalist' Exposed") that ran the following Sunday, Goodfellow was quoted as having told reporter Frederic Kelly that he never would have put Stone on the air "if I had any real strong feelings that it was only a trick. I thought he was on the up and up." And in a letter to the editor of the *Sun* that ran one week later, Goodfellow claimed that regarding Stone's earlier World Series predictions, "neither our viewers, critics nor ourselves could find fault with such stunning abilities. Consequently, Stone was invited back to attempt a similar prediction for the Super Bowl."

Fortunately, Goodfellow's letter was followed by this editor's note: "WJZ was warned Mark Stone might be a fake. *Focus* reports on Page D-3." The focus of Frederic Kelly's follow-up *Focus* article was me, as I had earlier that week provided him with photocopies of all of my, and Randi's, correspondence with Goodfellow and Baker. The article ended with the following quote from me: "It appears to me that mere naiveté does not fully account for the actions taken by WJZ with regard to Mr. Stone. By rejecting out of hand Randi's suggested protocol, WJZ deliberately chose not to properly control the conditions of Stone's performance, despite having been warned well in advance of Stone's penchant for such fakery. It would seem that the 'Stone affair' was intended all along to be not a test of 'psychic' ability, but simply a banal exercise in mutual exploitation—Stone, able to use his own gadgetry, could not 'miss,' and was assured (he thought) of national stardom; WJZ was assured of the high ratings it so desperately strives for."

During this same time frame, I generated a controversy with a letter to the editor of my own—on an entirely different topic—which was published in the winter 1978 *Skeptical Inquirer*. Earlier in the year, *SI* had ridiculed several prominent paranormalists by nominating them to receive Randi's annual "Uri Award." For many years, I had been a naive believer in UFOs myself. But I had never believed that I was able to communicate with the dead (or even with live aliens, for that matter) by using a Venus flytrap as a "medium"—as did one Uri Award nominee—or anything even remotely comparable in terms of departing from apparent reality. As a physician in training, I thought about how I'd react, and how I would expect my colleagues to react, should a patient present to us with such a claim. To my mind, mere "naiveté" or silliness didn't necessarily suffice as an explanation for such bizarre intellectual behavior as that exhibited by these career paranormalists. Thus, I submitted a cautionary note about singling out such individuals for ridicule, in which I included a speculative hypothesis:

. . . [I]t is to this label of naiveté that I address my remarks. . . . [While] making light of such persons by nominating them for a "Uri Award" may seem appropriate, one is obligated to consider the possibility that some of these people may be not merely naive but, rather, afflicted with a thought disorder that manifests in . . . a faulty sense of reality. "Ambulatory schizo-phrenia" is an entity in which the subject, generally free of symptoms, develops them only under certain circumstances. . . .

It is my opinion that much of the irrational behavior of many [I wish I had said "some"] paranormalists may be more compatible with a diag-nosis of ambulatory schizophrenia (or a close cousin thereof) than with mere naiveté. Whether I am correct or not, our duty to challenge paranor-mal claims by scientific investigation remains unchanged. However, as we continue to encounter bizarre intellectual behavior . . . [this] possibility . . . should be considered before bestowing a "Uri Award" for silliness or naiveté.

This letter has since been immortalized in George P. Hansen's infamous forty-five-page article, "CSICOP and the Skeptics: An Overview," in the January 1992 *Journal of the American Society for Psychical Research* (*JASPR*). Charged Hansen, "Gary Posner, an M.D. and leader of the Tampa Bay Skeptics, has claimed that believers in the paranormal may have a patho-logical medical condition, saying they may be 'afflicted with a thought dis-order that manifests in . . . a faulty sense of reality' and their 'irrational be-havior . . . may be more compatible with a diagnosis of ambulatory schizo-phrenia . . . than with mere naiveté.' . . . Posner made this statement despite the fact that surveys show that over half the population in this country has had psychic experiences. . . ." I then had to set the record straight in a letter to the editor of *JASPR*, in which I pointed out what any rational reader of my original letter should have been able to discern: that my "thought dis-order" comments were not offered as a blanket explanation for half the country's "belief" in such things as UFOs and ESP.

By the mid to late 1980s, my investigations into paranormal claims were increasing, and I graduated from mere letters to writing occasional articles for such publications as *Skeptical Inquirer* and *Free Inquiry*, and more recently the *Scientific Review of Alternative Medicine* (to which I am a con-tributing editor). In 1988 I was encouraged by CSICOP to form a local skeptics group, and Tampa Bay Skeptics was born that summer (I had moved to Florida in 1980). In 1994 I contributed a chapter to the book *Psy-chic Sleuths: ESP and Sensational Cases*, in which I critically examined the career of Florida-based "psychic detective" Noreen Renier. In 1999 I had the honor of conducting the definitive UFO-related interview with my "skeptics" mentor, Phil Klass, for *Skeptic* magazine. And thanks to the Internet, most of my writings, for what they're worth, are accessible from my Web site by anyone in the world.

From my beginnings as an uncritical "believer," I have metamorphosed over the years into a fully initiated member of the skeptics fraternity. And I have survived my hazing relatively intact. But, I must admit, I still retain one of my fondest childhood dreams. Whether my grandmother really saw one or not, I hope that an alien craft will make its presence unmistakably clear, in my lifetime, for all the world to see—even if that means (*especially* if that means) that my late-blooming disbelief in UFOs will be proven wrong.

GARY P. POSNER, M.D., practiced internal medicine for fifteen years before branching out into computer software in 1995. He is executive director of Tampa Bay Skeptics, which he founded in 1988, and edits its newsletter. He is also founder and national coordinator of a "Skeptic" Service for his fellow members of Mensa, a Scientific Consultant to the Committee for the Scientific Investigation of Claims of the Paranormal (CSICOP), a member of the Board of Scientific and Policy Advisors of the American Council on Science and Health, and a contributing editor of the *Scientific Review of Alternative Medicine*. E-mail: garypos@ aol.com. Web: http://members.aol.com/garypos.

IV

ASTRONOMY AND THE SPACE AGE

13

KILLER-COMETS, PSEUDOCOSMOGONY, AND LITTLE GREEN MEN

DAVID MORRISON

INTRODUCTION

Astronomy is among the oldest and the most popular of the sciences. In spite of the abstract nature of most astronomical ideas, we often see results from the Hubble Space Telescope or the latest planetary probes on the evening news or page one of the *New York Times*. Astronomers have accomplished wonderful things in the space age, probing the universe back to its origin, discovering planets orbiting distant stars, and sending spacecraft to eight of the nine planets in our solar system. This is heady stuff. It also provides many opportunities for misunderstanding and deception. Precisely because astronomy and space exploration are so unworldly, many people are ill-equipped to distinguish legitimate science from misinformation and fraud.

This essay discusses several cases of such confusion in astronomy and related topics, ranging from the origin of the universe to the search for extraterrestrial life. All of the cases involve historical and observational science, which is less well understood by the public than experimental, hypothesis-driven science, and hence more susceptible to confusion and misrepresentation.

I want to acknowledge the central role played by Carl Sagan in promoting a skeptical attitude toward these issues. Sagan was among the best-known scientists in the world during much of the past quarter century, perhaps unique in his ability to move from the academic and public policy worlds into the status of a media celebrity. Our community owes a great debt to Sagan for his wonderful ability to explain and inspire while rigorously maintaining a skeptical perspective. This is the more remarkable when we recognize that Sagan often found himself occupying the intellectual borderlands between science and pseudoscience in such areas as the search for extraterrestrial life. As a consequence of the skeptical analysis he applied to his own ideas and dreams, he did much to define the borders between science and pseudoscience. I wish it were he, and not I, writing this essay.

BAD SCIENCE, PSEUDOSCIENCE, AND NONSCIENCE

I will mention in this essay three different kinds of errors, a categorization that helps me to interpret some of these cases. The first is *bad science*, such as the cold-fusion claim of 1989, in which legitimate scientists seriously misinterpret their data. In such cases, the scientific community polices itself, usually through lively debate at one or more professional meetings. If this process works, the bad claim is soon recognized as unsupported and is withdrawn, often by the scientific team that made the error. We hear about such mistakes more often today because scientists are tempted to announce results by press release or on the Internet before they are subjected to peer review. I have seen tentative results posted on the Internet that became widespread news stories within twenty-four hours. It is not clear how one should respond when a reporter calls to ask for reactions to a new result that has never been reviewed by other scientists.

The second situation is what I call *pseudoscience*, such as the Velikovsky fad of the 1970s. Here sincere people, usually without research training, promote elaborate interpretation or theories outside the normal bounds of professional science. These are usually dressed up in the formalism of science, presented as technical-sounding papers or books bolstered by academic-style footnotes. When the pseudoscientist is attacked, or more commonly ignored, by science professionals, he or she often reacts with anger and accuses science of intolerance toward new ideas. In principle, however, pseudoscience is as subject to falsification as real science, and it can be subjected to experimental or observational testing.

My third category is *nonscience* or simply fraud, as exemplified by ancient astronaut theories or fad diets that are promoted without attempting to establish a legitimate scientific basis. Such nonscience is generally ignored by the professional community, which assumes that if it is not true it will go away. Experience has shown, however, that if effectively marketed, such nonscience can be widely accepted by the public. It is against such nonscience that Carl Sagan directed some of his most blistering attacks, promoting the idea of a "baloney detector" available so that every citizen could see through false claims dressed up as science.

In the real world, it is not always easy to distinguish among these three types of errors. Many professional astrologers, for example, probably believe that they are carrying on the traditions of an ancient and legitimate human endeavor. Some of them search for objective evidence of the value of astrology. These I would term *pseudoscientists*. I suppose that other professional astrologers recognize the lack of objective evidence for astrology, but they market its supposed predictive value as a way of making a living. To me, this is an example of nonscience. So-called creation science provides another example. While there are surely some persons who seek legitimate scientific evidence in favor of a creationist worldview, most of what is marketed as creation science is not science at all. It is religion packaged to look like science. As a matter of belief, it cannot be falsified. In my book, that makes it nonscience.

VELIKOVSKY'S PSEUDOCOSMOGONY

Twenty-five years ago, Immanuel Velikovsky had developed a substantial following, with "scientific conferences" and "technical journals" devoted to his catastrophist ideas about planets spinning from their orbits and careering through the solar system within historic times. He audaciously attacked the foundations of astronomy, planetary science, celestial mechanics, geology, and the interpretation of ancient linguistic, historical, and archeological data. Scholars in each of these disciplines were appalled. However, many journalists admired him, and there was a widespread feeling that Velikovsky had been badly served by attempts made by astronomer Harlow Shapley and other influential scientists to discourage the publication of his 1950 book *Worlds in Collision*.

Against this background, Carl Sagan and other scientists proposed that a symposium be held at the 1974 annual meeting of the American Association for the Advancement of Science (AAAS), with Velikovsky invited to present his views. In defending this decision, Sagan wrote that "no matter how unorthodox the reasoning process or how unpalatable the conclusions, there is no excuse for any attempt to suppress new ideas." Sagan biographer Keay Davidson explained: "The debate would constitute, in effect, an apology to Velikovsky [for previous slights from astronomers], giving him the opportunity to submit his ideas to direct scientific scrutiny. The debate's ultimate goal was not to reassess Velikovsky's ideas (hardly any scientist took these seriously), but, rather, to reassure the public of science's basic fair-mindedness."

The drama of the event centered on the confrontation of the imperious patriarch and his brash young critic. Sagan aimed his remarks primarily at the public and science journalists, and by most accounts he was the hands-down winner. But Sagan's critique of *Worlds in Collision* was more an example of science popularization than a serious technical discussion of Velikovsky's ideas. A few of Sagan's arguments, for example, concerning the probabilities of planetary collisions and the cooling rate of Venus, are not technically defensible. His long dissertation on manna (where he interpreted Velikovsky's language as requiring a total quantity of these hydrocarbons that exceeds the mass of the Earth) is perhaps excessively cute. These tactics infuriated the Velikovsky supporters, who perceived that Sagan not only was attacking their hero, but that he also did not take them seriously enough to engage in what they would consider a true scientific debate. Ironically, while many scientists criticized Sagan for stooping to debate with an obvious crank, Velikovsky fans castigated him for not engaging more seriously, for taking the easy way out by making the old man look ridiculous.

In the middle 1970s, radio astronomer James Warwick and I each made sincere efforts to connect with Velikovsky and his supporters, but with limited success. In my case, I tried to reformulate some of Velikovsky's claims in reasonable technical form so that they could be tested, and perhaps falsified, by the many discoveries about the planetary system being returned by NASA spacecraft. For example, Velikovsky explicitly wrote that the surface of the Moon was melted during the close planetary encounters of three millennia ago. In contrast, the Apollo samples showed that the youngest lunar lavas were more than 3 billion years old. Another claim by Velikovsky was that both Venus and Mars had been heated by planetary near-collisions 3,000 years ago and were visibly cooling, in contrast to data showing that neither planet had a significant internal heat source or was declining in temperature over time. Such arguments seemed more useful to me than calculating the postevent probabilities of planetary encounters, the approach that created such enmity toward Sagan. But my efforts were rejected with equal dispatch. I was booed at a Velikovsky symposium and was unable to get any such discussion into the pro-Velikovsky journals, so that my essay was published alongside Sagan's in *Scientists Confront Velikovsky*, the book (edited by Donald Goldsmith) that came out of the AAAS symposium.

The Velikovsky phenomenon is classic pseudoscience. Velikovsky himself was a medical doctor with no background to understand how fantastic his ideas appeared to physical scientists. Many of his supporters (a few of whom carry his torch even today) were on the humanities faculties of small colleges, more experienced in literary criticism than in astronomy or archeology. They have never understood how astronomers could reject Velikovsky without reading all his books and carefully studying his ideas. But someone with sound technical training and physical intuition can easily recognize pseudoscience like that of Velikovsky. You don't have to consume an entire meal of spoiled food to recognize the problem—one or two bites is enough.

How successful were the skeptical critiques of Velikovsky, and in particular the 1974 AAAS confrontation? Although none of Velikovsky's later books approached his initial success with *Worlds in Collision*, he had attracted a substantial following by the early 1970s. Journalists annoyed space scientists by citing his work in their reports on space probes to the planets, which Velikovsky invariably claimed confirmed his theories. The AAAS symposium helped deflate his image in the eyes of the press, and he never regained his credibility. On the other hand, his followers felt that the AAAS event was a calculated insult, and it increased their distrust of establishment science. Henry Bauer's widely read 1984 book *Beyond Velikovsky: The History of a Public Controversy* concludes that "Velikovsky was wrong" and "a crank," but Bauer spends much of its pages criticizing the science establishment for its treatment of Velikovsky. Judging by meetings held and papers published, his support group continued to expand up to the time of his death in 1979. It is thus difficult to know if the confrontational tactics of Shapley and Sagan had a positive or negative effect on either Velikovsky's public stature or popular understanding of how science works.

IMPACTS AND EVOLUTION

The real catastrophist revolution in twentieth-century science occurred after Velikovsky's death. The seminal 1980 work by Luis and Walter Alvarez identified an extraterrestrial chemical signature in the end-Cretaceous boundary layer and led them to suggest that an impact by a comet or asteroid had caused the mass extinction that ended the age of the dinosaurs. This daring hypothesis has been amply confirmed, and we now know a great deal about the impact that created the Chicxulub Crater in Mexico and precipitated an ecological catastrophe 65 million years ago. What was revolutionary was not the idea that the Earth is intermittently bombarded by space rocks (which is obvious from a look at the face of the Moon), but rather that an impact by an object only 15-odd kilometers in diameter could have such dramatic effect on Earth's biosphere, effectively redirecting the course of biological evolution.

For years after the Alvarez work, proponents of uniformitarian geology attacked the new paradigm. The new catastrophism was difficult to swallow for scientists who had built their careers on gradualist explanations for evolution, where even a mass extinction was thought to span millions of years. Yet here were these brash newcomers showing pictures of the ubiquitous impact craters found on other worlds, calculating the climatic effects of atmospheric dust loading, and claiming that most of the dinosaurs succumbed within an hour to impact-generated global firestorms. These were heady times, with a flood of new data and a number of hotly contested debates at scientific meetings. There was good science and bad science, and it required about a decade to determine which was which. On the whole, the press accurately reported this revolution, although they have artificially extended the debate. As long as one respectable scientist exists who disputes the extraterrestrial demise of the dinosaurs, some journalists will quote this dissent in the interest of creating a good story.

In a time of scientific revolutions, there is ample opportunity for bad science. One example is the minicomet hypothesis propounded by space physicist Louis Frank, who has asserted for more than a decade that the Earth is being bombarded by small (tens of meters) low-density comets. Based on two different spacecraft experiments, he believed he had detected the signature of these impacts in transient dark spots in the Earth's upper atmosphere. There is nothing wrong with the idea that the Earth is struck by comets, or that a heavy rain of such bodies in the distant past brought us the water in our oceans. The problem is that Frank's elusive minicomets represented a flux nearly a million times higher than was derived from other data. Frank argued that his comets were so black that they were invisible to astronomers, and that they had some sort of ill-defined stealth properties that allowed them to be swallowed by the atmosphere without producing signatures visible to surveillance satellites in Earth orbit. The idea of such an incoming flux was also inconsistent with the amount of water vapor in the stratosphere. But Frank persisted, even writing a popular book on the subject called *The Big Splash*. Since his research was carried out using NASA satellites and was presented at meetings of the American Geophysical Union (AGU), he enlisted the support of the publicity arms of NASA and the AGU, and his claims were widely reported. One by one his few supporters drifted away, but Frank remains committed even today to his bizarre hypothesis, which would now have to be classified as pseudoscience.

As scientists come to grips with the role of random impact catastrophes in planetary and biological history, we begin to see connections that might have been rejected previously. In arguing against Velikovsky, some planetary dynamicists postulated a solar system that had been stable since its formation 4.5 billion years ago. They were right about its stability on the time scales of interest to Velikovsky, but they should perhaps have been less dogmatic on longer spans of time. Today it is widely thought that the Moon was produced when the proto-Earth was struck by another proto-planet with the mass of Mars, a catastrophe that nearly destroyed our planet. Similar collision events probably stripped Mercury of most of its mantle and led to the capture of Neptune's large satellite Triton. Later, one or more smaller impacts may have sterilized our planet forcing a multiple genesis of life—with our DNA-based form of life simply the most recent to arise on this planet. This hypothesis of planet-sterilizing impacts is referred to somewhat euphemistically as the "impact frustration of life." Even more recently, new formulations of planetary dynamics are being used to explain the odd (to us) configuration of many external planetary systems, in which a large jovian-type planet appears to have migrated inward from its place of formation to end up even closer to its star than is the planet Mercury to our Sun.

The only terrestrial mass extinction that is unequivocally linked with an impact is the end-Cretaceous (K/T) event of 65 million years ago. There is evidence to support other impact-induced mass extinctions, but it is not yet conclusive. David Raup and Stephen Gould (among others) have suggested, however, that most extinctions might be the result of impacts or other catastrophes. If this is true, then we must change our perspective on traditional evolutionary theory. Species survival may depend on the ability to withstand rare violent environmental disasters that are unrelated to the everyday problems of finding food, evading predators, and producing offspring. These are fascinating ideas, which time will presumably sort out.

LIFE IN THE UNIVERSE

A quarter century ago, many scientists felt that we were close to understanding the origin of life on Earth. Astronomers were finding many organic chemicals in interstellar space. Lab experiments such as those first carried out by Stanley Miller and Harold Urey at the University of Chicago demonstrated the synthesis of organic compounds as complex as amino acids under conditions thought to simulate the early Earth. NASA had launched the twin Viking spacecraft toward Mars in an ambitious effort to detect life on that planet. The new field of extraterrestrial biology had even been given a name—exobiology.

Today we know a great deal more about life, especially at the molecular level, but we have not actually made much progress on the basic issues of its origin. The early atmosphere of the Earth now appears to have been much more oxidizing than the flasks of chemicals used in the Miller-Urey synthesis, and hence much less conducive to complex organic chemistry. The more we study terrestrial life the more remarkable it seems, and the greater the challenge to initiate self-reproducing, metabolizing entities from non-living precursors. Exobiologists were also disappointed when the Viking landers failed to find life on the martian surface.

In the absence of direct scientific evidence, opinions about the prevalence of life in the universe are influenced by beliefs and even wishful thinking. The situation is complicated by the popular confusion between the existence of extraterrestrial life and the evidence for alien visitors. Public opinion polls often ask if people believe in alien life. I am hard-pressed to understand either the question or the responses. Someone who recognizes the trillions of sunlike stars, a large fraction of which may have earthlike planets in orbit about them, is unlikely to conclude that terrestrial life is unique. In this sense, it is very difficult not to "believe" in alien life, even in the absence of any evidence for its existence. Unfortunately, the pollsters and journalists who ask such questions often associate a belief in alien life with either acceptance of UFO-spacecraft visiting Earth or expectation that the Search for Extraterrestrial Intelligence (SETI) is likely to succeed. Most scientists, however, would distinguish sharply among the concepts of alien life in the universe; microwave broadcasts from nearby intelligent aliens; and oval-faced, big-eyed creatures buzzing the Earth in their spaceships and abducting humans for bizarre sexual experiments.

One of the big space stories of the 1990s was the NASA report of possible fossil microbes in a rock from Mars (meteorite ALH 84001). This story was announced by the president from the White House, and it was given wide media play for weeks. We still don't know for sure if this is indeed evidence of life on Mars three billion years ago, but the scientific consensus has moved toward the negative. This initial analysis of ALH 84001 was not bad science, but nevertheless it may turn out to be wrong.

It is interesting to me that fossil microbes aroused such levels of public interest. We sometimes forget that just a century earlier, it was common knowledge among educated people that scientists had found evidence for contemporary *intelligent* life on Mars, thanks to the convincing case for martian canals made by Percival Lowell. What a comedown, from intelligent life to microbes, and from life today to life three billion years ago! People sometimes speculate on the impact that the discovery of extraterrestrial life would make on human societies and beliefs. I suggest that we look back a century for an answer. Were society and religion threatened when people accepted Lowell's case for intelligent Martians? Are they threatened today by the widespread public belief in UFOs and alien abductions? Not in any obvious way, as far as I can see.

A new thrust of Mars exploration is once more focusing on the search for life on that planet—either fossil or extant. We are also thinking seriously about the potential for terrestrial life—humans included—to adapt to space or to another planet such as Mars. This new interest has given rise to a new name—astrobiology. Jupiter's moon Europa, which is the only place in the solar system besides Earth that is known to have extensive liquid water, is also a prime target for astrobiological investigation. Beyond our solar system, the discovery of planets orbiting other stars raises the potential to search for other planets that support a biosphere. Even if we understand how to recognize that the Earth is a living world, we are not yet able to generalize about the possible signatures of alien life on distant planets.

While astrobiology and a more ambitious space program have rekindled interest in life beyond Earth, NASA's focus today is primarily on microbial life. The opposite end of the spectrum, of course, is to search for intelligent life. Intelligence may be rare in the universe, but intelligence is detectable (if the intelligent creatures are broadcasting microwaves) at much greater distances and in ways that are less ambiguous than the search for alien microbes. SETI is a logical part of any effort to search for extraterrestrial life. The odds of success may be low, but the payoff would be extraordinary. Even if only one in a billion living worlds were broadcasting microwave beacons, it would be easier to detect these beacons than to recognize the presence of life on worlds that had not developed such technology. Today, ambitious and technically sophisticated SETI searches are under way supported by private donors.

Some people have questioned whether SETI is real science. The issue focuses on whether the hypothesis of extraterrestrial intelligence is falsifiable. Baldly stated, this hypothesis is not. A negative result could mean that we looked in the wrong places, or at the wrong frequencies, or with insufficient sensitivity. Or it could mean that the aliens had not been broadcasting when we looked, or that they did not use microwaves for communications, or even that they had adopted the equivalent of cable broadcast so as not to radiate energy into space. We cannot hope to prove that the universe is uninhabited, or even that intelligence is rare. But any individual SETI search can be quite rigorous. It can search within a well-defined parameter space of frequency, intensity, and targets. The results are real science and subject to the usual rules of scientific evidence.

THE FACE ON MARS

In 1976, the Viking spacecraft orbiting Mars photographed a strange-shaped mesa about a mile across that looked remarkably like a human face. NASA released the image at once, noting that natural geological forms sometimes look like faces to human observers, especially in low-resolution images. Unfortunately, the Viking mission did not follow up with better photos, and there ensued a two-decade hiatus in successful Mars missions. This long data gap provided an opportunity for a cult to develop centered on the idea that this really was a human face, carved by intelligent Martians, perhaps part of a scheme to communicate with Earth. With the passage of time, the story grew more convoluted, complete with ruined pyramids and cities.

Richard Hoagland, author of *The Monuments of Mars: A City on the Edge of Forever*, has made a career out of promoting these ideas, together with conspiracy theories about the government suppressing evidence of aliens on Mars. According to him, the Mars Observer spacecraft, which failed when approaching Mars in 1990, was really a secret mission to contact the aliens, and its failure was faked. Hoagland also asserts that these martian features have geographic relationships that yield, to a chosen few, the mathematical foundation of an extraterrestrial technology. An effective marketer, he managed to get invitations to speak at a couple of NASA centers, and he announced some of his strangest beliefs about aliens at the National Press Club. His claims of association with NASA or the National Press Club make it more difficult for the public to sort out real science from false.

Initially, the Mars Face promoters appear to have been serious people who were trying to use image enhancement techniques to obtain all the information they could from the low-resolution Viking image. To me, this is an example of an idea that made the full transition from bad science to pseudoscience to nonscience. By the mid-1990s, image enhancement was passé. The story had expanded to include a crystal dome many miles high photographed on the Moon by Apollo astronauts, and cult members were pouring over transcripts from old NASA missions looking for oblique references to the presence of alien artifacts. The makers of the Face were also linked to crop circles in Britain, which showed that the alien presence was with us today, at least in the United Kingdom.

How should the skeptic respond to such an idea, which began as legitimate interest in an enigmatic martian feature, then morphed into the absurd? How do we react to a promoter who legitimizes his work by quoting associations with NASA while simultaneously accusing NASA of a massive cover-up? Sagan was often asked about the reality of the Face. He took the question seriously—not the nonsense about the pyramids and cities and secrets of unlimited energy, but about a possible artificial origin for this unusual geological feature. Like many scientists, he believed that Mars could have once supported abundant life, and he could not logically exclude the possibility of some surviving surface features that could date from the time when Mars was a living world. He wrote in *Demon-Haunted World*: "I might be wrong [about the Face on Mars]. It is hard to be sure about a world we've seen so little of in extreme close-up. These features merit closer attention with higher resolution. Even if these claims are extremely improbable—as I think they are—they are worth examining. Unlike the UFO phenomenon, we have here the opportunity for a definitive experiment. This kind of hypothesis is falsifiable, a [property] that brings it well into the scientific arena."

In his book *Captured by Aliens*, Joel Achenbach describes Sagan's role as "gatekeeper" of scientific legitimacy. Hoagland told Achenbach how, in a public meeting in 1985, Sagan stated that those planning NASA missions to Mars should be open to unexpected discoveries. This is the sort of comment Sagan made often, advising his colleagues to be receptive to new ideas. But according to Hoagland, when Sagan made these remarks, he briefly made direct eye contact with Hoagland among the journalists in the audience. Sagan's innocent comment thus became a coded message encouraging Hoagland to pursue his advocacy of an artificial origin for the Face. Hoagland argued to Achenbach that this "endorsement" legitimized his continuing crusade.

I have sometimes wondered if Sagan really entertained the possibility—even the extremely unlikely possibility—that the Face had an artificial origin. Or did he use this idea for its educational value—as an easily understood example of a question that could (and would) be tested by new data? Could he have been willing to keep the issue alive as a motivation for further exploration of Mars? Was he just being scrupulously honest and rational? Perhaps all of them.

The issue was (or should have been) settled in 1998 when the high-resolution camera on the Mars Global Surveyor orbiter obtained a beautiful photo of the mesa with linear resolution more than twenty times better than that of the old Viking image. Once one sees the real (and perfectly natural) geology of this heavily eroded landform, it is difficult to reconstruct in your mind just how facelike it appeared at low resolution. However, the Face cult had invested so much in their hypothesis that they could not accept the new information. Some said that NASA had faked the image. More imaginative was the suggestion that the earlier Mars Observer's secret mission had been to drop a nuclear bomb on the face to destroy it before other Mars missions could reveal its true alien heritage. (Why anyone imagines that an exploration agency like NASA would want to suppress information about life on Mars is another mystery, which I won't pursue here).

CREATIONISM AND THE BIG BANG

One of the most remarkable achievements of twentieth-century science has been the discovery that the universe had a beginning in time, a creation event, when the entire cosmos began as an incredibly hot, dense, rapidly expanding plasma of matter and energy. Such a creation was first suggested by the expansion of the universe of visible galaxies discovered by astronomers in the 1920s, but it was not until recent decades that this hypothesis was tested and "confirmed"—that is, raised to the level of a theory accepted by almost all astronomers and physicists. Key measurements included the discovery at microwave frequencies of the remnant fireball of the big bang event, the calibration using the Hubble Space Telescope of the distance scale and expansion rate of the universe, measurement of its density, and determination of the scale of fluctuations that gave rise to the formation of galaxies and supergalaxies. All of these observations are embraced by sophisticated mathematical models that represent one of the triumphs of general relativity. Today we can explore with some confidence conditions in the cosmic fireball in the first fraction of a second after its creation, and we can date this creation event to between twelve and fifteen billion years ago.

Ironically, this evidence for the creation of the universe has consistently been attacked by the proponents of biblical creationism, including the self proclaimed "creation scientists." This attack has received much less public attention than their assault on biological evolution, but it is firmly anchored in their beliefs, which require a young Earth and young universe (of order ten thousand years old). The expanding universe and big-bang cosmology were included right along with biological evolution and geological history in the areas of science proscribed in the infamous attack on modern science by the Kansas Board of Education.

Perhaps there should be more public discussion of the creationist threat to teaching modern astronomy. Some of these attacks are subtle, quoting the handful of cosmologists (such as Geoffrey Burbidge and Sir Fred Hoyle) who have continued to question basic tenants of the big-bang theory. It is ironic, however, that these big-bang critics are generally associated with an alternative model of the universe (steady-state cosmology) that is infinite in time, a point overlooked by those who use their names to try to discredit current cosmology. Some astronomers who favor the big-bang cosmology have also added inadvertently to public confusion. For example, Alan Sandage of Palomar Observatory, a leading observational cosmologist, has frequently described himself as a "creationist" in public talks and conversations with journalists. I am sure that Sandage was referring to the fifteen-billion-year-old creation event of the big bang, but I and other colleagues have not been able to dissuade him from this use of the creationist label.

While astrophysicists can apply reasonably robust theory to explore even the first fractions of a second of the big bang, they cannot reach all the way back to the mathematical singularity of the creation event itself. If there was ever a place where science reached its limits and left a clear role for a divine Creator, this is it. But that is no comfort to the young-Earth creationists, who insist on their own literal interpretation of the Judeo-Christian scriptures, in which this Creator did his job just ten thousand years ago, creating an essentially static, human-centered universe. It is the proponents of this narrow creationist perspective who dominate—and polarize—the public discussion.

CONCLUSIONS

Astronomy is exciting. Our recent progress in understanding the structure of the universe and exploring other worlds is remarkable. As Carl Sagan so often reminded us, people are fascinated by their cosmic connection, especially by the origin and distribution of life in the cosmos. There is a lot of excellent science available to the public today. But there is also an increasing amount of pseudoscience and nonscience that competes with the good stuff, especially on the Internet and talk radio. Many people are alienated from authority, mistrusting information that carries the imprimatur of the government or professional societies. In her recent book about "Star Wars," historian Frances FitzGerald describes the populist strain in the United States in terms of the virtues that are "quintessentially American: anti-elitism, distrust of the experts, a belief in democratic values, in plain speaking and common sense."

Unfortunately, efforts to communicate with the public are often confounded by semantics. What is the significance of geology shifting from a strictly uniforitarian to a more catastrophist perspective? Is the astronomical concept of creation twelve billion years ago compatible with biblical creationism? What does it mean to "believe in extraterrestrial life"? Words like *catastrophism, creation, theory,* and *belief* may mean different things to scientist and layperson. Often we speak past each other, not to each other.

One impediment to communication is the difficulty most people have with numbers, especially large numbers. We see this problem in several examples above. Planets changed orbits and even collided with each other four billion years ago, but not within historic times. The lunar surface was last molten three billion years ago, not three thousand. Comets strike the Earth and add to our water inventory, but nearly a million times less often than proposed by Frank. The universe experienced a creation event, but it was twelve billion years ago, not twelve thousand. Perhaps coincidentally, these differences are all about a factor of a million. How big is a million? Temporally, it is the ratio of the time to enjoy one meal to an entire lifetime. In distance, it is the number of people who would need to be laid end to end to stretch from Chicago to Denver. This is a big number. When something is off by a factor of a million, it is qualitatively as well as quantitatively wrong.

I conclude by quoting Sagan in *Demon-Haunted World*, "It is far better to grasp the Universe as it really is than to persist in delusion, however satisfying and reassuring [that may be]. Superstition and pseudo-science keep getting in the way [of understanding nature], providing easy answers, dodging skeptical scrutiny, casually pressing our awe buttons and cheapening the experience, making us routine and comfortable practitioners as well as victims of credulity." If scientists do not reach out and explain what they are doing to the public, there are others who will fill the vacuum. Promoting clear and skeptical thinking is an uphill struggle, but it is essential for the future of science in a democratic society.

DAVID MORRISON is a NASA space scientist and Fellow of CSICOP. He was one of Carl Sagan's first doctoral students and has provided a scientific update for the recent republication of Sagan's *The Cosmic Connection* by Cambridge University Press. Morrison is also coauthor of the popular series of college astronomy texts *Voyages through the Universe* (Fraknoi, Morrison, and Wolff, Saunders College Publishing) and *The Planetary System* (Morrison and Owen, Addison-Wesley).

NOTES

1. Emmanuel Velikovsky, *World in Collision* (New York: Doubleday, 1950). The book was originally published by Macmillan, but quickly transferred to Doubleday after scientists threatened to boycott Macmillan's textbooks.

2. Carl Sagan, "An Analysis of Worlds in Collision," in *Scientists Confront Velikovsky*, ed. Donald Goldsmith (Ithaca, N.Y.: Cornell University Press, 1977), p. 45.

3. Keay Davidson, *Carl Sagan: A Life* (New York: Wiley & Sons, 1999), p. 271. Davidson devotes six pages to the Sagan-Velikovsky confrontation, but William Poundstone, who also published a long biography of Sagan in 1999, does not mention the Velikovsky affair at all.

4. David Morrison, "Planetary Astronomy and Velikovsky's Catastrophism," in Goldsmith, *Scientists Confront Velikovsky*, pp. 145–76.

5. Henry Bauer, *Beyond Velikovsky: The History of a Public Controversy* (Urbana: University of Illinois Press, 1984).

6. L. W. Alverez et al., "Extraterrestrial Cause for the Cretaceous-Tertiary Extinction," *Science* 208 (1980): 1095–1108.

7. The flavor of the technical debate is well represented by the proceedings of two conferences held in Snowbird, Utah, in 1981 and 1988: Leon Silver and Peter Schultz (eds.), *Geological Implications of Impacts of Large Asteroids and Comets on the Earth, Geological Society of America Special Paper 190* (1982); and Virgil Sharpton and Peter Ward (eds.), *Global Catastrophes in Early Earth History, Geological Society of America Special Paper 247* (1990). More review papers can be found in: Tom Gehrels (ed.), *Hazards Due to Comets and Asteroids* (Tucson: University of Arizona Press, 1994).

8. Louis A. Frank with Patrick Huyghe, *The Big Splash* (New York: Avon Books, 1990).

9. N. Sleep et al., "Annihilation of Ecosystems by Large Asteroid Impacts on the Early Earth," *Nature* 342 (1989): 139–42; and C. Chyba, "Impact Delivery and Erosion of Planetary Oceans in the Early Inner Solar System," *Nature* 343 (1990): 129–33.

10. David M. Raup, *Extinction: Bad Genes or Bad Luck?* (New York: Norton, 1991).

11. David McKay et al., "Search for Past Life on Mars: Possible Relic Biogenic Activity in Martian Meteorite ALH84001," *Science* 247 (1996): 924–30.

12. Percival Lowell: *Mars and Its Canals* (New York: Macmillan, 1906), and *Mars as the Abode of Life* (New York: Macmillan, 1908). For a more recent discussion see William G. Hoyt, *Lowell and Mars* (Tucson: University of Arizona Press, 1976).

13. Richard C. Hoagland, *The Monuments of Mars: A City on the Edge of Forever*, rev. ed. (Berkeley, Calif.: North Atlantic Books, 1992).

14. Carl Sagan, *The Demon-Haunted World: Science as a Candle in the Dark* (New York: Random House, 1995), p. 55.

15. Joel Achenbach, *Captured by Aliens: The Search for Life and Truth in a Very Large Universe* (New York: Simon & Schuster, 1999).

16. Some excellent popular-level books on the origin of the universe are: Steven

Weinberg, *The First Three Minutes: A Modern View of the Origin of the Universe* (New York: BasicBooks, 1977); Michael Riordan and David Schramm, *The Shadows of Creation: Dark Matter and the Structure of the Universe* (New York: Freeman, 1991); George Smoot and Keay Davidson, *Wrinkles in Time* (New York: Morrow, 1993); and Timothy Ferris, *The Whole Shebang: A State-of-the-Universe(s) Report* (New York: Simon & Schuster, 1997).

14

CERTAIN UNCERTAINTIES

NEIL DeGRASSE TYSON

When reporting scientific discoveries, the popular press hardly ever conveys the inherent uncertainties in the data or its interpretation. This seemingly innocent omission carries a subtle, misguided message: if it's a scientific study, the results are exact and correct. These same news reports often declare that scientists, having previously thought one thing, are now forced to think something else; or are forced to return to the mythic "drawing board" in a stupor. The consequence? If you get all your science from press accounts then you might be led to believe that scientists arrogantly, yet aimlessly, bounce back and forth between one perceived truth and another without ever contributing to a base of objective knowledge.

A closer, more accurate look at the way science works reveals just the opposite.

New ideas put forth by well-trained research scientists will be wrong most of the time because the frontier of discovery is a messy place. But scientists know this and are further trained to quantify their level of ignorance with an estimate of the claim's uncertainty. The famous "plus-or-minus" sign, now given as part of the margin of error reported for polls, is, perhaps, the most widely recognized example. A scientist typically presents a tentative result based on a shaky interpretation of poor data. Six months later, different, yet equally bad data become available from somebody else's experiment and a different interpretation emerges. During this phase, which may drag on for years or even decades, news stories implying unassailable fact are written anyway.

Eventually, excellent data become available and a consensus emerges, which is a long-term process that does not lend itself to breaking news stories. Studies on environmental health risks or the effect of some foods on health and longevity, are especially susceptible to being overinterpreted. The financial consequences of premature news stories, and the attendant reactions on Wall Street, can be staggering. In 1992, a lawsuit was brought against two cellular phone companies by a Florida man claiming that his wife's death from brain cancer was caused by her heavy use of cellular phones. When this and several similar claims hit the news in late January 1993, the market capitalization of publicly traded cellular phone companies fell by billions of dollars in less than a week. Since you can get brain cancer without ever having used a cellular phone, and since the popularity of cellular phones was on the rise, you might expect some users to die from brain cancer just as some users might die from heart disease, or from old age. In this case, there was no definitive study to establish a cause and effect between cellular phone use and brain cancer, yet people reacted anyway.

Fortunately, most of the comings and goings in my field of astrophysics have so little impact on how people conduct their daily lives that I can spend more time joking about the problem than crying about it.

Initial uncertainty is a natural component of the scientific method, yet the scientific method is, without question, the most powerful and successful path ever devised to understand the physical world. When a published scientific finding is confirmed and reconfirmed and re-reconfirmed and re-re-reconfirmed, further confirmation becomes less interesting than working on another problem and new nuggets of knowledge are justifiably presented with little or no uncertainty in the basic textbooks of the day. Consistency and repeatability are the hallmarks of a genuine scientific finding, for if the laws of physics and chemistry were unpredictably different from week to week, or from lab to lab, then scientists would all just pack up and go home.

A modern astronomy textbook will discuss the well-known fact that the Sun occupies the center region of our solar system. You can bet that five hundred years from now, we will still be saying that the Sun occupies the center region of the solar system. Yet five hundred years ago this notion was a major source of debate—Earth was the object presumed to occupy center stage. Our modern textbook on astronomy will, however, speak only tentatively about the formation of galaxies in the early universe, or the nature of the ubiquitous dark matter, because major uncertainties remain in these areas. Suppose one day someone discovers that dark matter in the universe is actually made of chocolate pudding. Despite all of the problems this would create in theoretical astrophysics, no previously held consensus would be overthrown because no consensus exists.

Over their morning coffee, scientists have been known to completely ignore their uncertainties because, for the most part, scientists are people too. There are arrogant ones, lovable ones, loud ones, soft-spoken ones, and boneheaded ones. In published research papers, however, everyone is timid because of the semipermanence of the printed word and the overwhelming frequency of wrong ideas. Most results flow from the edge of our understanding and are therefore subject to large uncertainties.

Consider the origin of the Moon's craters. Any modern book will describe them, with certainty, as being caused by high-speed collisions with rocks and other debris from interplanetary space. But a century ago, they were described as being volcanic calderas. If the scientific community changed its mind once before then why should you believe us now? Because last century, volcanic calderas were a leading idea but had not achieved consensus and were thus not presented as a certainty in responsible scientific writings. In a chapter of *The Heavens Above*, a popular handbook of astronomy written in 1882 by two academics (J. A. Gillet, professor of physics at the City College of New York, and W. J. Rolfe, headmaster of Cambridge High School in Massachusetts), they describe the lunar surface:

> The smaller saucer-shaped formations on the surface of the moon are called craters. They are of all sizes, from a mile to a hundred and fifty miles in diameter; and they are supposed to be of volcanic origin.

Short of quantifying the uncertainty, which may be inappropriate for a popular book, the words "supposed to be" make an excellent literary substitute. And as late as 1923, Sir Richard Gregory, professor of astronomy, Queens College, London, wrote in the popular book *The Vault of Heaven*:

> The origin of the lunar craters is still obscure. Analogy suggests that the forces which cause volcanic eruptions on the earth have been at work on the moon . . . [although] some astronomers and geologists favour the view that the craters were produced by the bombardment of masses of rock when the moon was in a plastic condition.

More often than not, a scientist's printed word presents an honest, almost humble uncertainty that goes unnoticed when people reflect on the history of scientific misconceptions. What about that 1996 research paper in the journal *Science* that claimed to have found life in a Martian meteorite? The nine coauthors wrote, among other things, in their abstract:

> The carbonate globules [in the Martian meteorite] are similar in texture and size to some terrestrial bacterially induced carbonate precipitates. Although inorganic formation is possible, formation of the globules by biogenic processes could explain many of the observed features . . . and could thus be fossil remains of past martian biota.

From the oversized newspaper headlines that followed, you would never guess that the original research paper contained such unassertive language.

At mid-nineteenth century, there was a famous disagreement between the gentle geologists and the cocky physicists over the age of the Earth and the Sun. The geologists needed billions of years to account for Earth's surface features. The physicists, led by the brilliant William Thomson (who became Lord Kelvin), asserted an age of at least ten but no more than one hundred million years, based on thermodynamic calculations that invoke Earth's current internal temperature and the rate at which ordinary matter cools. A similar calculation for the Sun yielded similar results.

Lord Kelvin was off by a factor of fifty.

How embarrassing is this? Not bad at all. Kelvin's actual statements (this one taken from an 1871 lecture "On Geological Time") candidly alert the reader to inherent uncertainties in his calculations:

> Now, if the sun is not created a miraculous body, to shine on and give out heat forever, we must suppose it to be a body subject to the laws of matter (I do not say there may not be laws which we have not discovered) but, at all events, not violating any laws we have discovered or believe we have discovered, we should deal with the sun as we should with any large mass of molten iron, silicon, or sodium.

With no concept of the heat generated by radioactivity inside Earth or thermonuclear fusion inside the Sun, Kelvin had no chance of getting the right answer. But he humbly, and correctly, recognized that he might be missing yet-to-be-discovered laws of nature.

Another historical conundrum was whether the well-known force of gravity, discovered by Isaac Newton in the seventeenth century, applied to regions far beyond the solar system. As late as 1893, Charles Young, a professor of astronomy at the College of New Jersey (Princeton), wrote in *Lessons in Astronomy*: "It is probable (though not certain) that gravitation operates between the stars, as indicated by the motion of binaries." Once again the scientist conveys what is known, and is candid about uncertainties.

When this humble approach is abandoned, embarrassing claims can result. The nineteenth-century astronomy popularizer Agnes M. Clerke, who wrote brilliantly in her 1890 *System of the Stars* about all manner of astronomical knowledge, lapsed into hyperbolic denial on the nature of the spiral nebulae in the sky:

> The question whether nebulæ are external galaxies hardly any longer needs discussion. It has been answered by the progress of discovery. No competent thinker, with the whole of the available evidence before him, can now, it is safe to say, maintain any single nebula to be a star system of coordinate rank with the Milky Way. A practical certainty has been attained that the entire contents, stellar and nebular, of the sphere belong to one mighty aggregation, and stand in ordered mutual relations within the limits of one all-embracing scheme—

all-embracing, that is to say, so far as our capacities of knowledge extend. With the infinite possibilities beyond, science has no concern.

This passage is simply irresponsible. The lady doth protest too much. If the facts of the case were as secure as she implies then she would not have needed 114 words to say so. While not a research scientist, Clerke should have known better. She had enough command of astronomy to write authoritatively on the subject and to become one of the leading popularizers of her day, but she left no room for uncertainty, and bet on the wrong horse.

Forty-three years later, just three years before Edwin Hubble settled the debate on the nature of the nebulae, the astronomy professor Sir Richard Gregory candidly confessed in *The Vault of Heaven*:

> It can scarcely be said, however, that anything very definite is known concerning the form of the sidereal universe even at the present time.

This kind of writing does not make headlines, but it is honest and accurate.

A rare, but now-famous case of a misreported uncertainty coupled with an overconfident claim by a scientist took place in early 1998. The Central Bureau for Astronomical Telegrams (the clearinghouse for astronomers of the world who need to disseminate up-to-the-minute sky phenomena among colleagues) announced the discovery of a mile-wide asteroid whose orbit would bring it dangerously close to Earth in the year 2028. (Formerly sent around the world via telegram, these notices are now distributed instantly via e-mail.) The offending asteroid was coded 1997 XF11, which identifies when in the year 1997 the asteroid was discovered. The telegram reported on March 11, 1998:

> This object, discovered by J. V. Scotti in the course of the Spacewatch program at the University of Arizona on 1997 Dec. 6 . . . recognized as one of the 108 "potentially hazardous asteroids," has been under observation through 1998 Mar. 4. . . . An orbit computation from the 88-day arc . . . indicates that the object will pass only 0.00031 AU from the earth on 2028 Oct. 26.73 UT! Error estimates suggest that passage within 0.002 AU is virtually certain, this figure being decidedly smaller than has been reliably predicted for generally fainter potentially hazardous asteroids in the foreseeable future.

Converting to everyday language, the announcement declared that the asteroid would come within 30,000 miles of Earth (a cosmic hair's width), but with an uncertainty in the calculation that could place the asteroid anywhere within a 200,000 mile "error-circle" that happens to enclose Earth. When the substance of this telegram was further distributed via press release from the American Astronomical Society, passing along the terrifying words "virtually certain," a media deluge followed that overnight turned your neighborhood astronomers into the most sought-after people on your local news broadcasts.

The telegram went on to give the best available coordinates for the object, obtained from observers who were tracking it, preceded by a scientifically sensible appeal: "The following ephemeris is given in the hope that further observations will allow refinement of the 2028 miss distance." The next day, on March 12, 1998, another telegram appeared that announced the existence of what astronomers call a "prediscovery" photograph of the asteroid, obtained from archival survey images taken in 1990. This extended the baseline of observations to well beyond the original eighty-eight days. (Longer baselines always provide more accurate estimates than shorter ones.) Calculations that incorporated the new data narrowed the error-circle to a skinny ellipse that sat far away from Earth. Five weeks later, a telegram was issued that corrected the alarmist language of the first announcement and admitted that the original telegram's uncertainties could have been sharpened if a more complex method of calculation had been used.

The episode was widely reported as a blunder; but at worst, the original calculation was simply incomplete. At best, it was a valid scientific starting point. True, the survival of the human species was involved, but that's just a detail. More importantly, everything worked the way it was supposed to. The early estimate, and the better estimates that followed (within a day!) were a model of how science refines itself as it approaches an objective reality. After what had been twenty-four hours of sensationalist journalism across the country, the *New York Post*, a colorfully written daily newspaper in New York City, ran the inimitable headline: "KISS YOUR ASTEROID GOODBYE."

Formal accounts of the scientific method typically describe an hypothesis-posing, experiment-conducting process. You might see words such as *induction, deduction, cause,* and *effect.* What's missing is that science can be a creative process in which practically anything goes—from middle-of-the-night hunches to mathematical formulations driven by personal aesthetics. All that matters is that the results accurately describe and predict phenomena in the real world.

When conducting an experiment on the frontier of human understanding of the universe, you never know what the "right" answer is supposed to be. Sometimes you don't even know the right question. Often, guided by a particular vision of how the universe works, all you can do is make a series of measurements that you hope will lead you to the right answer. Answers to questions such as, "How far away is the Moon?" or "What is the mass of the Sun?" lend themselves to standard statistical analysis. But answers to questions like, "What kind of cheese is the Moon made of?" does not, because it starts with the false assumption that the Moon is a cheesy place, which will most likely thwart your acquisition of relevant data.

In most experiments, some data points will come out above the true value while some will come out below. These are ordinary fluctuations—a bar chart of these measurements would look like the statistician's beloved bell curve. The history of science has shown that if an experiment is well designed then most of the data will cluster around some value, presumably the right value. Unfortunately, this value may bear little correspondence to the real word if human bias is involved. An implicit goal of the scientific method is to minimize human bias, for therein lies some of the greatest sources of experimental blunder the world has ever known. When making multiple measurements scientists can unwittingly discard values that deviate strongly from their expectations. This selective editing of experimental results can skew data and fatally compromise the experiment. Once results are published, sometimes only the experimenter knows which data were included and which were discarded. In all fairness to the experimenter, however, some raw data do deserve to be discarded because of unavoidable experimental glitches. You just shouldn't get carried away. In any case, you must be honest about the breadth of measurements above and below the average value and report this uncertainty.

As already noted, the general public holds no greater scientific misconception than on the meaning of experimental uncertainty. Scientists are partly to blame. In research parlance our uncertainties are formally called "errors." Tell journalists that your experiment had errors and none of them will believe your result. Tell them instead that your experiment had quantifiable uncertainties and they will beat a path to your door.

The media hardly ever report the inherent errors in scientific discoveries. Instead of a range of uncertainty, reporters typically (and perhaps understandably) write about the meaning of the experiment's average value as given in scientific publications or press releases. Headline writers and general readers, however, are left vulnerable to drawing spurious conclusions. In one example from the mid-1990s, new, improved data led to the announcement that the oldest stars in the galaxy were born about 14 billion years ago, in a universe that's only about 12 billion years old. The press invoked the you-can't-be-older-than-your-mother principle, and portrayed the news as a cosmic controversy of the first rank. But when the numbers are accompanied by their published uncertainties—known as "error bars"— a sensible picture emerges that is quite undeserving of headlines. The age of the universe was 12 ± 3 billion years. The age of the oldest stars was 14 ± 2 billion years. The error bars suitably overlapped at 13 billion years, to where our current estimate of the age of the universe and the age of the oldest stars is converging.

After decades of ignoring the significance of measurement errors, the reported results of public opinion polls are now accompanied by "margins of error"—the sociologist's error bar. If opinion pollsters query only 100 of the quarter billion people in the United States they will (or had better) frame their claims with fat uncertainties. So when a news station reports,

"The incumbent leads the challenger 54 percent to 46 percent with a ±5 percent margin of error," then you have my permission to ignore all subsequent discussion and analysis of the significance of the incumbent's lead. Fortunately, there are well-tested statistical methods that account for the size of your polled sample compared with the size of the total population. If all quarter-billion people of the United States were polled, there would be no uncertainties except for the unavoidable fact that some people lie, and some people don't know who they will vote for until they enter the voting booth.

Often the most heated scientific controversies are conducted within the noise and confusion of messy data. Perhaps the most famous astronomical controversy of the second half of the twentieth century was over the numerical value of the famous Hubble constant, a measure of the expansion rate of the universe. Poor data allowed two warring factions to arise on opposite sides of the error bars. One group supported $H = 100 \pm 10$. Another group supported $H = 50 \pm 5$. What's a factor of two between friends in a universe where factors of thousands and millions are common?

The problem here is that somebody's error bars are way too small. Whose? Perhaps they are both too small. Regardless, experimental bias operating on messy data was at work. After the world's most aggressive supporter of $H = 100$ (University of Texas astronomer Gérard de Vaucouleurs) died in the 1990s, and after more and better data became available, the consensus converged around $H = 70 \pm 10$, falling comfortably between the extremes. Do we credit the new and improved value for the Hubble constant to better data? That would be good. Or did scientists continually reinterpret the data until things agreed, and then stopped trying? That would be bad. For the Hubble constant case, the former is more likely than the latter, but the latter remains a haunting specter over nearly all research questions whose answer you presume to know in advance of the experiment.

Speaking of scientists who take extreme views to their graves, the distinguished MIT mathematician Irwin Segal remained to his death a spirited opponent to the Big Bang model for the origin of the universe. He even offered a theory of his own to replace it. Whenever a new discovery in support of the Big Bang was reported in the news, he would write a letter to the editor explaining why the Big Bang was all-wrong. The problem was that readers got the (false) impression that Segal represented the other "half" of the responsible scientific view, when in fact his views were those of a vanishingly small minority. The German physicist Max Planck (father of the counterintuitive, but very real branch of physics known as quantum mechanics) perceptively penned in 1936:

> An important scientific innovation rarely makes its way by gradually winning over and converting its opponents. . . .What does happen is that its

opponents gradually die out and that the growing generation is familiarized with the idea from the beginning.

Unpopular scientific ideas have a certain appeal. Perhaps people just like to root for underdogs. But for each correct idea in science, a hundred (or a thousand) respectable ideas failed before it. Possible reasons for failure? New data didn't support the claims; logical inconsistencies emerged on further analysis; or predictions of natural phenomena were proven to be false. You would think this route to reliable conclusions would be valued in society's courts. Having never, until recently, lived more than a few years in the same place during my adult life, I had never been called for jury duty, which typically requires a minimum duration of residency. When I was finally called to serve, I went willingly and patriotically. After the classic long wait in the waiting room, I was finally called for selection and was questioned by an attorney: "What is your profession?" Astrophysicist. "What is an astrophysicist?" An astrophysicist studies the universe and the laws of physics that describe and predict its behavior. "What sorts of things do you do?" Research, teach, administrate. "What courses do you teach?" This semester I happen to be teaching a seminar at Princeton on the critical evaluation of scientific evidence and the relative unreliability of human testimony. "No further questions Dr. Tyson. Thank you."

I was on my way home twenty minutes later.

In courts of law, yes/no questions and multiple-choice questions are common. But science does not lend itself to such responses without incurring a major misrepresentation of reality. I was once called by a lawyer who wanted to know what time the Sun set on the date of a particular car accident at a particular location. This question can be answered precisely, but later in the conversation I learned that what the lawyer really wanted to know was what time it gets dark outside. He was going to compare the time of sunset with the time of the car accident, and had been assuming that everything gets dark the instant the Sun sets. His question was poorly formed for the information he was seeking. A better question might have been, what time do the dark-sensitive streetlights turn on? But even for that question, the presence or absence of clouds and the shadows of nearby buildings can affect the "right" answer.

Although I was tainted goods in the jury-selection box, I once managed to help convict a person who was charged with a fatal hit-and-run accident. The driver of the vehicle had a photograph of himself, claiming it was taken at the time of the incident and that he was nowhere near the scene of the crime. The defense attorney asked me if I could verify the claimed time of the image from the lengths of shadows from cars and people in the photo. I said sure. Given the location and the date, I provided him with the time of the photo, plus or minus twelve minutes. The time did not correspond with the alibi by several hours.

How certain can we be of a scientific measurement? Confirmation matters. Only rarely is the importance of this fact captured in the media or the movies. An exception was the 1996 film *Contact* (based on the 1983 novel of the same name by the celebrated astronomer Carl Sagan) which portrayed what might happen—scientifically, socially, and politically—if we one day make radio-wave contact with extraterrestrial intelligence. When a signal from the star Vega is discovered that rises above the din of cosmic noise, Jodie Foster (who plays an astrophysicist) alerts observers in Australia, who could observe the signal long after the stars in that region of the sky have set for Americans. Only when the Australians confirm her measurements does she go public with the discovery. Her original signal could have been a systematic glitch in the telescope's electronics. It could have been a local prankster beaming signals into the telescope from across the street. It could have been a local collective delusion. Her confidence was boosted only when somebody else on another telescope with different electronics driving an independent computer system in another country got the same results.

Null results matter too. Occasionally scientists will test for an effect that does not exist or that fails to reveal itself through the chosen methods. That same scientist may elect not to publish the nonresult. Another scientist may conduct the same experiment and find a statistical glitch that mimics a real effect. The second scientist elects to publish. The research literature now contains an innocent, yet guileful bias toward finding an effect when, in fact, none is present. Unfortunately, one of the cheapest, but blunder-prone ways of doing science is by conducting a survey of published surveys rather than by designing and conducting one's own experiment.

A seminal, but little-known null result draws from the history of attempts to measure the speed of light. In the early 1600s, Galileo sent an assistant to a distant hill to flash the light of a lantern. Galileo responded immediately with flashes from a lantern of his own. His attempt to time the delay proved futile. Human reflexes were inadequate for such a task. Of the speed of light, Galileo noted, ". . . if not instantaneous it is extraordinarily rapid."

Now those are some large error bars.

Galileo could have never predicted that over three centuries later, the International Committee on Data for Science and Technology, in an unprecedented decision, would *define* the speed of light to be the current best experimental value: 299,792,458 meters per second—exactly. The speed of light had such small error bars that by defining its speed by fiat, subsequent, improved precision in the speed of light would translate directly to a modification in the length of the meter. The meter is now defined to be the distance traveled by a beam of light in a vacuum during 1/299792458 of a second. The speed of light went from having big error bars to having no error bars. Galileo would be proud.

Occasionally, when you have a good theory and good observations and you understand the ways of the universe then magic can happen. When comet Shoemaker-Levy 9 was discovered in 1992, its orbit was computed after a sufficient baseline of observations had accumulated. Laws of physics that were known in the days of Isaac Newton enabled us to predict that the comet would come so close to Jupiter on its next pass that the most likely trajectory would intersect the planet's gaseous surface. How about the error bars? All paths within the uncertainties fell within the body of Jupiter. The inescapable conclusion: a titanic Jupiter-comet impact was imminent. We were certain enough to alert the media and mobilize all available telescopes to observe the event. Sure enough, two years later, on the comet's next orbit, it slammed into Jupiter's atmosphere with the destructive force of five billion atom bombs.

Ordinary uncertainties almost always lead to correct (and meaningful) answers, but systematic uncertainties are insidious. Your measurements may be statistically sound, but what if you measured the wrong object? Or the wrong phenomenon? What if the electrical current that fed your apparatus changed during the measurement? I was once observing our Milky Way galaxy from the Cerro Tololo Inter-American Observatory in the Chilean Andes. I was getting spectra of stars located near the galactic center when a 6.2 earthquake rolled through (not particularly uncommon in such a geologically active area). There was an expected loss of electricity in the obser-

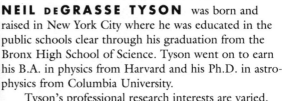

NEIL DeGRASSE TYSON was born and raised in New York City where he was educated in the public schools clear through his graduation from the Bronx High School of Science. Tyson went on to earn his B.A. in physics from Harvard and his Ph.D. in astrophysics from Columbia University.

Tyson's professional research interests are varied, but they primarily address problems related to star-formation models of dwarf galaxies, exploding stars, and the chemical evolution history of the Milky Way's galactic bulge. Tyson obtains his data from telescopes in California, New Mexico, Arizona, and in the Andes Mountains of Chile.

In addition to dozens of professional publications, Dr. Tyson has written, and continues to write for the public. And since January 1995, he has become a monthly essayist for *Natural History* magazine under the title "Universe."

Tyson's recent books include a memoir, *The Sky Is Not the Limit: Adventures of an Urban Astrophysicist*; the companion book to the opening of the new Rose Center for Earth and Space, *One Universe: At Home in the Cosmos* (coauthored with Charles Liu and Robert Irion); and a playful Q&A book on the universe for all ages titled *Just Visiting This Planet*.

Tyson is the first occupant of the Frederick P. Rose Directorship of the Hayden Planetarium and he is a Visiting Research Scientist in astrophysics at Princeton University, where he also teaches. He is also a Fellow of CSICOP.

vatory, but the data acquisition system and the computers were connected to an uninterruptible power supply that seamlessly kicked in during the power failure. I was able to save open files and backup my data. When power was restored, forty minutes later, I resumed taking data, only to discover that the telescope's spectrograph had shifted and was now sensitive to an entirely different part of the spectrum. Had I mindlessly kept working, and then averaged the night's data, the results would not only have been wrong, but meaningless, and I would not have known it for some time.

For some averages, you know right away they are meaningless. Try this one: If half the time I sit on the left side of the train and other half of the time I sit on the right side of the train, then on average, I sit in the aisle. Or how about my all-time favorite, which I credit to the mathematician and occasional humorist John Allen Paulos: The average American has one breast and one testicle.

ASTROLOGY

DOES ASTROLOGY WORK?
Astrology and Skepticism 1975–2000

GEOFFREY DEAN
and IVAN W. KELLY

If I doubt astrology to a believer, I am looked at with a shocked and bewildered stare, as if I were attacking apple pie and motherhood.
—Anthony Standen, *Forget Your Sun Sign*, 1977

END OF A SHOUTING MATCH

Astrology and skepticism are the oldest of opponents. Could astrology be true? Could the stars really correlate with human affairs? Such questions have been furiously debated without resolution for more than two thousand years. Astrology has been the world's longest shouting match.

Not any more. Since 1975 advances in relevant areas (astronomy, psychology, statistics, research design) and a decisive technology (home computers) have put astrology under the scientific microscope as never before. Today, most questions about astrology can be answered. The answers make good scientific sense and create a dilemma for astrologers.

In this article we track the progress of skeptical investigations since 1975. We ignore the usual tired arguments against astrology (sun signs do not agree with the constellations, there is no known way it could work) in favor of the only question that matters: Does astrology work? We start with the views of astrologers during this century.

VIEWS OF ASTROLOGERS

Astrologers leave you in no doubt that astrology works:

"Practical experiment will soon convince the most sceptical that the bodies of the solar system indicate, if they do not actually produce, changes in: 1. Our minds. 2. Our feelings and emotions. 3. Our physical bodies. 4. Our external affairs and relationships with the world at large." (Charles Carter, leading British astrologer of his day, *The Principles of Astrology*, 1925)

"No one has ever been known to make a serious study of Astrology and then reject it." (Nicholas de Vore, American astrologer and president of the Astrologic Research Society, *Encyclopedia of Astrology*, 1947)

"From being an outcast from the fraternity of sciences, it seems destined to assume an almost central role in scientific thought." (John Addey, leading British astrologer of his day, *Astrology Reborn*, 1971)

"Astrology throws light on every department of life; . . . From sex to career to character and future prospects—and more." (American astrologer Sydney Omarr, whose astrology columns were then appearing in nearly three hundred newspapers, *Astrology's Revelations About You*, 1973)

"There is no area of human existence to which astrology cannot be applied." (Julia and Derek Parker, *The Compleat Astrologer*, 1975, which sold over a million copies in ten languages. The first is a former president of the British Faculty of Astrological Studies.)

"Anyone who makes a serious and open-minded study of astrology becomes totally unable to scoff. Its truths are inarguable." (Mary Coleman, Australian psychologist-astrologer, *Astro-Pick Your Perfect Partner*, 1986)

"Despite the contemptuous guffaws of scientific orthodoxy, it [astrology] still continues to enthral the minds of some of our finest contemporary thinkers." (Charles and Suzi Harvey, former president and journal editor respectively, British Astrological Association, *Principles of Astrology*, 1999)

"Psychology textbooks of the future will look upon modern psychologists working without the aid of astrology as being like medieval astronomers working without the aid of a telescope." (Professor Richard Tarnas, American philosopher and astrologer, *Cosmos and Psyche*, 1999)

"Astrology's symbols are the soul's language of life. They reveal not only the mysteries of the universe but also the mysteries of each of our lives." (Gina Lake, American counseling psychologist and astrologer, *Symbols of the Soul: Discovering Your Karma through Astrology*, 2000)

In short, astrology is all-revealing, inarguably true, applicable to everything including past lives, enthralling to thinkers, soon to dominate scientific thought, and more. Just study it seriously and you will be convinced it works. Or so astrologers lead us to believe. Now a word from scientists who studied it seriously.

VIEWS OF SCIENTISTS

The following views reflect serious studies up to the 1980s:

"I myself, at the risk of appearing ridiculous even to my colleagues, have for fourteen years held my archives open for astrological evidence, . . . [but all were] the result either of a forced application of the rules to human careers already known, or of a careful culling of hits from preponderating numbers of misses. I do not think that any psychical researcher . . . has given attention to the claims of astrology and has not definitely cast the pretended science on the dust heap." (Walter Prince, presidential address to the Society for Psychical Research, 1930)

"The ancients were evidently unaware that [astrological judgments] were the result of reasoning by analogy, which so often proves a treacherous foundation. That is why the whole superstructure of astrology is so utterly worthless and fallacious." (August Thomen, *Doctors Don't Believe It*, 1938, a survey of medical superstitions)

"The casting of horoscopes provides a living to thousands of individuals and provides dreams to an infinitely larger number of consumers. . . . [But] since the most painstaking studies have shown the inanity of horoscopes, there should be a strong rising up against this exploitation of public credulity." (Michel Gauquelin, after analyzing the horoscopes of sixteen thousand famous people, *Dreams and Illusions of Astrologers*, 1969)

"The picture emerging suggests that astrology works, but seldom in the way or to the extent that it is said to work." (Geoffrey Dean and Arthur Mather, *Recent Advances in Natal Astrology*, 1977, a critical review by fifty astrologers and scientists of over 1,000 astrology books, 410 journal articles, and 300 relevant scientific works)

"We are convinced however that astrology does not work. Astrology cannot be used to predict events of any kind, nor is astrology able to provide any useful information regarding personality, occupation, health, or any other human attribute." (Roger Culver and Philip Ianna, *The Gemini Syndrome,* 1979, a review by astronomers of several years of data collection, tests, and most of the available evidence)

"Astrology is largely (but not entirely) superstition. However, because of the important areas which remain to be investigated, this conclusion may need future qualification. We should not be dogmatic." (Hans Eysenck and David Nias, *Astrology: Science or Superstition?* 1982, a review by psychologists of the most recent research)

Evidently astrology works if studied by astrologers but not if studied by scientists. Why the conflict? For non-scientists the question is not so much "does astrology work?" as "how can people disagree so completely over such a simple claim?" The disagreement was not properly resolved until the 1980s, when it became clear that everything depends on what is meant by "astrology" and by "astrology works."

WHAT IS MEANT BY "ASTROLOGY"?

In Western countries there are four levels of interest in astrology as shown in table 1. At the first level are the readers of sun-sign columns. They have little or no interest in serious astrology. For them astrology means entertainment. At the second level are those with enough interest to have their birth chart calculated and read. For them astrology means an intriguing way of exploring themselves.

Table 1. Four Levels of Interest in Astrology

Level of interest	Example	Seeks	Percent*
1. Superficial	Reads sun signs	Entertainment	50
2. Some knowledge	Has own chart	Ego boost	2
3. Deep involvement	Calculates charts	Meaning to life	0.02
4. Scientific	Performs tests	The truth	0.00002

*Of the population in Western countries. The figures vary from country to country and from decade to decade but the large difference between levels remains much the same. People who consult astrologers in person (as opposed to those who merely dial-a-horoscope or dial-an-astrologer) fall between levels 2 and 3; in the United States they number roughly one million a year, which seems like a convincing vote in favor of astrology. But even this number is only about 2 percent of the millions of Americans who at any one time are seeking answers to their psychological problems, and less than 1 percent of those who read newspaper horoscopes. So the popularity of astrological consultations is perhaps no more remarkable than the popularity of any one of 99 flavors of ice cream. If it is there then some people will try it. For comparison the proportion of people who are dentists is roughly 0.05 percent.

At the third level are those who read charts to find meaning in their lives. They see astrology as a form of religion that has little or no connection with sun-sign columns. In fact they tend to dismiss the latter just as skeptics do. At the fourth level are those who test astrology scientifically. They see astrology as a popular belief worthy of study whether or not the reasons for belief prove to be astrological.

As we progress through the levels there is a huge falling off in numbers but no worse than in other paranormal areas. More importantly, there is a crucial change in focus from entertainment to religion and research. In short, astrology means different things to different people, and there is more to astrology than being true or false.

WHAT IS MEANT BY "ASTROLOGY WORKS"?

One of the key inspirations of recent research was to divide astrology, however defined, into subjective and objective components as shown in figure 1. When this division is applied to the levels of interest shown in table 1, it resolves the previous disagreement over whether astrology works. At one extreme are astrologers who seek only spiritual insight. For them astrology provides subjective meaning and direction to life, so they conclude that it works. Here "it works" means "it feels good" or "it is meaningful." This kind of astrology does not need to be true, and attacking it would be like attacking Superman comics or a religious faith.

At the other extreme are scientists who seek factual proof. This kind of astrology needs to be true. (That is, it needs sound empirical support rather than speculation, so it reflects the actual state of things rather than fantastic imaginings.) But scientists find that astrology delivers negligible effect sizes, so they conclude that it does not work. Here "it does not work" means "it does not deliver results beyond those explained by nonastrological factors." In other words the disagreement over "Does astrology work?" tends to arise because people are talking about different things. The furious arguments, the shouting matches, all tended to be due to a mutual misunderstanding, but nobody noticed.

In between are those astrologers who see astrology as spiritual but grounded in the kind of factual statements ("Leos are generous") that fill astrology books. The outcome is a sleight of mind that allows objective findings to be welcomed if positive ("It confirms astrology!") and rejected if negative ("Astrology is not like that!"), and a nonfalsifiability whose problems escape notice (if no observation could prove astrology false, astrologers could never be wrong even when using the wrong chart). This sleight of mind was addressed by the emergence of a critical research base and by asking the right questions.

Figure 1. Subjective and Objective Components of Any Practice

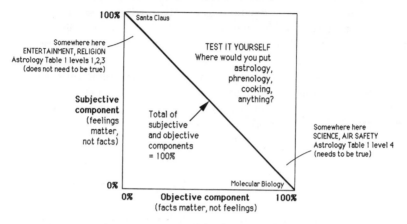

In principle we can take any practice and divide it roughly into two components, subjective and objective. If we make the total equal to 100%, the plot of one component against the other will then be a straight line as shown above. At the top, only feelings and values matter, as in pure faith-based religion. At the bottom, only facts and empirical truths matter, as in pure science. In between are those practices that are nominally a bit of both, such as astrology, phrenology, and cooking. Note that the objective component is determined by testability, not by truth. To be useful the objective component needs to be empirically true, but its truth does not affect its position on the line. Thus phrenology (whose claims tend to be testable) might appear in any position, depending on what we mean by phrenology, even though its claims are known to be completely false.

Similarly with astrology. Because astrology means different things to different people, there can be a huge gap between camps as shown above. The larger the gap the better the chance of misunderstanding, so the above plot provides a valuable corrective. Furthermore, where a false or problematic belief contains a subjective component, the plot shows how its acceptance might be due to its spiritual value, its social value, or its cultural value. A material feast cannot appease a spiritual hunger. Gullibility may play no role whatever.

EMERGENCE OF A RESEARCH BASE 1975–2000

Before 1950 almost no scientific studies of astrology existed. Something like a dozen major statistical studies by astrologers had appeared since 1900, but none were widely known, and their poor methodology (such as no controls) did not give meaningful results. By 1975 the situation had improved mostly due to the work of the Gauquelins. But the real turning point came in 1977

---

when a collaborative critical review by Dean and Mather gathered together the existing scattered studies. It took seven man-years to prepare. Among other things it found more than 150 empirical studies in astrology journals and more than twenty in psychology journals.

The same year saw the first astrological software for home computers. A birth chart could take hours to calculate by hand. Now it took only seconds. Astrological practice and research would never be the same again. Accordingly, when the research base provided by the above critical review appeared, it led to a minor explosion in critical books, research journals, groups, and studies. Today the above numbers of empirical studies are close to 400 and 100 respectively.

ASKING THE RIGHT QUESTIONS

The most significant additions to the research base were improved methods of testing, many more controlled studies, a resolution of what is meant by "astrology works," recognition of the crucial role of human reasoning errors, the use of meta-analysis to determine effect sizes, and the use of collaborative reviews to explore research issues.

Together they have shown that the questions to ask are not "Is astrology true?" but "To what extent is it true?" (answered by effect size), and "Does it need to be true?" (answered by breakdown into subjective and objective components). Not "How does astrology work?" but "What is meant by astrology?" (so we know what the issues are), and most crucial of all "Does astrology deliver benefits beyond those due to nonastrological factors?" (which cannot be answered until the other questions have been answered). The answers quickly replaced the astrologers' sleight of mind with a consistent verdict on astrology.

THE VERDICT OF RESEARCH SINCE 1975

Astrologers claim that the heavens indicate earthly circumstances so pervasively that no area of human affairs is exempt. They also claim that experience shows it works. But research tells a different story. Astrology means different things to different people, and at the emotional level it can enrich our lives in the same way that religion and poetry can (table 1 and figure 1). But at the factual level it fails to show any useful effects (figure 2). Other techniques have much larger effect sizes (table 2). Worse still, unaided human reasoning is subject to systematic errors that can fully explain why an experience-based astrology seems to work (table 3).

For example, they explain why tens of thousands of Western tropical

Figure 2. Does Astrology Work? A Visual Analysis of Effect Sizes

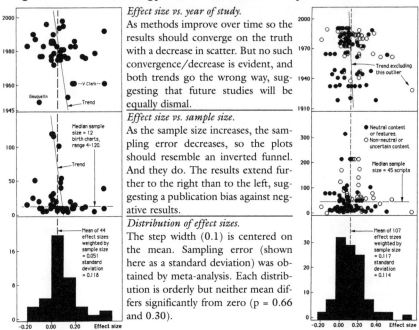

Effect size vs. year of study.
As methods improve over time so the results should converge on the truth with a decrease in scatter. But no such convergence/decrease is evident, and both trends go the wrong way, suggesting that future studies will be equally dismal.

Effect size vs. sample size.
As the sample size increases, the sampling error decreases, so the plots should resemble an inverted funnel. And they do. The results extend further to the right than to the left, suggesting a publication bias against negative results.

Distribution of effect sizes.
The step width (0.1) is centered on the mean. Sampling error (shown here as a standard deviation) was obtained by meta-analysis. Each distribution is orderly but neither mean differs significantly from zero (p = 0.66 and 0.30).

Left: Effect sizes for forty-four validation studies in astrology according to year, sample size, and frequency. Here effect size is the observed correlation between personality, ability, occupation, or case history and that predicted by astrologers. An effect size of 1 means perfect correlation (perfect prediction) as between feet and meters, 0 means zero correlation as between one coin toss and another, and –1 means perfect inverse correlation as between night and day. For individuals an effect size below 0.4 is of little practical use; 0.4 corresponds to 70 percent heads in coin tossing vs. 50 percent expected.

The forty-four studies were variously designed by astrologers, by skeptics, or by both in collaboration. All involve astrologers judging the whole birth chart, said to be essential for an accurate reading. Studies of anything less, such as sun signs, are not included. The studies include those where only top astrologers were used, or where more information was provided than in a typical consultation, or where the judgments were chosen to be especially easy, or where artifacts might reasonably be suspected, so the indications are optimistic. Yet meta-analysis shows that the differences between studies is due to sampling error (bottom plot), which is the inability of small samples to accurately reflect their source just as a hand of playing cards seldom has equal numbers of reds and blacks even though the pack does, so there is nothing left for astrology to explain. The other two plots are just as unremarkable. In short the plots offer no support for the validity of judgments based on the whole birth chart. Tests of isolated factors such as sun signs or aspects have shown them to be just as invalid.

Right: The same plots for 107 validation studies of graphology. They show close to zero support for the validity of judgments based on handwriting. Content (upper two plots), not graphology, explains what little validity there is, which is the opposite of what graphologists claim. The chances of proving astrology via graphology, or vice versa, are therefore not good. Source: *The Write Stuff* (1992), page 293.

Table 2. Thirty-four Ways to Convince Clients That Astrology Works

Do this	By using these strategies
Select initial hurdles	Preach to the converted (client predisposition)
	You never read the present chapter (ignorance is bliss)
	The best things in life are not free (charging a fee)
Stifle chances of being wrong	Appeal to birth chart complexity (nonfalsifiability)
	Avoid conflict, see what you believe (cognitive dissonance)
	Believe what you cannot prove (unavailable data)
	Remember the hits, forget the misses (selective memory)
	Ask only confirming questions, e.g., Are you awake? (stacking the deck)
	Ignore disconfirming evidence (confirmation bias)
	Deny that astrology can be tested (testability veto)
Use cues	Let context give the game away (vital statistics)
	Let body language be your guide (cold reading)
Make astrology look good	The importance of first impressions (halo effect)
	If it looks right then it is right (face validity)
	Style is more important than content (Dr. Fox effect)
	Underestimate chance effects (chance baseline shift)
	More is better (Aunt Fanny effect)
Make clients feel good	Use a kind heart to entice belief (tea and sympathy)
	The power of positive thinking (Pollyanna principle)
	It does us good if we think it does (placebo effect)
	Having control makes us feel better (misattribution)
	Just naming the unknown is enough (Rumpelstiltskin effect)
	Closeness is its own reward (rapport)
Make the chart fit	Find meaning where none exists (faces in clouds)
	Read specifics into generalities (Barnum effect)
	See only what you want to see (illusory correlation)
	Accentuate the positive (social desirability)
	Be seduced by resemblance (magical thinking)
	Afterwards we knew it all along (hindsight bias)
	Sound arguments yes, sound data no (stereotypes)
Make the client fit	Find something, anything, to match the chart (repertoire)
	Let client role-play their chart (self-fulfilling prophecy)
	Force client to fit their chart (Procrustean effect)
	Winter does not last forever (regression to mean)

Each strategy reflects the systematic error in human reasoning shown in parentheses, for which we have used the accepted name if there is one, or a provisional name if not. In the early days it was usual for skeptics to explain why clients were satisfied with astrology readings in terms of the Barnum effect, the reading of specifics into generalities ("you tend to be critical of yourself"), where sense appears to come from the reading when in fact it comes from our ability to make sense out of vagueness. Today, as shown above, many more reasoning errors are known to apply. They vary in effectiveness, and in a particular situation some may be irrelevant, but all lead to client satisfaction and none require that astrology be true.

But if clients are going to be satisfied, astrologers can hardly fail to believe in astrology. In this way a vicious circle of reinforcement is established whereby astrologers and their clients become more and more persuaded that astrology works. Note that there are no errors to persuade them that astrology does not work other than the informed critical mind, which of course is not an error as such but rather a defence against errors. An astrologer typically makes no effort to become informed or to acquire critical thinking skills, preferring instead to spend years learning to read charts, during which time they have ample chance to respond to the above reinforcement. Astrology in the consulting room does need to be true.

Table 3. Effect Sizes by Meta-analysis:
Astrology versus Other Techniques

RELIABILITY (agreement between repeat tests or between practitioners)

Test-retest agreement for IQ tests	.90	(63)
Test-retest agreement for personality inventories	.85	(43)
Agreement between practitioners on content:*		
Palmistry	.89	(4)
Graphology	.85	(12)
Inkblots (Rorschach)	.84	(24)
Lower limit of utility for testing individuals	.80	
Agreement between practitioners on interpretation:		
Graphology	.42	(15)
Inkblots	.36	(7)
Palmistry	.11	(1)
Astrology	.10	(25)

VALIDITY (agreement between measure 1 and measure 2)

Readability score vs. grade needed for understanding	.75	(19)
Wechsler IQ test vs. high school grades	.65	(5)
Eysenck Personality Inventory vs. self/peer ratings	.56	(13)
Lower limit of utility for testing individuals	.40	
Inkblots vs. IQ, personality test, clinical ratings	.34	(13)
Graphology vs. IQ	.29	(14)
Physiognomy vs. IQ, personality test, peer ratings	.15	(17)
Can subjects pick own astrology reading? **	.13	(17)
Graphology vs. personality test, ratings, work performance	.12	(107)
Sun sign prior knowledge vs. extraversion score	.09	(19)
Astrology vs. IQ, personality test, case history (from figure 2)	.05	(44)
Gauquelin planetary effects (eminent professionals)	.04	(11)
Gauquelin planetary effects (parents vs. children)	.02	(3)
Lunar effects on human behaviour	.01	(50)
Gauquelin sign or aspect effects for professionals	<.01	(30)
Phrenology measures vs. peer ratings	.00	(1)
Age (adults only) vs. work performance	−01	(425)
Palmistry vs. personality test, self-ratings	−05	(9)

Meta-analysis takes the effect sizes and sample sizes of all available studies and determines the most representative effect size. The first column of figures shows the representative effect size, and ( ) = number of studies on which it is based. Here effect size is the correlation (0–1) between the relevant variables (for an explanation see figure 2).

*For example on the abundance of palmar lines or on handwriting slope. Agreement between astrologers, say on whether sun is in sign X, has not been tested but (being a computational rather than a visual decision) should be close to 1.

**Most if not all of the effect is due to a failure to remove cues such as sun sign, which then give the game away.

The above table shows that astrological effect sizes are nowhere near commensurate with the claims of astrologers, and that nearly all other approaches do better than astrology, usually much better. Even physiognomy (which today is regarded as quackery) has a higher-effect size than astrology, which suggests that looking at faces is generally more useful than looking at birth charts. Phrenology is no better than tossing a coin, yet phrenologists were convinced it was true for precisely the same reason that astrologers are convinced astrology is true—by their experience. But the phrenologists were wrong. The suspicion that astrologers might also be wrong is confirmed by astrology's negligible validity (0.05). Even more telling is its negligible 0.10 for reliability, which is based on twenty-five studies and can therefore hardly be dismissed as untypical. What is the point of astrology if astrologers cannot even agree on what a chart means?

astrologers can say that in their experience Scorpios really are intense, while hundreds of thousands of Eastern sidereal astrologers can look at the same piece of sky, which they call Libra, and agree that in their experience it is not intense but relaxed. And what goes for signs goes for all the other factors over which there is disagreement, which is most of them. So much for experience. The claim that astrologers proudly and repeatedly make, that astrology is unassailable because it is experience-based, is simply mistaken—what they see as its strength is actually its weakness.

How have astrologers reacted to such charges? The philosopher Thomas Kuhn noted that when an idea is in crisis, its supporters retreat behind a smoke-screen of speculation that sounds good but is actually empty. Astrologers are no exception. Rather than accept the results of research, or specify how disagreements should be resolved, they retreat behind a smokescreen of speculation about the nature of truth and how astrology belongs to a reality beyond the reach of science, which is why it is so difficult to demonstrate. (More sleight of mind: How can astrology be so difficult to demonstrate when astrologers are so readily convinced that it works?) And what about the Gauquelin findings?

PRESENT STATUS OF THE GAUQUELIN FINDINGS

During forty years of immense labor, the most famous in modern astrology, the late Michel Gauquelin (1926–1991) and his wife, Françoise, tested astrological claims. Their findings were entirely negative except for two that pleased astrologers, upset skeptics, and puzzled everyone else: (1) Professional people such as scientists tend to born with a surplus or deficit of certain planets in the areas just past rise or culmination, but only if the people are eminent and born naturally. (2) Ordinary people with such features tend to pass them on to their children. Both tendencies are too weak to be of any practical use (table 3), and much additional work has been done, notably by Suitbert Ertel, yet they have proved to be extraordinarily controversial.

But the controversy seems unwarranted. Most Gauquelin birth data come from nineteenth- and early twentieth-century Europe, when popular almanacs contained planetary information, when almanac-based beliefs fitted the Gauquelin discoveries, when parents had ample opportunity to adjust birth data, and when motivation existed from family traditions. Planetary effects would then be the result not of astrology but of parental tampering. If this finding is correct, planetary-effect sizes for births on days where tampering is likely to be least, such as the undesirable thirteenth, should be less than on days where tampering is likely to be most, such as the desirable seventh. And they are, the means being 0.01 versus 0.03. Many other tests support this finding.

Figure 3. Will Astrology Last Forever?

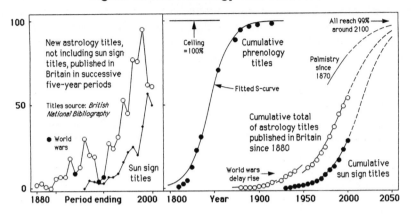

The growth of populations, whether of cathedrals, Christian saints, a particular model of a car or computer, or phrenology books, tends to follow a bell-shaped curve of increase-stability-decrease. The cumulative growth over the lifetime then traces an S-shaped curve that is followed remarkably accurately. If enough has been traced out, the S-curve will predict when the end is near, which for phrenology was around 1900 when it was effectively dead except for a few enthusiasts. As shown above, the growth in Britain of serious astrology books, and of sun-sign books (including Chinese horoscopes but excluding those for just one sign), fit S-curves that predict the end may be near roughly around 2100. Whether this is a genuine end, or merely the result of books being replaced by the Internet, is of course hard to say.

Phrenology had enormous appeal, as did a later popular version akin to fortune-telling, and at its peak was even more popular than astrology is today, which led phrenologists to predict that it would last forever. But ultimately people became suspicious of the hype and lack of substance. Once the social need for phrenology disappeared, it was effectively dead, and its decease was soon evident to everyone except phrenologists. Thus in their 1896 *Year Book* the British Phrenological Association still felt that "the nonacceptance of phrenology is next to impossible," while in his 1898 book *The Wonderful Century* the scientist and phrenology enthusiast Alfred Russel Wallace confidently predicted that "in the coming century phrenology will assuredly attain general acceptance," a prediction that is interestingly similar to one quoted earlier for astrology, see "Views of Astrologers."

Astrology does not face the religious opposition that phrenology did. Nevertheless it faces the same scientific opposition and the same taint of pop, plus mounting competition from a barrage of self-help psychologies (see any New Age bookstore). Phrenology has shown that popularity does not guarantee longevity, so we have no reason to suppose that astrology will resist the trends revealed above, tentative though they are, or that astrologers will be any less blind to an impending decease. Sociologists will watch with interest.

For astrologers the good news is that the existence of tampering confirms the reality of the Gauquelin findings. Given the social conditions at the time, we should expect to observe small planetary effects, and their absence would be more surprising than their presence. The bad news is that unless planetary effects can be demonstrated under conditions where tampering is absent, as when parents are excluded from the birth-reporting process, the Gauquelin findings can no longer be seen as providing support for astrology.

RESEARCH ISSUES YIELD TO COLLABORATION

Astrology and relevant fields are collectively too broad for any one person to address. The key is collaboration, which ironically has been taken up by scientists rather than astrologers. It was successfully used in the mid-1970s by Dean and Mather (fifty-two collaborators), in the early 1980s by Eysenck and Nias (nine collaborators), and variously in the 1990s (up to thirty-three collaborators). Example outcomes are given in the Further Reading section. The level of debate thus achieved is rare in astrology because astrologers tend to withdraw at any hint of critical scholarship or unwelcome news. Indeed, perhaps the clearest message to emerge since 1975 has been the lack (and even avoidance) of critical thinking skills among astrologers.

CRITICAL THINKING:
NO PROGRESS SINCE BABYLON

The serious literature of astrology totals nearly 1,000 shelf-feet of Western-language books and periodicals and is aggressively uncritical. It abounds with inconsistent and contradictory assertions in which the most elementary principles of technical writing (clarity, brevity, organization, adequate data, and reference to the work of others) are usually ignored. "It would not be unfair to term this literature a nightmare," said the British parapsychologist Carl Sargent in 1986.

Astrology on the Internet is even worse. During twelve months to February 1997, former American astrologer Joanna Ashmun sighted or read over twenty-five thousand messages on astrology e-mailing lists (about two-thirds their total traffic) and about the same number on the newsgroup alt.astrology (about half its total traffic). Toward the end she was receiving over 150 e-mails a day, averaging about 250 words each. Her verdict:

> The way astrologers treat researchers and skeptics is just the way they treat other astrologers who disagree with them—continuing on as if they and their disagreements never existed. . . . The thing that I find least comfort-

able about astrology discussions (and not just on the Internet) is their immateriality, their lack of grounding, their dearth of earth. . . . From experience with lists on other topics, I have to say that astrologers' posts are less literate than average and that this appears to contribute to outbursts of bad humor. They write badly and they read badly . . . there is almost no critical response; errors are ignored, corrections are not acknowledged. . . . Most astrologers would rather have an iffy quotation from Dane Rudyhar or C. G. Jung to support their opinions than some good numbers. . . . Many astrologers have university educations, quite a few have graduate degrees, and they must, therefore, have had to do some reading, writing, and scholarship sometime, but these presumed skills rarely escape to the mailing lists. (Source: *Correlation* 15, no. 2 [1996/97]: 35–51)

The same uncritical off-the-planet quality is evident even at the top. In 2000, at a huge international "Conference on the Future of Astrology" held in Los Angeles, "fifty-six of the world's finest astrologers" gave more than one hundred presentations. Inexplicably not one of them was addressed to the future of astrology, as if the various problems discussed here did not exist. But perhaps astrologers have no option, as we will see in the next section.

ASTROLOGERS FACE A DILEMMA

Since 1975 it has become clear that no astrological body could embrace science and stay in business. Any doubt on this point was dispelled in 1989, when the National Council for Geocosmic Research (a leading American astrology group) began a scientific research journal that folded a year later due to member protests; and again in 1999, when the editor of the British Astrological Association's journal of scientific research into astrology was sacked for printing articles too critical of astrology and astrologers (subseqent issues showed a notable loss of scientific rigor and the censoring of subsequent complaints).

Of course it is easy to argue that, to be credible, astrologers need to acquire the critical thinking skills that are part of any university course in the social sciences. And that if their astrology involves subjective components they need to refrain from making statements open to scientific challenge, whereas if it involves objective components they need to be familiar with research results and informed criticism.

However, the resulting credible astrologer faces a dilemma. Astrology seems unlikely to feel right unless astrologers and clients believe that the objective component is valid, for example that Leos really are more generous than non-Leos. Otherwise why bother with accurate birth charts? But research has shown that the objective component is invalid, and that numerous artifacts (such as those in table 2) readily explain why it seems to be valid. So the credible astrologer can claim only that "astrology uses interesting superstitions to stimulate self-examination," or that "astrology is basically tea and sympathy." The dilemma is why clients would then bother with astrology.

So what of the future? Based on past performance, the future is only too easy to predict: Vested Interests 1, Scientific Integrity 0. So legislation may be needed to protect consumers. Some speculations on longevity are given in figure 3.

DOES ASTROLOGY WORK? CONCLUSIONS FOR AND AGAINST

For: Astrology has many attractions beyond its historical importance. Our personal identity is helped by sun signs even if they are false. A warm and sympathetic astrologer provides nonthreatening therapy that is otherwise hard to come by, especially as no admission of some physical, mental, or moral weakness is required as with a doctor, psychiatrist, or priest. Astrology may even be the lesser (and cheaper) of available evils—if psychotherapy does not usefully do what it claims to do (help recovery from a neurotic disorder better than no psychotherapy), it becomes difficult to outlaw astrologers when psychotherapists go free.

Against: In terms of effect size there seems to be nothing in astrology that cannot be outperformed by almost any orthodox approach. Half a century of research using methods incomparably more powerful than those available to the Babylonians and Greeks has failed to find effects beyond those produced by nonastrological factors. Until professional astrologers make this clear, they will remain a contradiction in terms. Astrology will always have dangers, if only because the uncritical acceptance of unproven ideas can make people easy targets for abuse.

Over to the reader: Does astrology work? If your answer is yes, ask yourself if your kind of astrology needs to be true. If no, you are safe. If yes, you are on shaky ground, so ask yourself which proposition is the more likely: (1) That pervasive astrological influences exist which contradict known science yet on whose nature astrologers spectacularly disagree, or (2) that the many known errors in human reasoning (of which most astrologers are spectacularly unaware) explain astrological beliefs.

FURTHER READING

In accordance with our brief we have minimized the number of references in the text. The works below collectively cover the field and lead to the relevant references. Those with access to academic libraries should note that most of the important studies have been published in journals not abstracted by services such as Medline and PsycINFO.

Presently the most up-to-date scientific survey is the entry on astrology in *The Encyclopedia of the Paranormal* edited by Gordon Stein (Amherst, N.Y.: Prometheus Books, 1996), pages 47–99 (28,000 words, tables, figures, useful contacts, fifteen secondary references). The most recent example of collaboration is a collective interview of scientific researchers which occupies chapters 9 and 10 of *Astrology in the Year Zero*, edited by Garry Phillipson (London: Flare Publications, 2000). The other chapters (interviews with leading astrologers and a bibliography including most skeptical works) make this book an unusually well-balanced introduction to astrology.

For academics, a listing of critical reviews of astrology in the light of research findings is included in I. W. Kelly, "Modern Astrology: A Critique" (*Psychological Reports* 81 [1997]: 1035–66), who concludes that astrology is without the resources to solve its internal problems.

An important series of collaborative well-referenced articles appeared in the journal *Correlation* during 1994–1999. The topics (and outcomes) were the relevance of science (applies only where claims are testable), some conceptual problems of astrology (largely devastating), theories of astrology (none credible), and human reasoning errors (neglected by astrologers but

GEOFFREY DEAN received his Ph.D. from the University of London. Since 1974 he has conducted large-scale studies of astrology, and authored or co-authored many critical articles, debates, surveys, and prize competitions for research into astrology. He has also practiced as an astrologer. He is a freelance technical writer and editor in Perth, Western Australia.

IVAN W. KELLY received his Ph.D. from the University of Calgary. Since 1979 he has been professor of educational psychology at the University of Saskatchewan. He is chairman of CSICOP's Astrology Subcommittee and has authored or coauthored many critical works on astrology, human judgment, and alleged lunar effects on behavior. He lives in Saskatoon.

readily explaining their beliefs). For back copies contact astrological.association@zetnet.co.uk.

Critical articles, including an expanded version of the above collective interview and an updated version of Kelly's critique, can be found at www. smitpotze.demon.nl/Astrology-and-Science/index.htm, or via the keywords "Astrology and Science" should it change. A good starting point for articles by serious astrologers and links to other astrological Web sites is the British Astrological Association's www.astrologer.com/aanet.

16

THE BATTLE AGAINST PSEUDOSCIENCE
The Case of Astrology

JEAN-CLAUDE PECKER

For twenty-five years now, CSICOP and its widely read *Skeptical Inquirer* have fought the pseudosciences with a remarkable and indomitable energy. Paul Kurtz and his colleagues have accomplished in a quarter of a century unprecedented work in the necessary and permanent crusade against misinformation. They did it in the particularly difficult American society where many cults and uncontrolled beliefs are neighboring the most sophisticated style of life. But much remains to be done. To celebrate this twenty-fifth anniversary is an occasion to call for continuance and reinforcement of the battle. But the monster belongs to the family of the Lerna's hydra, which Hercules finally managed to kill, because he found it was necessary to kill its seven heads all at once. The seven heads and many more are there—pseudosciences, mystical cults, telekinesis, visits of aliens, homeopathy, etc.—and are still to be killed! CSICOP has managed to fight all of them, i.e., to fight everywhere for the use of reason instead of blind credulity, to fight for lucidity as one of the fundamental rights of humankind.

In this brief essay I shall attempt to show how one of the heads of the hydra, astrology, has been constantly killed since antiquity, and has constantly reappeared, helping the other pseudoscientific cults to survive.

1. THE OLD ASTROLOGY OF THE BABYLONIANS AND GREEKS

It is rather well known that, at the time of the Babylonians, astrology was flourishing, progressing at the same time as astronomy, together with the increased knowledge of obvious naked-eye astronomical phenomena, such as the succession of days and nights, the lunar months, the solar and lunar eclipses, the mapping of the thousand (or so) visible stars, the organization (completely arbitrary, but useful like a road map) of their asterisms into names of constellations, the introduction of the "zodiacal" band of constellations (traversed by the Sun in the course of one year). However, there was no idea of the distances of heavenly bodies. The question was not even asked. They were indeed part of the environment. Really, the Sun, the Moon, the planets, and the stars were in the sky, quite close obviously, and had some influence on the destiny of the only empire then known, that of the great kings of Babylon. The idea that the heavenly bodies were of a different nature than that of the sublunary world (subject to all kind of changes, generally unpredictable, perishable, fallible) then emerged. This later became an Aristotelian paradigm. Astrology was then not applicable to laymen, and less to women! The empire of the sky had no other possible counterpart, here down below, than the realm of the emperor. And "much ado" was done about something! Astrology was an essential device used by the influential rulers of the country to assert precisely and firmly their influence.

The oldest astronomical-astrological Chaldean tablets (as far as known) are dated back to Sargon the First (the Older), from Akkad, about 2,300 B.C.E. It was based on the strict methods of astronomy, more or less confirmed by the ability of the astronomers of that time to predict some phenomena (those in the sky), and was by no means a public and open field, as it is today. The Greeks, in the third century before our era, in their democratic mood, had extended to individuals the powers of astrology. This was an essential step, in that it became, if not yet quite popular, at least well accepted by the gullible elites. The Aristotelian paradigm (the "astral" and "sublunary" worlds are by essence different, but that very duality is an essential part of the cosmos) gave astrology some weight. And of course, the fraudulent excesses of astrologers became more common and visible. Astrologers became still more important under the Roman emperors. The emperor Tiberius was forced to issue an edict forbidding their activity. Tiberius allowed one exception to this rule, favoring, naturally enough, his own astrologer, Thrasyllus. In any case, whenever they were expelled from the door, they came back through the window! Some astronomers, such as Eudoxus, for example, were often critical of the very idea of astrology. The most accomplished (if not the best, at least the most systematic) astronomer of that time, Claudius Ptomelaeus (Ptolemy), who lived in the second century C.E., codified astrology in his work *Tetrabiblos*. He was not a strict Aristotelian, for he did not place a material mass at the center of the planetary orbs. But his astrology has no doubt dominated the minds of that period, at least among the pagans.

The unity of the universe, as opposed to this basic duality, is a concept which appeared much later, perhaps most clearly at the time of Tycho-Brahe (sixteenth century), although glimpses of this idea were already in the minds of early Christian thinkers, such as John Philoponus.

An important phenomenon was discovered during the second century B.C.E. by Hipparchus, a very important figure, certainly the most important one in Greek astronomy. Calendars are based on the definition of seasons. The spring equinox, which marks the beginning of what could be called the "true year," is the moment when the Sun crosses the celestial equator's plane, and when the length of night and day are therefore equal. It is the basis of the definition of longitudes on maps of the sky. Hipparchus discovered that the longitudes of stars had clearly increased since the time of a previous astronomer, Timocharis (150 years earlier) by a few degrees of arc. The longitudes of stars increased actually by 360° in approximately 26,000 years. Accordingly, at any time respective positions of heavenly bodies in the sky are identical with what they were 26,000 years ago. This shows that the constellations crossed by the Sun at a given season, defined from the time of the equinox, vary from year to year in a regular way, in a clear unavoidable succession. This is called the phenomenon of "the precession of the equinoxes."

This fact is of considerable significance. For example, let us consider the zodiacal sign of Taurus. It appears always, by definition, at the same time of the year, more than one month after the equinox. People "born under this sign" manifest some character of its symbolic feature: meaning that they are by their nature violent, impetuous, etc. Alas! At the time of the equinox, the asterism and constellation that gave the names to that sign have not yet been crossed by the Sun in its yearly path. The constellation Aries is there instead. Aries, the Ram, is a spring constellation, is a gentle animal, with which are associated all sorts of things linked with the spring, such as youth, a somewhat careless life, love, joy, etc. This is not at all the same connotation as it was 2,000 or more years ago. At that time, Aries was just at its old location of the spring equinox; and for that reason the equinox is denoted, as the Ram, by the letter Greek gamma (γ), which symbolizes the exact point (point γ) at which the Sun is crossing the celestial equator, and vaguely represents the head of a ram with its small horns. We may ask, what does it mean to associate the characteristics of Taurus with people who were actually born when the Sun was crossing the constellation Aries, the Ram?

This important fact, of course, passed unnoticed by astrologers until modern times; they obviously use the old tables, which ignored the phenomenon. We shall see the consequence of this discovery, in section 4 below.

2. CHRISTIANS AND ASTROLOGY, UP TO KEPLER'S TIME

Astrologers were easily confused with mathematicians and astronomers, which indeed they were too. The church fathers where shocked by what they viewed as degenerate forms of life surrounding the emperor. Moreover, they were not scientists; and they did not consider science in a favorable light. In a way, instead of "saving the phenomena" as the old Greek masters had taught their followers, they had first to "save the Scriptures." They were violently opposed to the astrologers within the emperor's court, but they had more serious reasons not to believe in astrology, and even to consider astrology as some sort of evil. Augustine (354–430, Bishop of Hippo), one of the more prolific and influential writers of the early church fathers, was violent in his attacks on astrology. He considered horoscopes as deliberate pagan swindles, and for several reasons. Astrologers, he conjectured, may very well have been in league with the Devil. It is one thing to monitor the tides by the Moon, it is quite another thing to interfere with the "free will" of men (women never had one), given to him by God, in the gardens of Eden, and so often badly used by him, against the wishes of a benevolent God. Not all Christians adopted this Augustinian viewpoint. Theodoret (390–458), for example, observed that there are indeed signs in the sky, which indicated when to plant, to seed, to build, to travel. But the bulk of Christendom followed Augustine in its ban of astrology. Since that time, the priests of the world who soon assumed power fought against the threats of astrology. Perhaps this was partly due to the influence of Arab thinkers, especially strong in Spain, and through them the influence of Ptolemaic conceptions. Still, Bishop Tempier, the most influential of Parisian astronomers, in an edict in 1277 solemnly condemned astrology, along with, I might add, Aristotelianism. However, this condemnation left the door open; for Tempier condemned only "illicit" astrology; prognostication about the "natural future" was quite acceptable (for example, by Pierre Abélard [1071–1142]). Nicolas Oresme (1320–1382) was violently opposed to astrology, especially to those astrologers who claimed that the eternal return is possible and implied complete predetermination of human destiny.

The Reformation did not accept the decrees of Rome, and astrology began to flourish in northern Protestant countries. It was at that time that Nostradamus (influenced by the Talmud) hid behind his predictions, a chronicle of his time, of a considerable historical value, I might add, but of no astrological significance. There is little doubt that Tycho Brahe (1546–1601) himself was known as an astrologer. Similarly for his follower and admirer Johannes Kepler (1571–1630), who profited successfully from it. It is well known that he cast the horoscopes of several influential people, including General Wallerstein, and that he gained considerable fame for this in spite of the errors of his prediction. Kepler himself said that he considered astrology and astronomy as two estranged sisters, and it was only fair that the richest one (astrology) help the poorest one (astronomy) to make a decent living.

The success of astrology was then linked with the echoes of success in other fields. Clearly, the opposition between the macrocosm and microcosm, the fundamental duality, linked instead of opposed the astral and sublunary parts of the world. People like Albert the Great, Roger Bacon, and especially medical scholars such as Mondeville were quite sympathetic to that idea, remarkably illustrated, notably, by the beautiful paintings of microcosm and microcosm in the *Très Riches Heures du Duc de Berry*. Indeed, alchemists, chiromancers, Tarot-card readers, and many other occultists used this analogy to construct the strangest theories. As bizarre as it may seem, astrology was at the root of these fanciful theories; and it served obviously as a scientific justification of them. Vice versa, the strength of magical cults and occultisms were reinforced by the public's faith in astrology as a scientific basis for interpreting nature. One cannot resist giving a few examples of such alleged correspondences, which permeate the thinking at that time. We shall limit ourselves here to some "zodiacal" correspondences.

> Aries (the Ram), the first sign of the "true seasonal year," corresponds to the head and the brain, to a few plants (primroses), a few minerals or stones (amethyst, red stones, red sands, sulphur, iron), to the color red, fire, to the tendency to blossom, to revolution, etc.
>
> Taurus (the Bull) corresponds to the neck, the larynx, the ears, to other flowers (almond flowers), minerals (alabaster, white coral, copper), colors (white, green), to the cold, to the instinct of power, etc.
>
> Gemini (the Twins) correspond to the waist, the nerves, hands, arms, to some minerals (beryl, opal, mercury), to some animals (the hare), colors (striped colors), to air, the positive characters, to a tendency to dualism, to intuition.
>
> Cancer (the Crab) corresponds to the stomach, breasts, flowers (lily of the valley, carnation), minerals (pearls, platinum, silver), animals (crayfish, octopus), colors (opalescence), and to . . . silence, hidden forces, invisible influences, etc.

There are many other examples that can be provided. The mixtures of words often contradict each other, and they can be interpreted in any way that you wish. Other astrologers may disagree with the above list of correspondences. There are so many different astrological systems that it is difficult to decide which is better. The subjective intuition of the astrologer in the last analysis is really decisive in his relationship to his clients. We are dealing with an art and a craft, not a science.

3. ASTRONOMERS OF THE SEVENTEENTH CENTURY: THE MUNDANE ASTROLOGY AND COLBERT

There were not any sound reasons to reject astrology before the sixteenth century. The distances of the heavenly bodies were unknown. Of course, astronomers had made estimates of the distances of these bodies; but they were only guesses. It is only since the seventeenth century that we began using optical instrumentation to determine with some precision the position of the stars and planets, or to have an idea of the great distance between the Sun and the planets, and of the enormous distances of the stars, where light may take billions of years to reach us. This evidence led us to the conviction that it is an absurd idea to conceive that the planets could influence the life of individuals on Earth.

But as illustrated by the "correspondences" above, astrological ideas nevertheless were in abundance; and sorcery was popular, at the court as well as the countryside, notably in the France of Louis XIV. Some noble ladies (including Mme de Montespan, the last wife of the king) were at a certain time fans of a poisoner named "La Voisin," and, in a mixture of sorcery, criminal tomfoolery, and astrology, they managed to send *ad patres* several old men, not necessarily only those they did not consider anymore as suitable husbands. This affair went to a special court, and was considerably commented on at the court of Versailles. La Voisin was condemned to the infamous death of witches—by fire. And finally Colbert decided to put an end to these bad stories, and forbade in the whole kingdom the practice of sorcery, astrology, and all the occult sciences. This decree by Colbert was certainly a turning point in the history of astrology. But astrology continued to flourish, hidden, as it does today.

4. ZODIACAL ASTROLOGY: THE PRECESSION OF THE EQUINOXES

Classical astrology is called a "zodiacal astrology," linking the birth of anyone to the position of the Sun in the zodiacal band. It incorporates today the precession of the equinoxes, which in itself is the basis of the "New Age" philosophy. According to computations (which were very badly done), the spring equinox, about four millennia ago, coincided with the constellation Aries, which gave its name to the astrological sign Aries. It moved (where it stayed for about 2,000 years) to the constellation Pisces, marked by the Christian era (a symbol for Christ was Ichthus [ιχθηζ in Greek], the fish). It now enters the sign of Aquarius. This entrance in Aquarius allegedly marks the New Age of Aquarius. One can object to a lot of things in zodiacal astrology, even if they attempt to take into account the precession of the equinoxes! They do so, however, very strangely indeed!

First, any astronomer knows there are thirteen, not twelve, constellations in the zodiacal band: the thirteenth one is Ophiucus (the Serpent-bearer).

Second, the Sun, in its yearly course, traverses the various constellations for different durations, not uniformly one month of three decans (periods of ten days)! For example, it stays almost two months in Virgo, and less than two weeks in Scorpio.

Moreover, from year to year, the Sun does not have the same trajectory in the sky, and it does not stay the same time in any one constellation.

Of course, astrologers tell us: "You speak about constellations; we speak about the signs, located elsewhere, and impregnated, so to say, millennia ago, by the naming of the constellations therein, itself imposed upon us by their shape." Well! Does that mean that, before the present naming of the constellations and of their signs (during the Babylonian era), the equinoctial precession did not exist? Why begin history at that particular time, particularly since the Solar System has existed for approximately 5 billion years?

Another argument is that the zodiacal constellations are defined very differently, even delineated differently, in China, in the West, in pre-Columbian America. Does this mean that the sky has different laws to rule different men and women on Earth? How unjust this is! What about the poor people born north of the Arctic Circle, in Murmansk for instance, who spend a large part of the year without seeing the Sun or any zodiacal sign in the sky? They have no horoscope. Do they not have the right to live?

There is no reason whatsoever to accept zodiacal astrology. It has no sound astronomical basis. The arguments against zodiacal astrology have been splendidly described in the writings of Michel Gauquelin, a statistician, now deceased. In doing so, he was, in a way, paving the road for his own type of astrology, astrobiology, so-called, which CSICOP and the *Skeptical Inquirer* have shown has not been replicated by independent researchers.

5. THE PLANETARY ASTROLOGY, AND ITS FATAL STATISTICS

Michel Gauquelin was interested in astrology. Through the analysis of hundreds of cases, he found that the location of the Sun in the birth sky of any person strongly influences his or her mode of life. He claimed, for example, that when the planet Mars is located in some particular areas of the sky, the people born at that time are more likely than others to become first-class sports champions. The analysis had been critically studied by Paul Couderc (in his book *l'Astrologie*); by Kurtz, Abell, and Zelen in the *Skeptical Inquirer*; by the Comité Para Belge (*Nouvelles Brèves*); and most recently the French Committee for the Study of Paranormal Phenomena, which is now combined with AFIS (the French Association for Scientific Information).

They later showed, in a rather decisive way (*The Mars Effect*, Prometheus Books), that the statistics introduced by Gauquelin were biased by some quite arbitrary posterior selection of the data. An unbiased statistical study shows there is no Mars effect; but there is some clear Gauquelin effect! Similar studies performed earlier by Gauquelin on other planets and other life stances were not pushed very far by Gauquelin. His case rested largely upon Mars. The evidence for it was very weak or nonexistent.

The influence of the planets can be discussed in another way. First of all one can ask: Why would not the approximately 10,000 smaller asteroids orbiting between Mars and Jupiter influence our destinies as much as the larger planets? One could also ask, Why not also the planets located around other stars, known now to be very numerous, no doubt billions, in space? The reply could be: "Well, of course, they are either too small or too far." But in that case, the astrologers, by their response, would accept the idea that the action of the planets are more or less linked with the mass and distance of the planets to the Earth, and is perhaps similar to gravitation. If that were the case, the influences of the forceps of the obstetrician, or of the building nearby, would be much larger than those of any planet, large or small! "If distance plays a role," according to the astrologers, "it cannot be in the same way as gravitation. There are some 'unknown' forces." But if so, do not these forces depend upon the distance, one way or another? If they depend upon the distance in a deeper way than gravitation, the argument just given (forceps, building) is still stronger. If, on the contrary, they do depend upon the distance in a way different than the gravitation, then the large planets around distant stars must be just as effective as the nearby planets; and, as they are many times more numerous, one sees the type of contradiction one is necessarily led to whatever the "nature" of the alleged force!

The natural conclusion is that there is no place for a force which would have the properties needed to explain the alleged astrological effects. The only conclusion is that there is no astrological effect. Astrology is pure fantasy. Clearly it had some influence historically on so many people, including kings and heads of state. This in spite of the fact that astrology has no objective value and no objective reality.

6. OUR BATTLE IS NOT OVER

The pseudosciences have more than seven heads. And CSICOP, for twenty-five years, has been fighting all these heads all at once. The general public has a complete misunderstanding of the scientific method, and charlatans of all sorts have exploited this ignorance and credulity, seductively using attractive language with their glib tongues, and with smiling faces, but charlatans nevertheless.

The problem is that when one does not understand the scientific methodology, one is easily convinced by any new arguments which sound scientific.The fight is perhaps not everlasting. At least we are in a crucial period, at the front against the threats of the "New Age," and we have to react to each step of the people we battle.

Astrology is a good example. I remember, before the founding of CSICOP, the actions that were led by my colleagues Bart Bok and George Abell in the United States, and Paul Couderc, Daniel Chalonge, and others in France—to mention only those who are no longer with us—and there are now many others everywhere who are critical of astrology.

In the beginning, we used the operational argument: "It does not work; read the press of January 1 of past years." We also said: "Why do you not take precession of the equinoxes into account? You should." But astrologers came again with computers, with refinement in the vagueness of the predictions, with a due account of the precession. Still, they did not explain what sort of force was transmitting the influence of heavenly bodies to humankind, apart from gravitation. They spoke a little of electromagnetism, but it was easy to refute. Now they speak about "spiritual" forces, and join the great river of the New-Agers. Unless, as we have seen, they change methods and link the position of the planet in the birth sky, instead of in the zodiac, to the character of someone (the Mars effect). Is not that battle endless? Perhaps not. We should remember the situation during the seventeenth century, when, in France, Colbert declared astrology illegal. Or decrees, later, punishing all those trying to extort money by false pretenses of a pseudoscientific nature. The hydra loses some heads. It is still alive; but, I feel it is definitely much weaker than it was some years ago. People who read their horoscopes in the newspaper claim it is only for amusement. They do not believe—oh no, they don't!—one word of it!

JEAN-CLAUDE PECKER, born in Reims, France, May 10, 1923, is an alumnus of the École Normale Supérieure. He taught physics at the University of Clermont-Ferrand (1953–1955), and was astronomer at the Paris Observatory (1955–1964) and professor at the Collège de France (1964–1988), now honorary (emeritus). He was director of the Nice Observatory (1962–1969), later of the Institut d'Astrophysique de Paris (1972–1979), and was general secretary of the International Astronomical Union (1964–1967). Professor Pecker is the author of many books, among them *The Orion Book of the Sky* (New York: Orion, 1960), *Space Observatories* (Springer Verlag, 1970), *La nouvelle astronomie, science de l'univers* (Paris: Hachette, 1974), *Sous l'étoile Soleil Le temps des sciences* (Fayard, 1984), and *The Future of the Sun* (New York: McGraw-Hill, 1992). He is a Humanist Laureate of the International Academy of Humanism.

POPULAR INVESTIGATIONS

17

ADVENTURES OF A PARANORMAL INVESTIGATOR

JOE NICKELL

Although I was not a founder of CSICOP, I had been investigating paranormal claims for several years before the committee was formed in 1976.

Like others, I had not always been a skeptic. I had a grandmother who helped keep me believing in Santa Claus until most of my schoolmates had become wise. She saw to it that "Santa" answered my letters, putting soot on the written responses to seemingly prove they had come down the chimney!

Later, my father having been an amateur magician, I also took up conjuring, which helped me further develop my critical-thinking skills. I performed "close-up" effects for friends and put on little shows at family gatherings. I sported a fake mustache affixed with spirit gum, and I recall thinking that someday I would be able to grow a real mustache and thus become a "real" (i.e., professional) magician.

About this time, when I was eight or so, I played fortune-teller at my school's annual fund-raiser, a Halloween carnival. Garbed in a turban and robe, my face darkened with "gypsy" makeup, I operated my prognostication booth for an evening. From a large container filled with folded slips of paper, the customer could draw his or her printed fortune. (These my mother and I made up, reproducing each in quantity on a vintage mimeograph.) I also exhibited a "love meter." Lent by a shop teacher, this resembled a big thermometer that supposedly registered, by touch, one's passion level. Actually, the bogus instrument was activated by a hidden rubber tube and bulb that I secretly squeezed. A few people even paid extra for a private session in the back of the booth where I utilized a fortune-telling card game to dispense more detailed blather. Although my customers included many good-natured skeptics, others expressed complete credulity for the pretended divinations. I thus learned an important lesson about the will to believe and the consequent need for skepticism, a lesson that has remained with me to this day.

Still another lesson came a few years later. I had discovered some seashell (brachiopod) fossils in a shalebank atop a hill near my eastern Kentucky home, and I took one rock slab to school to share with classmates. I was shocked by the response of my eighth-grade science teacher: He announced to the class that the find proved the truth of the biblical story about the Flood, over which Noah's Ark had supposedly triumphed. I recognized the absurdity of the teacher's comment, since the fossils were obviously millions of years old and long antedated the evolution of man. But the teacher was as beloved as he was ignorant, and I was a mere pupil, so I allowed the statement to pass. I now realize the incident was another milestone on the road to my enlightenment.

Always something of a jack-of-all-trades, I recall one of my first real paying jobs was as a chainman for a local surveyor, and from the age of about fourteen I also ran my own profitable business as a sign painter. I eventually had my own shop, station wagon, and part-time helpers. The demand was for a generalist rather than specialist, so "sign painter" really also sometimes meant commercial artist, gilder, advertising consultant, electric-sign salesman, billboard designer, sign fabricator and erector, calligrapher, show-card writer, silkscreen printer, and so on. Rather than tell a customer I couldn't do such-and-such, I would try to buy time to phone in an order for an instruction book and supplies, and then strive to be a quick learner.

I have often drawn on my early background in art, not only to provide illustrations to accompany investigative articles and books, but also as part of the investigative work itself (including subjects like the Shroud of Turin, spirit paintings, and other mysteries having some artistic component).

During college I majored in art, then English, and became active in the civil-rights and antiwar movements. I marched with Martin Luther King Jr., went south as a "community organizer" in the War on Poverty, and in 1967 was teargassed at the massive protest at the Pentagon (the subject of Norman Mailer's *Armies of the Night*). Late the following year I was living in Toronto as a federal fugitive—having refused to report for induction into the U.S. Army. My marriage also deteriorated and I eventually abandoned my unexciting job as an advertising writer to renew my interests in conjuring.

I was fortunate to get to know distinguished Canadian magicians like Sid Lorraine, ex-vaudevillian Harry Smith, and the talented young Doug Henning. Norman Houghton encouraged and tutored me and led me into the inner circle of mentalists, hypnotists, ventriloquists, and other allied artists.

My immersion in magic made me increasingly skeptical of paranormal claims. I had had a brief involvement with sixties' New Age pursuits, even doing Tarot-card readings for friends. However, as I had as a child, I noticed the tendency of people to interpret vague offerings as if they applied specifically to them—the so-called Barnum effect. Now I also saw how dishonest tricksters flourished in a climate of credulity, and I came to a deeper appreciation of Harry Houdini's use of his magician's knowledge and skills to expose phony paranormal claimants, including several spiritualist mediums.

I began my conjuring career as a magic pitchman in the carnival of the Canadian National Exhibition in 1969, working at a booth run by American magician Paul Diamond. I demonstrated and sold the seemingly miraculous magicians' "Svengali" deck of cards, the cut-and-restored rope trick, and the timeless effect known as the cups and balls, among other offerings. At this time, always attracted to the odd and curious, I also began studying the sideshows. I met "El Hoppo the Living Frog Boy" (depicted on a banner as a youth with a frog's hindquarters, but actually a gray-bearded man in a wheelchair, having a distended stomach and spindly limbs). I also witnessed "Atasha the Gorilla Girl," an attractive young lady who was transformed before the eyes of the crowd into a wild gorilla. Suddenly the beast shook open the cage door and lunged at the spectators, whose flight from the tent helped draw the next crowd (or "tip" in carny parlance). Of course the paranormal metamorphosis was a magician's illusion, and "Atasha" was slyly billed as being in "a legerdemain condition." I found the midway a wonderful skeptics' school that I continue to study in to this day.

From my instructive magical debut in the carnival world, I was soon coproducing a CBC radio special, "Houdini in Canada," for which I participated in a séance to contact the magician's spirit. (That ritual, often performed since his death on Halloween 1926, grew from an agreement between him and his wife, Beatrice, that the first to die would attempt to contact the other. The pact has led some to believe Houdini was a spiritualist, but a poster for his antimedium crusade is unequivocal: "Do Spirits Return? Houdini Says No—and Proves It.")

Work on the Houdini special also introduced me to James Randi, Houdini's great successor as escape artist and psychic investigator. Norm Houghton had learned Randi was in town and called to ask him to help a young friend. Randi graciously agreed, and my coproducer and I also interviewed him for another, shorter program about the then paranormalist du jour, Ted Serios. (The ex-bellhop-turned-wonderworker appeared able to project mental images onto film in a Polaroid camera, producing "thoughtographs" of exotic places, people, and other subjects. Magicians and photo experts studied films of Serios at work and concluded he employed a small optical device—essentially a combined magnifying lens and photo transparency—concealed in his hand. Randi duplicated the Serios effect, only one of many such effective vanquishings in Randi's continuing career.)

Research for the Houdini special also took me to Niagara Falls, Ontario, and the Houdini Magical Hall of Fame. In interviewing the owner I soon found him interviewing me and, learning of my experience as a magic pitchman, inviting me to demonstrate my ability. I was hired on the spot and moved there to work each of the next three summers (1970, 1971, and 1972) as resident magician.

On one occasion—the museum's highly publicized acquisition of Houdini's famous water-torture cell—Randi came to do a straitjacket escape while hanging upside-down from a crane over Center Street. He was at the museum on other occasions, even serving as a consultant for part of one summer. I took every opportunity to tap his extensive knowledge of paranormal claims. The museum also brought me into contact with other magicians, mentalists, "psychics," spiritualists, and others.

After my first summer at Houdini's—made even more profitable by my creation of the museum's Houdini Magic Kit—a girlfriend and I traveled for a few months in Europe, Asia, and North Africa. I paid particular attention to nighttime fire-breathing and Houdini-style chain-escape performances in Paris, a "dancing" bear in Istanbul, a charming little old wandering conjurer in Barcelona, and various entertainers—including a snake charmer—in Marrakech.

During the remainder of each year I performed on the school circuit in Toronto as either Janus the Magician or (for the youngest children) as Mister Twister the Magic Clown or again (for the older junior-high group) Mendell the Mentalist. The latter was a Kreskin-type act in which I performed marvels of ESP, then confessed it was all a trick. Without explaining the actual secrets ("magicians' code," you know), I used the opportunity to teach skepticism to my impressionable spectators.

My experiences in magic and mentalism helped feed my growing interest in paranormal claims, and I eagerly read such important books as Martin Gardner's classic *Fads and Fallacies in the Name of Science* and Milbourne Christopher's *ESP, Seers and Psychics: What the Occult Really Is.* Christopher (who also wrote *Houdini: The Untold Story*) related his experiences as head of the Occult Investigation Committee of the Society of American Magicians.

Inspired by the examples of Randi, Christopher, and others, I was soon conducting my own investigations, focusing on a curious "devil-baby mummy" in 1971 (an obvious fake with glued-on hair), and the much-publicized "haunting" at Toronto's Mackenzie House in 1972. The latter, my first major case as a paranormal investigator, was most instructive. Among the reported phenomena were mysterious footfalls on the stairs, occasionally heard by the caretaker and his wife when the house was otherwise empty. I discovered that the heavy thudding footsteps came from a parallel iron stair-case in an adjacent building! Some other ghostly sounds were similarly trace-able, yet during a decade of reported phenomena no one—neither reporter, "ghost hunter," nor curiosity seeker—had bothered to inquire next door.

These experiences tapped another deep interest: detective work. As a youth, I had avidly read the Sherlock Holmes stories and had my own "crime lab" (chemistry apparatus, microscope, fingerprint equipment, etc.). In late 1972 I completed a correspondence course in civil and criminal identification and investigation and the following year left my professional career in magic to work as a licensed private investigator with an international detective bureau. (Taking a cue from a Dashiell Hammett novel, I'll call it the Continental Detective Agency.) The irony that, at the time, I was wanted by the FBI was not lost on the supervisors in the Toronto headquarters.

By this time I had discovered that—like George Plimpton, the partici-patory journalist, and Ferdinand Waldo Demara, "the Great Impostor"—I had a bent, and perhaps a knack, for playing various "roles." I saw them as unique windows from which to view life. Although I was better at some things than others, I placed the greatest premium on what I could learn from each. My new job as a gumshoe offered many such opportunities.

I conducted background investigations, fixed and moving surveillances, bodyguarding, and other assignments, including mostly undercover jobs. These included stints as a forklift driver, mail clerk, steelworker—even lens polisher and tavern waiter. Several times I was on the inside of criminal oper-ations, including becoming a member of a warehouse theft ring that I then set up for an apprehension.

Grand theft, arson, insurance fraud—the subject matter was far different from that of most paranormal investigations, but I soaked up everything I could learn about detective work, relishing long-night stakeouts with an older detective who was willing to recount his exploits and offer tips to a young person who was eager to hear them. I was twice promoted but, when I decided it was time to move on, it was his favorable comments about my work that were among the greatest rewards.

I next turned up in the far north, in Dawson City, Yukon Territory, where from mid-1975 to the fall of 1976 I played several additional roles. Originally hired by Diamond Tooth Gertie's casino and dance hall as a blackjack dealer, I also operated a crown-and-anchor (wheel of fortune) game there and served as part-time master of ceremonies. During the winter (characterized by temperatures that dropped to the minus-sixty-degree-Fahrenheit range), I took a correspondence course from the Canadian Museum Association while working as an exhibit designer at the gold-rush museum. The following summer I again worked evenings at the casino while also employed during the days as a riverboat manager and (as events re-quired) a newspaper "stringer."

My boss at Yukon River Tours, "Captain" Dick Stevenson, was an inveterate dowser. On many occasions—while we traveled around, either on business (operating a tourist boat, maintaining an outdoorsman's camp, or tending to his smoked-salmon enterprise), or pleasure (hunting spruce hens or panning for gold)—Dick would whip out his copper witching wands to see if he should prospect further.

More than once I expressed my skepticism of dowsing and soon, with Dick's help, I had arranged to test four local diviners, assembling them on one of the famous old gold-rush-era claims on Bonanza Creek. I administered a simple test, which involved target objects placed in uniform small boxes that I obtained from a Dawson gift shop. Afterward we congregated in a log cabin on the property to check the scores. One of the dowsers, "Arizona" Wilkes, jokingly leaned a rifle against a table and quipped that the results had better be favorable. They weren't: Despite their braggadocio, the dowsers could not differentiate between gold nuggets, fool's gold, chromium nuts and bolts, or empty boxes. Their failure answered the question one of them had earlier voiced (in so many words), "If we're so smart, why ain't we rich?"

Wearing my reportorial hat (so to speak) I pecked out the story on my portable typewriter and sent it by airplane some three hundred miles south to Whitehorse. After it appeared in *Yukon News* I encountered the group of dowsers in the El Dorado tavern. Undaunted, they rationalized that the boxes had somehow shielded out the "rays" emanating from the test materials. No doubt they were long accustomed to counting their hits and explaining away their misses, and they were not going to change on my account.

In 1977, after receiving an unconditional pardon from President Jimmy Carter—on his first full day in office—I returned to the United States. For the next year I attended Paul Stader's Hollywood stunt school. Stunting was not my most successful role but I did take part in a stunt show and worked as an extra in a couple of movies. A highlight of this period was tracking down my mother's first cousin, Don Turner, who had been a professional stuntman during Hollywood's great era. One of Erroll Flynn's stunt doubles, actually mentioned by Flynn in his autobiography, *My Wicked, Wicked Ways*, Don regaled me with behind-the-scenes accounts of swordplay, horse falls, and other adventures. At Stader's gym, where our class practiced fight scenes, tumbles, high falls, and other basics, I was able to meet several active stuntmen and -women who dropped by from time to time—professionals like Julius Le Flore, who doubled Bill Cosby for a terrific twelve-story-high fall in *A Piece of the Action*, and Rita Egleston, who doubled Lindsay Wagner in the *Bionic Woman* series. From this make-believe, yet dangerous world, I learned many useful lessons—lessons to add to those gleaned from magic—about the interaction of illusion and reality.

To pay the bills while I attended Stader's classes three times a week, I worked as an armed guard following firearms training and qualification at the U.S. School of Law Enforcement. From there I entered the proverbial "school of hard knocks" where lessons were taught by pickpockets, muggers, robbers, drunks, shoplifters, and others of their ilk.

Much of my free time during this period was spent in carrying out a major new investigation. I began to conduct experiments, and write articles about the results, concerning the notorious Shroud of Turin. Supposedly the burial cloth of Jesus, historically it first appeared in medieval France as part of a faith-healing scam—or so the local bishop reported to Pope Clement VII in 1389. However, photographs taken in 1898 revealed that the image on the shroud was a "negative" (the darks and lights effectively reversed). That supposedly discredited the bishop's claim that the forger had confessed, since no artist working in the mid-fourteenth century could have been expected to produce such a "photographic" feature.

I set out to investigate how the image might have been formed. I first experimented with the possibility that it was an imprint produced by simple contact, but the results demonstrated there would have been severe wraparound distortions. I also experimented with "vaporography" (the notion that body vapors interacted with burial spices on the cloth to produce a vapor "photo"), but the result was a hopeless blur, not a clearly defined image. Eventually, I discovered that remarkably similar negative images could be produced by a rubbing technique that utilized a bas-relief sculpture to minimize distortions and a powdered pigment to duplicate the image's minimal depth of penetration into the threads.

My first investigative reports on the "Shroud" were published by Paul Kurtz, then professor of philosophy at the University of Buffalo and editor of the *Humanist*. We thus began a professional relationship that continues to the present. (In 1983 his Prometheus Books published my *Inquest on the Shroud of Turin*. This was followed by other Prometheus titles, presently nine of my sixteen books.)

During this period, while I lived in West LA, I also made a trip to the eastern edge of the state to examine the giant, ancient Indian ground drawings known as the Blythe Intaglios. I had begun working on a plan to recreate one of the even-larger Nazca figures in Peru, effigies so huge they can be seen only from the air, thus prompting crank notions they were created by "ancient astronauts." Arriving by bus in Blythe in 1978, I enlisted an Indian guide: a Native American cabdriver who knew where the landmarks were located and who was willing to take me there for a reasonable fee. However, he kept me waiting while he went on some unknown errand. When he eventually returned and I wondered aloud where he had been, he casually indicated a cooler he had had the foresight to fill with ice water. We were, after all, going into the Mojave Desert!

I later traveled for a while, and in Orlando, Florida, met forensic analyst

John F. Fischer, thus beginning another professional relationship, as well as a partnership that has involved us in many investigative exploits. We have worked together on a variety of forensic, historical, and paranormal cases, including "spontaneous human combustion," and the liquefying blood of San Gennaro. We have also coauthored numerous articles and books (most recently *Crime Science: Methods of Forensic Detection*, 1999).

In 1979, sensing the need to develop my research skills, improve my writing, and obtain scholarly credentials (to balance my checkered career), I returned to the University of Kentucky. There I worked as a teaching assistant while pursuing graduate studies in English Literature, including folklore, and received a master's in 1982 and doctorate in 1987. My dissertation focused on "literary investigation," including such cases as the disappearance of horror writer Ambrose Bierce, the "missing" edition of Ebenezer Cooke's eighteenth-century *Sot-weed Factor*, and the previously unidentified real-life model for the "Veiled Lady" in Nathaniel Hawthorne's *The Blithedale Romance*—all mysteries for which I provided solutions.

In the meantime, in 1982, I finally got around to reproducing the giant Nazca "condor" on a landfill near my childhood hometown, utilizing only materials and methods the ancient Nazca Indians might well have employed. Assisted by five family members, I laid out and marked the 440-foot-long figure, using only a pair of crossed sticks (for sighting) and two knotted lengths of cord (for measuring). We then flew over the area at about a thousand feet, the pilot banking the plane so my cousin John May could lean out and photograph our masterpiece straight-on, and me holding onto John's belt as a safety measure. *Scientific American* (June 1983) termed our drawing "remarkable in its exactness" to the original. Later our work was featured, with photos, in *Arthur C. Clarke's Chronicles of the Strange and Mysterious*.

My own report on our Nazca experiment represented my first article for *Skeptical Inquirer*, the official magazine of the Committee for the Scientific Investigation of Claims of the Paranormal (CSICOP). The following year, CSICOP named me one of its Scientific and Technical Consultants.

In 1988 at the instigation of Philip J. Klass, CSICOP's premier UFO expert, I was elected a Fellow and in 1993 became a member of the Executive Council. I was not at first certain I wanted to serve on the council, afraid it would divert time and energy from my main interest, investigation, but Randi took me aside and told me that the time had come for me to be centrally involved in the skeptical movement. Some time later, at a council meeting, I was expounding the view that CSICOP could do more to encourage the leaders of skeptics' groups and others who performed the myriad, often thankless tasks in the field. Warming to my subject, I mentioned how, once long ago, I had received a letter from Randi complimenting me on some of my investigations—a letter that, I said, kept me going for five years. Randi, who appeared to be "resting" but who was obviously taking in everything that transpired, opened one eye and quipped: "Remind me to send him a *ten*-year letter next time."

After receiving my doctorate, I stayed on at the university to teach technical writing, editing, and other subjects, and all during my time there continued to investigate paranormal claims, write articles and books, and appear on radio and television programs like *Larry King Live* (on crop circles), *Sally Jessy Raphael* (on ghosts), and the *Jerry Springer Show*. In fact, I appeared twice on *Springer* and lived to tell about it.

One of the episodes (March 16, 1992) featured "today's outrageous psychics." They included a pet prognosticator, an "aura" photographer, and the self-professed "world's greatest psychic," introduced as "Mr. B of ESP." With great fanfare he divined the contents of a padlocked and guarded refrigerator, supposedly utilizing his powers of X-ray clairvoyance. I was then brought on and my anger was palpable. I hinted at collusion. (Later, in the September 1999 *Skeptical Briefs*, I demonstrated that Mr. B's "hits" were not *visually* correct; for example, he mentioned a "carton" of milk but it was actually a jug, "apples" were in fact a single apple, and so on. Rather, the matches were only *cognitively* so, consistent with Mr. B having been verbally tipped off.)

As a consequence, I challenged Mr. B to a test, having brought with me a set of prepared envelopes in the event they were needed—as indeed they were. Mr. B failed to identify a single one of the three targets—simple three-letter words—and so I tore up my proffered $1,000 check. Although the audience was not on my side, I had nevertheless won a battle, and I have never more heard of the "world's greatest psychic."

Another case originated after I appeared on a special live broadcast of *Oprah* on Good Friday, 1995, to discuss miracles. There I met a daughter of Mario Rubio, the New Mexico woman who in 1978 discovered an image of Jesus (as she thought) in skillet burns on a tortilla. Such images, called *simulacra*, are usually the result of the mind's tendency to see patterns in randomness—the inkblot or pictures-in-the-clouds effect—but sometimes they are faked. After the show, as we waited in a limousine for a ride to the airport, I talked with a self-styled visionary who had also appeared on the program. She showed me a "miraculous" rose petal, bearing a likeness of Jesus, that supposedly came from the Philippines.

A preliminary inspection (with a penlighted loupe I always carry) made me suspicious, although I did not say so, of course. I did ask to borrow the object for further study. Later, stereomicroscopic examination with transmitted light showed that the markings, which were notably linear, were coincident with damage to the rose petal, while ordinary rose petals had no such markings. Experimentation with a blunt stylus enabled me to produce similar rose-petal portraits, and I concluded the questioned one was the result of a pious fraud, not an accident of nature. (See *Skeptical Inquirer*, November/December 1997.)

All during my time at the university, I worked closely with Dr. Robert A. Baker, a distinguished psychologist and author of such definitive books as *They Call It Hypnosis* and *Hidden Memories*. We collaborated on many projects, including investigating several hauntings. At one farmhouse in Indiana, where there were noisy disturbances, we had to have a little amnesty for the "ghost." A young boy, who was being gently interrogated by Dr. Baker, blurted out, "You aren't going to tell on me, are you?" As a result of such revelations, my great friend and fellow ghostbuster is fond of saying, "There are no haunted houses, only haunted people." He and I combined our talents and experiences to produce a paranormalistic handbook, *Missing Pieces: How to Investigate Ghosts, UFOs, Psychics, and Other Mysteries.*

CSICOP brought me to Buffalo in 1995 as Senior Research Fellow, launching a new phase of my career. Able to devote full time to the investigation of paranormal claims, I began a column for *Skeptical Inquirer* and also for our newsletter, *Skeptical Briefs*, called "Investigative Files." One such column (January/February 1997) resulted from my appearance on the *Mark Walberg Show* where a self-claimed psychic sleuth told an incredible tale. He boasted the psychic solving of over 110 murder cases, notably the Harrison, New York, deaths of two young women found suffocated in trash bags tied with rope.

The "psychic" claimed to have used a key found on one victim to locate a site in the south Bronx, unlock a door, and thus discover the murderer. I contacted one of the lead investigators on the "Bag Murder Case" and learned the true particulars. The key in question had not led the psychic anywhere; it simply took police to the apartment of one victim. In time the case was solved, the detective said, "due to diligent police work, not visions."

Another column (March/April 1997) featured my investigation of a "weeping icon" at the request of the *Toronto Sun*. A reporter called to tell me that they had been granted permission to actually examine the icon that evening. I packed my "weeping-icon kit"—containing stereomicroscope, camera with close-up lenses, various evidence-collection materials, and (I joke) a roast-beef sandwich, plus (no joke) a copy of my *Looking for a Miracle*. Alas, when we arrived at the small Greek Orthodox church, a line of pilgrims stretched far into the night and we were told the deal was off. I decided to bypass the line and rushed inside with a photographer following, striding past a woman who shouted, "Two dollars fifty cents"; I shouted back, "*Toronto Sun!*" and kept going.

Although I was not permitted to collect samples or even make a close inspection, I nevertheless observed that the flows were static, viscous, and (from a greasy-looking area where one rivulet was smeared) "suspiciously oily," I told the *Sun*. I was mindful of the trick of applying a nondrying oil (like olive oil) that will remain fresh looking indefinitely. I was also quoted as concluding that the phenomenon appeared "more carnival sideshow than miracle." It turned out that the priest, who had also preached at a church in the Bronx when an icon there "wept" a few years earlier, had been defrocked for running a brothel in Athens! I was invited to return to the church a year later, after the parent religious authority regained control of the church. This time, with a fraud-squad detective beside me and two constables posted outside, and with the major Canadian news media present, I took samples of the "tears" for the police crime lab. Much later, I learned from a laboratory official (whom I met at a forensic conference I addressed in Nova Scotia) that the substance was indeed a nondrying oil as I had suggested. However, the case went nowhere since it could not be proved who had actually placed the oil on the icon.

Another case required my immediate appearance in New York City. I was to view a video of an alleged telepathic interview with an alien at Area 51 (I don't make this stuff up) and to appear that evening (July 1, 1997) on the tabloid TV show *Extra*. Could I, a producer asked, catch a plane right away and bring my "Alien Timeline" chart (depicting the evolution of the mythological humanoid)? I could: I keep a small combination overnight bag/investigative kit in my car for such emergencies and was soon transported by plane and limo to the studio. (I have a dimmer memory of the overall taping, in which I described the questionable elements of the obviously bogus video, than I do a particular moment: suddenly the interviewer gave me a look of horror, and I just had time to wonder what for, when a toppling cast-iron light struck me on the head, knocking me out of my chair. I nursed a headache that evening, but did receive a nice filet-mignon dinner with wine as well as profuse apologies.

In addition to such cases that can prompt immediate attention, I also try to work the "cold case files" (to borrow a term from police parlance), unsolved mysteries like that of Nova Scotia's Oak Island. I researched the lost-treasure tale on an investigative expedition through Canada's maritime provinces in 1999 (see *Skeptical Inquirer* January/February, March/April 2000). My proposed solution to the case—that the tale was a Masonic "secret vault" allegory—would rely mostly on library research and the piecing together of many clues gleaned both before and after my trip. But I did want to set foot on the island and possibly talk to its controversial resident.

Referring to that man's legendary temper and an altercation involving a rifle, the island's security officer told me it would not be safe to trespass on the site. Indeed the causeway bridging Oak Island to the mainland is chained off and marked "Private/No Hunting or Trespassing/Danger." But a local fisherman said, "He won't shoot you, but he will probably turn you back." I decided to chance it. Halfway across the land bridge I encountered a barking dog, but the fisherman yelled to me, "She won't hurt you," and I was soon on the island petting her when the owner strode up. He listened to my excuses and finally asked my name. When I told him, he said, not encouragingly, "I read about you." He was obviously referring to a Canadian Press story that had circulated widely. The tongue-in-cheek article in Canadian newspapers advised:

> Maritimers better lock up their ghosts and keep mum about that favourite aunt or uncle who died in the flames of spontaneous human combustion.
> Professional skeptic Joe Nickell is touring the region . . . and not a lake monster, a beloved spectre or even the Oak Island treasure is safe from the penetrating glare of his cold, hard logic.

Nevertheless, I soon mollified the man and he graciously invited me to his home for an evening's study of artifacts, photos, papers, and a video made by lowering a camera down a borehole—the fruits of nearly thirty-five years of pursuing one of "the great mysteries of the world," as one writer termed it.

Paranormal investigation may occasionally seem more dangerous than it really is. However, I did have a moment's panic once when—at a Virgin Mary apparition site in Kentucky, attended by thousands of pilgrims—one young man pointed at me and declared, "It's him!" The Learning Channel film crew I was with rushed forward with me to shush the fellow before an ugly scene developed. As it happened, he had just seen me on television in Atlanta, recounting the results of a couple of days spent undercover at another Marian site. There, with the invaluable assistance of Georgia Skeptics, I had explained the "miraculous" phenomena typical of such sites.

I guess the worst that has befallen me as a P.I. was a badly broken leg—followed by botched surgery—in Spain in early September 1997. During the course of participating in a European skeptics conference there, I had just been to the cathedral at Santiago de Compostela, the end point of a famous pilgrimage that Shirley MacLaine went on for her book *The Camino*. The cathedral is built over the reputed relics of Saint James (one of Jesus' apostles), and a statue of the martyr is reputed to have special powers of protection and healing. Alas, although I had stood in the line that wound up stone stairs behind the statue and had hugged it as tradition directs, I was protected at best only briefly. I did escape injury when I tempted fate to step up on a narrow ledge to get a better photo, but later, merely strolling down the steps of my hotel in La Coruña, I slipped and broke both bones of my right leg completely in two, leaving my foot at a bizarre angle.

Most of my investigations have been less painful. I did recently inflict "stigmata" on myself with a sharp blade as part of an investigation into that phenomenon. And I risked infiltrating a spiritualistic circle, which met on regular occasions at a "haunted" mansion. I was welcomed as one with "good energies." At a table-tipping séance conducted by a professional medium for the group, I received loving messages from an aunt and uncle—both nonexistent.

I usually expect the worst in an investigation but am often happily surprised. So it was with my trip to West Virginia to review the 1952 mystery of the Flatwoods UFO monster. Would the locals be clannish and distant, even hostile, to an "outsider"? As I entered the village, a sign proclaimed, "Welcome to Flatwoods/Home of the Green Monster," helping to allay my trepidations. True, when I tracked down two of the original "monster" eyewitnesses they refused an interview, but others involved in the case could not have been more cordial and cooperative—photocopying material for me, taking me to the site of the alien encounter reported half a century before, even inviting me to supper. As I eventually concluded, the "monster" was indeed a frightening nocturnal creature—especially to several schoolboys and a local beautician—but it did not ride in on the meteor that initiated the comedy of errors. (See *Skeptical Inquirer*, November/December 2000.)

At one time or another I have caught hoaxers, exposed psychic tricksters and phony miraculists, obtained police warrants against a spiritualist, and challenged mystery mongers of all sorts, but I have also listened carefully and sympathetically to those who believe they have had a paranormal experience. I have slept in haunted inns, examined English crop circles, experienced "healing" therapies, and visited "miracle" sites in several states and countries.

I have collected samples from a "bleeding" door at a "haunted" farmhouse, used a stethoscope to listen for reported heartbeats in statues at a Marian site, experimentally replicated photos of supposed ghosts, hired a local guide to take me on a jet-ski search for a fabled lake monster, and gone aloft in a hot-air ballon to look for another—among countless other activities.

Over the span of three decades of paranormal research, I have striven to take a hands-on, investigative approach, decrying a debunking attitude as well as a too-credulous one. I believe mysteries should neither be dismissed nor hyped, but instead should be carefully investigated with the intent of solving them. Compared to armchair debunking, I believe case-by-case investigation is more likely to uncover the truth and to invite the confidence of others. I know it is the more adventurous approach.

REFERENCES

Baker, Robert A. 1996. *Hidden Memories: Voices and Visions from Within*. Amherst, N.Y.: Prometheus Books.

———. 1990. *They Call It Hypnosis*. Amherst, N.Y.: Prometheus Books.

Baker, Robert A., and Joe Nickell. 1992. *Missing Pieces: How to Investigate Ghosts, UFOs, Psychics, and Other Mysteries*. Amherst, N.Y.: Prometheus Books.

Christopher, Milbourne. 1969. *Houdini: The Untold Story*. New York: Thomas Y. Crowell.

———. 1970. *ESP, Seers and Psychics: What the Occult Really Is*. New York: Thomas Y. Crowell.

Fairley, John, and Simon Welfare. 1987. *Arthur C. Clarke's Chronicles of the Strange and Mysterious*. London: William Collins Sons.

Flynn, Errol. 1959. *My Wicked, Wicked Ways*. New York: Putnam.

Gardner, Martin. 1957. *Fads and Fallacies in the Name of Science*. New York: Dover.

MacLaine, Shirley. 2000. *The Camino: A Journey of the Spirit*. New York: Pocket Books.

Mailer, Norman. 1968. *The Armies of the Night; History as a Novel, the Novel as History*. London: Weidenfeld and Nicolson.

Milbourne, Christopher. 1970. *ESP, Seers and Psychics*. New York: Crowell.

——. 1969. *Houdini: The Untold Story*. New York: Crowell.

Nickell, Joe. 1983. *Inquest on the Shroud of Turin*. Amherst, N.Y.: Prometheus Books.

——. 1993. *Looking for a Miracle*. Amherst, N.Y.: Prometheus Books.

Nickell, Joe, and John F. Fischer. 1999. *Crime Science: Methods of Forensic Detection*. Lexington: University Press of Kentucky.

JOE NICKELL is CSICOP's Senior Research Fellow. A former professional stage magician, private investigator, and academic, he is the author (or coauthor or editor) of seventeen books. He investigates paranormal claims worldwide and writes the "Investigative Files" column for *Skeptical Inquirer* and *Skeptical Briefs*.

18

DIARY OF A CANADIAN DEBUNKER

HENRY GORDON

Author's note: This is a recounting of some of my experiences in the wacky world of the paranormal. As we know, our memories can be somewhat unreliable, so all that follows has been dredged up from my voluminous collection of documents, audiotapes, and videos. I've attempted to establish a chronological order to this "diary," but have probably strayed from the path here and there. In any case, the "facts" are there.

When I first became interested in the pseudosciences and the paranormal I took a different tack from their supporters, who often claimed to have been skeptics until they saw the light. Midway through the twentieth century I was a semibeliever. I wasn't too sure about UFOs. I thought von Däniken might have something there. Other claims also got me thinking.

But then I had some doubts. So I haunted the bookshops, searching for some literature that might answer my questions. Where were you, Paul Kurtz and Prometheus Books, when I needed you? Finally, success. In 1952 I found Martin Gardner's *In the Name of Science*, later published as *Fads and Fallacies*. Then, in the same year, came D. H. Rawcliffe's *The Psychology of the Occult*. My perspective changed.

My next step was to buy every book I could find by those who supported everything from ESP to UFO sightings to astrology, and so on. No shortage of material there. My object? The old business practice of learning what the opposition was doing. I haunted a very popular "spiritual" bookshop across the street from McGill University in my hometown of Montreal, and cut down expenses by perusing the books for hours at a time. What would usually hasten my departure was the smell of incense on the premises.

After a few years of study I had the temerity to go public, writing a weekly debunking column for a small local paper, the *Suburban*. But then came my first opportunity to inform the general public about some of the hanky-panky going on by the occultniks. On November 1, 1960, I was interviewed on the evening news, aired by the Canadian Broadcasting Corporation (CBC). The anchor, and my interviewer, at that time was a young man by the name of Peter Jennings. Yes, the same Peter Jennings who is the ABC anchor on the evening news. I was able to get that opportunity only because, as a professional magician, I had already done a couple of thirteen-week series on magic for the CBC, so the contacts were there. You might say that I got into my TV-debunking career through the back door. And, incidentally, at a much later date I was interviewed on Toronto's City TV by J. D. Roberts, who is now known as John Roberts, and who anchors the CBS evening news when Dan Rather is away. Amazing how these Canadians progress in the United States.

It really wasn't until 1966 that my broadcasting career really took off. I was on every available public affairs show in Canada, many on the CBC national network, the CTV national network, and others on local Montreal, Toronto, and Vancouver stations. These covered both radio and television, and are too numerous to list here—but I would like to mention just a few, which I believe attracted particular public attention.

In 1966 the popular CBC program *Seven on Six* had me on for about seven minutes. This was my first chance to go into a real debunking mode. In 1969 the media was beginning to take notice of the growing public interest in the paranormal, and I appeared on *The Occult*, also on the CBC. Nineteen seventy-five saw my first of several appearances on *Canada-AM*, on the CTV national network—a program that is still running daily.

In 1977 I was featured in my first series of programs, thirteen weeks on CBC network's prime TV program *Morningside*. That was a great opportunity to assert my skeptical views to a much larger audience. Other TV and radio series followed on local Montreal stations.

Andy Barrie, one of Canada's top radio broadcasters, was hosting a popular morning show in 1977, on CJAD, Montreal. Being a magician and a skeptic himself, he had me guesting on his program several times. He would sometimes broadcast from a leading downtown restaurant during the breakfast hour. One day he called me with a suggestion: "How about coming down there tomorrow morning and have me introduce you as a psychic, under an assumed name? We can talk about some of your great accomplishments and have you do one of your so-called psychic feats right on air and in front of the audience." This was some time after I had done my highly publicized stage performance as a psychic (more on that later).

I appeared at the restaurant wearing dark glasses and sitting beside Andy under dim lighting—because I was concerned about being recognized. The psychic feat I performed was to have Andy hold an empty wine glass, and then have it shatter at my command, ostensibly by psychokinesis. It worked. One of my better magical miracles, I must confess. The restaurant audience, too, was shattered. Andy was at the same time describing the happening over the air. He then asked the breakfasters what they thought of the visiting psychic. The applause was loud and unanimous.

After the final commercial break Andy informed the stunned audience, "You've been had. This is Henry Gordon, our well-known Montreal magician, who makes the point that you can all be taken in by this type of fakery." There was desultory applause as we went off air.

In the 1960s and 1970s, Allen Spraggett, a Canadian, was considered one of the continent's leading authorities as a proselytizer of all things paranormal. He had written books on the subject, was in constant demand as a speaker, and had a series of highly rated TV programs. In the 1970s and 1980s, Pierre Berton was hosting an outstanding series of syndicated TV shows titled *The Great Debate*, where well-known politicians, medical people, and so on, were pitted against each other, with the studio audience voting for the winner. When I was invited to appear against Spraggett in 1978 I was strongly advised by friends to decline. They justifiably felt that I couldn't cope with his deep experience and knowledge of the subject. So I decided to accept—and won the debate.

I was asked back in 1982 and managed to top another paranormalist named Howard Eisenberg, who was actually a tougher opponent than Spraggett. These debates led to media requests for me to appear on other programs and do *my* proselytizing.

The TV program that I found the most stimulating was *The Shulman File*, a long-running program on Toronto's City-TV station. The host was Morty Shulman, an acerbic, straight-from-the-mouth, no-nonsense type. Shulman was a physician, and had been Toronto's coroner. He brooked no nonsense from guests. Many leading politicians would not appear on his show because he would strongly challenge some of their mouthings. Several walked off the set during airings. So, when I was invited on the show I was relieved to find that Morty was a confirmed skeptic.

I was on the show a few times in the 1980s, usually with a few paranormalists. There was one time that I recall having a supporter, other than Shulman, around the table. And that was Paul Kurtz who, of course, needed no supporting. But the highlight, for me, was the evening when UFOlogist Stanton Friedman delivered one of his patented UFO lectures at Shulman in answering a question. When he finally finished, Shulman leaned toward him and said, "I've never heard such a pile of s——t in my life." My videotape of that program is a collector's item.

Those of us who are practicing skeptics know that many believers do not like to hear our opinions. It can be irritating to their belief systems—and understandably so. That point was brought home to me one day when I participated on CBC-Radio's long-running *Radio Noon*, on which we had a different theme each time I was on. On introducing me, the host announced, "We're going to talk about ghosts today, and here is Henry Gordon who has come to spoil our day again." He meant it to be tongue-in-cheek, but I assume there was some truth in the statement.

Most of the phone-ins were people who believed they had seen a ghost and wanted explanations—which was the usual procedure. But when I left the studio at the close of the show, the receptionist gave me the phone number and name of a woman who had asked that I phone her privately. She did not wish to call on air, knowing her voice would be recognized. She turned out to be one of Toronto's best-known city councillors. (My wife, Zita, and I were already residing in Toronto at that time.) She asked if perhaps I would like to visit her home and do some ghostbusting. It seems that a deceased relative was visiting, and she was looking for some explanations. I did visit, heard the details, ventured some explanations, was thanked, and left with the usual feeling that the woman's belief system would survive my rational reasoning.

My very first electronic media guesting in the United States was on the *Larry Glick Show* on WBZ radio in Boston in 1983. It was evidently a popular Larry King-type phone-in show at the time. Glick had called me at Salem, Massachusetts, where I was doing theatrical presentations for several weeks. (Again, more on that later.) I was back with Larry Glick a few months later.

Subsequently, the U.S. media market opened up for me. Many appearances on the *People Are Talking* TV show for the Westinghouse Group. Philadelphia, Baltimore, Boston in 1986. Boston again in 1987. Secaucus, New Jersey, in 1988. On one of these programs I was introduced as a psychic, did my schtick, and fooled the audience. The host, of course, was in on the spoof, and was about to reveal who I actually was when I interrupted him and volunteered to do a reading on him. He, of course, didn't object, thinking he would go along with it. But when I began to tell him some personal things about himself that I couldn't have possibly known—for example, that one of his eyes had been affected because he had been a forceps delivery when born, his jaw dropped until it almost hit his chest. When he finally told the audience and the viewers who I was, and the studio audience asked the usual questions, he kept interrupting to ask me how I could have known these facts about him. Well, as a psychic I would have said that the vision came to me, but as a debunker I revealed that, before entering the studio, I had merely questioned a few of the program's assistants and was lucky enough to find one who knew him personally, and who was kind enough to cooperate with some very useful information. In previous attempts like this, I had never been so fortunate as to be able to get information all the way back to a person's birth. Of such miracles do psychics make their reputations.

As far as I know, I was the only magician to participate on a one-hour TV program facing off with Uri Geller. He always kept clear of magicians, knowing they could embarrass him by explaining his "psychic" feats. Geller was to appear on WBZ-TV Boston in 1987 during a U.S. tour in which he had appeared with Larry King and other talk-show hosts—where he made believers out of them with his compass needle-moving effect. The program's producer called me in Toronto and asked if I could come on the program. I informed him that Geller would cancel if he heard of a magician coming on the show. Not to worry, he said, he'd tell Geller's agent that I was a columnist (which I was). Convenient to wear more than one hat.

I flew down; they smuggled me in a back door, and kept me away from the Green Room. Meanwhile, I cautioned the producer that when he gave Geller a couple of watches to resuscitate he should be sure that they were really defective.

As Uri and I sat side by side on a sofa, with a compass resting on a small table in front of us, we exchanged pleasantries. Somehow he had learned that I was a magician, but that was after the program had begun, and he accepted the fact gracefully. Then he went into his act, bent over the compass, grunting and waving his hands over it. But the needle stayed motionless. He expressed some surprise, and tried again. The compass refused to cooperate with Uri's mind power. The program's host changed the subject by handing him two watches to will back to life. This he couldn't do, but said he'd try again later.

After a break, Geller insisted on getting back to compass-busting. He had someone in his retinue bring in another compass, which was probably part of his traveling stock. But again, no luck. He was getting really disturbed. I suggested, "Uri, maybe your magnet isn't strong enough." "Magnet, what magnet?" he exploded, then returned to the watches. No success there either.

When we were about to go off air he insisted on getting back to the compass. No luck. His last words were, "I've been blocked!" He was. The powerful magnet I had strapped above my knee, under my slacks, was much stronger than his, and had already locked in the needle.

The two television programs which gave me the opportunity to present my rational views to a mass audience were during 1988, when I appeared on the *Oprah Winfrey* show and on Sally Jessy Raphael's program. On *Oprah* I debated with a couple of psychics and with a leading channeler. On *Sally Jessy* I argued with a couple who were supposed to be ghostbusters, but who were the usual type of ghost *creators*.

The foregoing were just a few of the highlights of radio and television programs I was on from 1960 until the late 1990s—close to 550 in all. Many of the radio appearances were by telephone from my office while plugging two of my books published by Prometheus Books, with Barry Karr setting up stations in almost every major city in the United States. We really did spread the skeptical word around.

In the 1970s Zita and I were hired to perform a magic act on several Holland America Lines cruises. Once on these ships, I was able to influence the cruise director to have me do a debunking lecture at least once on each cruise. It proved to be very successful, particularly when sailing through the Bermuda Triangle.

When CSICOP was formed in 1976 it opened new worlds for me. Up to that time I had been completely on my own. I knew of no other informed skeptics. There were no skeptical groups that I was aware of. In 1978 Paul Kurtz and Ray Hyman came to Montreal to attend a skeptical symposium at Concordia University in which I also participated. I subsequently became a CSICOP Scientific and Technical Consultant, and we arranged to set up a Canadian CSICOP branch. On July 13 of that year we had a highly publicized conference in Toronto, with CSICOP's executive council attending, in which CSICOP Canada was announced. This was the first time the Canadian public was informed of the existence of CSICOP. This group functioned for a couple of years, but then we later formed the Ontario Skeptics, and then other skeptical groups sprang up in this country, as they did around the world.

In 1979, in Montreal, I happened to be on a TV program that was seen by Dr. Leo Yaffe, a true skeptic who also happened to be the vice principal of McGill University. He phoned me to ask if I'd be interested in teaching a course on pseudoscientific subjects at McGill. I certainly was. "An Objective Inquiry into Psychic Phenomena" became an instant success at McGill. It continued into 1981 and probably would have run a few more years if Zita and I had not moved to Toronto during that year. To my knowledge that was the first course of its kind at a major university, but I certainly could stand corrected on that score. I did not attempt to contact any university in Toronto to continue teaching, because I was now involved in a new journalistic career.

My career as a columnist for a major city newspaper started in 1980 when I began writing a debunking column titled "ExtraSensory Deception" (later, the title of my first book for Prometheus). While in Toronto for a CBC-TV appearance, I dropped in to see the managing editor of the *Toronto Sun*, trying to interest him in publishing a debunking column. Not an easy thing to do. However, I did arouse some interest, and he asked that I send him a few sample columns when I returned to Montreal. I did, and got the job—mailing in my weekly columns.

Here again, I believe this was a first on this continent. And, here again, I could be wrong. But, with the media's propensity to push the paranormal, columns of this kind are few and far between, if they do exist at all. This column ran for almost two years, but the duration of a column usually lasts until its editor is replaced by someone of a different mind.

Ensconced in Toronto in 1981, I dropped in to the huge building housing the *Toronto Star*, Canada's biggest newspaper, and met with Gerry Hall, the editor of the *Sunday Star*. There was no space available for a column, but, as a freelancer, I was able to send in the odd feature article on the paranormal, superstitious beliefs, and so on. After establishing my credentials I was lucky enough to be assigned a space for a weekly column. Discussing a possible title for the column, I suggested a couple of mild ones, not wanting to rub some readers the wrong way. But Hall was not one to equivocate. "Let's call it 'Debunking.'" And we did. All of the columns are reprinted in Prometheus Books's *ExtraSensory Deception*. The column ran for three years—until Gerry was moved to a different department. The new editor, as is usual, cancelled the weekly column, but asked me to continue writing columns and features at irregular intervals. I am still writing for the *Toronto Star* as a freelancer, long after most of the regular editors are no longer with the paper. This doesn't give me any particular satisfaction, because most of the younger crop don't even know who I am. The world turns.

I've had some interesting experiences with the *Star*. There was the time I wrote two columns criticizing the chiropractic profession. The people from their college were up in arms and complained to the publisher. A meeting was arranged, including Gerry Hall, myself, the *Star* ombudsman, and the chiropractic people. They even brought their lawyer. After two solid hours of argument (which I taped) the ombudsman, slowly slumping behind his desk, finally asked them what they wanted. A retraction by me. No retraction, he said—what I wrote was accurate. They were granted a letter to the editor. They sent two of them—all packed with inaccuracies. The letters were published. The letters, and the tape, are among my souvenirs.

And then, there was the Benny Hinn matter, when this master manipulator of the evangelical stage brought one of his crusades to Toronto's Maple Leaf Gardens for a packed house of thousands. The *Star*'s religion editor asked if I'd accompany him and write a piece on the evening's event. The three-hour frenzy was something to behold. After two hours, the editor could take no more, and left me alone to carry on. I stayed to the bitter end, took notes, and taped all of the questionable proceedings. My scathing writeup, along with photos, took up an entire page of the *Star*. A couple of weeks later I had a call from—guess who—the ombudsman, and a letter in the mail. Hinn was threatening to sue the publisher, the religion editor—and me. As requested, I sent the ombudsman a summary of everything I had criticized—all of which I had on tape. I spoke to the paper's lawyer a few days later and asked if he thought they'd sue. He said, "I hope they try." They didn't. The Benny Hinn Crusade still comes to Maple Leaf Gardens regularly. And packs in the believers. Sad.

Previous to my radio appearance as a psychic in the late 1970s, I had pulled one of the most-publicized hoaxes ever staged in Montreal. I was able to convince the manager of the popular Saidye Bronfman Theatre that if he advertised me as a psychic appearing on his stage he'd have a packed house. He cooperated fully, advertising heavily, claiming that an unknown psychic who had been tested in European and American university parapsychology labs would be making his first public appearance on his stage. The theatre was deluged with calls from local radio and TV stations requesting interviews when I arrived in town. We had to turn them down, because I was personally too well known to the public, and it wasn't practical for me to appear in disguise and speak in a foreign accent for each booking, as I would do onstage.

Came the big evening in the summer of 1977, and the auditorium was packed. Management had to supply extra seating wherever space was available. A nervous Henry Gordon strode out onstage as Elchonen and proceeded to deliver a brief lecture and then to perform a series of psychic miracles. My years of conjuring experience stood me in good stead. The audience was overwhelmed. Remember, it consisted of a majority of believers who had attended the performance to reinforce their own belief systems. When I returned to the stage after an intermission, to explain the reason for this hoax, I was sans disguise and accentless. I then didn't have to reveal my little secret, because most of the assembly recognized who I was. Some were indignant at being taken in—others accepted it good-naturedly. I then did a few ESP demonstrations to round out the performance. Next day, the *Star*, Montreal's leading newspaper, carried a huge story on the event, with a front-page banner showing a photo of me in disguise with another of my normal visage. The *Gazette* also had a special feature with a huge photo. CBC-TV national network carried an interview a couple of days later. Details of this story were published in Prometheus Books's *Extra-Sensory Deception*.

I had earlier mentioned being in Salem, Massachusetts, in 1983. I had been called by the president of the John Proctor Society, a skeptical group, and was asked to do a series of stage presentations in Salem outlining the development of witchcraft, with the opportunity of debunking paranormal claims, and presenting some magic of my own. It sounded great, so I accepted. Zita and I were provided with a cottage on the bay and a car, and we settled down for a few summer weeks. Shows were staged at the Salem Theater several times a week.

But there were a few problems. The society printed large, expensive, four-color posters and put them up all over town. The next day they would disappear. This happened more than once. One day I was contacted and asked if I could attend a meeting of the city council. It seemed that I wasn't particularly welcomed in "Witch City." They wanted to know if I had a hidden agenda in coming to Salem. They were finally satisfied that I did not. One must understand: the economy of Salem depends an awful lot on the witchcraft history of the town, which makes it a major tourist attraction in the United States. Our visit ended on a happy note.

The "Shirley MacLaine" phase of my career occurred during the middle 1980s. This famous movie star and entertainer embarked on a side career of pushing the paranormal with a series of nonsensical books, personal appearances, and TV and radio talk shows. I immediately took enough interest in this phenomenon to begin audio- and videotaping every program I could catch her on. I bought every one of her books and read them from cover to cover—not an easy thing to do. The reading, that is, not the buying.

It was obvious that she was building quite a following among the public. And when she appeared with Larry King and on other prestigious programs, she was never asked the hard questions. They merely fawned over this impressive personality. I certainly never expected to have an opportunity to interview her personally, one on one. This sort of thing never happened to a comparatively unknown journalist. However, the skeptical gods must have been smiling on me. On a visit to Toronto to flog one of her books on a CBC-TV interview, the *Toronto Star* was able to arrange for me to interview her right after the program. That tape is another in my assortment of collector's items.

With all the MacLaine material I had accumulated, I realized that I had enough to write a book, met with Paul Kurtz, and Prometheus Books published *Channeling into the New Age: The "Teachings" of Shirley MacLaine and Other Such Gurus*. I don't believe Shirley is my biggest fan. When she did a tour of Australia with her stage show, she was interview by a leading columnist. He had asked her what she thought of my book. She answered that I was making a living out of criticizing her, and left no doubt about what she thought about me. Moneywise, I'd trade livings with her anytime. The column was sent to me by one of our Australian Skeptics buddies. Yep, another item for my collection. And, believe it or not, Shirley has not retired from the paranormal scene. I have her latest book. In two words, it's unbelievably idiotic. And it's on the *New York Times* best-seller list. I concede defeat.

My most interesting experiences as a columnist have been with the people I have interviewed. The sports personalities, about superstitions: John McEnroe, Jimmy Connors, Yogi Berra, and others. Paranormal personalities: Elizabeth Kübler-Ross; Edgar Casey's son, Hugh-Lynn Casey; J. B. Rhine; celebrated British "witch" Sybil Leek, in an interview that turned into a debate; Raymond Moody; and many others. Scientists: Tuzo Wilson, director-general, Ontario Science Centre; Isaac Asimov; Carl Sagan; Canadian Nobel Laureate John Polanyi; famed violinist Yehudi Menuhin, who had strong "spiritual" beliefs. Noted media guru Marshal McLuhan, whom I interviewed when he was the keynote speaker at a huge conference of parapsychologists and spiritualists in Montreal.

The assistance and information I've received from CSICOP during the past twenty-five years has been immeasurable. Residing just two hours from Buffalo has enabled me to have close contact with the staff over the years. Watching the construction of the Center for Inquiry building was a satisfying experience. And, in my humble opinion, CSICOP's spawning of skeptical groups all around the world is its crowning achievement.

CSICOP was the pioneer in organizing the battle against irrational thinking. But it is a never-ending one. Our goal in the future should be a concentrated effort to educate the average person in the use of critical thinking skills. A huge challenge—but worth pursuing.

HENRY GORDON is an author, a columnist, a broadcaster, a public speaker, and a magician. For many years he wrote columns for the *Toronto Sun*. He is a Fellow of CSICOP and president of the Toronto Skeptical Inquirers. In 1992 he received CSICOP's Responsibility in Journalism Award. Among his books are *Channeling into the New Age: The "Teachings" of Shirley MacLaine and Other Such Gurus* (1988), *ExtraSensory Deception* (1987), and *It's Magic!* (for children, 1989).

CREATIONISM

19

MY FAVORITE PSEUDOSCIENCE

EUGENIE SCOTT

Paul Kurtz's letter inviting me to contribute to this volume suggested that I describe "my own personal involvement" in the skeptical movement. My introduction to skepticism was a fascination with a particular pseudoscience, "creation science." From the day I first heard this phrase, I was hooked.

In 1971, I was a graduate student in physical anthropology at the University of Missouri. One day, my professor, Jim Gavan, handed me a stack of small, brightly colored, slick paper pamphlets from the Institute for Creation Research. "Here," he said, "Take a look at these. It's called 'creation science.'"

Wow. Here I was studying to be a scientist, and here were people calling themselves scientists, but we sure weren't seeing the world the same way. They were looking at the same data: the same fossils, the same stratigraphy, the same biological principles, and so on. But from these data, creationists were concluding that all living things had appeared in their present form, at one time, a few thousand years ago. I was concluding that living things had branched off from common ancestors over scarcely imaginable stretches of time. They were concluding that the entire planet had been covered by water, and that all the present-day geological features of Earth had been determined by this flood and its aftermath. I couldn't see any evidence for this at all, and much evidence against it. Why were we coming up with such different conclusions? The data weren't all that different, but the philosophy of science and the approach to problem solving sure were.

I began collecting creation science literature as an academic enterprise: an interesting problem in the philosophy of science and critical thinking. Due to the pressures of graduate school and my first teaching job, I wasn't able to pursue it especially deeply, but students would occasionally bring up the topic. I would tell them that even if proponents of creation science claimed they were doing science, one cannot claim that one is doing science if one is doing something very different from what scientists are doing. Creation science was a good foil to use in teaching students about the nature of science.

Philosophers of science can—and do—argue incessantly over the definition of science. I don't know how many academic papers have been written attempting to solve the "demarcation problem": what qualifies as science and what does not. Some partisans even go so far as to claim that science is impossible to define. I confess to having little tolerance for such "how many angels can dance on the head of a pin" type discussions. In my present job as director of the National Center for Science Education, I regularly encounter the public's misunderstanding of the most basic elements of science. I deal with people who nod in agreement with a typical creationist statement that "neither evolution nor creationism is scientific because no one was there to observe it." I deal with people who agree with creation scientists stating that "evolution isn't scientific because evolutionists are always changing their minds." A very popular view is that we should "give the kids all the options" in a science classroom, and teach them both data demonstrating that evolution took place and "the evidence" for the "alternate theory" that God created everything at one time in its present form—two mutually exclusive views.

Against such a background, the philosopher's discussion of the nuances of the demarcation problem becomes an intellectual luxury far removed from what people need to hear. Doubtless to the frustration of my colleagues in the philosophy of science, my job requires me to simplify—probably beyond what they consider acceptable. But in doing so, I can make a little progress in helping the public to understand why science works, and also why creation science isn't science. Maybe down the road the nonscientists I encounter can tackle falsificationism and the demarcation problem; right now, I'd be happy if they understood two basic rules of science that I believe the majority of scientists would agree upon—however much they might disagree on others. And—more importantly for this discussion—creation science can be rejected as science based even on this simplest of understandings of what science is.

THE NATURE OF SCIENCE

There are two basic principles of science that creationism violates. First, science is an attempt to explain the natural world in terms of *natural* processes, not supernatural ones. This principle is sometimes referred to as *methodological naturalism*. In time, a consensus of how some aspect of nature works or came about is arrived at through testing alternate explanations against the natural world. Through this process, the potential exists to arrive at a truly objective understanding of how the world works.

Please allow a digression here. I am not presenting a cut-and-dried formula—"the scientific method"—as if the process of science were a lockstep algorithm. It's much untidier than that. Of course science reflects the time and culture in which it is found. Of course scientists, being human, have biases and make mistakes. Yet the growth of knowledge in a field is not the result of individual achievement, but rather is a function of a number of minds working on the same and different problems over time. It's a collective process, rather than being the result of actions of a solitary genius. Individual scientists may be biased, closed-minded, and wrong, but science as a whole lurches forward in spite of it all thanks to its built-in checks.

An important check is that explanations must be tested against the natural world. Thus there is an external standard against which a scientist's views are measured, regardless of his biases or the biases of his opponents. Unpopular ideas may take longer to be accepted, and popular ideas may take longer to be rejected, but the bottom line determining acceptance or rejection is whether the ideas work to describe, predict, or explain the natural world. The Soviet geneticist Lysenko foisted a Lamarckian (inheritance of acquired characteristics) theory of heredity upon the Soviet scientific establishment because Lamarckian genetics was more politically compatible with Marxism than was Mendelism. His politically biased science set Soviet genetics back a full generation, but today Russians employ Mendelian genetics, not Lysenkoism. Wheat raised in refrigerators doesn't grow any better in Siberia than regular wheat, and after a series of five-year plans gone bust, eventually the Soviet government figured out that Lysenko had to go. Mendelism works; Lysenkoism doesn't.

Science is nothing if not practical. The explanations that are retained are those that work best, and the explanations that work best are ones based on material causes. Nonmaterial causes are disallowed.

The second minimal principle of science is that explanations (which is what theories are) are tentative, and may change with new data or new theory. Now, don't misunderstand me: I am not claiming that all scientific explanations *always* change, because in fact some do not. Nonetheless, scientists must be willing to revise explanations in light of new data or new theory. The core ideas of science tend not to change very much—they might get tinkered with around the edges—whereas the frontier ideas of science may change a lot before we feel we understand them well.

Here then are two critical strictures on modern science: science must explain using *natural* causes, and scientists must be willing to change their explanations when they are refuted. Viewed in the light of these two basic tenets of science, creation science fails miserably.

EXPLAINING THROUGH NATURAL CAUSE

When a creationist says, "God did it," we can confidently say that he is not doing science. Scientists don't allow explanations that include supernatural or mystical powers for a very important reason. To explain something scientifically requires that we test explanations against the natural world. A common denominator for testing a scientific idea is to hold constant ("control") at least some of the variables influencing what you're trying to explain. Testing can take many forms, and although the most familiar test is the direct experiment, there exist many research designs involving indirect experimentation, or natural or statistical control of variables.

Science's concern for testing and control rules out supernatural causation. Supporters of the "God did it" argument hold that God is omnipotent. If there are omnipotent forces in the universe, by definition, it is impossible to hold their influences constant; one cannot "control" such powers. Lacking the possibility of control of supernatural forces, scientists forgo them in explanation. Only natural explanations are used. No one yet has invented a *theometer*, so we'll just have to muddle along with material explanations.

Another reason for restricting ourselves to natural explanations is practical. It works. We've gone a long way toward building more complete and we think better explanations through methodological naturalism, and most of us feel that if it ain't broke, don't fix it. Also, being able to say, "God (directly) did it" is a "science stopper," in the words of philosopher Alvin Plantinga (1997). To say, "God did it" means one does not need to look further for a natural explanation. For example, creationist literature abounds with criticisms of origin of life research. Because scientists have not yet reached a consensus on how the first replicating molecule came about, creationists argue, this is an intractable problem that should just be attributed to "God did it." Well, if we stop looking for a natural explanation for the origin of life, surely we will never find it. So even if we haven't found it yet, we must nonetheless slog on.

Creation science, for all its surface attempts (especially in its presentation to the general public) to claim to abide by a strictly scientific approach, relying solely on empirical data and theory, eventually falls back to violating this cardinal rule of methodological naturalism. Sometimes one has to go a bit deep in an argument, but eventually, as in the well-known Sidney Harris cartoon, "then a miracle occurs."

For example, to a creation scientist holding to Flood Geology, Noah's Flood was an actual historical event, and representatives of all land animals plus Noah, his wife, their sons, and their sons' wives were on a large boat. Q: *All* land animals? A: Sure. The Ark is the size of the *Queen Mary*. Q: But there are thousands of species of beetles, alone! How could *all* land animals be on the Ark? A: Oh, Noah didn't take two of every *species*. He took pairs of each *kind*, and kinds are higher taxonomic levels than species. Q: But how could only eight people take care of a *Queen Mary*-sized boat full of animals? How could they feed, water, and clean out the stalls? A: They didn't have that much work, because the rocking movement of the boat caused most of the animals to estivate, or go dormant, obviating the need for feeding, watering, and stall-cleaning. Q: But the Ark floated around for almost a year before landing! Small mammals such as mice and shrews have a high surface area:body mass ratio, and have to eat almost their weight in food each day just to keep their metabolism up. These animals couldn't have survived estivation. A: Well, then, a miracle occurred.

Push a creationist argument far enough, and sure enough, it will become necessary to resort to a miracle. But miracle-mongering cannot be part of science.

In addition to the familiar creation science that got me interested in this particular pseudoscience, in the last ten years or so a newer form of antievolutionism has made its appearance: "Intelligent Design" (ID) creationism. ID harkens back to the 1802 position of clergyman William Paley that structural complexity (such as the vertebrate eye for Paley or the structure of DNA for his latter-day bedfellows) is too complicated to have come about through a natural process. Therefore it must have been designed by an "intelligence." The "intelligence" of course is God, and attributing natural causality to a supernatural power of course violates methodological naturalism. Recognizing that methodological naturalism is the standard of modern science, ID proponents argue that it should be scuttled and replaced with what they call "theistic science," which possesses the enviable ability to invoke the occasional miracle when circumstances seem to require it (Scott 1998). ID proponents are content to allow methodological naturalism for the vast amount of science that is done; they wish to leave the possibility of supernatural intervention only for those scientific problems that have theological implications, such as the big bang, the origin of life, the appearance of "kinds" of animals (the Cambrian Explosion), and the origin of humans. The strength of methodological naturalism is perhaps best illustrated by its general acceptance by both the ID and creation science wings of the antievolution movement—except when it comes to religiously sensitive topics.

THE IMPORTANCE OF CHANGING YOUR MIND

So creationists violate the first cardinal rule of science, the rule of methodological naturalism, but they also violate the second cardinal rule, that of being willing to change or reject one's explanation based on good evidence to the contrary. This is most clearly revealed by creationist treatment of empirical data. Now, the problem is not that creationists sift through the scientific literature to find data that support the creation "model," that in itself is not out of line. Scientists do seek confirming data (in the real world, as well as in the literature). But creationists *ignore evidence that disconfirms their view*, because they are not willing to change their explanations in the light of new data or theory.

Judges are not famous for their scientific acuity (witness Justice Scalia's dissent in the 1987 Supreme Court's *Edwards* v. *Aguillard* case), but one judge got it remarkably right. William Overton, in the decision in *McLean* v. *Arkansas* wrote,

> The creationists' methods do not take data, weigh it against the opposing scientific data, and thereafter reach the conclusions stated in section 4(a).
>
> Instead, they take the Book of Genesis and attempt to find scientific support for it.
>
> While anybody is free to approach a scientific inquiry in any fashion they choose, they cannot properly describe the methodology used as scientific, if they start with a conclusion and refuse to change it regardless of the evidence developed during the course of the investigation.
>
> A theory that is by its own terms dogmatic, absolutist and never subject to revision is not a scientific theory.

For decades now, creationists have claimed that the amount of meteoritic dust on the Moon disproves evolution. The argument goes like this: Based on scientific measurements, the amount of meteoritic dust falling on the Earth is X tons per year; a proportionate amount must also fall on the Moon. If the Earth and Moon were ancient as evolutionists claim, then the amount of dust on the Moon would be several hundreds of feet thick, since in the scant atmosphere of the Moon, the dust would not burn up as it does on Earth. When astronauts landed on the Moon, they found only a few inches of dust, proving that the Moon is young, so the Earth is young, so that there is not enough time for evolution, so that evolution didn't happen and God created the Earth, the Moon, and everything else in the universe ten thousand years ago.

Decades ago, creationists were told that the data they use for the amount of dust falling on the Earth was inaccurate. More accurate measurements of the amount of meteoritic dust influx to the Earth is degrees of magnitude smaller than the original estimates cited by creationists. Before astronauts landed on the Moon, satellites had accurately measured the amount of dust occurring in space, and NASA predicted the surface of the Moon would be covered by no more than a few inches of dust—exactly what astronauts found. Even though this information has been available for decades, and evolutionists time and again have pointed out flaws in the creationist argument, the dust on the Moon argument still is touted as "evidence against evolution." A normal scientific theory would have been abandoned and forgotten long ago, an empirical stake in its heart, but this creationist zombie keeps rising again and again.

It's hard to argue that one is doing science when one can never bring oneself to abandon a refuted argument, and creation science is littered with such rejects. More modern forms of creationism such as "intelligent design theory" have not been around as long, and have not built up quite as long a list of refuted claims, but things don't look very good for them at this point. Michael Behe (1996) has proposed the idea that certain biochemical functions or structures are "irreducibly complex": because all components must be present and functioning, such structures could not have come about through the incremental process of natural selection. The examples he uses in his book, *Darwin's Black Box*, such as the bacterial flagellum and the blood clotting cascade, appear not to be irreducibly complex after all. Worse, even granting the theoretical possibility that an irreducibly complex structure could exist, there is no reason it could not be produced by natural selection. A (theoretically) irreducibly complex structure would not have to have all of its components assembled in its present form all at one time. The way natural selection works, it is perfectly reasonable to envision that some parts of such a structure could be assembled for one purpose, other parts for another, and the final "assembly" results in a structure that performs a function different from any of the "ancestral" functions. As complex a biochemical sequence as the Krebs cycle has recently been given an evolutionary explanation of this sort (Melandez-Hevia, Waddell, and Cascante 1996).

I'm willing to give Intelligent Design (ID) a little more time to demonstrate that it is, as it aspires to be, a truly scientific movement. To be able legitimately to claim that ID is scientific, however, will require that its proponents be willing to abandon ideas in the light of refuting evidence—something that their ideological ancestors, the creation scientists, have been unable to demonstrate, and which we have seen precious little of from the leaders of the ID movement.

LOGICAL PROBLEMS

Needless to say, in addition to violating the two key principles of science, the science of creationism demonstrates other weaknesses, its logic being one. Creation scientists posit a false dichotomy of only two logical possibilities: one being special creationism as seen in a literal interpretation of Genesis, and the other being evolution. Therefore, if evolution is disproved, then creationism is proved; arguments against evolution are arguments *for* creationism. Creation science literature is largely composed of a careful sifting of legitimate scientific articles and books for anomalies that appear to "disprove" evolution.

But of course, to disprove one view is not to prove another; if I am not at home in Berkeley, that doesn't mean I am on the Moon. To accept the "if not A, then B" form of argument requires that there are only two possibilities. If the only two possibilities are that I am in Berkeley or on the Moon, then indeed, evidence that I am not in Berkeley is evidence that I am on the Moon, but clearly there are more than two alternatives as to my whereabouts. Similarly, there clearly are far more alternatives to scientific evolution than biblical creationism. There are several Hopi origin stories, several Navajo ones, scores of other Native American views, several dozen sub-Saharan African tribal explanations, and we haven't even looked at South Asia, Polynesia, Australia, or views no longer held such as those of the ancient Norse and ancient Greeks. Even if evolution were disproved, biblical literalists would have to find ways of disproving all of these other religious views, so the logic fails.

MORE THAN A PHILOSOPHICAL EXERCISE

For many years, then, my interest in creationism was largely academic. It was an interesting exercise in the philosophy of science. But a few years after I left Missouri, my professor Jim Gavan unwisely accepted an invitation to debate the ICR's Dr. Duane Gish. Gish had perfected a hugely effective technique for persuading the public that evolution was shaky science, and that folks should really consider his "scientific alternative." I and some of my Kentucky students drove from Lexington to Missouri to attend the debate, and it was an eye-opener. I counted thirteen buses from local church groups parked outside the big University of Missouri auditorium, and after seeing the enthusiasm with which the audience received Gish and his message, the cold water of the social and political reality of this movement hit me for the first time. It was no longer just an academic exercise. People were taking this pseudoscience very seriously.

The late Jim Gavan was an excellent scientist, a former president of the American Association of Physical Anthropology, a smart and articulate man well-grounded in philosophy of science. He had done his homework: he had studied creationist literature for several months, and came as prepared as anyone could be expected to be. Clearly, his scientific arguments were superior, but judged from the perspective of who won the hearts and minds of the people, Gish mopped him up.

So I realized that there was a heck of a lot more in this creationism and evolution business than just the academic issues. I went back to Lexington and my job of teaching evolution to college students with a new appreciation of a growing movement that had as its goal the undermining of my professional discipline, to say nothing of the scientific point of view. But still—there were pressures to publish, and a high teaching load, and I was still learning my job, so I didn't take an active role in the controversy quite yet.

Then in 1976, I went to Kansas University, in Lawrence, as a visiting professor. As I walked across campus one day, I saw a poster advertising a debate between two KU professors, Edward Wiley and Pat Bickford, and Duane Gish and Henry Morris from the ICR. My first thought was, Do these guys know what they are getting in for? I jotted down the names of the professors and called up Ed Wiley. I told him that I had a collection of creationist materials that I was happy to make available to him, and offered to discuss the upcoming debate with him some time. We met and shared resources, and because of Ed's strategy I began to think that maybe this debate would be different.

Gish's usual stock in trade was to attack Darwinian gradualism because virtually all of his evolutionist opponents defended it. Ed Wiley had recently arrived from the American Museum of Natural History, where he had been converted to some new approaches to evolutionary biology that Gish had not heard of yet. Whereas Gish anticipated that his opponent would defend Darwinian gradualism, Ed merely sniffed that Dr. Gish had not kept up on the latest scholarship and went on to explain punctuated equilibrium and cladism. Worse for Duane, not only did Wiley ignore Darwinian gradualism, he almost ignored evolution completely, concentrating instead on attacking creation science as being a nonscience, and as being empirically false.

This debate was a disaster for the creationism side. Gish didn't know what to say: his target had disappeared, and he was faced with new information with which he was totally unfamiliar (needless to say, by his next debate, he had figured out a "refutation" of punctuated equilibrium, and no other evolutionist opponent would ever catch him unprepared on *this* topic). It was pleasant to behold, especially after having seen my mentor and friend Jim Gavan skunked by Gish a couple of years before.

But the most memorable moment in the debate didn't have anything to do with science. Geologist Pat Bickford was paired with the avuncular founder of creation science, Henry M. Morris, and did a good job showing the scientific flaws of Morris's "flood geology model" (according to which all the world's important geological features were formed by Noah's Flood), although I don't know how many in the audience understood much of his technical presentation. As with the Gavan/Gish debate, the audience was dominated by people who had arrived on buses from regional churches, and they were there to cheer their champions Gish and Morris. I was sitting behind a young girl of eleven or so and her mother.

Bickford began his presentation by pointing out that he was an active churchgoer, had been one for many years, and found this not at all incompatible with his acceptance of evolution. The girl in front of me whirled to face her mother and said, "But you told me ————" and her mother, equally shocked and intent on hearing more, said, "Shhhhhhhh!" They had come to the debate convinced that one had to choose between evolution and religion. Bickford's testimonial exposed them to empirical evidence that this was not true. I suspect that they wondered what else they had been told that was not true. I noticed that they listened to Bickford far more intently than they had listened to Wiley, and left with a thoughtful look in their eyes.

But my true baptism into realizing the depth and extent of the social and political importance of the creation science movement came in 1980 in Lexington, Kentucky, when the "Citizens for Balanced Teaching of Origins" approached the Lexington school board to request that "creation science" be introduced into the curriculum. Because I had a collection of creationist literature collected over the years, I became a focal point for the opposition to this effort. After over a year of controversy, our coalition of scientists and liberal and moderate clergy (who objected to biblical literalism being presented in the public schools) managed to persuade the Lexington Board of Education to reject the proposal—by a scant 3–2 margin.

CREATIONISM AND PSEUDOSCIENCE

What happened in Lexington has happened in community after community across the United States, although the evolution side has not always prevailed. I learned from the Lexington controversy (and from observing creation/evolution debates) that creation science is not a problem that will be solved merely by throwing science at it. And I suspect that this is generally also the case with other pseudosciences. Like other pseudosciences, creation science seeks support and adherents by claiming the mantle of science. Proponents argue that creation science should be taught in science class because it supposedly is a legitimate science. This point must be refuted, and scientists are the best ones to make the point. But showing that creationism is unscientific (and just plain factually wrong) is insufficient, however necessary. People who support creation science do so for emotional reasons, and are reluctant or unwilling to relinquish their belief unless those needs or concerns are otherwise assuaged. I suspect the same thing can be said for believers in UFOs, or out-of-body experiences, or paranormal phenomena in general: these beliefs are meeting some emotional needs, and consequently will be very difficult to abandon.

In the case of creation science, the needs being met are among those associated with religion, which makes the adherence to creationism particularly difficult to give up. Creationism is most closely associated with a particular theology of special creationism; not all religion is inimical to evolution, as demonstrated both by scientists who are religious and religious non-scientists who accept evolution. But if your theology requires you to interpret your sacred documents in a literal fashion (whether the Bible, the Torah, the Koran, or the Vedas), in most cases, evolution will be difficult to accommodate with faith.

Some antievolutionists—most of the ID supporters, for example—think that evolution is incompatible with faith not because their theology is biblically literalist, but because they believe that a God who works through evolution is too remote; their theology requires a very personal God who is actively involved with individual human lives and who therefore gives purpose and meaning to life. The God of the theistic evolutionist, the one who uses evolution to construct living things much as Newton's God used gravitation to construct the Solar System, is too remote; evolution to them is a step down the slippery slope toward deism.

But whether in the form of biblical literalism or not, religious sensibilities are the engine driving antievolutionism. Religion is a powerful force in human lives. If religion didn't meet many human needs, it wouldn't be a cultural universal; obviously we are dealing with many complex psychological issues. No matter how sound Jim Gavan's science was during his debate with Gish, he failed to move most of his listeners because they came to the debate convinced that evolution was fundamentally incompatible with their religion. Pat Bickford's casual mention that he was a churchgoer was critical to the success of the Kansas debate, because it forced audience members to grapple with a new idea: that one could be an evolutionist and also a Christian. In Lexington, scientists could point out that creation science wasn't science, but the clergy could assuage the public's emotional concerns that by "believing" in evolution, they were giving up something important to them. Scientists alone could not have won the day. If ninety-five clergymen hadn't signed a petition stating that evolution was fine with them, and that they felt that the schools should not be presenting a religious doctrine as science, community sentiment would not have allowed the board of education to make the decision it did.

Those of us concerned about pseudoscience and its attraction to the public would be well advised to consider the emotional needs that are met by beliefs in ESP, alien abduction, astrology, psychic powers, and the like, and address them as well as criticizing the poor science invoked to support the pseudoscience. We skeptics sometimes feel that the people we are trying to reach are impenetrable—and some of them are! The public is divided into three parts: confirmed believers, confirmed skeptics, and a much larger middle group that doesn't know much science, but doesn't have the emotional commitments that might lead it to embrace a pseudoscientific view. In the case of creation science, the emotional commitment (among many) is to the particular theology of biblical literalism; in the case of UFO abductees, it may be a need for a quasi-religious benevolent protector (or conversely, the fear of an omnipresent threat against which one is powerless). I have found that I am most effective with that large middle group, and hardly ever effective with the true believers; I suspect most skeptics have had similar experiences.

But after all, reaching that large middle group is also the goal of the proponents of pseudoscience. If, like most skeptics, you feel that we'd all be better off with more science and less pseudoscience, then that is where we should be focusing our energies, rather than fruitlessly arguing with people who will never agree with us. But to reach that group that is potentially reachable, we must also be aware that a scientific explanation is necessary but not sufficient to change someone's mind; if I have learned anything from over twenty-five years in the skeptic business, it is that it is necessary to deal with the emotional reasons that make our species susceptible to these beliefs, as well as the scientific.

REFERENCES

Behe, M. 1996. *Darwin's Black Box.* New York: Free Press.
Plantinga, A. 1997. "Methodological Naturalism Is True by Definition." *Origins and Design* 18, no. 2: 22–34.
Scott, E. C. 1998. " 'Science and Religion,' 'Christian Scholarship,' and 'Theistic Science': Some Comparisons." *Reports of the NCSE* 18, no. 2: 30–32.
Melandez-Hevia, Enrique, Thomas G. Waddell, and Marta Cascante. 1996. "The Puzzle of the Krebs Citric Acid Cycle: Assembling the Pieces of Chemically Feasible Reactions, and Opportunism in the Design of Metabolic Pathways During Evolution." *Journal of Molecular Evolution* 43: 293–303.

EUGENIE SCOTT is the executive director of the National Center for Science Education, Inc., a nonprofit membership organization which promotes evolution education and education in the nature of science. A physical anthropologist by training, she is a former university professor and the president of the American Association of Physical Anthropologists 2001–2003. She is a Fellow of CSICOP.

VIII

ALTERNATIVE MEDICINE

"ALTERNATIVE MEDICINE"
How It Demonstrates Characteristics of Pseudoscience, Cult, and Confidence Game

WALLACE SAMPSON

CHARACTERISTICS OF A PSEUDOSCIENCE

We speak and write of pseudoscience but there is no agreed-upon set of criteria to define it. Literally a false science, or a pretender to science, it is difficult to define by strict criteria. There have been several attempts at laying out sets of characteristics by which it can be recognized.

In *In the Name of Science* (1952) Martin Gardner wrote of two books introducing the concept: D. W. Hering's *Foibles and Fallacies of Science* (1924), and J. Jastrow's *The Story of Human Error* (1936). Gardner then outlined characteristics of scientific cranks. They work in isolation. They tend to paranoia, claiming to be ignored or persecuted. They focus attacks on scientists, accepted theories, or authorities. They speak before organizations they themselves form. They publish outside normal channels, often creating their own journals and publishing their own books. They write in complex jargon.

Physicist Irving Langmuir also outlined a set of characteristics of pseudoscience in a talk before a group at the General Electric Corporation in December 1953, defining the phenomenon as "Pathological Science." In that talk he recalled his examination of the claims of Davis and Barnes. Davis's claims and observations were similar to those of Blondlot, who claimed to have discovered "N" rays—X-ray-like rays he claimed to have found but which were proved to be visual hallucinations or misinterpretations.

Davis's claim was that he could count many or fewer flashes on a scintillation plate caused by alpha particles that did or did not combine with electrons at certain presumed energy levels, and that the changes were created by changes in voltage. But those voltage changes were too small to have created the claimed effects. When Dr. Langmuir controlled the apparatus so that the observer could not tell whether the voltage had been changed, Davis could not tell the difference among several runs. Apparently Davis had counted imaginary or background noise as the flashes he had expected to see.

Langmuir set down characteristics he called symptoms that he saw distinguished pseudoscience from science.

1. A causative agent of barely detectable intensity produces a maximum effect independent of the intensity of the cause.
2. The effect stays at the limit of detectability; many measurements may be necessary because of low statistical significance.
3. Claims of great accuracy.
4. Fantastic theories contrary to experience.
5. Criticisms are met by ad hoc excuses.
6. Ratio of supporters to critics rises up to somewhere near 50 percent and then falls gradually to oblivion.

These criteria were derived from his experience with anomalous physics experiments, so one has to extend their borders some to embrace the pseudosciences in biology and medicine. But most characteristics are shared.

Physicist Russell Turpin of the University of Texas expanded on Langmuir's definitions with the following points:

1. Subjective measurements made with subjective end points. (The Blondlot and Davis experiments were both victims of such subjectivity.)
2. Small differences. (The advocate may magnify small differences and perceive them to be of great importance.)
3. Tighter controls turn results more negative. ("The death knell for the finding.")
4. Negative results count more against a proposal than positive ones count for it. (This is a variation on the requirement that true findings should be reproducible in various labs and clinics, and not be successful in only the proponent's lab. It is hard to establish a number at which one draws the line for validity, but certainly a narrow majority of positive experiments does not validate a finding, and may invalidate it.)
5. No direct evidence. (An example is an association without establishing proof by experimentation or prospective clinical trials.)
6. Absence of deepening evidence. (With time, more information should become confirmatory, especially when the problem is approached from different angles.)

7. Predicted phenomena remain slippery. (The strength of a finding or proposal should be a basis for predictions, which then should be explored and confirmed.)
8. Poor investigation of alternative explanations. (An obvious simple explanation is rationalized away in favor of the advocate's favored one.)
9. Revolution without support. (Evidence from other fields and subsequent research should support the finding or theory. If not, the finding is likely to be erroneous. A corollary is the saying, *Extraordinary claims require extraordinary proof.*)

No scientific or other body has approved any of these criteria or constructed a list of steps through which one can proceed to disprove a proposal, nor is there likely to be any such attempt. Scientists and clinicians must simply use them and use rational judgment in their evaluations. In view of these varied criteria, how do the various "alternatives" match up? We can answer by examining three examples, probably the three about which the most has been written.

One principle to keep in mind is that methods may be helpful to certain individuals and not to others. In medicine, not every method must apply equally to all subjects—in fact most do not. But the question has to be turned around. If one claims that the method works for even a significant minority, that claim can be put to a series of tests to find out, and be proved. Excuses are themselves signs of pseudoscience.

If a method has even one of the characteristics, the likelihood of the claims being true is low. That is what the Langmuir and Turpin lists really tell us. The more a method or claim is characterized by multiple indicators, the more likely the claim is a pseudoscience.

Since the business of defining a pseudoscience is not formalized, and ways of classifying claims also are not, the results of evaluations must remain matters of opinion for now. But more rigor may not be necessary. That is because the burden of proof remains with the claimant, and if that burden is not met, then the likelihood is that one is dealing with pseudoscience.

We can start with three aberrant health and medical methods about which we know a great deal: chiropractic, acupuncture, and homeopathy. Applying Turpin's criteria, we start with subjective measurements. For the chiropractic method, there is no objective measurement of manipulative techniques. Investigators have measured some forces and angles of manipulation, but repeatable data in different operators' hands do not exist. At least thirty-seven different techniques have been described, and none is accepted as indicated over another in specific situations. None of these is superior to the simplest conservative and hands-off management. Measurements remain highly subjective and indirect.

Regarding outcome measurements, the presumed subluxation of chiropractic theory has never been proved to exist, and therefore there is nothing direct or objective to measure. Measurements are subjective or indirect—pain, days off work, expense, and so forth.

Small differences are characteristic of most chiropractic research. One positive result from a published study was by Meade, published in *Lancet*, and showed only about a 10 percent difference between chiropractic and physical therapy in terms of pain relief and time off work. But physical therapy is ineffective in this situation also, and most recent trials of back manipulation for pain show no difference from controls.

Tighter controls resulted in the negative studies. There is no direct evidence of improvement, or deepening evidence after one hundred years of existence. Evidence and predictions remain slippery with chiropractors changing from testing one treatment and condition to another with no consistency of effect for any. Chiropractors fail to admit that their results could be due to chance or to misinterpretation (causality error, regression to the mean, etc.), or conditioning. Despite all these defects, chiropractors continue claiming success, demonizing medicine for medication deaths, and calling for more research to confirm their borderline findings. Chiropractic scores on all indicators.

Acupuncture fares better, because needle insertion points can be defined. But in practice and reality, there is hardly a point on the human body not claimed to be a "point" and little agreement exists among operators as to which point to use for which condition. In fact, medical conditions (diagnoses) in traditional Chinese medicine (TCM) are independent of scientific classification and understanding—fanciful and fallacious.

Applying the criteria here, we find similar results. Acupuncturists rarely treat measurable disorders, relying instead on subjective pain, nausea, headaches, and the like, and on the patient to score the results. This allows for breaks in blinding to have significant effects.

Differences remain small. Our recent review (D. Ramey and W. Sampson, "Analysis of Systematic Reviews of Acupuncture," submitted for publication) shows a preponderance of negative studies for almost all conditions, and a slim majority of positive studies for only two specific conditions—nausea of chemotherapy and postoperative dental pain. Even for those, there are enough negative studies and nonreproducible ones to cast serious doubt on effectiveness.

Two meta-analyses of acupuncture for pain showed that the most positive studies were the least well controlled. The best-controlled studies were negative. Thus, there is little to no direct evidence, and no deepening evidence after thirty years of studies since the most recent wave of popularity began.

Predictions remain slippery—in fact, no predictions can be made from acupuncture theory.

Regarding alternate explanations, some researchers acknowledge that the "placebo effect" may explain positive results. But all effects can be explained by the same alternative explanations. As for chiropractic, even more telling, there are no clearly positive results to explain.

Homeopathy is the least popular of the three and is the easiest to dispose of because of its absurd implausibility. The first claim is that substances with effects similar to the subject's symptoms are curative. The second is that solutions of decreasing strength can be made more potent by their serial dilution and a specific way of agitating them. (Modern homeopathic solutions are not even "potentized" the way originally described, but they are mixed in standard chemical vortex mixing equipment.)

Nevertheless, homeopathy fulfills all the criteria of relying on qualitative end points—diarrhea, asthma and hay fever symptoms, and fever of flu. Differences remain small. No reported result exceeds about 10 percent from a placebo, and then often by selecting end points after the fact of the experiments. We have examined the top ten best-rated homeopathy papers and found most to have been either misrepresented or to be defective in serious ways, causing them to be uninterpretable. The two well-regarded reviews found again that the tighter the controls the more negative the studies.

There has been no deepening evidence, and no prediction of advances. Results remain static over the fifty years of modern investigation. Homeopathy advocates do not allow for alternative explanations, but go to extreme lengths to marshal odd theories to explain their debatably positive results. Theories include hormesis (small doses having effects opposite of large doses) or several different presumed mechanisms for how water maintains a structure so the molecules can "remember" what to do. None of those mechanisms could possibly explain the effect, which in any case does not exist.

I would add to the above criteria of pseudoscience that of being based on a discredited, resurrected theory. From chiropractic's theories of nerve dysfunction caused by vertebral subluxation, traditional Chinese medicine's Q'i ("life force") imbalance, and homeopathy's laws of similars and infinite dilution, to perpetual motion and alchemy, the theories are old to ancient and long discredited. Yet advocates resurrect them as agents of a forgotten mystical science ignored by the Establishment.

In summary, even without considering the aberrant behavior of advocates and practitioners, the three leading "alternative" medicines of the "CAM" (complementary and alternative medicine) movement fall clearly into the category of pseudoscience. For other methods such as herbs, mind/body action, prayer/spirituality effects, and odd psychotherapies, similar cases can be made.

CHARACTERISTICS OF THE CULT AND THE CON

"Alternative" medicine has not been seriously considered a confidence game, although many may feel that belief in some methods is akin to religious or cult conversion and belief, so firmly do people hold to implausible ideas.

One can consider these together because cults and cons operate in similar ways, the main difference being that cons usually involve one or a few people, and cults operate with leaders and larger followings. Con artists and cult leaders use some similar tactics. The objective study of cults is difficult because of the inability to study them in any blinded or objective way, except by infiltration and misrepresenting oneself in an ethnographic type of relationship (joining the cult).

The study of cults and sects suffers also from a politically correct opposition to considering them as different or abnormal. Some claim that most religions started as cults, became sects, and then became accepted variants. Thus, studying or labeling a medical cult is fraught with difficulties of accusations of prejudice and bias. Also, there are few references on cults—one of the most recent being Margaret Singer's *The Cults in Our Midst* (Jossey-Bass, 1995)—that display how they and their leaders operate.

Con artists' and cults' operations involve first seeking out the vulnerable—the isolated, homesick college student; the aging senior living alone; a trusting uninformed female customer; the person with a chronic illness; the cancer patient; the elderly recently widowed spouse. All of these are vulnerable to cons and cult recruiters.

Second, they soften up the mark or subject by appearing innocent or dumb, helpless or loving, interested or accepting, thus gaining sympathy and confidence (thus the term). In the case of cults, operatives instill distrust of the family or former friends, and isolate the person from contact. In the case of medical cults and illness, the person is given only supportive information, and encouraged not to believe the physician. The isolation is associated with demonizing the family or former associates, medicine, and physicians. The mold is set for conversion, or for the take.

Sociopaths operate either solely, in small groups, or as leaders of cults. They establish their own rules of behavior, believing that they are above the law or that for some reason the law does not apply to them. They are rewarded financially and through the thrill of outwitting the law, and outwitting their marks.

Alternative advocates use similar techniques on the public in less apparent and more devious ways. Their tactics reveal more intention than manifestations of simple mistaken observations and errors, and an intent more sinister than the antics of cranks. When faced with noncompliance to the rules and customs of organized medical science, advocates assemble forces and conspire to change the rules of scientific evidence, and to change the laws.

When faced with accomplished or impending disproof by basic science knowledge or controlled clinical trials, the "alternative" advocates write articles denying the applicability of scientific trials to their claims. They retreat into ideological pillboxes claiming that there are different paths to knowledge, "different ways of knowing." They claim that statistics and consistency could not be applied to their methods because the methods are tailored to the individual.

They soften the opposition by demonizing medicine as too cold, removed, impersonal, reductionist—and a medical monopoly. The perceived crisis is financial, due mostly to technological advances and booming personnel salaries from near-poverty level to levels of living wage. Alternative ideologues take advantage of the popular perception of the 1970s through the 1990s as a "crisis in medicine." Technology advances and personnel salaries booming from poverty-level to a living wage caused a gross inflation in costs. Ideologues blamed medicine and doctors. Surveys reported that 40 million U.S. residents lacked medical care. The figure applied to the number uninsured, but most if not all of those had sufficient care through public clinics and hospitals.

But the myth persisted, nevertheless. The continued demonizing of medicine by government and pseudoscience guilds such as chiropractic was an accidental association but they softened up public and professional resistance. The medical profession's natural self-criticism abetted the process as most physicians and nurses continually accepted blame while looking for ways to improve.

In order to further their cause, advocates intentionally distorted language to make their claims more acceptable. We are now aware that the terms *alternative, complementary, unorthodox, unconventional, nontraditional, homeopathic/naturopathic, politically suppressed, culturally bound,* and *holistic* were invented specifically to produce a sympathetic, esthetically pleasing visceral response.

The words replaced the negative *implausible, unproved, disproved, dubious, fringe, quackery, pathological, sectarian, cultlike,* and *pseudoscientific*. CAM advocates made it socially and politically unacceptable to use the latter terms by stating they indicated bias.

They then turned to debasing and demonizing medicine with their own pejorative antonyms: *orthodox, conventional, traditional, allopathic, culturally dominant, politically dominant, Establishment, medical monopoly, culturally disabled, reductionist,* etc. CAM advocates do not admit that their terminology reflects bias.

The intent of these maneuvers was to "demystify" science and medicine and to change them to "complementary and alternative medicine"—a utopian, egalitarian set of relationships with a linguistically and emotionally acceptable description. The press accepted their terminology without question, repeating it daily, fertilizing the public's altered perceptions.

Not satisfied with changing the language through massive popular misuse, advocates in the Office of Alternative Medicine approached the National Library of Medicine (NLM) in 1994 to change its classification system. As the NLM changed its new medical subject headings (MeSH) to "alternative medicine," ten or more sectarian methods such as chiropractic and homeopathy were reclassified from "therapeutic cults" to "alternative medicine," changing for decades to come the way the U.S. population and the rest of the world would perceive quackery. "Ineffective" and "quackery" are now successfully converted to "complementary and alternative medicine" or "CAM." So far as is known, there was not a voice raised or a motion made in opposition to that action. Few even knew it had happened.

Advocates admit that these language twists were intended to result in changes of applicable laws. New laws redefined practice boundaries to include ineffective methods now known as "complementary" or "culturally imbedded." By the year 2000, eleven states had passed "access to medical treatment" acts which allow any licensed practitioner to use any method on a patient provided the patient is informed and certain other conditions are met. These acts have expanded the definition of medical practice well beyond the previous standard of scientific proof and ethics. The Federation of Medical Boards and other state boards are at this time investigating the possibility of changing regulations to allow anomalous and ineffective practices under their new names.

And it did not end there. In a move both gross and occult, the movement co-opted the more sensitive, qualitative aspects of medical practice for its own, as if medicine had never known of them. Support groups, weight-loss clinics, religious prayer, exercise, and relaxation techniques had all been part of the supporting structure of medicine. Hospitals began as religious institutions and nurses as nuns or "sisters." Massages were routine in hospitals from before the 1920s through the 1950s. For centuries physicians have recommended rest, relaxation, smoking and alcohol cessation, and regular exercise for heart conditions, intestinal disorders, and anxiety. Suddenly these functions were found in the definition of "unconventional" in the famous Eisenberg survey published in 1993 in the *New England Journal of Medicine*, and are now considered "complementary."

Langmuir and Turpin did not comment on such actions as being pseudoscientific. These were political and propagandistic actions of ideologues and advocates who assumed political power, and took advantage of the Establishment's blind spots and self-criticism to change how people would perceive them. Call it political wisdom, or call it a con, it is an action of major proportions with implications not only for the public's health, but also for the economics of medicine and society.

This language distortion and the rise of CAM may be one of the largest cons of the twentieth century, ranking in terms of people affected with the propaganda-bound ideological myths of midcentury. There are 300 million people in North America and an equal number in western Europe. If the majority of people in the Western or developed world now know implausible, ineffective, and fraudulent practices by the blander terms "alternative," "complementary," and "unorthodox," then as many people in the Western world have been conned as were conned by the major political tyrannies of the twentieth century. The presence of believing, deluded advocates and a massive public following must be considered a major cult.

The effects cannot be compared to the massive suffering engendered by political cons. But they certainly outdo in dollars and numbers of people affected, major literary and other cons such as the Hitler diaries, the French oil "sniffer plane," the Howard Hughes biography, and Carlos Castaneda's eight-volume fictional Don Juan series that was passed off as anthropological truth and a Ph.D. thesis.

These are fascinating yet serious thoughts for rational and democratic societies to ponder. People can be fooled into having their thoughts twisted by a cult leader and a midnight talk show to believe that a spaceship following a comet contains aliens coming to rescue believers after death. That belief resulted in mass suicide of the Heaven's Gate cult members. Cultic behavior also caused the Jonestown affair.

Similar mechanisms are at work in the rise of the CAM movement—a subject that will have social scientists and physicians researching and writing voluminously two generations from now. The CAM movement is all three—a pseudoscience, a cult, and a con. The principles are the same, it is just the manifestations that change.

WALLACE SAMPSON is the editor of the *Scientific Review of Alternative Medicine*, and a member of the board of directors of the National Council Against Health Fraud. Dr. Sampson is a highly respected and well-known authority in numerous medical fields, including oncology, hematology, and pathology. He has held, and currently holds, responsible positions in a wide variety of medical institutions and activities. He was formerly the associate chief of hematology and medical oncology at the Santa Clara Valley Medical center, and a clinical professor of medicine at Stanford University School of Medicine. Dr. Sampson is also a prominent and active member of numerous professional organizations devoted to the protection of consumers from fraudulent healthcare products and claims. He is a Fellow of CSICOP.

IX

SKEPTICISM
AROUND
THE WORLD

21

A DOZEN YEARS OF DUTCH SKEPTICISM

CORNELIS de JAGER and JAN WILLEM NIENHUYS

The Netherlands has a historic reputation as being receptive to free-thought, free inquiry, and skepticism. For example, Spinoza (1632–1677), René Descartes (1596–1650), and Pierre Bayle (1647–1706) lived and wrote there. As a matter of fact, the most famous and influential Dutch skeptic who explicitly doubted the paranormal was the reverend Balthasar Bekker (1634–1698). He wrote a book (*De Betooverde Wereld* [The Enchanted World], 3 vols., 1691–1693) that caused an uproar because in it he argued that witches, magic, and ghosts were merely superstitions. Indeed, Bekker's book may have prevented more superstitious murders than all twentieth-century skeptics together. Thus Dutch skepticism didn't start with the establishment of the Stichting Skepsis on November 27, 1987, but it was given a significant boost in the twentieth century by its creation. Before that time there were isolated skeptics like Piet Hein Hoebens and J. H. Ottervanger (died 1963) and an antiquackery organization that had been flourishing with ups and downs since 1881. After Skepsis was founded there still remained some rationalists active outside of Skepsis.

What a dozen years of organized skepticism in the Netherlands has achieved is that many people, especially in the media, now know where to find us if they need another view. The media often want to avoid the appearance of taking sides. So they often let a "skeptic" give comments rather then saying "nonsense" themselves. It's a bit of a trick to say then the necessary without compromising scientific accuracy and without actually supporting crazy ideas by discussing them seriously.

The main activity of Skepsis was and is publishing a quarterly magazine, *Skepter*. Skepsis also published a number of booklets on subjects like alternative medicine, spiritism, and reincarnation or just the lectures given during our annual congresses. Board members of Skepsis have written two books on skeptical matters, namely a survey of the paranormal in 1988 and an encyclopedia of pseudoscience in 1997, which was moderately priced (thirty dollars) and sold so well that a third and improved printing was brought out in 1998. Many articles were published by skeptics in newspapers and other periodicals. One Skepsis sympathizer published a book debunking the medical claims of a well-known Dutch psychic healer. Other sympathizers published a book in which the so-called Saas-Fee photograph of a UFO was analyzed to be most probably a hoax. Recently these publishing activities have been supplemented by a Web site (www.skepsis.nl) that contains hundreds of articles from *Skepter*.

One of the principal aims of Skepsis is to investigate pseudoscience and claims of the paranormal. Such investigations have been done on a small scale. A book review often entails such an investigation. A typical small investigation was a localized UFO panic in Amsterdam. Much more laborious was an analysis of the two thousand psychic clues that were sent to the police after a spectacular abduction and murder case. Most of the work to analyze this veritable mountain of rubble was done by the Dutch Institute for Parapsychology. The relevance for the solution of the crime was nil (the case was eventually solved when the criminal started to spend the ransom money), and there was even hardly any remarkable coincidence that might raise the interest of a parapsychologist.

There were more such small investigations. Most of them have only local significance. For some reason an investigation of whatever phenomenon loses force across national borders. A debunking of English crop circles or German earth rays doesn't impress anyone in Holland, and conversely, when the Dutch Academy of Sciences crushes dowsing in the Netherlands with an extremely thorough investigation (which is what they did in 1954), it has no impact in Belgium.

GRAPHOLOGY

The example of graphology is instructive. Graphological analysis is widespread in France and somewhat less so in Germany, but in the Netherlands a certain A. Jansen wrote a Ph.D. thesis titled *On the Validation of Graphological Judgments* (1963). This dissertation happened at a crucial moment in the evolution of Dutch scientific psychology, and the result of Jansen's dissertation was that the empirical school of psychology gained the upper hand in the Netherlands, and that graphology in the Netherlands lost in respectability.

In the 1950s 75 percent of Dutch companies used graphology to judge job applicants and personnel. One by one people using this method stopped doing so or went out of business, and in 1987 the percentage was down to 8. When one of us (Nienhuys) examined all 1991–1992 issues of a well-known weekly with many ads for higher personnel, he found seventeen thousand ads, of which 1.39 percent asked for handwritten letters. About half of the 118 companies did so because they intended to use such handwritten letters for graphological analysis. For the other half a readable handwriting was deemed important for the job, or neat handwriting was considered on the same level as a tie or clean fingernails. One organization tried to filter out analphabetics! Of four recruitment agencies that had placed such ads, three had discontinued using graphology by the time (1993) they were asked why they had done so.

Graphological analysis had therefore descended in the Netherlands into the occult realm, something akin to astrology and palm reading. Skepsis's treasurer Dick Zeilstra created singlehandedly Grafospect, the institute for scientific graphology, member of the NNBG. None of his customers asked what NNBG meant (Dutch nonexisting graphologists). These customers were recruited by small ads, and they all received (for a mere ten dollars) the same Forer type of character analysis ("You don't accept statements from others without sufficient evidence, you tend to be critical of yourself, and you are averse to superstition," etc.). All twenty-one customers except one thought the description fitted them very well or completely, and about half thought they had acquired a deeper understanding of themselves.

The graphology story shows several things. A well-designed scientific study can, given proper circumstances, squash an entire branch of pseudoscience or occultism. But the effect of such a study need not extend beyond national borders. And lastly, you can't get rich by distributing moderately priced Forer analyses.

DOWSING

We will now describe in some depth a few investigations that may have some relevance beyond Dutch borders. Two of these are related to astrology, but we start with the Skepsis dowser investigation. The word *dowser* evokes images of people with forked sticks looking for water or diagnosing health aspects of locations. Many dowsers don't use forked sticks but a so-called pendulum: a string of maybe not more than 30 centimeters (what the ancients used to call a "foot") with a small weight attached. This pendulum is held in one hand and then small motions of the weight, with an amplitude of a few centimeters, are supposed to provide an answer to various questions.

A discussion with a dowsing clairvoyant in a national weekly magazine in 1992 led to a general challenge: participants could earn up to 10,000 guilders (about 5,000 dollars) if they were succesful in a Skepsis test of dowsing. The test material consisted of six small boxes. An object (usually the dowser's favorite crystal or a holy Tibetan relic provided by Skepsis) was hidden in one of these boxes and the pendulum had to tell which box. Getting five hits in ten tries counted as a success. A successful dowser would at first get a refund of travel costs and a choice between 100 guilders or a second test. Likewise, success in the second test would result in a choice between 1,000 guilders or a third try. As the probability of passing a single test was only about 1.5 percent, Skepsis didn't have to worry much about losing a lot of money by a freak accident.

It is clear that such a design is much simpler than trying to find out whether dowsers can locate water or whatever in a more or less natural setting. Skepsis took various precautions to minimize any natural flow of information. The boxes were filled with cotton wool and also glued to a board, to prevent cues like rattling. One of the boxes was filled in a separate room by one experimenter (who used a die to determine his or her choice). Then the whole board was carried out into an intermediate space and then brought by a go-between into another closed room where the dowser would perform his or her guesses in front of two other experimenters. All candidates where allowed to practice first. They expected to score about eight (out of ten) correct, but nobody scored more than three times correct, and altogether there were fifteen hits in seventy tries, which is not anything remarkable. The only remarkable "effect" we noticed was that the dowsers were clearly averse to chosing the same box on consecutive tries.

How did the candidates react to this? Two were quite satisfied with their efforts. No candidate concluded to have been completely mistaken about their own abilities. Five had various cop-outs: the color of the boxes was wrong, said one lady, who earlier had confided to us that she had often observed in the supermarket that her pendulum always told her that foods in green pots or packs were unwholesome. Some thought the floral decorations on the boxes were too distracting, or the central heating pipes in the experimental room were uncomfortable, or maybe the cotton wads blocked the aura of the object. Or the mental pressure of having to perform was too much. One lady insisted that the experimental room (a basement in an observatory that had been built several centuries before) had to be rigged by secret magnets in the floor, because her pendulum rotated counterclockwise.

It has become clear to us that most of these dowsers have no idea of what constitutes an adequate testing method. That is why a general challenge to paranormalists only occasionally results in a testable claim and almost never produces a proposal for a good test. On some occasions dowsers have contacted us with vague general claims. But when we then outlined how to go about proper blinding and randomizing we received either no answer or an answer that they had followed our directions and discovered that the effect was an illusion. In one case an engineer told one of us (Nienhuys) that he had set up his own test situation by having a computer operate a switch. To his great surprise he only obtained random results when he didn't know the (pseudo-) random sequence selected by his computer.

Actively approaching purveyors of the paranormal seldomly yields results. Such people are often too busy saving humankind and feel no need to prove themselves. One guy was selling (at a guilder per gram) salt that he had programmed by means of a pyramid to imbue it with a creative healing intelligence. He had a marvelous a priori cop-out: double blind doesn't work, because the salt's intelligence must be able to interact with human intelligence and of course this can't happen when the human cannot be sure that she's dealing with intelligent salt.

THE ASTROTEST

Skepsis has been trying for a long time to get associations of astrologers to issue a joint declaration with Skepsis to the effect that newspaper horoscopes are for amusement only. This joint declaration was never issued: at the last moment the astrological associations forbade their boards to support such declarations. Even though this enterprise came to nothing (in 1992 Skepsis sent a letter on its own to newspapers and magazines, which was of course ignored), the negotiation led to a certain mutual understanding with these organizations.

In the spring of 1994 Rob Nanninga, Skepsis's secretary, proposed a matching test on the occasion of a discussion about the predictive value of astrology in a Dutch national newspaper. Astrologers would be provided with the exact data of the birth of seven people (place, date, and time to the nearest five minutes), and with life descriptions of these people, namely the answers to long lists of questions. The astrologers taking part in the test would be allowed to submit their own questions. An amount of 5,000 guilders (then somewhat less than 2,500 dollars) would be divided among those people who would be able to match all birth data to the questionnaires. This didn't seem too much of a risk as there are 5,040 ways to match seven items to seven other items, and only one of them would be correct.

The gathering of data wasn't really simple. To prevent age being a clue (with the answers to over fifty questions about one's life it shouldn't be too difficult to guess a person's age within a decade), it was decided that all seven people used for the test should be born in a single year. When these were found in 1948 the chairperson of the national astrologers association protested: in that year the birth times were usually not noted down precisely enough. So Nanninga had to collect a new sample from 1958. For the purpose of such a test it is not good when important points on the horoscope are close to the points where adjoining signs meet (so-called cusps). Also it was thought wise to take care that none of the seven subjects could be matched in a very obvious way to his or her horoscope.

All these preparations took half a year to work out, and eventually forty-four astrologers responded, but two among them had worked together and both of them sent in their joint solution, so there were effectively forty-three independently submitted answers. The astrologers were generally quite experienced: members of astrological associations, teachers of astrology, or at least former students of astrology courses or well-read in the subject (over fifty books), and most of them were professionally active. At least half of them expected to share in the prize money by scoring precisely seven correct matches and the others were also fairly optimistic (one astrologer expected to have precisely six correct!). In reality only one scored three correct, and half scored not a single correct answer.

Outsiders might think that there is some system in astrology, so maybe the astrologers would agree a little with each other, if not with reality. There were 903 pairs of independent astrologers, but the numbers of pairs that agreed on 0, 1, 2, etc. horoscopes showed nothing but chance results. Only one pair agreed completely.

The last part of the investigation consisted of asking the astrologers themselves what they thought about it. Half of the participants never answered this question, and only four admitted that astrology wasn't as powerful as they had thought it to be. There were lots of reasons why the test hadn't worked: the horoscopes resembled each other too much: the faraway planets were mostly in the same sign, because all subjects were born in the same year. A strange excuse for people who will claim at other times that a difference of a few minutes in birth time can result in a totally different horoscope. Also the persons resembled each other too much: they all considered themselves as reliable persons. Some astrologers conjectured that our subjects didn't really know themselves or had lied about themselves. Most questions, however, related to verifiable facts. And even if all data had been false this wouldn't explain the utter lack of agreement among the astrologers. The most preposterous excuse came from the astrologers' chairperson. She herself had approved the Skepsis questionnaire, and according to her, psychological tests are worthless. All the same she protested afterward that the questionnaire wasn't scientific at all, because it hadn't been seen by an expert!

This is of course not really surprising. Astrologers are unusually gifted in the cop-out department. Around the same time one of us (Nienhuys) took part in a TV program in which the abilities of an astrologer and a tarot reader were tested. On the advice of Nanninga the broadcasting organization had asked them to predict passing or failing an exam for a driver's license. Usually about two-thirds of the examinees fail in the Netherlands.

The astrologer (a well-known author of weekly horoscopes) had predicted a 30 percent failure rate, so naturally her prediction failed badly. She instantly made up a perfectly logical explanation: when astrology was invented by the ancient Babylonians, there weren't any automobiles yet.

THE MARS EFFECT

A major effort that has occupied both of us is the investigation of the Mars effect. Parts of this research have been published in various places, so we will give a survey that shows the connection between these activities. In the beginning of 1991 a Dutch association for "critical astrology" and Skepsis cooperated in organizing a symposium in Utrecht. This symposium featured among others Geoffrey Dean, Suitbert Ertel, and Michel Gauquelin, and the afternoon program was about the work of Gauquelin and related matters. During this symposium one of us (De Jager) made a short presentation on the subject of "spurious periodicities." In the next half year this line of investigation was pursued vigorously together with Piet Jongbloet, an expert on human reproductive biology, and Carl Koppeschaar, a science journalist with an extensive knowledge of astronomy.

Gauquelin claimed that sports champions were more often born at times that Mars is rising or culminating in the south. This supposed effect wasn't very large: the "good" Mars positions were found in about 17 percent of "ordinary" people and in about 22 percent of the champions. Because "Mars rising" rather often more or less coincides with the "sun rising" on the one hand, and on the other hand births show a daily peak around sunrise, there is a small so-called astrodemographic effect which raises the expected percentage from a theoretical 16.667 to a somewhat higher value. Our idea was that for very vigorous women giving birth to very healthy babies (i.e., future champions) a combination of a more pronounced seasonal and daily rhythm and an accidental synchronicity of Mars with these rhythms in the beginning of the twentieth century might have produced what is known in astronomy as "spurious periodicities." The results of these investigations were presented during the 1991 European Skeptical Conference in Amsterdam. By that time we had had access to many data, also of champions declared by Gauquelin to be "controls" (often after he had seen their Mars positions), and we had formed an opinion that Gauquelin's findings were merely chance flukes compounded by various unknown experimental errors.

Many of these data derived from an investigation of Ertel in 1988 of Gauquelin's files. Ertel had discovered then a rather serious selection bias, but had tried to save the Mars effect by showing an "eminence effect" in all Gauquelin's champions: the ones whose names had been published, the ones who had been used as "controls" (about whom only collective statistics had been published), and also further additional names. Ertel claimed that champions mentioned more often in certain reference books had higher "Mars percentages." However, Koppeschaar discovered that Ertel's evidence for this was not really very impressive.

In the process of preparing the proceedings of the 1991 conference one of us (Nienhuys) had to read so often manuscripts, galley proofs, and revisions of five different articles on this subject that he decided to write an introductory survey. He tried to support Koppeschaar's analysis by statistical arguments, and found that Ertel's eminence effect was absent from the total of all French champions (2,040 out of the total of 4,391 of all Gauquelin's champions) and that its presence in the non-French champions could be explained as a result of a confounding of "unpublished" with "unquoted." The "unpublished" non-French (among whom were large numbers of Italian soccer players) had a grand total of six citations in Ertel's sources, no doubt because Ertel hadn't bothered to avail himself of any comprehensive Italian sports encyclopedia.

This small investigation—an afterthought to an editing process—was of pivotal importance for Nienhuys. When Ertel organized a European meeting of the Society for Scientific Exploration in Munich in 1992, he invited De Jager to present the Dutch findings, but then accepted that Nienhuys went instead. The editor of the *Journal of Scientific Exploration* then asked to be allowed to publish papers on this subject, which resulted in further research. Nienhuys found (after studying Ertel's 1988 paper carefully, and running computer programs on Ertel's database of 4,391 champions) that Ertel's eminence effect also disappeared when the reference books that Ertel had borrowed from Gauquelin were disregarded.

The next stage was an invitation by Paul Kurtz, received in the first week of January 1994 by express mail, that Nienhuys would look into the final report of the French committee that had performed a new experiment to test Gauquelin's hypothesis. Rumors about what would be in that report had been circulating already since the beginning of 1991, but no rumor could prepare for the dynamite in the report.

In the very end the French turned out to have collected 1,120 champions, of which 18.66 percent were "Mars champions." As the base rate turned out to be 17.7 percent, this was a nonsignificant result. Moreover the French committee was more or less forced into including also a large number of the champions on which the whole "Mars effect hypothesis" was based. In scientific research it's definitely a no-no to undertake a decisive test of a claim or conjecture, and then include the data that gave rise to the claim, in this case the sportsmen and women whose names were published by Gauquelin in 1955. If these are disregarded the French result is: 826 champions and a Mars percentage of 17.43.

But it was not this confirmation of science in general and the U.S. test performed around the birth of CSICOP in particular, that formed the dynamite. It was the fact that Gauquelin had been extremely unscientific in his dealings with the committee, and in fact with its secretary, Claude Benski. By some kind of oversight Gauquelin had not received a list of criteria and names selected according to those criteria, back in 1986. The French committee seems to have had serious internal communication problems, because they went ahead writing to town halls in 1988, without anybody bothering about the absence of any Gauquelin reactions to the list of 1986. When Gauquelin was sent the preliminary findings in the fall of 1990 he protested bitterly. But then Benski asked him to write down what he thought was wrong. Benksi even paid a personal visit to Gauquelin to discuss matters. Gauquelin responded by making proposals that turned out to be extremely biased. More negotiations and meetings were planned, but these had come to an end when Gauquelin committed suicide in May 1991.

During the checking of the French report Nienhuys compared all findings of the committee with what he knew (from Ertel's data and Gauquelin's publications) about Gauquelin's own data. Perusal of the source books used by the committee showed that many selection errors were made, but that these weren't biased either way. Gauquelin predominantly pointed out errors that worked against his hypothesis. In about 140 cases the French committee reported other dates and times of birth than had been found long ago by Gauquelin (so much for the accuracy of city hall officials and sports dictionaries) and here Gauquelin showed his bias most clearly: he proposed to correct all twenty cases where the correction would raise the Mars percentage and he remained silent about all seventeen cases where such a correction would have the opposite effect. And Gauquelin offered to provide virtually all of the missing thirty-nine data that would raise the Mars effect, but in case of the remaining 134 he only provided additional information in about a third of the cases.

All this checking and computing (including three trips to France) took Nienhuys until the summer of 1996. Meanwhile Ertel had submitted to the *Journal of Scientific Exploration* a paper containing a more or less libelous attack on the honesty of Paul Kurtz. *JSE* allowed Paul Kurtz to submit a rejoinder, which was jointly written by Kurtz, Ranjit Sandhu, and Jan Willem Nienhuys. The research for this rejoinder showed not only that Ertel's calculations were nonsense, but it turned up another interesting fact. Among the names published by Gauquelin there were many whose data might have seemed doubtful at the time they were collected. The Mars percentage among these (almost 165 names) is over 30. Conversely, a similar group in the French investigation who were absent from Gauquelin's files, even though it is almost certain that he searched for them, had a Mars percentage of 6. In other words, Gauquelin may have been biasedly throwing away data that seemed unreliable to him.

So the Mars effect seems now compounded of several experimental errors: first, in 1955, selection of a chance result which happens to be the most impressive among hundreds of similar results. At that time biased computations were probably flattering the outcomes already. Next were biased choices of quality criteria; then biasedly throwing out "unreliable data"; and finally actively trying to modify test results.

The end of the Mars effect debate is not in sight, unfortunately. Professor Ertel keeps churning out long papers with ever newly contrived arguments. When he responded to a critical review of a book of his in *Skepter*, he included a graph showing the Mars effect as a function of citation frequency. Both of us saw immediately that there was something wrong with this graph. Given the size of the error bars, the claimed precision was so incredible that it smacked of fakery. When this criticism was pointed out in the German magazine *Skeptiker*, Ertel responded by suing the magazine (he lost) and by expounding the moral failings of skeptics in a long article in *Correlation*.

A lesson that we have learned from the Mars saga is that one should study one's opponent well. Those who dealt with Gauquelin might have profited from a thorough study of all his writings, rather than rushing headlong into some kind of test. And people who have had dealings with Ertel (including ourselves) might have been more careful in sharing results with him if they had read a 1978 analysis of a so-called textual dogmatism test developed by Ertel:

> many breaches of the elementary rules of statistical testing . . . replacing proofs by suggestions . . . juggling the numbers around until finally an optically impressive distinction is created that cannot be interpreted anymore . . . project his own methodological errors onto his opponents . . . the *nec plus ultra* of lack of taste and ridiculous argumentation . . . theoretical amateurishness . . . a fabric of the most crude subjectivism and horrifically unscientific behavior . . . also in the manner in which he counters criticism . . . slipping in well calculated "misunderstandings" as proofs for a priori disqualifications of criticism . . . on purpose withhold important details and key informations . . . repeatedly misquoting . . . specific argumentation strategy, namely a tendency to personalize general methodological problems. (Keiler 1978, especially pp. 166–80, 208–209)

PRACTICAL (PARA)PSYCHOLOGY

Skepsis has conducted other investigations as well. Together with a small group of parapsychologists we examined the conjecture that the output of a physical random generator might be influenced retroactively on the moment a human observer looked at the output, long after the data were copied onto diskettes. Our subject had been very succesful in earlier uncontrolled tests.

He observed 150,000 random bits. The original data and the control data were kept in a locked strongbox. Finally the experimental bits were compared with the control bits. The difference just failed to reach the traditionally basic 5 percent significance level. In most respects this is the best experiment performed by Skepsis.

Together with the largest national newspaper and a group of parapsychologists we organized a contest to "predict the news of 1995." For this the contestants (altogether more than one thousand) had to assess twenty-five news items varying from a serious accident with a nuclear reactor to the exchange rate of the dollar. They had to assign these events a probability varying from 10 to 90 percent. After a year it turned out that contestants who said they had used paranormal means scored a bit worse than contestants who said they had used their wits. The nice thing in such a contest is that there is always a winner: the person who has by accident or by design scored most points.

A minor problem with this experiment was how to assign the rewards. If anybody wants to repeat a similar experiment, here is how. Suppose someone assigns a probability P that a certain event happens, and probability Q that it doesn't happen. Of course, P and Q sum to 1. The most obvious reward function is then the logarithm of P if the event happens, and the logarithm of Q if the event doesn't happen. In this manner one cannot possibly improve one's expected reward (in fact the amount of information or negative entropy) by assigning wrong probabilities.

A major problem with this experiment was that the contestants were allowed to hand in "free" predictions. About 2,400 of such free predictions were handed in. About half of them concerned Dutch royalty, politics, soccer, war, the weather, and accidents—in that order of frequency. The parapsychologist partners in this experiment had promised to provide an analysis of these free predictions, but their report was never finished.

The activities of Skepsis have not only been in the realm of more or less scientific investigations. Various forms of quackery pose a real threat and in this field Skepsis has been active as well. Our secretary Nanninga discovered in his hometown, Groningen, a lady, Wies Moget, who practiced a viciously paranoid form of psychotherapy for real and alleged incest victims. One reason to take action was that municipal officials sent welfare clients to this Moget and paid their bills too, quite contrary to usual practice. These officials weren't interested in Nanninga's findings, and so he published a well-researched article about it in several newspapers and periodicals. Moget hit back with the ultimate unscientific weapon: she sued for defamation—and lost. The government aid to Moget was stopped, but Moget had more friends and she is still in business. The details of this story can be read (in English) on the Web site of Skepsis, so we won't repeat it here.

THE FUTURE

What is the future of Skepsis and the skeptical movement? We don't know. For the moment we have our hands full with what comes our way. We try to expand our fields of interest, but we cannot stray too far from our traditional fields. A major shortcoming of the skeptical movement in general is that it operates on the fringe of science. Our own commitment to the skeptical cause is part of a wider commitment as science teachers, but this is of course not true for all skeptics. Others are motivated by compassion for the hapless victims of occultist and superstitious exploitation. We are a kind of consumer protection organization.

It is our experience that talking about morals, religion, and related matters quickly degenerates into endless and inconclusive discussions. That is the main reason why we have always avoided broadening skepticism into the religious realm. This means that modern skepticism probably never will develop into a movement with a wide appeal and a strong moral force.

In a discotheque there are large crowds who dance and have fun, small numbers of people who make the music, and a single doorman who keeps out the worst troublemakers. That's us.

ACKNOWLEDGMENT

The authors thank Rob Nanninga for his helpful remarks.

REFERENCES

Benski, C., et al. 1996. *The "Mars Effect": A French Test Of Over 1000 Sports Champions*. Amherst, N.Y.: Prometheus Books.

Ertel, S. 1988. "Raising the Hurdle for the Athlete's Mars Effect: Association Covaries with Eminence." *Journal of Scientific Exploration* 2: 53–82.

———. 1993. "Puzzling Eminence Effects Might Make Good Sense." *Journal of Scientific Exploration* 7: 145–54.

———. 1993. "Comments on Dutch Investigations of the Gauquelin Mars Effect." *Journal of Scientific Exploration* 7: 283–92.

———. 1997. "Gauquelins Mars-Effekt: Illusion oder Irritation? Zum übereilten Abgesang von Dr. J. W. Nienhuys" (Gauquelin's Mars Effect: Illusion or Irritation? On the Overhasty Farewell Song of Dr. J. W. Nienhuys). *Skeptiker* 10, no. 3: 88–89, 91–92.

———. 2000. "Debunking with Caution—Cleaning Up Mars Effect Research." *Correlation* 18, no. 2: 9–41.

Ertel, S., and K. Irving. 1996. "Biased Data Selection in Mars Effect Research." *Journal of Scientific Exploration* 11: 1–18.

Keiler, P. 1978. "Wie 'wissenschaftlich' ist das 'DTA- Verfahren'?" (How "Scientific" Is the "DTA-Procedure"?). In P. Keiler and M. Stadler, *Erkenntnis oder Dogmatismus? Kritik des psychologisches Dogmatismus-Konzepts* (Knowledge or Dogmatism? Criticism of the Psychological Dogmatism Concept), 132–209. Cologne: Pahl-Rugenstein.

Kurtz, P., J. W. Nienhuys, and R. Sandhu. 1997. "Is the 'Mars Effect' Genuine?" *Journal of Scientific Exploration* 11: 19–39.

Nienhuys, J. W., ed. 1992. *Science or Pseudo? The Mars Effect and Other Claims.* Utrecht: Skepsis.

Nienhuys, J. W. 1993a. "Comments on Puzzling Eminence Effects." *Journal of Scientific Exploration* 7: 155–59.

———. 1993b. "Dutch Investigations of the Gauquelin Mars Effect." *Journal of Scientific Exploration* 7: 271–81.

———. 1996. "Wie der Mars-Effekt zustande kam" (How the Mars Effect Came into Existence). *Skeptiker* 9, no. 4: 124–27.

———. 1997. "Ertels 'Mars-Effekt': Anatomie einer Pseudowissenschaft" (Ertel's "Mars Effect": Anatomy of a Pseudoscience). *Skeptiker* 10 (3): 92–98.

———. 1997. "The Mars Effect in Retrospect." *Skeptical Inquirer* 21, no. 6: 24–29. (Also on www.skepsis.nl)

CORNELIS DE JAGER is professor of space research at the Astronomical Institute at Utrecht, Netherlands, and is on the advisory council of the Planetary Society. His research focus is on solar physics. A minor planet, 3798 de Jager 2402 T-3, discovered on October 16, 1977, was named in his honor. De Jager is president of the European Council of Skeptical Organizations, and a Fellow of CSICOP.

JAN WILLEM NIENHUYS is a mathematician who used to teach at the Eindhoven University of Technology. He is a board member of Skepsis and presently is a full-time skeptic and freelance writer.

22

A NEW HOPE
From a Good Idea to Real Change

MASSIMO POLIDORO

I taly has a long tradition of skeptical thinkers, in fact the origins of philosophical skepticism can be traced back to the Greco-Roman world, when philosophers like Pyrrho of Elis, Sextus Empiricus, and Carneades defined and advanced the skeptical outlook. When, subsequently, skepticism went into decline in Christian Europe for over a thousand years, it was again from Italy that the seeds of modern skeptical and scientific thought were sown.

From Padua, in fact, Galileo Galilei demonstrated between the sixteenth and seventeenth centuries that we should doubt received authority and base our views of the physical cosmos not on what Aristotle or the Church said, but on empirical observation. This was a key factor in the growth of scientific methods of inquiry, where hypotheses are tested by both evidence and mathematical inferences. As a consequence of his modern views, Galileo was imprisoned by the ecclesiastic authority until the end of his life.

It was only in the twentieth century, however, that skepticism became an organized world movement. Soon after the formation of CSICOP in the United States, in 1976, the idea that similar organizations could develop in other countries as well took shape. In Italy, the central motor behind this idea was scientific journalist Piero Angela, who conducted for RAI TV a critical investigation of parapsychology: it was the first time in Italy that paranormal claims were being seriously questioned. The TV series, and the book that ensued from it, generated a large amount of interest and controversy and a group of scientists, including three Nobel Prize winners, signed a document prepared by Angela in which the idea to form in Italy a committee with aims similar to those of CSICOP was launched. CSICOP itself worked hard to get a group started in Italy and Paul Kurtz visited the country twice, repeatedly trying to stimulate the birth of a new organization there.

It was only in 1988, however, that things finally took the right turn. Taking advantage of a visit to Italy by James Randi, Angela gathered all the Italians then subscribing to the *Skeptical Inquirer* (about thirty people) and a plan was quickly formed. Lorenzo Montali, then a young student, would go for a three-month stay at CSICOP's headquarters in order to understand how a similar committee should work and operate. As for myself, also a young student at the time, I was offered the chance to live the dream of my life: to become James Randi's "sorcerer's apprentice," learn the "fine art of baloney detection," travel the globe testing psychics and dowsers, and then bring that experience back to the Italian committee.

CICAP (the Italian Committee for the Investigation of Claims of the Paranormal) was thus born: we were backed from the start by some of the most prestigious names in science, and this certainly made it easier to be listened to by the media. However, we were only a handful of volunteers and the work to be done quickly increased. A bulletin had to be prepared, printed, and distributed; subscribers had to be kept informed and updated; investigations had to be conducted; journalists had to be called; lectures had to be organized. None of us had previously done anything of the sort, but we did our best, made mistakes of course, and in time we learned what to do and what to avoid in order to reach the best results.

In 1990 CICAP published only two issues of a small newsletter, had about two hundred members, organized about ten lectures, and went on TV possibly three or four times. Also, the only skeptical book existing at the time was still the one published in 1978 by Piero Angela.

Ten years later, in 1999, CICAP was publishing six issues of a bimonthly magazine, plus various other monographs, collections of articles, and other publications; had about two thousand members, organized in eleven regional groups all over Italy; presented about four lectures a month all over the country and hosted a national conference that gathered about seven hundred participants and had all the newspapers and TVs in Italy talking about the event: in total, that year CICAP was on national TV about fifty times. Also, the committee helped the birth in Rome of Avverbi, the first Italian publishing house willing to give voice to critical examinations of paranormal claims. The result was the publication (through various publishers, in addition to Avverbi) of over sixty skeptical books in fewer than four years.

One of the most important tools for the development of CICAP turned out to be, undoubtedly, the Internet: on the one hand it allowed all the members to be constantly in touch with one another and, thus, it rendered possible to organize and promote an unprecedented amount of undertakings; on the other hand, the Internet released the committee from the tyranny of television's imperatives. Our Web site (www.cicap.org) quickly became our most powerful advertising instrument, to the point that we now usually receive about one hundred requests a week for a sample copy of our magazine (20 percent of which then transform into real subscriptions).

At times it seemed very hard to continue: when funds were short and volunteers were just a handful; when the publishers didn't think that skeptical books could sell or when the press didn't seem to be interested anymore in our work; when the attacks from the opponents were particularly hard and it looked as if our work was useless. At these times we asked ourselves why did we have to put up with all that, why did we have to invest so much time, effort, and money in something that didn't seem to give results.

But we persisted, because—at first only occasionally, but then ever more often—we could see that what we did was important to a lot of people. More and more we received the compliments not only of the scientists but of the public as well, a part of which appeared to be quite conscious of the importance of our efforts. We finally received solid proof that we were on the right track when, in 1998, after launching a fund-raising campaign in order to buy an office for CICAP, the donations actually started to arrive and, in the spring of 2000, we were finally able to buy a two-floor office in Galileo's Padua, of course.

This marks the beginning of a new approach in the work of CICAP: plans are underway to start a series of courses and workshops with the aim to form and prepare new and competent experts; another road to cover is in the schools, with lectures for the students and refresher courses and teaching kits for teachers. Also, we are planning a monitoring group that will keep an eye on every newspaper and TV channel, report on every false or unfounded claim presented as truth, and be ready to write and call journalists and editors in order to present them with correct facts and data. In time, such an approach can only lead journalists to be more careful in presenting their news.

This, then, is the story of how what seemed to be just a good idea became, through the perseverance and enthusiasm of a small group of friends, a solid reality in the cultural panorama of Italy and a hope for a less superstitious society.

In the end, in fact, I personally think that the aim of a group like ours does not have to be that of "converting" people to science, or keeping them away from "dangerous" beliefs. This, in fact, is what currently happens in Italian society, where the Vatican condemns New Age and paranormal beliefs but, at the same time, promotes unfounded paranormal claims as diverse as stigmata, exorcism, miraculous healings, Padre Pio's supernatural powers, the Shroud of Turin, weeping icons, and the blood of St. Januarius.

Skepticism should not be another form of religion but rather a sensible approach to life. Everyone has the right to believe whatever he or she likes; we only want people to be correctly informed in regard to paranormal and pseudoscientific claims. Only then will one possess all the information needed to make up his or her mind and, in the end, be able to choose whether to believe an unfounded claim or not.

Personally, I am an optimist and I always try to see the good in everything. However, if we look at what is happening in today's societies the future seems to be darker. Today, we witness a large sector of politics embracing antiscientific trends and fundamentalistic religious views in a fearsome mix-up.

What the skeptical movement can do in such circumstances is very limited, unfortunately, but our contribution can be very important. By providing a trustworthy reference point for the public and the media, we can help keep lit the light of reason and hope that our small candle in the dark will soon transform itself into the light of day in what is still, in Carl Sagan's words, a "demon-haunted world."

MASSIMO POLIDORO is the executive director of the Italian Committee for the Investigation of Claims of the Paranormal (CICAP), the editor of *Scienza & Paranormale*, and a Fellow of CSICOP. A psychologist and author, his areas of expertise include psychology and techniques of deception in parapsychology; the history of Spiritualism and psychical research; and magic, in particular Harry Houdini. He is the author of thirteen books, including *Final Séance: The Strange Friendship Between Houdini and Conan Doyle* (Prometheus Books, 2001). Web site: www.massimopolidoro.com; e-mail: polidoro@cicap.org.

23

A SKEPTIC IN A STRANGE LAND

MARIO MENDEZ-ACOSTA

Skepticism is an uncommon attitude in Mexico. This doesn't necessarily mean that superstition is any more rampant than in any other contemporary country, or that pseudoscience is accepted as equal to real knowledge. But it certainly means that most thinking persons, including scientists, teachers, and intellectuals, do not consider that opposing or criticizing crackpot ideas is a really important issue, or is something worth doing instead of doing science, promoting culture, or discussing contemporary knowledge. Sometimes the skeptic is criticized for "playing along" with the paranormalists' game when taking part in debates against them. But the serious problem is that pseudoscience is growing mainly because it is largely unopposed. It slowly gnaws at high standards in journalism, in academia, and in the general public's understanding of science. Even within the academic scientific community, the task of opposing pseudoscience is seen as something of secondary if not of marginal relevance. But at the same time, the public continues to gradually lose its taste for good scientific information, something that in the long run threatens even the scientist's own livelihood.

Yet, in spite of this, nothing compares in personal satisfaction with being a skeptic in this sometimes all-too-gullible society. Seeing once and again the desolate faces of the purveyors of hogwash as you proceed to destroy their claims in public, or through the electronic media, especially when they expect no opposition with valid and convincing arguments, is one of the greatest intellectual pleasures that one can imagine. This is especially true when the proponents of magical thinking are aware that they are deceiving the public.

288

The joy of being a skeptic, where pseudoscience is not perceived as a threat to civilization, surfaces almost every day, whenever an unknown person stops you on the street and congratulates you for something you said on a TV talk show, sometimes many years ago, a statement that turned that person into a skeptic himself. Of course, confrontations with UFOlogists or paranormalists are not easy in today's world of strident and high-profile debates in front of a jeering public or in marathonic TV shows. These can become very trying experiences, and some of my colleagues have become really reluctant to partake in any more of these *Jerry Springer*-styled shows. Yet, the seed is sown and, although outnumbered, there is always at least one new true skeptic in every crowd, somebody that understands what we are trying to convey and sees through the cloud of fallacies of the charlatans and begins his or her own career as a part-time debunker.

Perhaps the greatest problem for the skeptic in Mexico is the extraordinary lack of critical information available about most paranormal claims. Most of it consists of isolated paragraphs included in popular science books or magazines. There are very few openly skeptical books published in Spanish, and skepticism sometimes has to be introduced through the back door of scientific publications—although once it makes it there, it can become very effective. Plain criticism of popular pseudosciences like homeopathy or UFOlogy is considered an unfair and rancorous attack on them. And many TV and radio talk-show hosts, and even a large segment of the public, usually demand that a proponent of a pseudoscience be present in any program whenever any critical issue is addressed. Unfortunately, the contrary is almost never true, so that when proponents appear in the media to attack, directly or indirectly, the scientific point of view, no one expects a scientist—or a skeptic—to be there in order to defend the rational point of view—this is often confused with "intransigence" and "closed-mindedness."

There are a few arguments that we usually manage to convey to the Mexican public. One is to state the fact that the public has the right to learn about critical information concerning any claim about science, health, or the general scientific worldview—even if this means bad news for their dearly held beliefs. No one will openly renounce such a right—so that fact can open ears to the skeptical point of view. Everybody agrees that they have the right to be playing with a full deck of cards, and they also agree that the critical outlook is all too scarce. Thus, if the skeptic manages to establish his position in society as a reliable source of critical information concerning the paranormal, alternative medicines, and other strange claims, then he is successful in accomplishing his job.

Another argument that can become quite convincing is to emphasize that the common denominator of all pseudoscientific and paranormal claims lies in the fact that, almost without exception, they always promise to yield something in exchange for nothing, or almost nothing: knowledge without study; the accomplishment of something without strenuous effort; information concerning the future; or better stated, knowledge about the effects without knowledge of their causes.

Ignorance is bliss, at least in the short run, and the lack of adequate information about the origin, tenets, and foundations of many pseudosciences becomes sheer bliss, even for many professionals in medicine. Medical doctors often appear along with homeopaths on talk shows, and the general attitude of some uninformed doctors is that this popular pseudoscience really counteracts the effects of many maladies, at least some of the secondary causes that contribute to the onset of a disease. Some of this may be due to the placebo effect. But they have never heard about the preposterous theories behind the claims, and, being of good faith, they may even believe that it's "rational," although perhaps somewhat primitive. When confronted with the basic tenet of homeopathy, that illnesses cause germs and not vice versa, they reel back in disbelief. When I get to read to them what James Tyler Kent, a classic British homeopath, has to say about this (from a little book that is still used as a text by homeopaths in any of the two official homeopathic medical schools that exist in Mexico) they are amazed: Kent claims that "bacteria are the result of illnesses. We will . . . demonstrate, with absolute certainty, that microscopic organisms are not the cause of diseases, but they are its companions, they come just after them, they are the sweepers, the garbagemen of a sick organism, and they are completely harmless." It's then when it dawns upon those honest physicians that all is not right in their tranquil view of what alternative medicines really mean.

It's interesting that homeopathic practitioners—like the dean of the School of Homeopathy of the otherwise-prestigious Polytechnical Institute of Mexico, when confronted with this sort of evidence, avoids discussing the basic arguments of what homeopathy professes. Instead, he goes on to claim grandiose fabrications that allowed him to affirm that skeptics are "ignorami," because they overlook, for example, the fact that modern homeopathy is based on advanced physical concepts like "fluoroscopy, magnetic nuclear resonance, atomic absorption, and other spectrometric and telemetric methods that show that the changes caused by homeopathic dilutions in water really exist." This is what this same fellow stated on a letter he sent to the director of the science magazine *Ciencia y Desarrollo* (Science and Development, where I'm a contributor) demanding that I be silenced. This fancy-sounding gibberish is difficult to simply dismiss firsthand for an educated layman or even a genuine physician. What the skeptic has to do in response is to immerse himself in the study of atomic physics in order to refute such claims. Even a qualified physicist cannot answer them without first understanding what it is that homeopaths are trying to sustain.

The organized skeptic movement in Mexico was founded in 1979 by an American conjurer and writer, resident in Mexico, the late Craige McCombe

Snader Jr., a scholar in the history of magic and a wonderful man. He had been in touch with Paul Kurtz. It wasn't until 1989 that the group was legally incorporated. It organized a world conference in cooperation with CSICOP in that same year; and it has since convoked more than two hundred national and local conferences. It has published a newsletter and a magazine on skeptical UFOlogy. We have conducted two long-running radio shows on skepticism and humanism; and we have appeared on more than twenty televised debates against UFOlogists and paranormalists and we have been interviewed by Spanish-language American networks and even by the A&E TV network (on one of the many UFO sightings reported in Mexico).

One of the most powerful sources of irrationality in Mexico is the relentless activity—by means of the most important national TV network—of a UFOlogy cult that masquerades as a crack team of scientific researchers. This group is headed by Jaime Maussán, a TV moderator who once anchored the Mexican version of *60 Minutes*, and who has managed to amass a huge fortune by exploiting popular belief in UFOs—imagine Mike Wallace transformed into a true believer in a strange paranoid UFO cult. He has a weekly hour-long program that airs Sundays on prime time. Maussán manufactures and sells hundreds of different TV videos on UFOs and other phenomena—as occurred with the Chupacabras craze. The network has no moral restraints about broadcasting obvious fabrications.

The strategy against this sort of organized misinformation has been to counteract the claims by means of the press, scientific publications, and specialized magazines, and by participating in debates on several talk shows—where Maussán and his followers are routinely invited as "experts," whereas skeptics are unfairly characterized as "bitter spoilers" of fun. This occurs in spite of the fact that the skeptics' UFO subcommittee includes some of the most widely known and respected UFO investigators. Incidentally, all the members (like skeptics in other countries) began as believers in the extraterrestrial hypothesis and had published in pro-UFO magazines, but eventually became skeptical after many years of thorough investigation.

Yet, time and patience do prevail. Prophecies of doom and of imminent landing of extraterrestrials have failed to materialize. The world didn't end in August 1999, as the disciples of Michel de Nostradamus prophesied it would; civilization didn't collapse because of the Y2K scare, as sensationalist writers warned, like the American writer Edward Jourdon, whose translated book *Time Bomb 2000* was widely read in Mexico and promoted this craze. In Mexico, it was the same Maussán who jumped on this wagon. His endorsement of the infamous Hale-Bopp comet's gigantic companion spaceship—that finally caused the tragic mass suicide of the members of the Heaven's Gate Cult—has become one of our best weapons against him. For once, he and his crack team of colorful cranks remained silent, obviously disturbed. Since then, debating against them has become much easier.

The UFO cult in Mexico is supported by the teachings of a Spanish priest, Salvador Freixedo, who claims that extraterrestrials have already landed, and that there are more than two hundred different civilizations visiting us, most of them hostile. This cult claims that there are alien bases beneath every U.S. military facility all over the world and that there are straight-lined tunnels linking each. Incredibly, many who believe this preposterous tale manage to pass as genuine journalists to hold high-profile jobs in the media and are well received by the public. The depth of human folly makes one wonder why there is an urge to escape reason.

This is the burden of the skeptic: to worry about the increase in gullibility and the decline of rationality. Concern about these matters doesn't affect most educated people, who chuckle about such weird beliefs, dismiss them as innocuous eccentricities, and go on with their business of living, as if nothing of consequence was happening.

Strange new beliefs appear every year. Today is the time again for belief in wondrous "activated" water, which is able to heal everything that ails you; it even works as a potent antiseptic! Tap water is another popular nostrum in Mexico—it is easy to obtain and can do no real harm. Sanitary authorities can easily grant a registration for bottled water and there are no complaints! In the early nineties a savvy though callous businessman, Hector Cha'n, began selling plain water from his farm in rural central Mexico. He claimed that water from Tlacote could heal anything: cancer, AIDS, arthritis, you name it! At first, he gave it away free, filling large containers that people from all over the country carried to his ranch. Visitors waited their turn for days, without any shelter in an incredibly long line along the highway that led to his house. This started an international craze. Cha'n—recently deceased—falsely claimed that Magic Johnson himself visited his ranch and took away hundreds of gallons of the magic liquid. The water was exported to Argentina. At Buenos Aires airport, desperate crowds waited several days for the release of a sequestered shipment of Tlacote water. Finally, the authorities yielded and allowed importers to sell the precious bottles of the liquid from Tlacote to the whimpering crowd. Cha'n claims that his water was "lighter than common water." Tests made in several laboratories could not find any difference from tap water; furthermore, it wasn't even sanitary. Cha'n switched his claim and said that his water was a gift of God. Who can argue against that? (Why doesn't God cure the ailments directly?) As usual, our group managed to publish several articles in the press debunking this claim. We also appeared on several TV shows and sent information to Argentina, where the local skeptics did a good job in unmasking the hoax. All this somehow led us to something that we considered to be our most important impending task: the establishment in Mexico of a mechanism for enforcing accountability among alternative medicine healers.

Recently the federal government created a special board to hear complaints concerning medical malpractice, especially within public-health organizations; and it aimed to service the poorest segment of the population. This included a crackdown on doctors that prescribed quack cures over the radio; and for the first time very effective lawsuits could be brought to bear against inept physicians. Some of these have resulted in heavy sanctions being imposed. Practicing medicine without a medical degree was also prohibited. All this sounds fine—okay, but there is a problem. Now it just so happens that real doctors can go to jail if they goof up, and they cannot prescribe medicine on radio or TV. But if you are an alternative medicine therapist, a magic or mental healer, or just a common crank, you are not accountable to that board, and you can say what you want through radio or TV. Of course, if you really want to, you can sue fake healers. The penal code states that the false claims of healers are equivalent to fraud. You can accuse them of that, but you have to go to the tribunals and to the criminal district attorney to lodge your charges. You need to bring with you a good lawyer along with hard evidence. Perhaps in time, with good counseling, and after spending considerable sums of money, you may get justice!

With the backing of some nongovernment organizations, the skeptics of Mexico are attempting to change the law, to enforce accountability on the acts of anyone who diagnoses and prescribes without examining the patients,

MARIO MENDEZ-ACOSTA was born in Mexico City in 1946. He studied civil engineering at the University of Mexico, and got a master's degree in planning at that same institution. He started as a journalist in 1979, writing for one of the journals of the Mexican government's science agency (Conacyt). That very same year he started the Mexican skeptic group SOMIE, which he still heads. From 1982 to 1992 he was a current-affairs TV commentator on Channel 13 in Mexico City. In 1992 he became a political columnist for *Excelsior*, a Mexican daily newspaper. From 1995 to 2000 he conducted two daily radio talk shows on science, humanism, and skepticism, and has appeared on more than fifty TV shows debating and debunking UFOlogists and other paranormalists. He currently writes the skeptical column "Science and Its Rivals" for *Ciencia y Desarrollo* (Science and Development), another science journal of Conacyt, and also the skeptical section "The Skeptical Eye" for the National Polytechnic Institute's science journal. He is the author of *Biography of Life* (1997), a book of essays on evolution and biology, and *Self-Medication and Alternative Medicines* (2000), a skeptical view of contemporary medical pseudo-sciences and irrational health practices. In 1997 he was named a Fellow of CSICOP. He received the National Journalism Prize in both 1989 and in 1993 and is currently executive president of the Mexican Journalists' Club.

especially if they suffer any damage to their health. This was brought about by a well-known radio host—a brave woman who is also active in the civil-rights movement—and who suffers from chronic hepatitis C. While listening to another radio program, she heard a widely known quack prescribing the drinking of your own urine as an infallible recipe against illness. This illustration provides an interesting case of how normal people may suddenly become aware of the need to counter the claims of the charlatans. This very same group was until then seen as some sort of amusing cranks. When illness is at stake they become something more dangerous—purveyors of false and injurious nostrums. What an important role for skeptics to play in exposing such spurious claims.

24

SKEPTICISM IN RUSSIA
Past and Present

VALERII A. KUVAKIN

Skepticism as an idea and general attitude toward the outside world and human knowledge per se did not develop a specific intellectual school in Russia. We can find, however, in the history of Russian culture a number of strong proponents of skeptical philosophy as a mode of thought.

One of the earliest forms of domestic skepticism was expressed within the broad heretical movements of the eighteenth and nineteenth centuries. The leaders of the most influential trend in heresies—*zhidovsvueshie*—attacked the official institution of the Orthodox Church. They denied the icons, the dogma of the Holy Trinity, the necessity of monasteries and many religious practices, and they called for the reformation of Christianity on the basis of reason, philosophy, astronomic and historical knowledge, and humanist ideas.

More sophisticated skeptical approaches took place in Russia during the reign of Peter the Great (1682–1725) when theistic patterns of thought were replaced with a geocentric picture of the universe and science competed with religion.

The central figure of the Age of the Russian Enlightenment (from the early eighteenth to the first quarter of the nineteenth century) was Mikhail Lomonosov (1711–1765), the founder of Moscow University. He was a strong defender of the separation of the church from the university and science from religion. As a pioneer of the naturalistic (materialistic) tradition in Russian philosophy he was extremely skeptical of the doctrine of phlogiston. In fact, Lomonosov rejected the existence of any phenomena or substances outside nature, which was understood as eternal, endless, evolving, and self-creative, and available to human investigation. The realism of his epistemological position included the idea of the fallibility of human knowledge, though it did not undermine the possibility of general progressive penetration by human reason into the nature of the universe. In his words: "I shall not attack people who have made a contribution to the republic of science for their mistakes, but shall try to put their good ideas to use. . . . Noticing their mistakes is not worth much; to do things better—that is what befits a worthy man."[1]

In the nineteenth century skepticism in Russia played a role basically in two fields: (1) in freethinking—as skepticism toward religion, and (2) in the natural sciences—as methodological skepticism, an important aspect of human knowledge. The first kind of skepticism was exemplified by Mikhail Bakunin (1814–1876), whose atheism was stamped with a persistent, strong, and sometimes even violent critique of religion and the church. He considered the church as a main enemy, along with the state, of human beings, the source and instrument of their slavery. "Man," he wrote, "emerged from animal slavery, and passing through divine slavery, a transitory period between his animality and his humanity, he is now marching on to the conquest and realization of human liberty."[2] Two social thinkers and anthropologists, Nikolai Chernyshevsky (1828–1889) and Pyotr Lavrov (1823–1900) were no less influential Russian skeptics.

Skepticism among the leading figures of Russian science developed rapidly in the last third of the nineteenth century. This is usually associated with naturalistic materialism. This outstanding group of skeptically minded scientists included, among others, Ivan Sechenov (1829–1905), Dmitry Mendeleev (1834–1907), Ivan Mechnikov (1845–1916), Ivan Pavlov (1849–1936), and Vladimir Vernadsy (1863–1945).

The great chemist Dmitry Mendeleev, who is broadly known in Russia as a discoverer of the periodical law of chemical elements, was one of the first organizers of the scientific investigation of the claims of the paranormal. In 1875, the Russian Physical Society, headed by Mendeleev, set up a commission to study spiritual phenomena. And in 1876 he published his book *Materials for a Judgment about Spiritism* (*Materialy dlya suzhdeniya o spiritizme*) in which he concluded, from the commission's investigation and his own observations, that so-called spiritualist phenomena came from unconscious movements or deliberate deceits, and that spiritism was superstition connected with archaic consciousness and backwardness. He described spiritualism as a "form of mysticism," the condition of "the childhood of thought."

Ivan Sechenov's works in psychology played a no less important role in debunking paranormal prejudices. As a father of objective psychology and a reflective theory of knowledge he demonstrated the naturalistic character of all kinds of psychological acts. In his famous *Reflexes of the Brain* Sechenov developed the idea of the unity of animate and inanimate nature, the conception of life as a natural process taking place in the form of interaction of the organism and the environment. He proceeded from the Darwinian conception of the evolution of the living world, recognizing man's genetic kinship with the animal kingdom, and considered the brain as the material organ of consciousness. Sechenov's objective psychology did not leave room for any supernatural phenomena in the field of human conduct and mental activity.

The twentieth century was marked within Russia by the deep and dramatic conflict of social relationships and cultural traditions. Religious philosophy and Marxist-Leninist ideology clashed, and were interpreted as the major symbols of the Russian past and future. But both of them turned out to be dogmatic, fanatic, and intolerant of all other worldviews. In spite of such unfavorable circumstances there were some exceptions; for example, the existential skepticism of Lev Shestov (1866–1938). The peculiarity of Shestov's philosophy was that he strove for ultimate skepticism. This entailed not only scientific methodology, but metaphysical and theological assumptions as well. Total skepticism led him to doubt the ability of reason to develop durable knowledge. In his struggle against *veritates æternae* and the search for truth he appealed to the realities of borderline cases, uncertainty, and the unknown, which, he said, "can have nothing in common with the known," and "can in no way . . . be reduced to the known."[3] Searching for the "living truth" he hoped to find it by "unusual" means in "unusual" realms of human existence. That is why he insisted that "philosophy must . . . teach man to live in uncertainty . . . and that man is afraid of uncertainty and hides from it behind various dogmas."[4]

The domination of Communist ideology in the Soviet Union deformed all spheres of human activity. It put the color of militancy and suspicion on freethinking and atheist studies; scientific researches were considered as one of the fronts of "the class struggle." Only in the 1980s did we begin to see a softening of this hard line in party policy. Dr. Sergeí Kapitza made one of the breakthroughs in the field of free inquiry in his long-running television series *Obvious and Improbable* (*Ochevidnoe—neverojatnoe*). This popular talk show brought to the attention of viewers the most advanced frontiers of science in the world. He offered his Russian audience the importance of critical thinking, common sense, skepticism, and freedom of scientific inquiry.

The landmark in the Russian history of freethinking, free inquiry, and skepticism occurred in the early 1990s, after the crash of the Communist ideological and political system. For the first time in their history the Russian people gained unprecedented freedom of thought and speech. The rapid pluralization of post-Soviet society gave birth to a complex and contradictory situation. On the one hand, a number of forgotten antiscientific religious and New Age practices—from archaic magic to satanic healers, astrology, and psychic phenomena—"fruit formerly forbidden" (by the

Communist Party) was now offered to an unsuspecting public. On the other hand, freedom of conscience and exposure to scientifically based worldviews restored (in a new and democratic form) the ideas of secular humanism, rationalism, and skepticism as an alternative to both traditional and dogmatic orthodox religion and the now-discredited Marxist ideology.

One of the first steps in creating skeptical groups in post–Soviet Russia was related to activities of the Russian Humanist Society, which was formed in 1995 as a voluntary organization, dedicated to promoting and disseminating the ideas of secular humanism, rationalism, and scientifically oriented skepticism. Actually, this process began in 1988 when Russian philosophers began meeting Western humanists and skeptics, and they in turn visited Russia time and again. This culminated in 1997 with the creation of a Center for Inquiry at Moscow State University.

I am glad to say that I have been involved in these new and daring initiatives. Among our activities are the founding of a new journal, *Common Sense*, which provides articles and reviews of skepticism and secular humanism. We have convened conferences at Moscow and St. Petersburg Universities; we now have members coming from all over the former Soviet Union. We are also in the process of developing a new literature by translating and publishing books and monographs on skepticism and secular humanism in Russian. Moreover, we have founded two student freethought groups at Moscow State University.

For a long period of time we had been isolated from the world intellectual community, and hence it is refreshing to be exposed to the deeper trends of scientific and skeptical thought. Unfortunately, there is a good deal of cynicism and pessimism among the Russian population, first with the disillusionment with Communism for having failed its ideals, and second with the slow pace at which economic transformation has uplifted the lives of ordinary people. Russia is now importing many schools of philosophy and theology—including postmodernism—and some of these are antiscientific, for they deny the possibility of gaining objective knowledge about the world. Others demean human power, and deny that we can resolve social problems or provide new ideals for the future.

Humanist Manifesto 2000 offers an optimistic and realistic defense of the possibilities of ameliorating the human condition; scientific naturalism, which it defends, is an important viewpoint that needs an audience in Russia. I am pleased to say that many distinguished Russian scientists and philosophers endorsed this *Manifesto* (such as Garry Abelev, Vitaly Ginzburg, Yuri Efremov, and Alexander Razin).

I am particularly pleased that I (and my colleagues) have been able to attend international conferences and to visit the Center for Inquiry in Amherst, New York, and we look forward to continued cooperation. The best antidote for nonsense—old and new—is critical thinking, and we welcome working with our fellow skeptics in this endeavor. The best hopes for the future, in our view, are science and reason and the defense of democracy—views essential to secular humanism.

NOTES

1. Mikhail Lomonosov, *Izbrannye filosofskie proizvedeniya* (Selected Philosophical Works) (Moscow, 1950), pp. 92–93.
2. G. P. Maximoff (ed.), *The Political Philosophy of Bakunin* (New York: Free Press, 1953), p. 74.
3. L. Shestov, *Sobranie sochineniy* (Collected Works), vol. 4, 2d ed. (St. Petersburg, 1911), pp. 23, 27.
4. Ibid., p. 84.

VALERII A. KUVAKIN, Ph.D. in philosophy, is a professor at Moscow State University; the founder (1995) and chairman of the Russian Humanist Society; the editor of the quarterly *Zdravyj Smysl* (Common Sense), subtitled *Magazine for Skeptics, Optimists, and Humanists.* He is a member of the Committee for Debunking of Antiscience and Falsification of Experimental Data under the Presidium of the Russian Academy of Science. Professor Kuvakin is the author of more than twelve books, including *A Critique of N. Berdiaev's Existentialism* (1976), *Religious Philosophy in Russia* (1980), *Marxist Philosophical Thought in the USA* (1980), *What Philosophy Is?* (1988), *Vladimir Lenin's Worldview* (1990), *Personal Metaphysics of Hope and Wonder* (1993), *Your Heaven and Hell: Humanity and Inhumanity of Human Being* (1998) (all in Russian, the last one is going to be published by Prometheus Books as *In Search of Our Humanity* [2001]), *A History of Russian Philosophy: From the Tenth Through the Twentieth Centuries,* 2 vols. (Prometheus Books, 1993). He is the editor of more than ten books, including five Russian editions of works written by American scholars and originally published in the United States: James Lawler, *I.Q., Heredity, and Racism* (1984); Howard Parsons, *Man in the Contemporary Word* (1987); Paul Kurtz, *Forbidden Fruit* (1993); Paul Kurtz, *The Transcendental Temptation* (1999); and Paul Kurtz, *The Courage to Become* (2000).

25

LIBERATION FROM THE DARK DUNGEONS OF BLIND BELIEF

SANAL EDAMARUKU

A sunny September morning in 1995. Driving to the Rationalist head-quarters I noticed extraordinary long queues in front of two temples on the way. Unusual for the morning hour, the streets were full of people talking, whispering, laughing, running. There was excitement in the air. Our office was in a state of high activity when I reached it. Everybody tried to talk to me at the same time. Phones were ringing unendingly, messages were heaping up on my desk, and the tapes of the answering machine were full. Two journalists were waiting for me; a TV team was expected to come at any moment. "The greatest miracle of the century" was in full swing. In thousands of temples in India, the statues of the elephant god Ganesh and other deities belonging to the Shiva family were drinking milk. Since it was found at dawn, the news spread like wildfire. People forgot about going to work or to school and flocked to the nearest temple, carrying milk in vessels, glasses, and packets to offer it to the gods. They fed the statues with spoons. Ganesh and his colleagues seemed endlessly thirsty. Every spoon of milk touching their mouths would disappear in seconds. No one could explain how and why. Chanting praising the elephant god echoed in nearly every temple. And spoon by spoon, vessel by vessel, the gods guzzled thousands of liters of milk until milk went out of stock in the country. Never before in living memory had anything like this happened: a miracle which was not a secluded or local phenomenon but ubiquitous; it could be witnessed by everybody, everywhere, and was openly happening before the eyes of millions of people.

300

But what exactly was happening? Together with journalists and TV people—meantime, a second team had arrived—we went to a small temple in the neighborhood to investigate the phenomenon. One of the first things that came to our notice was a white stream of milk running through to the open drainage. It was not easy to proceed to the center of the temple courtyard where about twenty statues of different gods were beleaguered by an excited crowd trying to feed them with hundreds of spoons. Thanks to the TV cameras we were considered privileged and finally got access. But still the pushing and pulling crowd and the highly charged atmosphere made it difficult to watch closely and calmly what was going on. We noticed that a good part of the offered milk was simply spilled and ran down over statues and flower garlands. The pulpits where the statues were erected were full of milk and overflowing. But it also seemed as if some of the statues did consume milk. It looked unreal, but it happened in front of our eyes and the running cameras. Back at headquarters we obtained a Ganesh statue from a nearby astrologer's home and started our work. And it soon became clear what caused the illusion: The moment the wet statue and the milk in the spoon came into contact, the milk disappeared from the spoon as if being sucked in, but it was only flowing down the multiple curves of the odd-shaped Ganesh statue. Since it was made of white marble like most of the statues, it needed very close watching to see the thin and nearly transparent stream of milk running down.

Two hours later we provided our observations to the waiting media. We presented five conclusions:

- First, not only the statues of Ganesh and the deities of the Shiva family "consumed" milk, but also other statues; for example, those of Jesus and Mahatma Gandhi, as well as any other objects with a smooth surface over which milk can flow down; for example, a cobbler's iron shoe-molder or a banana.
- Second, statues were "drinking" not only milk but also any other liquid; for example, coffee, mineral water, or beer.
- Third, the flow of the liquid started automatically only when the statue was wet with the same liquid that it was fed. Due to the principle of surface tension liquids have a tendency to form a singular unit when two units meet each other, here the liquid already present on the statue and the liquid on the spoon. The slightly projected liquid surface in the spoon breaks at the point of contact and following a primary siphoning as it flows down over the surface of the statue. Milk in small quantities or over white marble is almost invisible. In most cases the statues were also covered with flower garlands which did not allow a close inspection of them.
- Fourth, the principle of capillary action is responsible for the primary siphoning, which initiates the downflow of the milk.

- Fifth, automuscular movements can make the feeder tilt the spoon without noticing, thereby adding speed to the downflow of the milk from the spoon.

We not only explained the scientific principles behind the illusion, but also were able to demonstrate its functioning by having our Ganesh statue "drink" milk and blue ink in front of running TV cameras. By evening our explanations were presented on the major television networks—DD Metro and Star Plus—and on several other channels. I also gave telephone interviews for international news on the BBC and CNN. The next day's newspapers front-paged reports about the sensational events in India's temples and focused on the explanations given by us and supported by several scientists. After hours of enthusiasm, the miracle spectacle died down, demystified by our massive media presence.

We felt exhausted but were satisfied that we had been able to stand this unexpected fire test. We had responded powerfully to an extraordinary situation. With the cooperation of the media we were able to stop the frenzy of millions and lead the country back to normalcy. But at the same time it was shocking and alarming to see how fast superstition and illusion can take control of the reins. It was like a strange dream: one fine September morning the whole country awoke with the absurd idea that marble statues were able to drink milk. And stimulated by this illusion millions of people, among them many who were not strong believers or habitual temple visitors, began with seriousness and dedication to perform a ridiculous new ritual. What was the secret behind this sudden outbreak of mass madness?

Our inquiries at several local temples revealed that all of them had received phone calls from one of the central temples the night before the events announcing that a miracle was going to happen and instructing the priest to pour milk over the deities and to feed them with a spoon as soon as dawn broke. The priests followed these instructions so that the early morning visitors found the statues indeed drinking milk—and this news spread like wildfire. In search of the origin of the initiating phone calls, we phoned the Birla Temple in central Delhi. The priests here had also received a phone call during the night asking them to perform the ritual without delay and then to call up all the other local temples in Delhi. They found the miracle working and passed the information on, as they had been asked to do. Similar telephone chains had worked in other cities. There had obviously been a well-organized and precisely timed central telephone coordination. At places without telephone connection, the miracle began only after people returned from nearby towns and broke the news. Temples in the United States and the United Kingdom were not in the "net" and did not participate in the milk miracle until after they had received the first TV reports from India.

An important clue for our investigation came from a small news item appearing on the local page of the city newspaper of the Hindu holy city of Hardwar in Uttar Pradesh. It said that in Hardwar milk had already gone out of stock the evening *before* the milk miracle. That meant that in Hardwar the Shiva family of deities got thirsty half a day earlier than in the rest of India. Could this have been the trial run for the big miracle? With considerable effort we were able to determine in which temples in Hardwar the milk miracle had happened the previous evening and we could even identify the sadhus who initiated it. And here the story came full circle: These very sadhus had been at Delhi one week before. They had held a demonstration in the center in support of the prominent godman Chandraswamy who faced arrest in a sensational case of cheating amounting to millions of rupees and involving important politicians. The sadhus had threatened dire consequences if Chandraswamy was touched and the godman himself had threatened earlier that he would invoke the gods if he was arrested. In fact, even on the day of the milk miracle he claimed that he had invoked the god Ganesh to demonstrate his power. In some temples sadhus began chanting slogans in praise of him, but nobody took it seriously. The story which we had pieced together was confirmed and documented when I later went to Hardwar again to talk to the sadhus—this time with a BBC television team, who recorded the investigation for the TV channel UK Horizons. We also managed to get an audience with Chandraswamy himself in his Delhi ashram; after some months in jail, he was back home again. I somehow slipped through the thorough screening without revealing my identity and was granted the rare honor to interview the beleaguered godman. He was not very talkative, but he gave us, with the majesty of a living god, the understanding that he was the creator of the milk miracle. Chandraswamy's men had initiated the drama. But it followed its own dynamics. Catching the imagination of millions, it soon went beyond their control.

What would have happened if we had not stopped the miracle frenzy with scientific explanations that day? The highly charged atmosphere bore danger of political manipulation in favor of the radical Hindus. In fact, there have been certain efforts in that direction. Some hours before our explanations appeared on national TV, claims received currency that the gods were showing the miracle to motivate a political change. The possibilities were multifaceted. Had the milk miracle continued for some more days it might have altered the political map of Southwest Asia.

Sometimes the efforts of skeptics and rationalists can have enormous consequences. Those dramatic moments when history stands atilt and awaits a significant shift may be rare. But our work has the potential of slowly and steadily transforming tradition-bound societies. The fight against superstition and blind belief is a fight against powerful adversaries.

In a country like India with nearly half the population illiterate, sadhus, gurus, astrologers, spiritual frauds, and charlatans have enormous influence on every aspect of life. Most of the marriages are still fixed by matching horoscopes, often without any prior meeting of the spouses. Poor peasants spend a major part of their earnings in order to take part in a miraculous pilgrimage or to satisfy the demands of a guru. Ailments are allegedly cured by miracle-healers chanting mantras. Countless numbers of people die after consuming the contaminated water of "holy" rivers. Tantriks perform strange rituals, sometimes even human sacrifices to prevent allegedly threatening catastrophes. Helpless old women are killed with stones and axes because they are suspected of being witches casting evil spells on the village. Poltergeists frighten families from their homes. Sorcerers are hired to settle scores with neighbors and competitors by practicing voodoo against them; their victims sometimes die of sheer fright. Recently a little girl, in a bizarre ritual, was "married" to a dog to prevent her family from accidents.

The skeptical and rationalist activities began in India in the last decades of the nineteenth century. In the beginning these were confined to pockets of urban elite. A dramatic change occurred in the early 1960s when Abraham Thomas Kovoor, a dynamic college professor in Sri Lanka (Indian by birth), began giving public lectures across the length and breadth of India debunking all major superstitions and challenging all those who claimed supernatural powers to be tested by him under fraud-proof conditions. He announced a huge award for anybody who would stand his test, but no self-styled representatives of the spiritual world dared to face up to his challenge. This gave great credence to Kovoor. In the comparatively short span of his career he made a decisive mark in the history of Indian rationalism. Kovoor died in 1978. His will is a document of his uncompromising commitment to rationalism. To ward off the fear of life after death and to ridicule the ritualistic ceremonies to keep the soul in peace, he refused a traditional burial and instead donated his body to a medical college for the students' anatomy lessons. His skeleton was later donated to the science laboratory of the college where he had taught. His eyes were donated to two blind men for corneal transplants.

The skeptical work of the Indian Rationalist Association did not stop with Kovoor's death. It reinvigorated it in memory of his impressive example. I myself drew great inspiration from Kovoor whom I knew personally. He was a close associate and friend of my father, Joseph Edamaruku, who, in fact, had been initiating his campaign in India and worked hand in hand with him. The Indian Rationalist Association, which grew from a few thousand members in 1983, has today grown into the largest and most vigorous organization of its kind. Our countless activists, including many students, are dedicated to debunking any paranormal claim that comes to public light. Hundreds of "poltergeists" and "ghosts" have been debunked over the years, many sadhus and gurus claiming supernatural capacities have been publicly exposed, and several powerful godmen have been caught red-handed during their acts of deceit.

Responding to the challenges of the special situation in India, our fight against superstition has developed new dimensions of skeptical work. Fighting superstition in India is closely related to social transformation. Eighty percent of India's population lives in villages. We go from village to village and meet people in their familiar surroundings and in their day-to-day life, in their superstitious and oppressing small world. We try to help them find the courage to open their eyes and to overcome fear of the fantastic evil powers, and we try to expose the real evil powers that are hiding beneath the umbrella of their blind beliefs. This is a sensitive and time-consuming process as there are several millions of villages in India. Of course, we use all possible means of modern communication, including TV and the Internet, for our campaigns. But to counter deep-rooted superstitions it is not enough to logically disprove them. We try to initiate the experience that it is possible to challenge the authority of the supernatural and remain unharmed.

Our working patterns could most likely be successfully adopted in other Third World countries as well; for example, in many African, Asian, and Latin American countries. But it would require a large well-networked organization of local rationalists who are familiar with the local life, know the local superstitions, and speak the local dialect. At this moment the work of Indian rationalists is unique and drawing much attention and curiosity from all over the world.

Rationalist volunteers receive special training as "Guru-Busters," and they conduct antisuperstition campaigns all over the country. Great Britain's Channel Four has produced a documentary featuring one of our journeys through the villages of Kerala. This met with considerable international interest and has been telecast in fourteen countries. Sometimes our activists dress up like gurus and seek to impress the villagers by performing some of the famous guru tricks. Like other "miraclemen" they bow their heads in respect and prepare to depart with their earnings. But instead, the rationalists remove their saffron robes and explain to the stunned audience the scientific principles and sleights of hand which had just been used to dupe them. Those who had fallen prey to these performances are encouraged to try to perform the "miracles" themselves. First hesitantly, and soon with confidence and growing pleasure, the villagers walk on fire; take burning camphor pieces in their hands; crush the specially prepared little balls between their fingers which the rationalists distribute, in order to "create" holy ash from thin air. All these tricks of the trade had been veiled in obscurity until we explained how they were performed and how it gave fake authority to the holy men. When the spell is broken, the villagers feel great relief and become curious and courageous. Imitating the feats, they overcome the barriers which had confined their lives. The spirit of discovery spreads, mostly "infecting" young people first and slowly conquering the entire community. For many people the encounter with rationalism in action is a turning point in their lives. The truth about their earlier superstitious beliefs becomes a question of greatest importance for them—an existential question. Once initiated, this process often continues by itself and can transmit a spark of doubt to other villages and groups of people. Sometimes we hear stories of gurus and sadhus who visited a village and were chased out by the enlightened peasants.

An eyewitness reported an event on an intercity bus in Uttar Pradesh on the next morning after the milk miracle. Somebody presented the explanation I had given in the evening news debunking the miracle; in a few minutes the whole bus was involved in a heated debate which threatened to turn violent. The driver stopped the bus until the excitement subsided. Finally the rationalist view, reported the witness, prevailed. The idea that there is nothing supernatural to be afraid of is explosive and sets strong feelings free, mostly positive, sometimes also negative if the process of deformation of the personality has already progressed too far and the urge to defend the supernatural authority against all evidence becomes irresistible. People who have reached this stage may sometimes turn fundamentalist.

Gurus, sadhus, and astrologers are not simply a village phenomenon. Sometimes even prime-ministerial residences are altered and reconstructed, perhaps spending millions of rupees because an astrologer feels that the main entry is on the wrong side and violates the rules of *vastu* (the ancient Hindu religious teaching about the right way of constructing a building to guarantee health, happiness, and success for its inhabitants). There have been prime ministers and presidents in India who would not make a move without the advice of astrologers or who publicly bowed their heads before their favorite godmen. Some godmen have reached national fame and influence by winning politicians as their devotees. One of them is Chandraswamy, and there are many others. The famous godmen drew their power by using the same bag of tricks which are used by village sadhus. For example, Guru Sadachari several years ago charmed his devotees by producing fire by "mental powers" (actually by using chemicals), and he had half the Indian cabinet at his feet and enormous political influence. A photo collection shows him with Indira Gandhi, who invited him to perform special poojas (Hindu prayer rituals) for her, and he influenced a wide range of politicians across party lines. That did not save him from jail, but that is another story.

Another extraordinarily powerful godman is Sai Baba. His devotees include top politicians, diplomats, high bureaucrats, and industrialists, and he enjoys inordinate respect among a section of media people. He claims to have supernatural powers and proves them by producing things from thin air: holy ash for the poor and jewelry for the rich and famous. His trick is very simple, a sleight of hand, which can be done by anybody after some training. We have demonstrated and explained it in hundreds of public lectures and TV interviews and challenged him to show his miracles under fraud-proof conditions. Of course he did not accept the challenge. Finally we could obtain—and widely circulate—a video clipping, watching him closely as he "produced" a golden chain—and catching him red-handed as he plucked it from the bottom of a plaque where it was carefully pasted. The fame of Sai Baba's miraculous capacities has suffered since then and the exposed trickster today avoids the limelight.

Politicians who present themselves as devotees of godmen, priests, sadhus, and astrologers may be as superstitious as uneducated villagers or may be coolly calculating that it brings multiple advantages for rulers to demonstrate closeness to the guardians of the supernatural. In any case, they lend an enormous credibility not only to their personal gurus but also to the whole clique of holy charlatans. The nexus of political power and spiritual fraud is strong and resistant. The symbiosis is too advantageous to be given up easily. But the Indian Constitution, clearly committed to secularism, is a powerful weapon against these charlatans and the educated part of the public are strong supporters of our rationalist efforts. Thanks to them we have won many battles. When Delhi's health minister tried in 1998 to realize his pet project to integrate a Mantra Healing Centre into a reputed state-run medical college, we were able to force him to withdraw his proposal, and it vanished shortly thereafter. Often powerful politicians attempt to come to the rescue of spiritual frauds in distress. Some years back the office of the then prime minister tried by all means to cancel a program on the state-owned television network because the prime-ministerial astrologer cried for help. He had been prepared to appear in a sensational debate with me about astrology. But he anticipated that it would damage his reputation if he could not escape. Thanks to public pressure the debate did finally take place and was telecast. And the astrologer's prediction, for once, came true: it did ruin his reputation.

Power-hungry and corrupt politicians are not the only ones who promote and protect superstition and exploit the gullibility of people. Another mighty adversary of our work is a section of the media. Superstition is big business. Many new TV channels compete with each other in presenting "real-life" stories and serials based on witchcraft and ghost possession. Some newspapers cannot resist sensational cover stories that present the "truth" about rebirth and other best-selling paranormal claims. Given this media propaganda, it is becoming fashionable in some circles of the educated and well-to-do urban elite to be "a little bit" superstitious. These people would never entrust a street sadhu with the treatment of any serious illness that might befall them, nor would they miss a good business deal because of some bad omen or take any other personal hardship in pursuit of their spiritual destination. For them the miraculous world of the irrational is an exciting entertainment, an extravagant pastime, a little luxury which they allow themselves. Despite higher education, they are often very passionate defenders of bunkum and proud devotees of a star godman or godwoman. The more "rational" among them appreciate our work, but they add with a twinkle, that a little bit of superstition should be allowed; it doesn't do any harm, and finally, we are Indians!

This cynical approach corresponds with an alarming development in the West. Christian miracles (like the virgin birth) don't quench the thirst for the extraordinary in the Western world for many, but tourism has discovered India's exotic mysteries. Indian godmen and godwomen have opened ashrams and have gained not only riches but also respectability in the West. Mantra healing, vastu architecture, astrology, and other phonies are treated like serious scientific disciplines. The world's "spiritual leaders"—which include a wide range of India's holy charlatans—are considered respectable authorities on questions of global peace.

While hypocritical and corrupt politicians, unscrupulous media circles, and neospiritual snobs in both the East and the West try to make India a spiritual Wonderland—a natural preserved area for all kinds of spiritual frauds—the majority of the Indian population has to pay the heavy price. Instead of being given a helping hand and allowed to enter the twenty-first century of science and reason, they are shoved back into their cages, like strange animals in a zoo.

Over the years we have educated many young rationalists to undertake our village-level campaigns. But I still find it fascinating to participate in such campaigns personally. During a recent miracle-debunking session in a remote village, when I explained to the village crowd the fundamentals of

SANAL EDAMARUKU lives in New Delhi, leads the Indian Rationalist Association, and is well known for his antisuperstition campaigns. He organized two International Rationalist Conferences, in 1995 and 2000, and is the president of Rationalist International. He also oversees the publication of rationalist and skeptical books in India. E-mail: Edamaruku@ rationalistinternational.net

the scientific approach they have to develop, these rustic peasants showed their appreciation with warm hugs. Such moving experiences encourage me much more than the glittering TV shows and the widespread applause that we get in organized urban public lectures. Those are the moments when I realize the value of the struggle that we take forward.

26

SCIENTISTS, EDUCATORS, AND JOURNALISTS AGAINST THE DEMON'S TEMPTATION

LUIS ALFONSO GÁMEZ

arl Sagan calls them demons; I prefer to talk about "she-demons." It is not a matter of gender. The devil has settled in the collective subconscious of Judeo-Christian civilization as a vicious and physically unpleasant creature, while a she-devil seems to combine perversity, great charm, and seductive power. Hence, I think her image is similar to that offered by pseudoscience: the access to magical knowledge which does not require study or perseverance, is reachable by anyone capable of reading a couple of books, and in many cases brings fame and easy money. For them, the study of the paranormal is more worthy than the effort wasted on standard studies, such as attending graduate courses, or pursuing a doctorate program. Nothing is needed to become an expert on the paranormal. That is why there are so many of them. However, a special kind of character is needed. Pseudoscience kills, purely and simply.

To pseudoscience we owe, for example, the early deaths of people who fell into the hands of psychic healers and who refused conventional medicine such as heart operations and cancer treatments which might have saved their lives. Thanks to the advice of faith healers, many hundreds of diabetics are hospitalized in comas after interrupting their insulin treatment following the recommendations of their "therapists." Many cancer patients abandon scientific medicine and trust homeopathic potions or place spheres under their pillows instead—as some Spanish esoteric magazines have recommended. Many families were destroyed when one of their members denounced sexual child abuse—with repressed memories recovered in a hypnotic session introduced as the only "proof." We owe all this, and much more, to pseudo-science: innocent people are bilked of billions of dollars by false prophets and with total impunity; many companies select their personnel based on handwriting analysis following the advice of graphologists or the horoscopes of astrologers instead of paying attention to genuine capabilities; the wasted curiosity of thousands of young people who fall into the hands of mystery-mongers who offer simplistic explanations of reality; huge amounts of money that some governments have wasted on ill-designed research, money which could have been used for better purposes.

Surely many or most people are sensible and don't believe in demons or anything like them. But if you look around and ask your neighbors, friends, and family you will stumble upon another reality: 46 percent of the people in Spain usually read their horoscope, 37 percent think that UFOs are extraterrestrial spaceships, 32 percent are sure that there are spirits around them, 23 percent believe in reincarnation, and 15 percent of the population consult quacks when they have an illness. As in other countries, most Spaniards hold some form of esoteric belief. Statistical surveys indicate that, at least among the general public, pseudoscience is advancing at a steady pace. Some people are not concerned, but I submit that pseudoscience is dangerous not only for its disciples, but for the entire society.

This age, as Richard P. Feynman says in his book *The Meaning of It All*, is a scientific age. If you believe that a scientific age is an age in which science is developing at the fastest possible pace, then this is undoubtedly a scientific age.[1] If this is the case, how can you explain the boom in pseudoscience? Why do people fall into the hands of rogues and racketeers? In my opinion, the science-literacy tripod is sustained by scientists, journalists, and educators. Three legs hold up scientific education which unfortunately is faltering—be it by action or inaction, this tripod has allowed widespread irrationality to develop.

Until recent times, the scientific community in Spain ignored the people who financed their research. They locked themselves inside their laboratories and refused to engage in the popularization of their findings. They thought that making their research understandable to those without scientific ability was not part of their duty. Popularizing science was, and is, something secondary, and it carried a stigma. Perhaps some consider this attitude deplorable, but I can still remember when twenty years ago *Cosmos*, the excellent TV series of Carl Sagan, provoked distrust among some scientists who accused Sagan of *trivializing* science by providing it a spectacle. This is a serious mistake: doing science is not the same as interpreting it for the general public. This surely is one of the reasons for the growth of pseudoscience, and for the negative attitude of scientists against those (such as Sagan) who *wrap* science in fancy paper and ribbon so that it attracts the attention of the broader public.

In 1999, Michael Crichton—a physician and anthropologist, but best known as a best-selling author—delivered an address at the annual meeting of the American Association for the Advancement of Science. He exhorted his fellow scientists to abandon their ivory tower and present science in an understandable way, "to assume your responsibilities and provide your knowledge to the people who demand it."

This is nothing new. As early as 1923, American journalist H. L. Mencken said:

> There was a time, and it was much less than a century ago, when any man of sound sense and fair education could understand all of the concepts commonly employed in the physical sciences, and even most of those used in the speculative sciences. In medicine, for example, there was nothing beyond the comprehension of the average intelligent layman. But of late that has ceased to be true, to the great damage of the popular respect for knowledge. Only too often, when a physician of today tries to explain to his patient what is the matter with him, he finds it impossible to get the explanation into terms within the patient's understanding. The latter, if he is intelligent enough, will face the fact of his lack of training without rancour, and content himself with whatever parts of the exposition he can grasp.
>
> But that sort of intelligence, unluckily, is rather rare in the world; it is confined, indeed, to men of the sort who are said to have the scientific mind, i.e., a very small minority of men. The average man, finding himself getting beyond his depth, instantly concludes that what lies beyond is simply nonsense.
>
> It is this fact which accounts for the great current prosperity of such quackeries as osteopathy, chiropractic and Christian Science.[2]

It is sad to see that so many things have changed so little in the past seventy years. Perhaps they have gotten worse because science has become *hyperspecialized*—to the point where communication is difficult not only between scientists and nonscientists, but even among scientists themselves. And we will pay for this error, if we are not already paying for it, in the form of the lack of understanding, the lack of popular knowledge about the work of scientists, the failure to demand sufficient support for research to avoid missing the train to the future. It is very hard to convince the taxpayer of the need for spending more money for something so misunderstood, with an unknown purpose and an unknown utility.

But the scientist must do more than explain to the public what science is and how it works, and present the results of research. The scientist has to be involved in establishing the boundaries between science and pseudoscience, and in the criticism of pseudoscience. Many researchers consider it a waste of time, believing that the fight against superstition requires them to transform into a sort of Don Quixote—fighting an endless battle against the windmills of irrationality. For those who think so, fighting against pseudo-science is a waste of time. They are wrong. Science popularizers, thinkers, and scientists like Isaac Asimov, Mario Bunge, Martin Gardner, Stephen Jay Gould, Paul Kurtz, James Randi, and Carl Sagan, among others, understood a quarter of a century ago that fighting against pseudoscience will play a key role in determine our future.

If there is something worthwhile, it is telling people about their errors and in calling things by their correct names. As the Spanish-Argentinian scientific journalist Mario Bohoslavsky said, in denouncing deceit, we bet the millions of years passed from Lucy to Stephen Hawking, from the print of the first hominid who walked over Olduvai to the prints left by Neil Armstrong on July 21, 1969, on the Moon. If pseudoscience continues to grow and if critical scientific thinking is diminished in our society, then any madness is possible, and new Hitlers can appear at any time.

Moreover, "when dreams become more important than reality we stop traveling, building, creating. . . ." The phrase is not mine, but Vina's, a character in one of the episodes of the original *Star Trek* series, which represents the apathy into which an alien species has fallen because they can bring into reality all their wishes with the power of their minds.[3] Miraculous pills, quasi-magic medicines, extraterrestrial saviors, the future written in the stars . . . all this reduces the need for action and our ability to engage in skeptical analysis, with all the dangers that represents for democracy. We may start by believing the first peddler who sells angel amulets or reads fortunes, and end up by following a fanatic who will establish an inhumane regime, rewriting history to his taste, while we are unable to react because our critical thinking has atrophied.

Mencken's observations about the cryptic character of scientific knowledge is as current as the talk delivered by Thomas Henry Huxley in 1880 at the opening of the Sir Josiah Mason University College, in Birmingham, England. Huxley's address sought to vindicate integral education; it was as much literary as scientific. What Huxley had in mind was not the endless recitation of formulas and principles that some have suffered at school, with the consequent mutilation of human curiosity. Science should not be taught as a succession of facts unrelated to their historical contexts or the process of scientific discovery. Students should be encouraged to ask questions and not simply swallow everything the teacher says, or accept it as holy word. It is only by posing questions that knowledge can advance. This ignorance of the methods of scientific inquiry has contributed to the advancement of pseudoscience and superstition, especially among young people.

While I was a student at the University of Deusto, in the early 1980s, a Jesuit priest taught a course on the history of art. Brother Fernández saw in some prehistoric art samples phalli and vulvae, which caused laughter among the hundreds of students. Later in the semester, he proposed that we should deliver papers. One of the accepted subjects was the stones of Ica. These engraved stones are possessed by a Peruvian doctor, who claims that dinosaurs and humans coexisted. These views were popularized in Spain by a UFOlogist-journalist who claims he can talk to both God and his own dead father. According to their owner, the stones of Ica are the legacy of an extinct prehuman civilization that coexisted with the dinosaurs!

Based on these claims, a student presented a paper in class never questioning the authenticity of the stones. Once she completed her talk, I assumed that my first task was to raise some skeptical doubts. The first part of the debate was intense but I achieved my goal by questioning the scientific validity of the claim. I kept exposing weak points in the story of the stones of Ica during this second talk, transgressing the instructions of Brother Fernández, who intercepted me at the door of the classroom, asking me to tone down my criticism, as he knew the owner of the stones, and they were friends. I could have stopped, but I was concerned that future teachers were being exposed to patently pseudoscientific claims. Even more surprising was the passive attitude I observed in most of my peers, who did not question the claim that humans coexisted with dinosaurs. I would like to think that they considered it absurd, but I am not quite sure about that.

As some of my peers at the university were, many youngsters are seduced by impostures. Tricksters offer a *marvelous* vision of reality which curiously has not received enough attention from educators. I say *curiously* because some experiences prove that the academic approach to pseudoscience (not the one showed by Brother Fernández) has had positive effects among the students; for many of them it is a sort of vaccine.

There are various ways to approach the paranormal in the classroom: one is through didactic exercises that allow the student to test how reliable some pseudoscience postulates are—those centered around astrology are the most frequent—illustrations of criticism by experts, dissecting some subject. Another is to submit them to debate. Still another is to stimulate interested students to write objective papers, with bibliographical citations for and against certain beliefs, and ask for both defenders and critics of the claim. From my point of view, discarding fuzzy subjects in class by simply labeling them as silly is a mistake; this only reinforces the legend of the existence of an *official science* which denies *paranormal reality.*

Moreover, from a utilitarian point of view, opening the classroom to a critical analysis of pseudoscience is a way to teach science. Proving that parapsychology, UFOlogy, astrology, or graphology and whatever *logies* you want are nothing more than beliefs without scientific support demands more action than simply saying that this or that is "absurd"; it is best to give proofs. For example, highlighting weak points in astrology requires some comparison between magical postulates and tested hypotheses of astronomy and physics; dissecting homeopathy implies learning chemistry and biology; examining fictionalized archaeology demands resorting to history, geology, art. Good criticism of pseudoscience brings an added value: it is accompanied by scientific popularization and can help to attract young people to the true knowledge. Martin Gardner states it clearly: One of the best ways to learn about any branch of science is discovering what is wrong with lunatics.[4]

Although the role of professionals in science and education is important, their work will be useless if the third leg of the tripod fails, as it usually does. I am talking about journalists, who have failed miserably in the struggle against pseudoscience. Unfortunately, they have been and still are the main vehicle for superstition and nonsense. In Spain there is no TV station, radio, or newspaper without a column on horoscopes; several have more than one; and paranormal wizards appear in the audiovisual media more than scientists. It is true that since the mid-1980s, when the organized skeptics movement began to exert some influence—paranormal subjects are treated in the Spanish media from both points of view, the believer and the skeptic; though unfortunately the opinions of the proparanormalists are presented more prominently than those who defend scientific rationality. But this is not enough. For this implies that the deceiver has the same respectability and credibility than those who denounce their deceptions; it's like placing a UFOlogist who claims that the transistor is an alien invention on the same level as a NASA physicist!

More serious than this uncritical attitude, although not as frequent, is the conscious manipulation of facts, the twisting of reality in order to reinforce a myth even after it has been debunked by science. If there is an example of this, it is the Shroud of Turin, which, according to the proponents, wrapped the body of Jesus Christ and provides physical proof of his resurrection. Many lies have been said about this cloth, the most prominent being that an analysis reportedly done by NASA in the later 1970s proved the tridimensionality of the image. Actually, the analysis was performed by a group of believers related to the Holy Shroud Guild, to which some individuals belonged who were associated with NASA. Walter McCrone, one of the world's leading forensic microanalysts, was expelled from the group after he revealed that what looks like blood was really paint pigment. Despite all this, we hear again and again that NASA studied the cloth—false!—and that the relic has been subject to many scientific investigations—again false!—which confirm its authenticity. This misstatement was recently reported in some Spanish newspapers.

The problem that we face is that many journalists suspend critical thinking when they are confronted by surprising claims, and they do not apply the same standards when contrasting claims of a defender of any mystery from, for example, those of a politician. Curiously, tricksters enjoy a sort of privileged status and they are usually well treated. A journalist can spend hours, even days trying to evaluate the data obtained about economic, political, or cultural news. However, when the subject is flying saucers, relics, alternative medicines, or paranormal powers, the same professional often becomes a mere transmitter for the claims. Nothing else. No second opinions. This attitude, unthinkable in other fields, is one of the main characteristics of information about the paranormal offered by many mass media, especially in those media which do not have a specialist in scientific information. This must change, both from the standpoint of public interest, which has the right to receive information not based on mere rumor or deception, and journalism, which is discredited when it becomes an echo of mere rumors or plain lies.

"Two Israeli Scientists Confirm that the Holy Shroud Comes from Jerusalem," published the Spanish newspaper *Abc* on June 18, 1999.[5] According to the text, two investigators from Hebrew University of Jerusalem had found "traces of pollen from *Gundellia* flowers, a plant that only grows in the hills of Judea." Not surprising. For *sindonologists* appear from time to time announcing yet another astonishing discovery reinforcing the Shroud's reality. What makes this article particularly worthless is that the journalist described the Shroud as "the holy Shroud which covered the body of Jesus after his crucifixion," or again that Jesus' "body was wrapped on the unction stone after being washed" and that the Shroud had been "subjected to more than a thousand scientific investigations," concluding that the Israeli study described in the article "reinforces the thesis progressively less debated in the Catholic Church and among historians and scientists about the authenticity of the cloth."

All these statements are false and come from a journalist—not from the scientists involved in the pollen study. Curiously the article did not even mention the most definitive scientific test done on the Shroud: the carbon 14 test performed by laboratories in Oxford, Arizona, and Zurich dated the origins of the cloth to the fourteenth century. This report was published, with twenty researchers as authors, in *Nature* in 1989; nobody has refuted it. The article in *Abc* exemplifies how false legends are fed by the Spanish media. The radiocarbon analysis, as other analyses (as by McCrone and Joe Nickell) prove that the Holy Shroud is a forgery and not an object of miraculous origin. This evidence is systematically ignored or only marginally cited. Why? I guess that the Roman Catholic majority of the Spanish population has some bearing, and many believe that questioning the authenticity of the relic would imply that one is attacking their religion.

Let us go back to the true mission of a journalist: verify the facts before publication. Are there any reliable sources to which a professional can turn to for help in his daily work when confronted with a paranormal claim? Yes. Obviously the journalist must be aware that any information coming from believers—UFOlogists, alternative doctors, parapsychologists, etc.—should be placed under some quarantine. Whenever any information looks like self-pleading, the best you can do is call upon the director of the nearest science museum, a university, or perhaps a skeptics organization. Spanish journalists today frequently refer to ARP—the Society for the Advancement of Critical Thinking, which was founded in 1985 and which provides some expertise in most branches of the paranormal. Its members include leading scientists, science popularizers, and educators who are prepared to provide scientific evaluations. ARP has the experience of years in contrasting information in this field, for example, when reports of flying saucers appear at five in the evening, and when the journalist must race against the clock in order to shed some light on the event before press time.

In recent years as a practicing journalist, I have been confronted by what I have called "*5 P.M. flying saucers*" three times, all of them with success. This is not because I am clever, but because I apply the same criteria that I use when I have other news stories to report. By this I mean that I try to verify the possible causes before mentioning a UFO. Moreover, I have been lucky enough to contact the right person in record-breaking time. The telephone book is of capital importance. Once I was confronted with a flying saucer report in real time during the opening of the Second National Congress on Pseudosciences, organized by ARP in Pamplona in 1995. During the press conference in which we presented the program, a journalist asked: "What can journalists do when faced with an apparently paranormal event?" The answer was that they must consider all the alternative explanations before declaring it unexplainable. Well, that same evening, only two hours before the opening of the congress, a UFO sighting was reported over Pamplona.

Was it an interplanetary conspiracy to ridicule the skeptics? Well, it was a dose of our own medicine. Racing against the clock, journalist Victoria Toro; astrophysicist Javier Armentia, president of ARP; and I started to look, not for the most probable explanation, which we almost knew, but for actual data, for the proofs which made it clear that the object floating over the city was a big stratospheric balloon. We got it, and published a press release with all the data within two hours. We also took some photographs which proved it was a balloon. To be honest, I don't think we are more clever than anyone: the key is not to believe anything at face value without some verification and to know whom to phone, and to be cautious if we have not been able to verify the claim.

We have left for a further exploration a second issue: the role of specialized journalists. Given the lax controls applied to pseudoscientific claims in the mass media, the attitude of scientific journalists must change. Until recently many thought that paying attention to pseudoscience, even from a critical point of view, was a waste of time. In this case the journalistic leg of the tripod has failed miserably when it has tried to expose false science. That is why I submit that journalistic integrity must be given high priority. We need to convince scientific journalists that criticizing pseudoscience is part of the popularization of science; wearing blinders about pseudoscience should end.

Dedicated to fight irrationality since we first contacted CSICOP in 1983, Félix Ares, promoter of the Spanish skeptic movement, and I are now glad to see that skeptics are no longer the only people concerned about the advance of irrationality. It happened during the First Congress of Social Communication of Science, which took place in Granada in March 1999 and was attended by more than 550 people from fifteen countries. One of the main conclusions of the congress was the expressed view that "it is urgent to increase the scientific culture of the people. Scientific information is a very fertile seed for the social, economic and political development. Knowledge must be considered of the greatest strategic value, as it was repeatedly remarked during the congress. The collaboration between scientists and the rest of the society is an exceptional celebration of democracy. Moreover, that new culture would help stop fraud disguised as science, increase the critical capacity of the people, avoid fear and superstition, and would make the humans more free and brave. The enemies to vanquish are the same faced by philosophy, art, or literature, i.e., uncouthness, obscurity, barbarism, misery, and human exploitation."

These are hopeful words that have begun to have an effect. The skeptics taking part in scientific conferences, with support from ARP, demonstrate how the perception of the risks of pseudoscience among Spanish scientists, educators, and journalists is changing, and how it is necessary to unite our efforts in the struggle against nonsense. The key point is that the advance of the irrational can only be stemmed by those who believe in science and reason.

NOTES

1. Richard P. Feynman, *The Meaning of It All: Thoughts of a Citizen Scientist* (Reading: Hellix Books, 1999), p. 133.

LUIS ALFONSO GÁMEZ (1962) is a scientific journalist with the newspaper *El Correo* (Bilbao, Spain). A bachelor of history and master of journalism, he was one of the founders of the Spanish skeptic group ARP (Society for the Advancement of Critical Thinking) and has been coeditor of its magazine *El Escéptico* (The Skeptic).

2. H. L. Mencken, *A Mencken Chrestomathy* (1949; reprint, New York: Vintage, 1982), p. 627.

3. Marc Daniels, director, "The Menagerie," *Star Trek*, Episode 16 (Paramount Pictures). Aired in the United States on November 17 and 24, 1966. 103 minutes.

4. Martin Gardner, *On the Wild Side* (Amherst, N.Y.: Prometheus Books, 1992), p. 257.

5. Juan Cierco, "Dos científicas israelíes confirman que el santo sudario procede de Jerusalén," *Abc* (Madrid) (June 18, 1999).

X

SOME PERSONAL REFLECTIONS

27

SKEPTICISM AND SCIENCE

VERN L. BULLOUGH

Science is much revered and also much misunderstood. One image of the scientist is of a dedicated individual working alone in his or her lab coat trying to find answers to the world problems as recounted in children's books about George Washington Carver or Madame Curie. Another image is of the crazed scientist Frankenstein creating a new monster in his laboratory. Neither view is accurate in this age of big science where billions, if not trillions, are spent on supporting the massive enterprise which is modern science. Every discipline and profession sometimes seems to be making a claim to having a scientific basis, even though many of those making such claims know almost absolutely nothing about science or the scientific method. This is why CSICOP becomes so essential and why its twenty-fifth anniversary is deserving of celebration. But in spite of the success of CSICOP, there is probably more pseudoscience around than when the organization began. No sooner is one new fad put down than it is succeeded by two or three others.

As one who has occasionally taught the history of science, probably for the most part to students who knew little about the subject, I was always somewhat shocked each year to find out how often the new batch of students in my class mixed pseudoscience with science. I was also distressed at how they were often opposed to science. They were following a kind of deconstructive rote learning in claiming that science was what they said it was, not a special kind of knowledge or method. In a sense this was a backhanded tribute to the influence of science and scientific discoveries on their lives which has revolutionized the way we live, but not yet changed the way we think.

I spent much time trying to explain that the key to science is the methods by which the investigators arrive at conclusions, that is gathering evidence, replicating or verifying findings, and examining for logical consistency. This is core science but I also pointed out that many scientific theories have not yet been completely supported by painstaking data-gathering or experiments, although to be seriously considered such theories do meet the very minimal test of falsification, that is the ability to falsify the theory by seeing whether it can be refuted or sustained by empirical evidence. A theory is meaningless if there are not conditions under which it can be disconfirmed.

Students seized on my explanation to point out "discarded" scientific assumptions which in the past claimed to have the support of science such as the supposed inferiority of people with African heritage, the supposed lower intelligence of women, the belief that homosexuality was a pathological condition, and any number of other erroneous assumptions as pointed out by Martin Gardner and others. I emphasized that while science is rational, and empirically based, scientists, as human beings, are not always able to be entirely rational but have certain preconceived opinions and assumptions. They see things through the prism of their cultural assumptions, and in the past they tended to interpret things through male eyes. The important thing to be emphasized, is that such erroneous interpretations could be and were corrected with additional research, and also, it must be admitted that old data could be reexamined and looked at through different eyes. I also pointed out that science was an ever-expanding exploration, that we no longer see the universe through the eyes of Isaac Newton although our new views have incorporated his. Also our interpretation of evolution is continually being modified, most notably in recent years by the acceptance of the influence of catastrophic events, an explanation which had been a dominant belief in the early nineteenth century, then discarded, and then reinvigorated in the last part of the twentieth century. This emphasizes that the scientific enterprise is not static but ever growing and changing.

It was also necessary for me to emphasize that when new phenomena appear, it is often difficult to explain what is happening. During the past twenty years, for example, there have been arguments among different segments of the scientific community over whether or not global warming or global cooling was taking place. Most now seem to agree that global warming is what is happening, but the causes are still a matter of debate. Is it part of a natural cycle of warming and cooling that the earth has undergone over its long history, or is it being accentuated by man-made pollutants? Most scientists seem to agree that man-made pollutants are a factor but there are many supposed pollutants, and which might be the most important is still a matter of some disagreement. Science cannot speak with a united voice on such issues at present because there are so many variables involved. This lack of unity in the scientific community opens the way to all kinds of pseudoscientific "experts" to chime in.

Still another factor is what might be called the misuse or abuse of science. One of the best examples is the discovery and widespread use of DDT, which ultimately had disastrous effects on fish and wildlife and the environment in general. Another example is the problem of used nuclear fuel. While scientists involved were often giving warnings to the public about potential dangers, their words of caution were generally ignored. In the aftermath, however, a kind of demonizing of science took place as if the scientists were responsible for the decisions made by industry and government.

Generally my students came to accept my explanations on such issues but they were still fascinated by the claims of pseudoscience. The problem with giving them satisfactory answers other than generalized principles was that most scientists ignored or simply dismissed the claims of pseudoscience. Perhaps one reason for this is that science has increasingly become more and more specialized and many of the claims of pseudoscience go beyond the expertise of the specialists. Others, who could perhaps deal with pseudoscience, had neither the time nor the inclination to do so. There was no grant money and no real benefit to their careers for them. The mass media, even those who had science editors, seemingly jumped on every bandwagon for every newly proclaimed discovery or every new sure cure for all the world's problems, often without making any qualifications. Scientists, when they did speak out, were often fooled by what magicians pointed out were simple magical manipulations as in the Uri Geller case and others. Sometimes also an individual with any kind of doctoral degree was regarded by the public as an authority. The number of engineers who are involved with the creationist movement is fascinating, as if a degree in electrical engineering also qualified them as expert biologists.

Religion remained a significant factor in the issue of pseudoscience since many of those making the most exaggerated claims, especially in health, come from religious groups. Miracles and the belief in miracles has been an essential Christian belief in the past (and for that matter most religions), and for many believers it still is. Miraculous cures do come about, which scientific medicine cannot always explain. There are a lot of holes in our knowledge base, but as we have expanded it the number of miracle cures has decreased. There is also the placebo effect, which right now bedevils some of the major drug manufacturers who have to test their products for FDA approval. The testing of many would-be miracle drugs has often revealed that those taking the placebos undergo the same changes as those taking the drugs. In fact, statistically, drugs have to go well beyond the norms anticipated for placebos to have any value at all. It seems clear, however, that many of the alternative medical cures rely on the placebo effect in their advertisements and that individuals unacquainted with this effect associate the cure with the drug.

Although alternative medicine might well hold some real cures, it is only recently that an effort has been made to scientifically test this possibility. Unfortunately, the fact that those testing are often confirmed believers in the alternative drugs undoubtedly influences the outcome as well.

When all of this has been said, it becomes easier to understand why pseudoscience often is believed, and why it is important to counter it with the best data available. Most scientists, unless they are personally involved in a particular topic, stay clear of controversy, reluctant to denounce what they believe is unscientific. This is particularly true if the pseudoscientist is in his own profession and in a powerful position. One of the best examples of this is in the field of nursing where a few individuals in dominant major universities such as Columbia University and New York University turned out new Ph.D.s indoctrinated in the teachings of therapeutic touch and Rogerian grand theory, the pseudoscientific assumptions of which have been publicized in the *Skeptical Inquirer*.

In my studies of nurses, I found few who believed such theories, and they had often been exposed in various nursing journals. The problem is that, even though the theories were criticized and mostly found wanting, few journals were willing to keep reprinting new exposés on the same old topics. They wanted to go on to other things since they had been there and done that. The dedicated believers, however, continued to propagate erroneous theories in small enclaves where they hold power, and so the theories persisted. Nursing is not alone in this position. The same sort of pseudoscience has often been propagandized in African American studies, Chicano studies, and even women's studies and other disciplines, new to the college setting where individuals became all-engrossed in their own disciplines, determined to correct the erroneous assumptions of the past, and downplay traditional approaches. They are eager to assert their independence and pass off as valid untested theories and radical reinterpretations. In a sense it is similar to the phenomenon which took place in many of the traditional disciplines in the humanities in the 1980s and 1990s, in part as a reaction to the increasing emphasis on science in the curriculum. Deconstructionism became the new bible for a generation of graduate students and inevitably of new faculty members who tried to weed out all the old assumptions and theories only to find themselves a few years later confronted by a new generation who no longer subscribe to deconstructionism and regard their work, particularly if they were on the extremes, as not particularly valid.

If criticism cannot come from within, then it has to come from without, and this is the role and task of CSICOP, the *Skeptical Inquirer,* and the various societies and publications around the world which have followed their example. In a sense it is our job to publicize not only the errors of pseudoscience but also to sell the message of what science is all about. Being negative is not enough; we also have to be positive. If we only attack and dismiss without being positive, we will lose the battle. It is only through being skeptical that there is any progress, but too much skepticism can become almost nihilism. It is also important to remember that.

Science has its own establishment, and some of us are part of it, but to be effective, we have to be willing to be critical of the establishment, although we work within it. All in all these are difficult tasks, but science is the better for having had organized skepticism for twenty-five years.

REFERENCES

Bullough, Vern L., and Bonnie Bullough. "Therapeutic Touch." *Skeptical Inquirer* 17, no. 2 (winter 1993).

Bunge, Mario. "Absolute Skepticism Equals Dogmatism." *Skeptical Inquirer* 24, no. 4 (July–August 2000)

Raskin, Jef. "Rogerian Theory." *Skeptical Inquirer* 24, no. 5 (September–October 2000).

VERN L. BULLOUGH is a State University of New York Distinguished Professor Emeritus, a Laureate in the Academy of Humanism, and a Fellow of CSICOP. Much of his early writing was on medicine and science in the medieval and early modern period, but in recent years he has concentrated on sex and gender issues. He is the author, coauthor, or editor of approximately fifty books and over a hundred refereed articles. He was dean for ten years at the State University of New York College, Buffalo, and before moving to Buffalo had founded the Center for Sex Research at California State University, Northridge. Among other things he is also a nurse (he is a Fellow of the American Academy of Nursing) and is currently an adjunct professor in nursing at the University of Southern California.

28

LET US REFLECT
How a Thoughtful, Inquiring Watchman Provided a Mark to Aim At

MICHAEL SHERMER

On Wednesday, August 9, 2000, I appeared as a guest on Boston's WTKK, 96.9 FM talk radio, hosted by a genial but verbose woman named Jenine Graf. The interview was set up by my publicist at the University of California Press to promote my new book on Holocaust denial, *Denying History*, but since presidential candidate Al Gore had just selected the orthodox Jewish Senator Joseph Lieberman as his vice-presidential running mate, the subject everyone wanted to discuss was politics and religion.

Most callers were impressed and pleased with Gore's choice, many extolling the virtues of biblical ethics and how it is good not only that our politicians endorse their favorite biblical characters (George W. Bush said Jesus is his favorite philosopher, Al Gore called himself a born-again Christian), but that they actually reintroduce biblical ethics into politics. To one caller I responded: "Oh, do you mean such biblical ethical practices as stoning to death disobedient children?" The caller promptly challenged me to produce the said passage. As I was nowhere near a Bible, he said that if I could post it to the Skeptics Society Web page (www.skeptic.com) within the next twenty-four hours he would donate $100.00. If I could not produce the passage, then I had to donate $100.00 to his favorite charity, a Jewish organization called Jews for the Protection of Firearm Ownership.

The host of the show took the caller's phone number and insisted that we actually play out this little bet, and that she would have the two of us on the show the next night to settle it. The next morning I phoned the religion editor of *Skeptic* magazine, Tim Callahan, whose two books *Bible Prophecy* and *The Secret Origins of the Bible* have pushed him to the forefront of biblical scholarship. I figured that Tim would know where that passage came from, and sure enough, a few minutes later he phoned back with the answer—Deuteronomy 21:18–21 (Revised Standard Version):

> If a man has a stubborn and rebellious son, who will not obey the voice of his father or the voice of his mother, and, though they chastise him, will not give heed to them, then his father and his mother shall take hold of him and bring him out to the elders of his city at the gate of the place where he lives, and they shall say to the elders of his city, "This our son is stubborn and rebellious, he will not obey our voice; he is a glutton and a drunkard." Then all the men of the city shall stone him to death with stones; so you shall purge the evil from your midst; and all Israel shall hear, and fear.

Within an hour my Web meister Nick Gerlich had the passage up on our Web page, and early that evening I found myself back on the air with Graf and the challenging caller. I fully expected that he either would not appear on the show or that he would waffle and not pay up. I was wrong on both counts. Not only was he on the air, he spoiled Graf's hope for a good talk-radio on-air confrontation when he said: "There is nothing to dispute. I was wrong. I will pay the Skeptics Society $100.00." And he did. I was blown away. This almost never happens. It takes a lot of intellectual courage and honesty to admit you are wrong, and this gentleman did so with grace. He did wish to make a couple of other points, which included the fact that Jesus' new philosophy of ethics overrode much of Old Testament morality when he called for more ecumenical acceptance of others and more humane responses to sinners and wrong-doers. (I even received a call the next morning from a woman making the same point and kindly offering to pray for me to accept Jesus into my heart as my savior.)

I agreed with the radio caller, but pointed out that Christians typically pick and choose biblical passages, including and especially from the Old Testament, without consistency, and that there are many more Old Testament rules that make one blanch and feel embarrassed for believers. For example, for emancipated women thinking of adorning themselves in business attire that may resemble men's business ware (or for guys who dig cross-dressing), Deuteronomy 22:5 does not look kindly on such behaviors: "A woman shall not wear anything that pertains to a man, nor shall a man put on a woman's garment; for whoever does these things is an abomination to the Lord your God."

Even worse than stoning disobedient children (for it also encompasses a wide range of misogynistic attitudes) is how to deal with virginal and nonvirginal women. According to Deuteronomy 22:13–21, for all you men who married a nonvirgin, you've got to turn in your wife immediately for a proper stoning (for those not accustomed to reading between the biblical lines, the phrase "goes in to her" should be taken literally, and "the tokens of virginity" means the hymen and the blood on the sheet from a virgin's first sexual experience; the key passage about stoning her to death is at the end):

> If any man takes a wife, and goes in to her, and then spurns her, and charges her with shameful conduct, and brings an evil name upon her, saying, "I took this woman, and when I came near her, I did not find in her the tokens of virginity," then the father of the young woman and her mother shall take and bring out the tokens of her virginity to the elders of the city in the gate; and the father of the young woman shall say to the elders, "I gave my daughter to this man to wife, and he spurns her; and lo, he has made shameful charges against her, saying, 'I did not find in your daughter the tokens of virginity,' And yet these are the tokens of my daughter's virginity," And they shall spread the garment before the elders of the city. Then the elders of that city shall take the man and whip him; and they shall fine him a hundred shekels of silver, and give them to the father of the young woman, because he has brought an evil name upon a virgin of Israel; and she shall be his wife; he may not put her away all his days. But if the thing is true, that the tokens of virginity were not found in the young woman, then they shall bring out the young woman to the door of her father's house, and the men of her city shall stone her to death with stones, because she has wrought folly in Israel by playing the harlot in her father's house; so you shall purge the evil from the midst of you.

For those of you who have succumbed to the temptation of the flesh at some time in your married life, Deuteronomy 22:22 does not bode well for you: "If a man is found lying with the wife of another man, both of them shall die, the man who lay with the woman, and the woman; so you shall purge the evil from Israel." Do Jews and Christians *really* want to legislate biblical morality, especially in light of the revelations of the past couple of decades of the rather low moral character of many of our religious leaders? Most don't, but believe it or not some do, even advocating returning to stoning as a proper form of punishment.

I think I've made my point, but while I'm ranting let me point out that the religious right who are lobbying for the Ten Commandments to be posted in public schools, the very first one prohibits anyone from believing in any of the other gods besides Yahweh ("Thou shall have no other gods before me," a passage indicating that polytheism was commonplace at the time and that Yahweh was, among other things, a jealous god). That is to say, by posting the Ten Commandments we are sending the message that any nonbeliever, or believer in any other god, is not welcome in our public schools. I seem to recall that the First Amendment of the Constitution had something to say about such religious exclusionary practices.

To be fair to believers, not *all* biblical ethics are this bad. There is much to pick and choose from that is useful for our thinking about moral issues. The problem here is consistency, and selecting ethical guidelines that support our particular personal or social prejudices and preferences. If you are going to claim the Bible as your primary (or only) code of ethics, and proclaim (say) that homosexuality is sinful and wrong because the Bible says so, then to be consistent you've got to kill rebellious youth and nonvirginal premarried women. Since most would not endorse that brand of consistency, why pick on gays and lesbians but cut some slack for rebellious youth and promiscuous women? And, on the consistency issue, why aren't men subject to the same set of sexual guidelines as women? The answer is that in that culture at that time it simply was not appropriate. Thankfully we have moved beyond that culture. What we really need is a new set of ethics, an ethical system designed for our time and place, not one scripted for a pastoral/agricultural people who lived four thousand years ago. How about we think through these moral issues for ourselves instead of turning to what is largely an antiquated book of morals?

This is, in fact, one of the primary goals of the modern skeptical movement that has grown dramatically over the past quarter century. Skepticism, of course, dates back to the ancient Greeks, well captured in Socrates' famous quip that all he knows is that he knows nothing. Skepticism as nihilism, however, gets us nowhere and, thankfully, almost no one embraces it. The word "skeptic," in fact, comes from the Greek *skeptikos*, for "thoughtful"—far from modern misconceptions of the word as meaning "cynical" or "nihilistic." According to the *Oxford English Dictionary*, "skeptical" has also been used to mean "inquiring," "reflective," and, with variations in the ancient Greek, "watchman" or "mark to aim at." What a glorious meaning for what we do! We are thoughtful, inquiring, and reflective, and in a way we are the watchmen who guard against bad ideas, consumer advocates of good thinking who, through the guidelines of science, establish the mark to aim at.

Since the time of the Greeks, skepticism (in its various incarnations) has evolved along with other epistemologies and their accompanying social activists. The Enlightenment, on one level, was a century-long skeptical movement, for there were no beliefs or institutions that did not come under the critical scrutiny of such great thinkers as Voltaire, Diderot, Rousseau, Locke, Jefferson, and many others. Immanuel Kant in Germany and David Hume in Scotland were skeptics' skeptics in an age of skepticism, and their influence continues unwaned to this day (at least in academic philosophy and skepticism). Closer to our time, Charles Darwin and Thomas Huxley were skeptics par excellence, not only for the revolution they launched and carried on (respectively) against the dogma of creationism, but also for their stand against the burgeoning spiritualism movement that was sweeping across America, England, and the Continent. (Darwin was quiet about it and worked behind the scenes; Huxley railed publicly against the movement, bemoaning in one of the great one-liners in the history of skepticism: "Better live a crossing-sweeper than die and be made to talk twaddle by a 'medium' hired at a guinea a séance.") In the twentieth century Bertrand Russell and Harry Houdini stand out as representatives of skeptical thinkers and doers (respectively) of the first half, and in the first year of the second half of the century, Martin Gardner's *Fads and Fallacies in the Name of Science* launched what we think of today as "the skeptics."

We are at an appropriate time for reflection with this volume celebrating twenty-five years of skepticism. The date corresponds with the founding of CSICOP and the publication of *Skeptical Inquirer*, but no institution leaps into existence out of a sociohistorical quantum foam fluctuation, so I date the modern skeptical movement to 1950 with the publication of an essay by Martin Gardner in the *Antioch Review* entitled "The Hermit Scientist." The essay is about what we would today call pseudoscientists, and was Gardner's first-ever publication of a skeptical nature. It launched not only a lifetime of critical analysis of fringe claims, but in 1952 (at the urging of his literary agent John T. Elliott) the article was expanded into a book-length treatment of the subject under the title *In the Name of Science*, with the descriptive subtitle "An entertaining survey of the high priests and cultists of science, past and present." Published by Putnam, the book sold so poorly that it was quickly remaindered and lay dormant until 1957, when it was republished by Dover and has come down to us as *Fads and Fallacies in the Name of Science*, still in print and arguably the skeptic classic of the past half century. (Gardner realized his book had made it when he turned on the radio "at 3 A.M. one morning, when I was giving a bottle of milk to my newborn son, and being startled to hear a voice say, 'Mr. Gardner is a liar.' It was John Campbell Jr., editor of *Astounding Science Fiction*, expressing his anger over the book's chapter on dianetics.")

What caught the attention of a youthful Martin Gardner half a century ago? The "hermit scientist," working alone and usually ignored by mainstream scientists: "Such neglect, of course, only strengthens the convictions of the self-declared genius," Gardner concluded in his original 1950 paper. "Thus it is that probably no scientist of importance will present the bewildered public with detailed proofs that the earth did not twice stop whirling in Old Testament times, or that neuroses bear no relation to the experiences of an embryo in the mother's womb" (referring to L. Ron Hubbard's dianetics theory that negative engrams are imprinted in the fetus's brain while in the womb).

Gardner was, however, half wrong in his prognostications: "The current flurry of discussion about Velikovsky and Hubbard will soon subside, and their books will begin to gather dust on library shelves." While Velikovskians are a quaint few surviving in the interstices of fringe culture, L. Ron Hubbard has been canonized by the Church of Scientology and deified as the founding saint of a world religion.

In the first chapter of *In the Name of Science*, Gardner picks up where he left off, noting that "tens of thousands of mentally ill people throughout the country entered 'dianetic reveries' in which they moved back along their 'time track' and tried to recall unpleasant experiences they had when they were embryos." Half a century later Scientology has converted those reveries into a worldwide cult of personality surrounding L. Ron Hubbard that targets celebrities for membership and generates hundreds of millions of dollars in tax-free revenue as an IRS-approved "religion."

Today UFOs are big business, but in 1950 Gardner could not have known that the nascent flying saucer craze would turn into an alien industry, but it was off to a good start: "Since flying saucers were first reported in 1947, countless individuals have been convinced that the earth is under observation by visitors from another planet." Absence of evidence then was no more a barrier to belief than it is today, and believers proffered the same conspiratorial explanations for the dearth of proof: "I have heard many readers of the saucer books upbraid the government in no uncertain terms for its stubborn refusal to release the 'truth' about the elusive platters. The administration's 'hush-hush policy' is angrily cited as proof that our military and political leaders have lost all faith in the wisdom of the American people."

From his perspective in 1950 Gardner was even then bemoaning the fact that some beliefs never seem to go out of vogue, as he recalled H. L. Mencken's quip from the 1920s "that if you heave an egg out of a Pullman car window anywhere in the United States you are likely to hit a fundamentalist." Gardner cautions that when presumably religious superstition should be on the wane how easy it is "to forget that thousands of high school teachers of biology, in many of our southern states, are still afraid to teach the theory of evolution for fear of losing their jobs." Today, bleeding Kansas enjoins the fight as the creationist virus spreads northward.

I devote an entire chapter in my forthcoming book *The Borderlands of Science* (Oxford University Press) to Martin Gardner and his seminal work, but suffice it to say here that *Fads and Fallacies in the Name of Science* has been a cherished classic read by legions of skeptics and scientists, and that it laid the foundation for a bona fide skeptical movement that found its roots in the early 1970s. There has been some debate (and much quibbling) about who gets what amount of credit for the founding of CSICOP and *Skeptical Inquirer* (much of this played out in the pages of *Skeptic* magazine in our interviews with the major players). This is not the place to present a definitive history of the movement, but from what I have gleaned from first- and secondhand sources is that Martin Gardner, magician James Randi, psychologist Ray Hyman, and philosopher Paul Kurtz played key roles in the foundation and planning of the organization, with numerous others, such as Phil Klass and Marcello Truzzi, in important supporting roles.

Regardless of who might be considered the "father" of the modern skeptical movement, everyone I have spoken to (including the other founders) agrees that it was Paul Kurtz more than anyone else who actually made it happen. All successful social movements have someone who has the organizational skills and social intelligence to get things done. Paul Kurtz is that man. But he had a lot of help, and the many contributors to this volume reflect that support. First among equals in this stellar pantheon is Barry Karr, who impressed me with his organizational genius and plain old hard work. For a social movement to survive it must be able to make the transition from the first generation to the second, and I have no doubt that CSICOP will flourish in the next quarter century thanks to the next generation of skeptics such as Karr and many others.

The founding of the Skeptics Society by myself, Pat Linse, and Kim Ziel Shermer in 1992, then, was also not without precedent and historical roots, and while this history has yet to be written, suffice it to say that without the likes of Gardner, Randi, Hyman, and Kurtz there would be no Skeptics Society and *Skeptic* magazine. And what an experience it has been. Twenty-five years ago I was twenty years old and in my third year of college at Pepperdine University, a Church of Christ-based institution located in Malibu and overlooking the Pacific ocean. Although the site was certainly a motivating factor in my choice of a college, the primary reason I went there was that I was a born-again Christian who took his mission for Christ seriously. I thought I should attend a school where I could receive some serious theological training, and I did. I took courses in the Old and New Testaments, Jesus the Christ, and the writings of C. S. Lewis. I attended chapel twice a week (although truth be told it was required for all students). Dancing was not allowed on campus (the sexual suggestiveness might trigger already inflamed hormone production to go into overdrive) and we were not allowed into the dorm rooms of members of the opposite sex.

Despite the restrictions it was a good experience because I was a serious believer and thought that this was the way we should behave anyway. But somewhere along the way I found science, and that changed everything (although not overnight). I was thinking of majoring in theology, but then I discovered that a Ph.D. required proficiency in several dead languages (Hebrew, Greek, Aramaic, and Latin). Knowing that I was not especially good at learning live languages, let alone dead ones, I went into psychology and mastered one of the languages of science: statistics. Here (and in research methodology courses) I discovered that there are ways to get at solutions to problems for which we can establish parameters to determine whether a hypothesis is probably right (e.g., rejecting the null hypothesis at the .01 level of significance) or definitely wrong (e.g., not statistically significant). Instead of the rhetoric and disputation of theology, there was the logic and probabilities of science. What a difference this difference in thinking makes!

By the end of my first year of a graduate program in experimental psychology at the California State University, Fullerton, I had deconverted out of Christianity and stripped off my silver ichthus, replacing what was for me the stultifying dogmas of a two-thousand-year-old religion with the worldview of an always changing, always fresh science. The passionate nature of this perspective was enthused most emphatically by my evolutionary biology professor, Bayard Brattstrom, particularly in his after-class discussions at a local bar that went into the wee hours of the morning. This is where the action was for me.

About this time (1975–1976) Uri Geller entered my radar screen. I recall *Psychology Today* and other popular magazines published glowing stories about him, and reports were afloat that experimental psychologists had tested the Israeli psychic and determined that he was genuine. My advisor—a strictly reductionistic Skinnerian behavioral psychologist named Doug Navarick—didn't believe a word of it, but I figured there might be something to it, especially in light of all the other interesting research being conducted on altered states of consciousness, hypnosis, dreams, sensory deprivation, dolphin communication (John C. Lilly), and the like. I took a course in anthropology from a woman whose research was on shamans of South America and their use of mind-altering plants. It all seemed entirely plausible to me and, being personally interested in the subject (the Ouija board consistently blew my mind), I figured that this was rapidly becoming a legitimate subfield of psychological research. After all, Thelma Moss had a research laboratory devoted to studying the paranormal, and it was at UCLA no less, one of the most highly regarded psychology programs in the country.

Enter James "the Amazing" Randi. I do not recall exactly when or where I first encountered him. I believe it was on the *Tonight* show when he was demonstrating how to levitate tables, bend spoons, and perform psychic surgeries. He didn't convince me to become a full-fledged skeptic overnight, but it got me thinking that if some of these psychics were fakes, perhaps they all were (and if not fakes, at least self-deceived). Herein lies an important lesson. There is little to no chance that we can convince True Believers of the errors of their thinking. Our purpose is to reach that vast middle ground between hard-core skeptics and dogmatic believers—people like me who thought that there might be something to these claims but had simply never heard a good counterexplanation. There are many reasons why people believe weird things, but certainly one of the most pervasive is simply that most people have never heard a good explanation for the weird things they hear and read about. Short of a good explanation, they accept the bad explanation that is typically proffered. This alone justifies all the hard work performed by skeptics toward the cause of science and critical thinking. It does make a difference.

Fast-forward ten years. My first contact with organized skepticism came in the mid 1980s through the famed aeronautics engineer and human-powered flight inventor Paul MacCready. I originally met Paul through the International Human Powered Vehicle Association (the IHPVA), as he was interested in designing them and I was interested in racing them (I had a ten-year career as an ultra-marathon cyclist). One day he phoned to invite me to a lecture at the California Institute of Technology being hosted by a group called the Southern California Skeptics (SCS). This was an offshoot of CSICOP and one of many that had spontaneously self-organized around the country throughout the 1980s. The lectures were fascinating, and because of my affiliation with Paul I got to meet some of the insiders in what was rapidly becoming the "skeptical movement." Paul was friends with such science megastars as Richard Feynman, Stephen Jay Gould, and Murray Gell-Mann, and with the likes of Randi and Penn and Teller affiliated with the movement it seemed like it was a happening place to be. In 1987 CSICOP hosted a convention at the Pasadena Civic Center that featured Carl Sagan as their keynote speaker, and he was so inspiring that I decided to return to graduate school to complete my doctorate.

By the end of the 1980s, however, the Southern California Skeptics folded and the skeptical movement came to a grinding halt in the very place that so desperately needed it. In 1991 I completed my Ph.D., was teaching part time at Occidental College, and was nosing around for something different to do. I had just published a paper in a science history journal on the Louisiana creationism trial, that featured the activities of SCS which had organized the amicus curiae brief signed by seventy-two Nobel laureates (Murray Gell-Mann encouraged his fellow Nobelists) and submitted to (and read by) the United States Supreme Court. One of SCS's former volunteer staff members, Pat Linse, heard about the paper, tracked me down, and dropped by to pick up a reprint copy. During that visit she expressed her frustration—and that of many others—that skepticism in Southern California had gone the way of the Neanderthals. Subsequent meetings with her and others inspired us to jump-start the skeptics movement again by launching a new group and bringing out James Randi for our inaugural lecture in March 1992. It was a smashing success as well over four hundred people crammed into a three-hundred-seat hall to hear the amazing one astonish us all with his wit, wisdom, and magic.

With that successful event we were off and running. I starting planning a newsletter, but when Pat saw a sample copy of a bicycle magazine I was publishing (*Ultra Cycling* magazine, the publication of the Ultra-Marathon Cycling Association and Race Across America that I had cofounded in the early 1980s), which was sixty-four pages long, perfect bound, with a duo-tone coated cover, she said that if we could splurge for a skeptical publication of that quality she would generate the appropriate artwork and typography. Since Pat is a professional artist who was working for movie studios generating film posters, she was more than capable of backing up her offer, which I accepted. Our original cover was to feature Randi, and Pat produced a striking portrait of him, but just before publication Isaac Asimov died, so Pat generated a new cover portrait and that became the cover of volume 1, number 1 of what we came to call *Skeptic* magazine. (My originally planned title—*The Journal of Rational Skepticism*—was voted down by Pat and my wife, Kim Ziel Shermer, who reasoned that shorter is better. They were right.)

A detailed history of the demise of SCS and the founding and evolution of the Skeptics Society and *Skeptic* magazine can be told another day by another chronicler with more distance and objectivity. For the purposes of this volume—in essence a celebration of twenty-five years of CSICOP—let me close by paying tribute to the giants on whose shoulders I and others in this "next generation" of skeptics have stood. If Martin Gardner was the pen of this revolution, then James Randi was its sword, as he was in the trenches fighting the good fight and inspiring us all to maintain the courage of our convictions in the face of overwhelming odds. But now that I am running a sizeable organization myself I have come to respect more than ever before what Paul Kurtz has done for our movement. He may not be as prolific and famous a writer as Martin Gardner, or as public and visible an activist as James Randi, but in terms of the day-to-day grind of keeping a movement afloat through the constant battering and assaults that come from variegated sources, there is none to compare to Paul Kurtz. So I close with several excerpts from what I still consider to be one of the finest tomes in our genre and arguably his greatest work, *The Transcendental Temptation*.

The temptation, says Kurtz, "lurks deep within the human breast. It is ever-present, tempting humans by the lure of transcendental realities, subverting the power of their critical intelligence, enabling them to accept unproven and unfounded myth systems." Specifically, Kurtz argues that myths, religions, and claims of the paranormal are lures tempting us beyond rational, critical, and scientific thinking, for the very reason that they touch something in us that is sacred and important—life and immortality: "This impulse is so strong that it has inspired the great religions and paranormal movements of the past and the present and goaded otherwise sensible men and women to swallow patently false myths and to repeat them constantly as articles of faith." What drives this temptation? The answer Kurtz provides is both insightful and beautifully described:

> Let us reflect on the human situation: all of our plans will fail in the long run, if not in the short. The homes we have built and lovingly furnished, the loves we have enjoyed, the careers we have dedicated ourselves to will all disappear in time. The monuments we have erected to memorialize our aspirations and achievements, if we are fortunate, may last a few hundred years, perhaps a millennium or two or three—like the stark and splendid

ruins of Rome and Greece, Egypt and Judea, which have been recovered and treasured by later civilizations. But all the works of human beings disappear and are forgotten in short order. In the immediate future the beautiful clothing that we adorn ourselves with, eventually even our cherished children and grandchildren, and all of our possessions will be dissipated. Many of our poems and books, our paintings and statues will be forgotten, buried on some library shelf or in a museum, read or seen by some future scholars curious about the past, and eventually eaten by worms and molds, or perhaps consumed by fire. Even the things that we prize the most, human intelligence and love, democratic values, the quest for truth, will in time be replaced by unknown values and institutions—if the human species survives, and even that is uncertain. Were we to compile a pessimist's handbook, we could easily fill it to overflowing with notations of false hopes and lost dreams, a catalogue of human suffering and pain, of ignominious conflict, betrayal, and defeat throughout the ages.

Kurtz sounds like a pessimist, right? Wrong. He's a realist. Actually, as he continues the discussion, despite this cold reality he remains optimistic:

I am by nature an optimist. Were I to take an inventory of the sum of goods in human life, they would far outweigh the banalities of evil. I would outdo the pessimist by cataloguing laughter and joy, devotion and sympathy, discovery and creativity, excellence and grandeur. The mark made upon the world by every person and by the race in general would be impressive. How wonderful it has all been. The pessimist points to Caligula, Attila, Cesare Borgia, Beria, or Himmler with horror and disgust; but I would counter with Aristotle, Pericles, da Vinci, Einstein, Beethoven, Mark Twain, Margaret Sanger, and Madame Curie. The pessimist points to duplicity and cruelty in the world; I am impressed by the sympathy, honesty, and kindness that are manifested. The pessimist reminds us of ignorance and stupidity; I, of the continue growth of human knowledge and understanding. The pessimist emphasizes the failures and defeats; I, the successes and victories in all their glory.

Now that is elegant prose. And not a bad case for skepticism and humanism, either! Arguably, however, the most important point Kurtz makes in *The Transcendental Temptation*, at least for our purposes in this volume, comes toward the end in his discussion of the meaning and goals of skepticism. It is an admonition we should all bear in mind, a passage to be read once a year:

The skeptic is not passionately intent on converting mankind to his or her point of view and surely is not interested in imposing it on others, though he may be deeply concerned with raising the level of education and critical inquiry in society. Still, if there are any lessons to be learned from history, it is that we should be skeptical of all points of view, including those of the skeptics. No one is infallible, and no one can claim a monopoly on truth or virtue. It would be contradictory for skepticism to seek to translate itself into a new faith. One must view with caution the promises of any new secular priest who might emerge promising a brave new world—if only his path to clarity and truth is followed. Perhaps the best we can hope for is to temper the intemperate and to tame the perverse temptation that lurks within.

Amen, brother!

MICHAEL SHERMER is the publisher of *Skeptic* magazine, the director of the Skeptics Society, the host of the Skeptics Science Lecture Series at Caltech, a columnist for *Scientific American*, and the cohost and consulting producer for the Fox Family television series *Exploring the Unknown*. He is the author of *Why People Believe Weird Things*, *How We Believe: The Search for God in an Age of Science* (both published by W. H. Freeman), *Denying History* (University of California Press), and *The Borderlands of Science: Where Orthodoxy Meets Heresy* (Oxford University Press). His next book is *Heretic-Scientist: The Life and Science of Alfred Russel Wallace*, and he is currently researching and writing *Why We Are Moral: The Origins of Morality and the Science of Ethics*.

29

THE IMPORTANCE OF SKEPTICISM

STEVE ALLEN

It has long been known that in our individual lives, at the beginning of which we resemble nothing so much as a tiny accidental smear of tapioca on a glass plate, we gradually relive the physical history of our species. At the stage when we, like other animals, leave the environment of the mother, which is called birth, we are introduced into the world in such a blank condition that it may be said that even the individual who may eventually be recognized as the most intelligent person who ever lived nevertheless on day one knows nothing.

Something like the same mysterious grand process takes place as regards our sciences, arts, and other disciplines in which the general rule is simplicity at the start and increasing complexity along the line of development.

Is it not strange, therefore, that the modest observation I have just made, now so widely accepted by people of a thousand-and-one philosophies, applies to every area of human development with the single exception of religion?

It is no reasonable objection to refer to specific forms of belief concerning which we are obviously able to recognize certain points of origin by referring to such historical characters as Joseph Smith, Mary Baker Eddy, Mohammed, or Jesus Christ. All of these, and the literally thousands of others considered the founders of their religions, did indeed proclaim a new order, but in no case were their teachings new in any overall sense; they all built on previously existing beliefs, customs, and moral exhortations. Parenthetically, Christians themselves have long told us that Jesus personally did not found his church; that was done by his individual followers over a considerable span of time after his death.

It does not inescapably follow, from any of this, that just because it is very likely that religion, too, like all other human activities, emerged, in its many different forms in different parts of the earth, by a long slow process, therefore they must consist entirely of nonsense and fanaticism. That individual believers have been guilty of these two grievous faults has never been denied but I am making here a general observation that does not address the validity of any particular form of religious faith.

Historians, philosophers, and other scholars have bequeathed to us the fruit of their inquiries on such important questions, and we are, of course, free to add our own. Fortunately it is quite a simple matter to identify certain common life-factors which are perfectly consistent with the hypothesis that religions in general started as a way of attempting to make sense of natural phenomena. Anyone, for example, who has ever gazed into the fiery pit of a volcano, which now, because of the wonders of modern photography, everyone can do, has very likely entertained at least the thought that the belief in a literal, fiery hell might have originated in such a physical cause.

Those who have witnessed violent outbreaks of nature—hurricanes, tornadoes, tidal waves, earthquakes, floods, wild storms with their sometimes lethal lightning bolts, avalanches—can be forgiven for imagining that such fearful destruction of precious property and lives are due to the gods or God, or in believing that the gods were furious with human creatures and intent on punishing them for their sins. Any of us who have ever lost a dearly beloved one or whose communities are mourning a heroic leader can understand the longing that some part of the departed soul still exists and that death is not the final chapter of human existence.

Thoughtful analysis of such common questions is invariably a sign of intelligence on the part of those who attempt—urged on by nothing more than their reasoning powers—to deal with life's many mysteries.

Those societies are most healthy that give birth to freethinkers, rationalists, and skeptics. It is a good, not a bad thing to ask for evidence rather than to uncritically accept everything on authority. Certainly no society that inhibits this process of inquiry can any longer boast that it is free.

Another relevant factor is that every one of us often has difficulty in responding to criticism. In some cases the problem is so extreme that we are literally unable to see any justification for the accusations made against us, and this may apply to serious as well as trivial concerns. If we are members of any larger societal group—a political party, a church, a corporation, a bowling team—our sense of loyalty may make us rationalize the group's offenses, if not deny them entirely. Strangely enough, this is especially the case in religion.

If we were really concerned about moral virtue and nobility of conduct, we would not only do a better job of behaving appropriately ourselves but we would be particularly sensitive to breaches of conduct committed by our fellow believers.

Unfortunately what tends to happen when criticisms, even justified criticisms, against our group are made is that we succumb to a "circle-the-wagons" mentality and often defend the indefensible.

It is to the great credit of the freethought movements, over the centuries, that their adherents often have had the courage to openly criticize religious beliefs that are patently false and acts which are shameful. One of the reasons they are prepared to engage in such critiques is that they tend to be more familiar with history than the average believer. Rationalists are inclined to honor the search for truth wherever it may lead, whereas those who are already committed to a religious or political creed customarily behave like attorneys for the defense.

It is odd that most of us recognize such reprehensible behavior as it applies to groups that we perceive as rivals, yet we often are relatively blind to our own faults and the faults of those who share our creedal assumptions.

The same unfortunate drama is often found within the corporate or industrial world. Witness the fate of those often heroic defenders of public welfare who discover that something evil is being perpetrated by the company that employs them. In a more rational society they would be honored. In the world in which we live they are vilified, often hated, spied upon, and treated as pariahs. Witness what the automobile industry did to Ralph Nader, or what the tobacco industry did to its internal critics while brazenly denying its responsibility for the countless deaths it caused every year.

In the history of religious institutions, it has often been the courageous and outspoken heretics and freethinkers who have provided a fundamentally important moral service to society by pointing out hypocrisies and errors. The least that the rest of us should consider is the *evidence* in support of the indictment that they may present.

Society should always leave room for skeptics and skepticism and this should apply to all areas of human interest. Skepticism, of course, is commonly misunderstood—particularly in cases where the skeptical reasoning process inclines to atheism. Opponents here argue that if either (a) there is no God or (b) we believe there is none, then there is no foundation whatever for morality. Since this is simply not the case it ought *not* to be accepted as a reason for rejecting skepticism.

There are relevant clues in studies made of prison populations. Most inmates are firm believers in the Deity. There are relatively few atheists or agnostics in prison. The other side of that same coin is that although I have known many atheists and agnostics in my life, I have never encountered evidence that they are any worse, judged according to moral criteria, than believers.

One does not have to be a professional theologian to clarify simple moral questions concerning right and wrong. A concerned five-year-old child has some capacity for moral understanding. In fact, the child could perhaps do it even better because he is unlikely to be infected by the virus of political or social bias or economic self-interest that so often confuse the moral judgments of those to whom many turn for guidance.

This is a point of such profound importance that I must return to it. Every culture is enriched by its literature. One of the most morally instructive examples of the literary art is Ibsen's play *An Enemy of the People*. The story is about a medical man who works in a popular European resort which is about to celebrate an annual fair, an event that brings in large amounts of money to local merchants. The doctor happens to discover a bacterium in the community's water supply, one that will undoubtedly sicken and perhaps even kill residents or visitors.

The danger is so severe that the doctor does the only thing he can do, as a concerned citizen. He tells the local powers that under no circumstances must they proceed with their plans for the annual event because of danger to the public health. He is promptly told to keep his mouth shut. But he protests, "People may die." His critics make it clear that they really do not care that serious illness or deaths are likely to result from the contaminated water supply. They are more concerned about the fact that what the doctor is advising is "bad for business."

We would be very ill-advised to assume that this is just a fascinating story about a place long distant in time and space. Precisely the same drama is acted out literally every day of our experience.

In the evaluation and analysis of such social phenomena I have found the skeptical method to be very helpful. But it is, of course, merely another name for the scientific method. In an instructive audiotape for children called *Gullible's Travels* that I produced for Prometheus Books, I've written a song called "Look for the Evidence." Skeptics insist that we do that.

For convenience we often treat as separate things that in physical reality are merged together. For example, we refer to *nature* and *science* as if they were two distinct entities. In reality the raw materials with which science works are the very things that constitute nature. Science obviously employs mathematical symbols and logical concepts in describing the regularities it detects within nature, but it also deals with concrete things—the variety of plants, of animals, the humans, the daily processes of birth and death of innumerable living creatures, water, air, sunsets, clouds—in other words, the only reality of which we can have any degree of reliable knowledge. Those fundamentalist religious believers, therefore, who seem to relish speaking contemptuously of science reveal an astonishing insensitivity to the world that they tell us God created. If we grant their assumption that all material reality was created by God, then it follows that anyone who criticizes real science is in a sense criticizing the Creator!

In a time of such astonishing expansion of scientific knowledge it is depressing that superstition is still common; this is all the more reason why skepticism is needed today as in the past. No matter how patently absurd a given claim might be it may appeal to some segments of society. These segments which believe in a specific absurdity may be a minority; however, if we add them up they constitute together a large part of the American population. Skepticism must be recognized as a high social virtue, and therefore it should be encouraged.

Many believers assume that the skeptical impulse is directly and inescapably at odds with religious belief. On the contrary, approaching religious subject matter with the methods of reason or even, at a more modest level, simple common sense can do religion a great service. A particularly admirable current example is *Papal Sin—Structures of Deceit* by Garry Wills (Doubleday). It is by no means Wills's purpose in presenting his fascinating study to induce Catholics to leave the Church. He refers in complimentary terms to St. Augustine, Cardinal John Henry Newman, Lord Acton, and Pope John XXIII. But he quite correctly points out that errors made by the Church in past centuries still affect Vatican thinking in the present period.

Speaking from personal experience as one raised in the Church and who served it faithfully for many years, I am encouraged that I can still maintain cordial dialogue with some of its priestly representatives, while at the same time remaining a committed skeptic.

STEVE ALLEN (1921–2000) was known as television's renaissance man. He authored more than fifty books and composed over 8,500 songs. Allen was the original creator and host of NBC's long-running *Tonight* show and the award-winning PBS series *Meeting of Minds*. You can learn more about this legendary entertainer by visiting his official Web site at SteveAllenonline.com.

WHEN CORPORATIONS EMBRACED "TRANSCENDENTAL TECHNOLOGIES"

BÉLA SCHEIBER

It was in the 1970s when CSICOP organized and began publishing the *Skeptical Inquirer* under the name of the *Zetetic* that I started my career in the telecommunication industry as a systems analyst. I mention this only to establish myself as someone who has had twenty years in the business world. This form of experience, I believe, is underrepresented in this volume as most of the other distinguished contributors are primarily connected with the academic community.

While the skeptic publications have primarily focused on such topics as alternative medicine, parapsychology, UFOs, and other curious beliefs within our culture, the approach has been nearly always academic. There has been very little published within the skeptic community regarding the infiltration and influence on corporations of the type of poor thinking that is in fact part and parcel of the same class of irrational beliefs.

Perhaps it was something peculiar about the 1970s that while CSICOP was being conceived, John Paul Rosenberg was formulating his own plans. Rosenberg, having brushed shoulders with Scientology, became an instructor for a spiritual-like discipline known as Mind Dynamics. Not content with being an instructor he changed his name to Werner Hans Erhard and in 1971 decided that what the business world needed—and would pay for—is a savior who could persuade their employees to be more motivated and thereby positively influence the bottom line. After all this was the pre-desktop, Internet era where productivity depended on attitude, and manipulating the beliefs of the employees was viewed as a means of achieving that goal.

Erhard created what was to become the most copied and influential model of corporate effort to enhance human performance, EST (Erhard Seminars Training), which was to peak in the late 1980s. It is of some interest that in the booming economic times of the 1990s corporations turned increasingly away from influencing workers' motivation as a means of increased profits toward mergers, downsizing, and "right-sizing" (same as down-sizing but with less guilt) to influence Wall Street perceptions. Also, concurrently, productivity became viewed more as an outcome of technology than of individual motivation.

R. D. Rosen's book *Psychobabble* (1975) captures the many sophistries within EST. Examples from the book directly attributed to Erhard include: "Thinking won't get you there, but most people don't think well enough to see that thinking doesn't work"; and "Once you get It, you have to prove that you've got It. But proving you've got It means you haven't got It. So the only thing to do once you've got It is to give It up." What is "It"? From Rosen, attributed to Erhard: "IT is you experiencing yourself without any symbology or any concept. Normally, I experience myself through my thoughts; I think who I am. Sometimes I experience myself through my body; I sense who I am. Sometimes I experience myself through my emotions; I feel who I am. Well, IT is you experiencing you directly without any intervening system."

EST became very popular among entertainers and some intellectuals by the end of the 1970s. Perhaps it would have faded away eventually had it not been for a new alternative culture that was soon to become the symbol of irrational thought to many and a way of life for many more. The emergence of the "New Age" came just at the right time for EST. Shirley MacLaine told the world in her book *It's All in the Playing* that, "The way I look at it, this is all my dream. I'm making all of it happen—good and bad—and I have the choice of how I'll relate to it, and what I'll do about it. What is the lesson in this? Perhaps we are all telling the truth—our truth as we see it. Perhaps everyone has his own truth; the truth as an objective reality doesn't exist."

While Shirley MacLaine was promoting her views others moved in to define the "New Age" more in terms of "unlimited potential," "transformations," and "empowerment" of the self. Soon the concept of limitations was discarded. In fact the popular mantra was that we are limited only to the extent that we believe we are. David Spangler in the 1988 publication of *The New Age Catalogue* partly defined the New Age "as a metaphor for the expression of a transformative, creative spirit rather than as a future event." In the same volume, the editor, Paul Zuromski, wrote, "The goal [of New Age] is an understanding of who you are, learning why you're here and exercising your unlimited potential in this lifetime."

By the early 1980s all the components were in place: Corporations wanted to enhance their profits and were desperate to find a means that would accomplish that goal; EST was running into some difficult times and Erhard reinvented it as The Forum and created in 1984 Transformational Technologies; the "New Age" subculture began to offer the public the hope of an unlimited potential through empowerment and transformation. Soon, CEOs and directors of corporations took notice and began to explore the possibilities of sending employees to enhancement seminars. Erhard, through his Transformational Technologies, began licensing other entrepreneurs to design their own training programs based on EST/Forum.

The "human transformation" movement had arrived. The September 25, 1988, issue of the Business World supplement of the *New York Times Magazine* gave extensive coverage in their article "Scenario for a New Age," in which they listed Owens Corning Fiberglas Corporation, Apple Computer (in its previous incarnation), NEC, Pacific Bell, and Scott Paper as being involved. The March 23, 1988, *Washington Post* reported that "Members of the Pentagon Meditation Club hope to deploy a spiritual 'peace shield' around the planet through what they call their 'Spiritual Defense Initiative.' " The president of the club is shown holding a device described as a " 'peace shield gauge,' which measures a person's aura."

The National Academy of Sciences brought together many distinguished experts to formally evaluate the claims and the impact of these human performance seminars. In their report published in 1988, *Enhancing Human Performance: Issues, Theories, and Techniques*, they state that the "American Society for Training and Development 'estimates that companies are spending an astounding $30 billion a year on formal courses and training programs for workers. And that's only the tip of the iceberg' (*Wall Street Journal*, August 5, 1986)."

My personal interest in all of this first emerged when, as a relatively new employee of Mountain Bell (later to become US West), I was requested to attend a seminar entitled "I'm O.K.—You're O.K." Within the first hour I became suspicious and started to ask some skeptical questions. The attendees were expected to consider a very simpleminded approach to human behavior and somehow transform this into productivity on the job. That was the beginning of my reputation with my coworkers as a troublemaker. There would be more over the next eighteen years. Interestingly, in every one of these episodes my closest coworkers agreed with me but were not motivated to speak up. What the managers and directors were oblivious to was that most everyone I spoke with considered these seminars as a way to get away from real work and have lunch at the company's expense.

Soon after the above incident everyone in my office had to attend a lecture on personality types. Afterward we had to complete a personality test that was then mapped onto a circle subdivided into twelve zones (sounds a bit astrological), each representing a "personality trait." This was supposed to give us insights into our strengths and weaknesses. We then had to turn this information over to our supervisors—which I refused to do. In preparation to confronting my supervisor I called the company that devised the test and asked them several key questions such as: How was the test devised and what publication could I go to for information on its validity? Answers were not forthcoming. I then informed my supervisor that at the risk of being judged based on an unproven personality assessment profile that it was inappropriate for him to see my results. My coworkers again showed no interest even after I informed them that I called the company that devised the test and they could not cite a credible reference.

Perhaps the most bizarre effort on the part of US West management to enhance employee performance began July 24, 1989, when *all* programmers, systems analysts, and managers (at least in my district in Denver) were required to attend an all-morning lecture in a large auditorium. I could not believe what followed. I felt as if I was attending a religious cult revival. The keynote speaker was Dean Anderson and his magic was called "Optimal Performance" (OP). The official schedule we received at the door was as follows: "Introduction and History—8:30–8:45; Group Exercise—8:45–9:15; Organization Development—9:15–9:25; Training Overview—9:25–9:40; Logistics—9:40–9:50; Sharing of Optimal Performance Experiences—9:50–10:20; Creating Conditions for Success of Optimal Performance—10:20–10:50; Closing—10:50–11:00." None of the sessions above had anything of objective quality about them. The entire two-and-one-half-hour production had the appearance of being carefully choreographed. "Spontaneous" outbursts came from the auditorium as one after another audience member rose from his or her seat and gave a testimonial. Surprisingly testimonies even came from upper-level managers on how their lives had changed since they met Anderson and had been exposed to his training. These leaders of one of the largest telecommunication companies of the 1980s appeared to be mesmerized by the speaker without any questioning. At the end we were told that it was mandatory that all managers (programmers and systems analysts were considered managers) register for OP training. We were told that 100 percent compliance was necessary for the training to have a real impact on productivity. More on the training later.

I came well prepared for the above session. Having had previous experience with "transformational training," and having researched its history and methods, I always carried in my briefcase several copies of the April 1, 1988, EEOC official letter to their field offices on handling " 'New Age' Training Programs [Which] May Conflict with Employees' Religious Beliefs." This letter included a six-page policy statement (Number N-915.022; Date 2/22/88). Some relevant quotes follow: "Employers are increasingly making use of training programs designed to improve employee motivation, cooperation, or productivity through the use of various so-called 'new age' techniques." "A large utility company requires its employees to attend seminars based on the teaching of a mystic, George Gurdjieff. . . ." "Another corporation provides its employees with workshops in stress management using so called 'faith healers' who read the 'auras' of employees." "Specialists in employee training say that 'most of the nation's major corporations and numerous government agencies have hired some consultants and purveyors of similar 'personal growth' training programs in recent years." "The programs utilize a wide variety of techniques: meditation, guided visualization, self-hypnosis, therapeutic touch, biofeedback, yoga, walking on fire, and inducing altered states of consciousness." "These programs focus on changing individual employees' attitudes and self-concepts by promoting increased self-esteem, assertiveness, independence, and creativity in order to improve productivity."

The EEOC policy statement states that individual conflicts with these types of seminars "can be resolved under the traditional Title VII theory of religious accommodation." The problem raised is "whether the employee must prove that some aspect of the training program is actually based on religion or has religious content in order to establish a need for religious accommodation. It is necessary, therefore, to examine the nature of an employee's religious belief requiring accommodation under Title VII." The murky issue of an employee's religious belief is well handled in the document by its use of the Supreme Court's determination in the case of *United States* v. *Seeger*.

The most valuable EEOC interpretation from the Supreme Court's ruling on religious accommodation was that, "Moreover, the Commission has held that protected religious belief also includes the *freedom not to believe* [author's emphasis]." More employee protection was given in the EEOC policy document: "That the employer or the sponsor of a 'new age' program believes there is no religious basis for, or content to, the training or techniques used is irrelevant to determining the need for accommodation. If an employee believes that some aspect of the training program conflicts with his/her own beliefs, an employer may only inquire as to what the employee's beliefs are and consider the sincerity with which the employee holds those beliefs. . . . An employer may not reject an employee's request for accommodation on the basis that the employee's beliefs about the 'new age' training seem unreasonable."

At the end of the session, while most everyone was leaving for lunch, I went to the front of the auditorium with several copies of the above document in hand and presented them to the US West organizers of the event. I pointed out to them that they should carefully read the EEOC policy statements and that it might be in conflict with their directive of mandatory compliance. The next day I received some confirmation that my effort was a success. A notice was sent to everyone that attendance in the OP seminar was strongly recommended but not mandatory. Again my coworkers were a disappointment with only four refusing to attend the seminar and three of them claimed religious conflict as they were Jehovah's Witnesses. I simply refused to attend and waited for the inquisition which never materialized.

OP involved the creation of several subgroups from the pool of employees. Members of these smaller groups each attended a "Core Training" seminar lasting two full workdays at a remote setting where they had to get in front of everyone and discuss, among other personal items, their fears, even if their fear was to discuss their fears, with strangers. Everyone had to eat together. A very thick student manual was distributed. Under the heading of "Finding Solutions to Problems: There are no problems in the universe, only problem-makers" is written: "The important understanding here is that there is no problem 'out there.' There are only a series of stimuli. In fact, we don't even experience the stimuli 'out there.' We experience them in our own minds. This brings up the question of 'What is reality?' Do we ever really experience it? If it is only a montage of feelings, sounds, sights, tastes, and smells that we process in our minds, then how do we know 'it' even exists out there?" Shades of EST!

Near the end of the training booklet there is a naked appeal for further development of the student: "Other trainings are taught outside the corporate environment in retreat settings, and focus on the deeper aspects of personal growth and transformation. Please feel free to contact us if you feel that any of these programs would support your further integration of the Optimal Performance material." One can only imagine how expensive "deeper aspects of personal growth" can be.

Follow-up four-hour refresher courses every week over several months were required after the Core Training.

In my opinion the most destructive aspect of the training was the divisiveness it created in the office. Fortunately this did not last long. Because the management was persuaded to believe that only 100 percent participation could be of value to the company, those who would not participate were labeled "reptiles." Part of the OP training was dividing people into three states: reptile (the worst), biocomputer, and evolutionary cocreator (the best). It did not help matters any when I explained that 100 percent participation was impossible in the long run because new people were constantly being hired or being transferred to the district and we could not maintain the training forever.

Perhaps the most bizarre contrivance of the OP training was the requirement that once a month those who went through the initial, formal training had to go bowling, golfing, or to a movie with Dean Anderson during working hours at company expense. Ostensibly this was required to maintain the bonding. I, however, suspected otherwise.

The entire OP episode lasted less than six months and Anderson reportedly walked away with over half a million dollars (this data was carefully extracted by me from several people close to the situation).

The magical effect Dean Anderson had on some people was made clear in a January 16, 1990, internal memo sent to everyone after the OP training had already ended: "Attention! Here is a special announcement for you to share with your group: Dean Anderson is a daddy. Linda gave birth to Terra Lyn Anderson on January 10th. . . . Dean said he predicted Terra's birthdate last summer as 1/10; what insight that guy has. By the way, Terra Lyn translates to 'beautiful earth.' "

The above characterization of events within one company is, of course, limited in its usefulness as a serious study of the corporate environment. Having been exposed to these programs within my company made me curious as to how widespread they are.

Using the April 25, 1988, issue of *Forbes* magazine's list of "The Forbes 500" U.S. companies, I selected two hundred to survey. The magazine supplied the addresses and I directed my letter of inquiry to their respective human resource director. Along with a cover letter and a return envelope I enclosed a survey composed of a matrix with the following entries along the left side: Win/Win, Human Potential, The Forum, EST, Visualization, Lifespring, Krone Training, New Age, Fire Walking, Wonder Link, Neuro-Linguistic Programming (NLP), WISE, Transformational Technologies, Subliminal Techniques, and Relaxation/Meditation. Confidentiality was promised. I asked the personnel filling out the form to indicate which, if any, of the above techniques were (1) currently used, (2) previously used, (3) found to be effective, and (4) if management was required to attend. Two of the techniques listed do not exist and were listed as controls to eliminate any respondent that would check them (Wonder Link and WISE).

The results of this survey, while clearly not rigorous scientifically, produced the following. Out of two hundred surveys mailed forty-four were returned. Out of the forty-four, twenty-six checked that they are or had used at least one of the techniques listed. Understandably the language of the survey allowed for differing interpretation and some of the techniques listed were broad categories while others were specific (e.g., Transformational Technologies is a specific type of training but may be interpreted as a generalized reference to any alternative training).

The top three techniques used were the Forum (thirteen, 50 percent of the twenty-six), Win/Win (thirteen, 50 percent of the twenty-six), and Relaxation/Meditation (ten, 38 percent). Seven of the thirteen corporations indicated that The Forum was found to be effective and two of them required management to attend. Curiously fire walking had zero participation even though Tony Robbins was actively using it in his seminars in the 1980s.

Perhaps what was most interesting were the comments from those who indicated they used none of the techniques: "We do not use any of these. Our approach to teaching motivation is that managers/leaders must understand that individuals choose to be motivated by a variety of intrinsic and extrinsic factors. No one can motivate another except by coercive means." "We make sure that the job and its contents are motivational. Outside programs have not met with any ongoing success." Proudly one proclaimed: "We use no motivational training" in dark blue large script. One respondent, a Ph.D., gave his company's name as well as his own with the following statement: "We've used some rudimentary NLP, but not extensive or required. Many of the programs you list (e.g., Lifespring) are considered disasters or useless (EST, meditation, etc.). We prefer more substantive programs which teach a skill or technique."

One person who marked that his company had used The Forum and found it to be effective and required management to attend provided his name and address. I contacted him by telephone for an interview. His response to my questioning was interesting. He called The Forum "nonsense" and said that while "70 to 80 employees participated," in his opinion the "people use it as a fix."

BÉLA SCHEIBER, after receiving his master's degree from the University of Colorado in Boulder, embarked on a career in the space program working on the Skylab mission in Houston, Texas. This was followed by a twenty-year second career in the telecommunication business as a systems analyst. It was soon after his second career began that his primary interest in skepticism developed at which time he founded the Rocky Mountain Skeptics. Now that he has retired he devotes most of his time to his third career as an author and lecturer on topics related to skepticism. He has recently published the book *Therapeutic Touch* and is on the editorial board of the *Skeptical Inquirer* and the *Scientific Review of Alternative Medicine* as well as president of the Rocky Mountain Skeptics and a member of CSICOP's Executive Council.

RELIGION

31

CONFESSIONS OF A SKEPTIC

MARTIN GARDNER

My first awareness of the enormous influence that pseudoscience can have on the minds of intelligent but gullible persons began in my undergraduate years at the University of Chicago. I had grown up in Tulsa, the son of a devout Methodist mother and a geologist father who was a great admirer of the pantheism of John Burroughs. Through the influence of a Sunday school teacher and camp counselor I became a convert to an ugly Protestant fundamentalism that caused my father great distress. For a short time I took seriously the many books defending creationism by a Seventh-Day Adventist crank geologist named George McCready Price. His major work, *The New Geology*, is still the inspiration behind the writings of today's flood theorists who believe the universe was created in six literal days, just as it says in Genesis, and that fossils are relics of life that perished in Noah's flood.

Courses in geology and biology at the University of Chicago opened my eyes to the glaring fallacies in Price's books. It was then brought home to me that one should never accept extraordinary scientific claims without first learning something about the science involved. Indeed, a great way to master the basics of a science is to investigate crazy conjectures to discover where they go wrong. In any case, after finding how ignorant Price was, and finding the evidence for evolution overwhelming, my fundamentalist faith slowly eroded. I felt a kinship with Charles Darwin who also was a believing Christian until his faith dissolved and he decided to call himself an agnostic.

In my theological novel *The Flight of Peter Fromm* (there is a Prometheus Books paperback edition) I put Peter, whom I don't resemble in looks or personality, through the convoluted mental stages I went through before I finally decided, like Darwin, that I could not call myself a Christian without being hypocritical. Unlike Darwin, that I somehow managed to preserve a kind of theism, though a theism far outside the circle of any established religion. It is what today is called philosophical theism in the tradition of such thinkers as Kant, Bayle, William James, Charles Peirce, Ralph Barton Perry, John Fiske, Edgar Brightman, John Hick, and, above all, my mentor, Miguel de Unamuno, the Spanish philosopher, novelist, and poet.

My atheist and agnostic friends never cease to be amazed and dismayed over how I manage to be such a thoroughgoing skeptic of the paranormal and still retain a belief in God. It's as if they think that anyone who doubts Uri Geller's ability to bend spoons with his mind must also doubt the existence of God! As I argue in my confessional, *The Whys of a Philosophical Scrivener*, I see not the slightest conflict between philosophical theism and unbounded respect for science. My belief in God, I freely confess, rests entirely on emotion. There are no logical proofs that God exists, and not the slightest empirical evidence for a deity. Indeed, the prevalence of irrational evil—thousands killed by a sudden earthquake or by prolonged famine—is a powerful emotional reason for disbelieving in God.

Although Kant, following Hume, demolished the traditional proofs of God, he also stressed the emotive power of the argument from design. The seeming design in the structure and habits of life-forms, which so many theologians once took to be proofs of a creator, evaporated in the light of Darwin's revolution. Today, the old design argument has returned in the form of the anthropic principle. So many physical constants are so finely tuned that if they varied by a tiny fraction it would have been impossible for stars and planets to form. A popular way to get around this as evidence for design is to posit a multiverse in which billions, perhaps an infinity, of universes explode into being, each with a random set of physical constants. Naturally we could have evolved only in a universe with constants that allowed life to arise.

Even if there are no other universes, the fine tuning of constants provides no logically binding proof of intelligent design.[1] One merely assumes that this is just how the universe is. As Gilbert Chesterton once put it, to an atheist the universe is the most exquisite machine ever constructed by nobody. It is here that emotions play a crucial role. One is either undismayed by the thought that the universe we see is all there is, with no transcendent meaning or purpose, or one is deeply moved by realizing that in the microsecond after the big bang, the laws of nature were such that you and I were potentially *there*. The waves and particles of quantum mechanics were of such a fantastic nature as to make inevitable, as the hot universe cooled, that galaxies would form, their matter would condense into suns and planets, and on at least one insignificant little planet, in one of billions of galaxies, life would get underway and finally produce such curious creatures as you and me. Contemplating this awesome scenario one may feel a strong desire to hang the process on a wholly other Creator. With such a desire travels faith.

It is important to understand, my atheist friends, that this leap of faith in no way dims a respect for science. I will go even further. Although there are no logical proofs or empirical evidence for or against the existence of a Creator, I believe that atheists and agnostics have the better arguments. Even atheists can be profoundly disturbed by the unfathomable mystery of why there is something rather than nothing, or as Stephen Hawking recently phrased it, why the universe bothers to exist, and at the same time feel no need for a quixotic leap of faith. I confess I am more comfortable discussing such questions with an atheist than with true believers in a great religion or in some grotesque religious cult.

Although I do believe, for emotional reasons only, in a transcendent Creator, wholly beyond our comprehension, I do not think this God would stoop to such droll antics as popping down on Earth to invade the womb of a virgin, then grow up to become a charismatic faith healer who claimed to be God's son, and went about performing such conjuring tricks as walking on water, turning water to wine, multiplying loaves and fishes, finding a coin in a fish, withering a fig tree, raising corpses from the dead, and finally dying a horrible death to save us from hell before he floated back to heaven. I cannot believe in a God whose creation is so imperfect that he is compelled to poke a finger into our cosmos to adjust the orbits of planets (as Newton believed) or to help dinosaurs evolve into birds or cause apelike creatures to turn into humans.

Consider my admiration for two British writers who had little in common except their ability to write well and to produce entertaining fiction. I refer to H. G. Wells and G. K. Chesterton. I am aware of all of Chesterton's faults, especially his mild anti-Semitism and his ignorance of science, but I share his constant sense of wonder toward the mysteries of the universe and toward finding himself alive. Late in life Chesterton converted to Roman Catholicism. Wells, after a youthful flirtation with the concept of a finite God, became an atheist. His understanding of science was extensive. Although he caricatured Chesterton as Father Amerton in his utopian fantasy *Men Like Gods*, and although Chesterton constantly attacked Wells, the two men were friends. As I say in my *Whys*, if you can imagine how I can admire both Wells and Chesterton, two men so far apart in their opinions, you will understand how I can combine theism with skepticism and an acceptance of science as our only road to knowledge about how the universe behaves.

I have written introductions to books by both Wells and Chesterton, and in 1999 I annotated Chesterton's masterpiece, *The Man Who Was Thursday*. Written long before he and his wife became Catholics, in my opinion Chesterton's nightmare, as he called it, is a profound philosophical novel grappling with God's relation to Nature, with the terrible problem of evil, and with the reality of free will.

But enough of theology. My first writing about pseudoscience was an article titled "The Hermit Scientist" that appeared in the *Antioch Review* (winter 1950–51). A high school friend, John Elliott, was then a literary agent in Manhattan. He persuaded me to expand my article into a book. I spent many months in the New York Public Library researching crackpots. The result was a hardcover volume titled *In the Name of Science*, published by Putnam in 1952. Sales were mediocre and the book was quickly remaindered. The late Hayward Cirker, founder and president of Dover, picked up the book and issued it as a paperback with the new title *Fads and Fallacies in the Name of Science*. Sales skyrocketed, thanks mainly to tireless attacks on the book by guests on an all-night radio talk show hosted by Long John Nebel.

Nebel was the Art Bell of his day. Although he himself did not take his guests seriously, his show, like Bell's, featured dialogue with every type of crank willing to go on the air. For many months my book was mercilessly pilloried by believers in the various pseudosciences that my book attacked. I recall one night when I was up at 2 A.M. to give a milk bottle to our first child, I turned on the radio. The first words I heard were "Mr. Gardner is a liar." They were spoken by John Campbell, then editor of *Astounding Science Fiction*. Campbell had published an article on dianetics by L. Ron Hubbard, and was firmly convinced that dianetics was a great new scientific breakthrough. As a result of such nightly attacks, *Fads and Fallacies* became one of Dover's all-time best-sellers. It has never since been out of print.

At the time I wrote that book I would have ridiculed the suggestion that any of several pseudosciences to which I devoted a chapter would last more than a decade. One chapter, for example, was about the early sightings of what were then called flying saucers. I never would have guessed that UFOlogy would become the nation's leading mania, comparable to visions of Mary and angels that were so widespread in the Middle Ages and Renaissance. Joan of Arc talked with an angel. People today talk with aliens who abduct them in spacecraft from other worlds. As I write, I see no signs that the mania is abating.

Another chapter in my book was an attack on L. Ron Hubbard's *Dianetics*. This was before he transformed dianetics into a bizarre religion, complete with gods and reincarnation, that he named Scientology. Hubbard's contention that embryos make recordings, called engrams, of what their mother is saying or hearing long before they develop ears, struck me as a belief so absurd that I couldn't imagine that Hubbard's delusions (assuming he really believed them at the time, which many doubt) would become the basis for a wealthy, powerful, worldwide cult—a cult that would capture some of the best actors in Hollywood.

Still another chapter in my book described the equally mad views of Wilhelm Reich. When the *Village Voice* gave away copies of *Fads and Fallacies* to new subscribers, howls of fury arose among Village Reichians. They wrote letters to the *Village Voice* complaining about my many errors. I managed to silence them with a letter pointing out that I had submitted the chapter to Reich himself before the book was published. If you check that chapter you will see that it never criticizes Reich. It merely describes his views. I did have a sentence saying that Reich was either misguided or he was the greatest scientist of our time.

Reich, of course, was not in the least offended by this statement because he took for granted the second alternative. He found only one trivial mistake of a date, which of course I corrected. At several spots in the margin of my manuscript he wrote "Good!" because he liked the accuracy of what I said. Although orgonomy no longer has the passionate following it once had, it is far from dead. It still generates books and periodicals and conferences, and has at least one active orgone rainmaker, James de Meo, about whom I have written in *On the Wild Side*, another Prometheus book.

The final chapter of *Fads and Fallacies* was about Joseph Banks Rhine, the father of modern parapsychology. Although I do not believe there is any sound evidence for the reality of ESP, PK, and precognition, I am all in favor of parapsychologists continuing their efforts. Enormous progress has been made in their awareness of the need for rigid controls. No longer do top parapsychologists claim that PK will bend keys and spoons or project thoughts onto Polaroid film. As controls have tightened, claims by parapsychologists have become far less extraordinary. Rhine's sensational results have never been replicated, nor has anyone produced reliable evidence that a psychic can rotate a delicately balanced needle under a bell jar, an experiment Rhine repeatedly tried, but with failures he never reported. Perhaps some fine day parapsychologists will devise an experiment that can be regularly repeated by skeptics, though I suspect that a hundred years from now their claims will be in the same limbo they are now.

I have no objection to cranks of all sorts publishing books and papers because there is always the possibility, however slight, that they might hit on something fruitful. It is well to remember that the situation today is a far cry from the infant days of science when a Galileo could be condemned on religious grounds. Indeed, the Catholic Church recently admitted it erred in persecuting Galileo, and the present pope has announced, to the vast surprise of conservative Catholics, that evolution can be taught as a fact in Catholic schools. Today science is a vast network of thousands of researchers in touch with one another and eager to overturn popular speculations. The quickest way to fame for a scientist now is to find evidence that falsifies a widely held belief.

In 1976 Paul Kurtz, then a philosopher at the State University of New York at Buffalo and editor of the *Humanist* magazine, decided that the nation needed a skeptic's organization and a periodical devoted mainly to combating the steady rise of superstition and bogus science. Today astrologers far outnumber astronomers worldwide. On chain bookstore shelves books on astrology, the occult, and pseudoscience far outnumber books on all the sciences combined. Kurtz called a meeting attended by psychologist Ray Hyman, magician James Randi, sociologist Marcello Truzzi, and myself. This was the beginning of CSICOP. Its first periodical, the *Zetetic*, was for a short time edited by Truzzi.

It soon became apparent that Truzzi's plans for the magazine were not the same as those of others on the founding board. Truzzi regarded "debunk" as a dirty word. He wanted our periodical to provide scholarly discussions between skeptics and fringe scientists. He disliked calling anyone a crank. Marcello has always had a friendly, at times admiring, attitude toward pseudoscientists and psychic con artists. He seldom perceives them as any sort of threat to science or to the public. Indeed, in recent years he has become a personal friend of Uri Geller; not that he believes Uri has psychic powers, as I understand it, but he admires Uri for having made a fortune by pretending not to be a magician.

For the rest of us on the founding board, to expect our periodical to treat outrageous pseudoscience with respect was like expecting a liberal or socialist magazine to seek articles by right-wing extremists. Of course dialogue is possible with competent scientists who hold controversial views, such as superstring theorists, or defenders of the many-worlds interpretation of quantum mechanics, but we believe that dialogue with, say, an astrologer or homeopathic doctor or a historian who denies the Holocaust would be as fruitless as exchanging ideas with a flat earther. The dispute with Truzzi could not be resolved, and Truzzi resigned from CSICOP. He took with him the name *Zetetic*, which had previously been the title of his own periodical. We changed the name of ours to the *Skeptical Inquirer*.

I soon began contributing to this magazine a regular column called "Notes of a Fringe Watcher." Four book collections of these columns have appeared. Prometheus Books published three of them: *The New Age* (1988), *On the Wild Side* (1992), and *Weird Water and Fuzzy Logic* (1996). A fourth collection, *Did Adam and Eve Have Navels?* was published in 2000 by W. W. Norton.

As I see it, our organization and its magazine are not intended to persuade believers in bad science to abandon their beliefs. Like true believers in a religion or a cult, their minds are usually set in concrete. As John Dewey once observed, it is almost impossible to argue persons out of a firmly held belief no matter how preposterous. You can only hope, if they are young, that they will outgrow it.

To me the main purpose of our magazine is to alert officials of both print and electronic media to the gulf that exists between reputable science and the world of cranks and charlatans. Most media bigwigs, and an astonishing number of actors, artists, musicians, and others active in the liberal arts, know almost nothing about science, and are unable to distinguish genuine science from the claims of cranks. Maybe, just maybe, we can play a role in enlightening the media and stemming the rising flood of bogus science. It seems hopeless to expect book publishers and TV producers to downplay pseudoscience and the occult as long as an uneducated public relishes such fare. However, we have had a few small successes, such as persuading some newspapers to print a disclaimer above their horoscope section saying it is intended for amusement purposes only.

Perhaps some day, if more famous scientists are willing, like Carl Sagan and Robert Park, to speak out against bad science, more courageous newspapers will drop their horoscopes. Years ago I had lunch with the managing editor of the local newspaper in the town where I live. I did my best to persuade him to adopt our horoscope disclaimer. He refused on the grounds that the paper would lose subscribers; besides, he said, no one takes horoscopes seriously. Reading them is like reading a fortune cookie. Not long thereafter it became known that President Reagan and his wife, Nancy, had long believed in astrology. (See Reagan's chapter on astrology in his autobiography, *Where's the Rest of Me?*) Not only did the president and his wife read their daily horoscopes, but the president's appointments were being scheduled on days selected by Nancy's astrologer in California!

A democratic government clearly functions best when there is an informed public. That the president of a great nation could believe in astrology, and that members of Congress can constantly support funding with our tax money of dubious science are striking testimonies to how much an organization like CSICOP and its magazine are needed.

Philosophers of science often speak of the "demarcation problem," by which they mean the difficult task of formulating sharp criteria for distinguishing good science from bad. There are no such criteria. Science and pseudoscience are portions of continua that fade into one another. In gray areas where the two overlap one should be open-minded, and debunking is out of place. Not for a moment would we think of calling a physicist who believes in superstrings or the multiverse a crank. On the other hand, at extreme ends of the spectrum, are the obvious cranks who do not deserve to be treated like reputable scientists.

The author of a book claiming that the entire universe was created ten thousand years ago with light from distant galaxies "on the way," or perhaps traveling millions of times faster than it does today, is fair game for humorous debunking. A homeopathic "doctor" who is convinced that his drugs have great curative powers when they are diluted to a point where no molecule remains does not deserve respect. Far-out alternative medicines, even when they are as harmless as the distilled water of homeopathy, can cause great harm and even death when ignorant patients rely on them for ailments that require mainstream medicine or surgery. Christian Scientists who allow their children to die rather than take them to a physician not only deserve contempt; they deserve prison.

To treat obvious cranks without ridicule is like treating with respect a native Nazi, proud of his Hitler mustache, who thinks we should send all our Jews to Israel and all our blacks back to Africa. As H. L. Mencken once said, and I am fond of quoting, a good horselaugh is worth a thousand syllogisms.

NOTE

1. Richard Swinburne, Oxford University's Greek Orthodox theologian, is the leading defender of the view that although God's existence cannot be proved, the universe's fine tuning, among other things, renders theism more probable than not. See his *Existence of God* (1979) and *Is There a God?* (1996). Strong attacks on his probability arguments for God can be found in J. L. Mackie's *The Miracle of Theism* (1982), and Michael Martin's *Atheism: A Philosophical Justification* (1990).

MARTIN GARDNER was born in 1914 in Tulsa, Oklahoma. He became a freelance writer after four years in the U.S. Navy during the Second World War. For more than twenty-five years he wrote the "Mathematical Games" column in *Scientific American*, columns now collected in sixteen volumes. He is the author of some seventy books about science, mathematics, philosophy, and literature. Gardner is a Fellow of CSICOP.

32

THE BREATH OF GOD
Identifying Spiritual Energy

VICTOR J. STENGER

ABSTRACT

If other forms of energy exist beyond those recognized by physics, these should still be detectable in controlled experiments by the observation of apparent violation of energy conservation. This includes the psychic energy associated with paranormal phenomena, the vital energies supposedly manipulated in alternative medicine, and even supernatural or spiritual energy. So far all the data are consistent with conservation of the known forms of energy. Furthermore, observations indicate that the total energy of the universe is zero, and so no outside energy was necessary to bring it about.

MATERIAL MODELS

Soon after subscribing to *Skeptical Inquirer* in the early 1980s, I was surprised to discover that much of what appeared on its pages was related to my own work as a high-energy particle physicist and astrophysicist. At that time I was heavily involved in the collaborative efforts being carried out on a grand scale to explore the fundamental nature of matter and the physical universe. The data gathered at large particle accelerators had just been successfully interpreted in terms of a new synthesis called the *standard model*. In this model, which remains today fully consistent with all observations, matter is composed of *quarks* and *leptons* that interact locally with one another by the exchange of other particles called *gauge bosons*.

The atomic nucleus was found to consist of *up* and *down* quarks, the lightest of three generations of quark pairs. The electron that swirls about the nucleus proved to be the lightest of three electrically charged leptons. The photon, the particle of light, turned out to be just one of a set of twelve gauge bosons.[1]

No one believes that this model will be the final one. For one, it does not include gravity, which remains well described by Einstein's 1916 theory of general relativity. Physicists still seek a fully unified picture in what they hope will be the final synthesis, the "theory of everything," although I am personally holding off my bets. The current most promising approach is *m-theory*, in which the fundamental objects are m-dimensional *m-branes*.[2] A particle is a 0-brane, a string a 1-brane, and so on. A politician is a p-brane. Whatever the dimensionality, the approach remains one in which localized, discrete bits of matter form the primary elements of nature.

Combining the results from nuclear and particle physics with a great variety of astronomical observations, cosmologists have begun to draw a comprehensive picture, at least in broad terms, of the evolution and structure of the universe. The big bang, now well established by ever-improving agreement between theory and observation, has been enhanced by the *inflationary model* that offers plausible solutions for most of the remaining problems of the original theory.[3] Inflation is also strongly supported by the data, but will be severely tested in the next year or two as accurate new measurements are made on the structure of the cosmic microwave background. Recent observations on distant supernovae indicate that the expansion of the universe is accelerating under the action of some yet-unidentified "dark energy," that constitutes the bulk, over two-thirds, of the mass-energy of the universe.[4]

As a result of all this progress over the recent decades, we can now safely say that the wide range of observations of thousands of scientists worldwide, with the best instrumentation modern technology can provide, reveal a universe that contains matter and nothing more. No data or theories currently require the introduction of either supernatural forces or immaterial substances.

SOMETHING MORE?

Many supernatural and paranormal claims do not fit within this new synthesis of physics and cosmology. They assert something more, that the universe contains other ingredients beyond the known particles and forces in physics. By itself, of course, this does not imply a contradiction. Perhaps these nonnatural effects are so tiny as to be very difficult to detect. Or, perhaps the detectors of physics and astronomy are not suitable for these phenomena, just as a telescope cannot be used to see bacteria.

Indeed, the observations reported by parapsychologists are not made with high-tech instruments. Rather they are based on unusual human experiences, reported as anecdotes, or simple experiments that can be done on the dining table in your own home. Even the experiments conducted in the handful of university parapsychology laboratories are crude by the standards of the conventional science being done on the same campuses.

To be found so easily and cheaply, paranormal forces, if they exist, must exert powerful control over normal matter. If paranormal claims are valid, then the picture of the universe that is rapidly evolving in all the major physics laboratories and astronomical observatories around the world is wrong or at best grossly incomplete.

The common thread I see running through most paranormal claims is the hypothesis that the universe contains a nonmaterial component that plays a significant role in the lives of humans—possibly providing the animating source for life and consciousness.[5] This substance is often identified as some form of force or energy not presently registered in the scientific inventory.

Although infrequently described so explicitly, mind-over-matter and mind-to-mind communication can be thought of as resulting from the flow of "psychic energy." Perhaps the stars control our lives by means of the transmission of "cosmic energy." Acupuncture, therapeutic touch, and other complementary healing techniques work by bringing the body's "vital energy" into better balance.[6] Similarly, trivial electromagnetic phenomena, such as infrared "auras" and Kirlian photography[7] are promoted as evidence for a human "energy field." Energy seems to be a unifying concept among many paranormal claims.

ENERGY AND SPIRIT

The English word *energy* comes from the Greek *energeia* for activity. Webster gives 1599 as the earliest date for its use, but energy did not play an identifiable role in physics until 1847. At that time, Helmholtz introduced the law of *conservation of energy*, also known as the *first law of thermodynamics*, which has proven to be one of the most powerful principles of physics.

Most people presume that life and consciousness require some activating agent beyond cold, impersonal matter. I suppose it would be consistent with the root of the term to call this a kind of energy. However, what is being proposed by paranormalists appears to be little different from the traditional notions of "spirit" or "soul." This strikes me as yet another example of an old idea being given a new, scientific-sounding name to make it sound like something new and give it modern authority.

The term "spirit" also has a classical root, deriving from the Latin *spiritus* for breath. Breath was associated with "soul," the source of life, in many ancient cultures, including the Hebrew. In Genesis, God breathes life into

Adam. Modern supernaturalists seem to being saying that they can feel the "breath of God" upon their cheeks.

Although many skeptics prefer not to bring religion into the discussions of paranormal claims, a connection between religion and the paranormal is impossible to avoid because of the connection with the supernatural, either direct or implied. No matter how much the editors of skeptical publications may wish to avoid offending potential subscribers, science and religion are two "magesteria" that cannot help but overlap when discussing paranormal claims.

The paranormal concepts of psychic, cosmic, and vital energies arise out of traditional religious beliefs, usually referred to as "deeply held." To challenge paranormal claims is to challenge religious beliefs, perhaps the very existence of soul.[8]

Indeed, many of the original paranormal researchers, such as Oliver Lodge, William Crookes, and Joseph Banks Rhine, seem to have had strong religious motivations for their efforts to demonstrate the reality of psychic phenomena.[9] I suspect many of the current investigators have similar motivations and that much of their mostly private funding is donated in the hope of "proving" religious beliefs. The religious overtones of astrology, UFOlogy, alien abductions, and much of alternative medicine are also evident.

If the existence of ESP could be shown, then this would be interpreted by many as evidence for the long-sought spiritual element to the universe. Although natural explanations would still have to be ruled out, these are not very likely to be found based on what we already know about the physical universe. Psychic energy is not part of the current standard model and no conceivable extension makes any room for it. And, as I have written about extensively, quantum mechanics also offers no refuge for mystical beliefs.[10] But, none of this means we might not find psychic energy if we look in the right place.

Before we start a search, we need to identify some of the properties of the object we are seeking. If what we are looking for is a form of energy, then it should have the properties of energy. So, what are the characteristics of other forms of energy that have been identified in physics?

Until the end of the eighteenth century, heat was regarded as physical substance, *caloric*, that flowed in and out of bodies. However, this substance was not, to my knowledge, ever directly equated with energy. The connection between heat and energy came about when Thompson and Joule refuted the caloric model by showing that heat was associated with kinetic energy, that is, motional energy.

Another generic form of energy is *potential energy*. This is the energy a body may have stored that can be later converted into other forms. Thus the gravitational potential energy of a falling body is converted to kinetic as the body falls closer to Earth. Electrical potential energy is converted to light and sound in a lightning discharge, each of the latter being forms of kinetic energy.

These examples illustrate an important point. Classical physics never regarded energy as a substance of some kind, but rather as a measure of motion or capacity for motion; this is consistent with its root meaning of "activity." Even when Einstein showed that energy and mass were related by $E = mc^2$, this did not mean that energy was now to be regarded as a material substance. Rather, matter was understood as containing within its *rest mass* m a certain stored capacity mc^2 for inducing motion. For example, in chemical and nuclear explosions, rest energy is converted to kinetic energy.

Physicists often use words loosely; their equations and symbols encompass the facts anyway, so they see no need to act like philosophers about the precise meanings of words. This, unfortunately, is a major source of the serious lay misinterpretations of physics that are exploited by merchants of paranormal wares.

In the case of energy, physicists tend to talk as if it were some kind of physical essence that, for example, is radiated away from a heated body or a light source. Actually, in this case material particles are radiated: photons that carry in their kinetic energy a capacity for inducing motion in other material bodies. For example, light falling on a roof will increase the molecular motion in the house, warming it up. Energy is conserved as it moves from photon kinetic energy to molecular kinetic energy.

If you wonder whether light should properly be termed "matter," note that it has the identifying properties of matter: inertia and gravitation.

Parenthetically, modern relativistic physics can be formulated without ever introducing the term "energy." All the properties of energy can be incorporated in inertial mass, as defined by Newton's laws of motion. Kinetic energy is equivalent to the difference between inertial and rest mass. That is, it can be viewed as the additional mass a body has when it is moving. However, physicists have chosen to break with Newton's original inertial definition and reserve the term mass for rest mass, the mass measured when a body is at rest. This is arbitrary and has unfortunately resulted in the common confusion that energy is a property that is somehow independent of matter.

THE SIGNATURE OF ENERGY

The crucial significance of the concept of energy in physics rests on the fact that it is conserved. Until Helmholtz discovered the principle of conservation of energy, physics had no use for the term. The concept of energy is intimately bound to the concept of energy conservation. If forms of energy beyond those already familiar to physics exist, these must be added to the energy conservation equation. If they are not part of the equation, then perhaps they should be called something other than "energy" so as not to confuse them with energy as used in physics. (I doubt we can talk physicists into dropping the use of the term, unnecessary though it may be to their theories.)

Radiated energy will spread out over an ever-increasing area as it moves away from its source. If the source sends its energy uniformly in all directions, the energy intensity (energy per unit area) will fall off as the square of the distance from the source. Beaming can also occur, where the fall off with distance is much slower. However such a beam then has to be carefully aimed to hit its target and even then some spreading occurs that eventually reduces the intensity at some distance.

When Einstein was told about Rhine's work on ESP at Duke, the famous physicist said he would not believe it until the effect was shown to fall off with distance. This prompted Rhine to carry out a series of ESP experiments in the 1930s in which the distance between sender and percipient was varied. The anticipated "distance effect" was not seen; in fact, no convincing effect was seen at any distance.[11] Rhine concluded that psychic phenomena were not bound by energy conservation. Perhaps ESP was supernatural. The more economical explanation that the phenomenon did not exist apparently never occurred to him.

Actually, contemporary parapsychologists have come up with a less mystical rationalization for the missing distance effect in ESP: information that is encoded in radio signals does not decrease as you get farther from the source. They suggest that the ESP signal should analogously show no distance effect.

The analogy is strained. The energy intensity of radio propagation still decreases with distance, and the signal goes away at some point when it becomes indistinguishable from background noise. In any case, I think Einstein's point was that had a distance effect been seen, that would have been pretty good evidence for the reality of psychic energy. And, it still would be, because this is a signature property of energy.

Energy conservation, or a distance effect, is also not found in astrology. There what matters are the alignments of heavenly bodies irrespective of distance. Even if astrology's "cosmic energy" is not associated with gravity, and so not dependent on the mass of the body, we should expect a reciprocal square dependence in the ratio of the effects of two planets or stars. For example, Mars would have over six hundred times the effect of Saturn and billions of times the effect of any star.

Again, the point that I am trying to make here is not that the absence of a distance effect disproves the existence of paranormal phenomena. Rather, the observation of a distance effect would provide an indication of the presence of some form of energy that would be strong evidence *for* the paranormal. This essay is meant to be positive; I am looking for a way to discover psychic or spiritual energy that would be convincing to a skeptical physicist. Solid, scientific evidence for the apparent violation of energy conservation would be a sign of some previously unknown form of energy, within our universe or without.

For example, consider a body at rest and completely isolated from all known sources of energy. Suddenly it is observed to start moving. Such an observation would indicate an apparent violation of energy conservation. A moving body has kinetic energy, but the original energy was zero. If this happens when someone casts his thoughts in the direction of the body, and conventional explanations (like trickery) can be ruled out, then this would be evidence for psychic energy converting into kinetic energy.

As we have seen, the term energy is frequently used in paranormal theories as equivalent to the ancient notion of soul or spirit as the motivating element of life. The notion of conservation of energy can still be maintained in these theological terms. The breath of God, which we suppose carries the motivating energy, simply comes from outside the universe. This is no more difficult to conceive than a child propelling a boat in the bathtub by blowing on its sail. God's breath could have provided the energy for the parting of the Red Sea for Moses.

Unfortunately, we have only anecdotal evidence for these kinds of observations. None are scientifically documented. Indeed, paranormal phenomena seem to become neutralized in the presence of knowledgeable and especially skeptical observers. If such events could be captured on sophisticated instruments in properly controlled experiments, then we would have to take them seriously.

Let me give another example. Suppose the Virgin Mary were to appear for a minute in an open field in the presence of nonbeliever scientists. Magicians James Randi and Joe Nickell are also present to detect any trickery. Instruments record the event so it cannot be attributed to a collective hallucination.

The lady steps on a scale and is found to weigh 50 kilograms. This corresponds to a rest energy of 4.4×10^{18} Joules. The scientists and magicians can find no source of energy anywhere near this amount. The Heisenberg uncertainty principle allows a certain quantum fluctuation of energy over a one minute period, but this is only 5.5×10^{-36} Joules. So this can't account for the energy observed. Most of those present would likely conclude that they witnessed a miracle.

While this example would make many of us believers, the simple observation of the violation of energy conservation in, say, a particle physics experiment, would not lead us to immediate conversion. Perhaps the energy came from another universe, or another dimension, a possibility that has been recently proposed. Or, we may just be missing something purely material. For example, when nuclear beta-decay was first observed in the early twentieth century, energy did not seem to be conserved. It was later discovered that a previously unknown particle, the neutrino, was carrying away the missing energy. Such natural explanations would still have to be ruled out. I did not say that detecting spiritual energy would be easy!

CRITERIA

From my reading of the literature of parapsychology, I conclude that psychic energy has not yet been conclusively detected in any experiments or observations. In the history of paranormal studies, going back over a century now, one can find at any given time one or two experiments that proponents claim are solid evidence for psi. Typically these fade away and are replaced by new claims. Today, remote viewing and random-number generator experiments are fashionable. While proponents insist the evidence is strong, it does not convince most scientists. Here again is where particle physics comes in to account for my personal skepticism.

For forty years I was involved in a field where extraordinary new discoveries were being made regularly, often several a year. I personally played a small role in some of these, including most recently the evidence for neutrino mass found in Japan in 1998. Colleagues of mine were involved in the first observation of the top quark a few years earlier. In these cases and many others, the physics journals did not permit publication until a certain threshold of statistical significance was passed, along with other stringent criteria.

The statistical criterion for publication of a new phenomenon in physics demands that if you were to repeat the experiment ten thousand times, the observed effect, or something greater, would not occur more than once on average as a random artifact. This must be demonstrated quantitatively, which today requires extensive calibrations of the detectors and elaborate computer programs that simulate all conceivable backgrounds.

Some psi proponents have argued that the criteria that should be applied in parapsychology are those of psychology or medicine, not physics. In these fields, the statistical threshold has been traditionally 1/20 rather than 1/10000. This low standard is justified in two ways: First, 1/10000 is impossible to achieve in most cases; second, the primary goal of psychology and medicine is to help people. Making extraordinary new discoveries is a secondary goal.

While these justifications have merit, the fact remains that 1/20 is a rather loose criterion, far too loose even for the purposes stated. The implication is that up to one in twenty results published in medical and psychological journals could be a statistical artifact. In fact, given the propensity of investigators to not publish negative results, the number could be even greater. No wonder the public is often confused by news reports of studies that say one thing, only to be contradicted by studies that say the opposite. Many of the studies should not have been published in the first place.

In any event, authors cannot reasonably claim that they have demonstrated the existence of psychic, vital, or spiritual energy when the statistical significance is at the ridiculously low 1/20 level. The demonstration of any extraordinary phenomenon demands extraordinary criteria. I can guarantee that psi will not be accepted into the consensus of science until it is demonstrated with much greater significance and independently replicated, in quantitative detail, to at least the same level of significance.

THROUGHOUT THE COSMOS

Given the great difficulty of designing foolproof, and cheatproof, experiments involving people, I have grave doubts that this level of significance will ever be achieved by this approach. But why should we rely on human experiments? If humanity never evolved, or if the earth were destroyed tomorrow by a cosmic cataclysm, neutrinos and quarks would still exist. Similarly, if spiritual energy exists, it should not matter whether or not humanity does. The breath of God should be detectable throughout the cosmos, not just on Earth.

As I have already remarked, those instruments that explore the cosmos have not yet revealed any mysterious sources of energy that might even remotely be considered supernatural. Although the nature of the dark energy is still uncertain, such a component to the universe is allowed by existing theories and remains in the physical realm. The processes observed at the greatest distances from Earth, and deep into the past, still exhibit energy conservation.

This undisputed fact has led many theists to look to the origin of the universe as evidence for an external source of energy that could be associated with a creator God. Surely, the argument goes, energy had to be pumped into the universe at the beginning. Else, where did all the current matter and energy come from?

Well, it turns out that as best as we can tell from observations, the total energy of the universe is zero, within allowed quantum fluctuations. The positive kinetic and rest energy of all the matter in the universe seems to be exactly balanced by the negative gravitational potential energy of that matter.

This observation is equivalent to the one you will read in articles about cosmology that the universe on the average is flat. That is, although an arbitrary curvature of spacetime is allowed by Einstein's equations of general relativity, the overall curvature that seems to exist in fact is zero. The energy of a flat, empty spacetime is zero, give or take the tiny zero point energy expected by quantum mechanics.

A flat universe is predicted, indeed required, by the inflationary big bang cosmological model. In this model, the universe underwent a rapid exponential expansion during its first moments that stretched out its original curvature, whatever it was, to zero. The observation of a nonflat average geometry to the universe would doom inflation, and perhaps also open up room for a creator.

Recently, a brief interim occurred in which inflation seemed to be in deep trouble. Observations indicated that the matter of the universe, including the yet-unidentified *dark matter*, could provide no more than about 30 percent of the mass needed to give a flat universe. But then, in two independent investigations on supernova in distant galaxies, the remarkable, unanticipated discovery was made that expansion of the universe is accelerating.[12] Some additional component to the universe, which I have previously mentioned—the dark energy (or "quintessence"), is producing a negative pressure that is pushing the galaxies apart. Furthermore, the amount of this dark energy seems to be just what is needed to give a flat universe. Thus, the energy conservation equation is once again in balance, with only a slight quantum fluctuation away from zero energy, allowed by natural processes, needed to produce the universe as we know it.

CONCLUSIONS

The great majority of humanity believes in the existence of forms of energy beyond those currently recognized by physics. In this essay I have tried to indicate how these might be detected to the satisfaction of the scientific community. Energy conservation is one of the great principles of physics. The observation of an apparent violation of energy conservation in a carefully controlled experiment would imply the existence of another form of energy. The source of this energy could be within our universe, in the form of "psychic" or "vital" energy, or some source of energy from outside the universe.

I do not hold out much hope for these energies to be found in experiments involving humans with the significance required for such an extraordinary discovery. Such experiments are too hard to control, too easily contaminated by psychological factors or trickery. However, if the phenomena exist, they should be evident elsewhere, on Earth and in the cosmos.

The observation of an apparent violation of energy conservation at a particle accelerator or astronomical telescope would not constitute immediate evidence for the supernatural. Obviously, natural explanations would have to be sought and ruled out. In any case, the discovery would be remarkable.

One obvious place to look for a violation of energy conservation is in the energy balance of the universe as a whole. For many years it seemed that the universe contained too little matter for negative gravitational potential energy to cancel the positive kinetic energy in the motions of galaxies. The universe seemed to have positive energy that would have had to be inserted from the outside at sometime in its history. However, increasingly precise observations have indicated that invisible components of matter exist, dark matter and dark energy, that provide an exact balance between positive kinetic and negative potential energy. Thus the total energy of the universe appears to be zero and no input of energy from outside, either natural or supernatural, seems to have been needed to bring the universe into being.

The author is grateful for comments and suggestions from Keith Douglas, Ron Ebert, Taner Edis, Bill Jefferys, Edward Oleen, Bill Spight, Ed Weinmann, and Roahn Wynar.

NOTES

1. Many books contain descriptions of the standard model. For my own account, see Victor J. Stenger, *Timeless Reality: Symmetry, Simplicity, and Multiple Universes* (Amherst, N.Y.: Prometheus Books, 2000).

2. Brian Greene, *The Elegant Universe: Superstrings, Hidden Dimensions, and the Quest for the Ultimate Theory* (New York: W. W. Norton, 1999).

3. D. Kazanas, "Dynamics of the Universe and Spontaneous Symmetry Breaking," *Astrophysical Journal* 241 (1980): L59–63; A. Guth, "Inflationary Universe: A Possible Solution to the Horizon and Flatness Problems," *Physical Review* D23 (1981): 347–56; A. Guth, *The Inflationary Universe* (New York: Addison-Wesley, 1997); Andre Linde, "Particle Physics and Inflationary Cosmology," *Physics Today* 40 (1987): 61–68; Andre Linde, *Particle Physics and Inflationary Cosmology* (New York: Academic Press, 1990).

4. Peter M. Garnavich et al., "Supernova Limits on the Cosmic Equation of State," *Astrophysical Journal* 509 (1998): 74–79.

5. H. Bergson, *Creative Evolution* (New York: Macmillan, 1911); H. Driesch, *History and Theory of Vitalism* (New York: Macmillan, 1914); L. Richard Wheeler, *Vitalism: Its History and Validity* (London: Witherby, 1930).

6. B. A. Brennen, *Hands of Light: A Guide to Healing Through the Human Energy Field* (New York: Bantam New Age Books, 1988); Joanne Stefanatos, "Introduction to Bioenergetic Medicine," chapter 16 of *Complementary and Alternative Veterinary Medicine: Principles and Practice*, ed. Allen M. Schoen and Susan G. Wynn (Mosby-Year Book, 1997); M. Rogers, "Science of Unitary Human Beings," in *Explorations of Martha Rogers' Science of Unitary Human Beings*, ed. V. M. Malinski (Norwalk: Appleton-Century-Crofts, 1986); L. Rosa et al., "A Close Look at Therapeutic Touch," *Journal of the American Medical Association* 279 (1998): 1005–10; George Ulett, "Therapeutic Touch: Tracing Back to Mesmer," *Scientific Review of Alternative Medicine* 1, no. 1 (1997): 16–18; Béla Scheiber and Carla Selby, eds., *Therapeutic Touch* (Amherst, N.Y.: Prometheus Books, 2000).

7. John O. Pehek, Hay J. Kyler, and David L. Faust, "Image Modulation in Corona Discharge Photography," *Science* 194 (1976): 263–70; Barry Singer, "Kirlian Photography," in *Science and the Paranormal*, ed. George O. Abell and Barry Singer (New York: Scribners, 1981).

8. Jerome W. Elbert, *Are Souls Real?* (Amherst, N.Y.: Prometheus Books, 2000).

9. Paul Kurtz, *The Transcendental Temptation: A Critique of Science and the Paranormal* (Amherst, N.Y.: Prometheus Books, 1986); Victor J. Stenger, *Physics and Psychics: The Search for a World Beyond the Senses* (Amherst, N.Y.: Prometheus Books, 1990).

10. Victor J. Stenger, *The Unconscious Quantum: Metaphysics in Modern Physics and Cosmology* (Amherst, N.Y.: Prometheus Books, 1995).

11. C. E. M. Hansel, *The Search for Psychic Power: ESP and Parapsychology Revisited* (Amherst, N.Y.: Prometheus Books, 1989).

12. Garnavitch et al., "Supernova Limits on the Cosmic Equation of State."

VICTOR J. STENGER is professor emeritus of physics and astronomy at the University of Hawaii and visiting fellow in philosophy at the University of Colorado. Professor Stenger has been a visiting professor at the University of Heidelberg, Oxford University (twice), Rutherford-Appleton Laboratory, and the Italian National Institute for Nuclear Research. He has authored or coauthored over fifty papers in major physics and astrophysics journals on his research and given over one hundred talks at international conferences which are published in the proceedings of these conferences.

Professor Stenger has also had a successful parallel career as a philosopher, skeptic, and popular writer on subjects ranging from alternative medicine to psychic phenomena, quantum mysticism, cosmological mythologies, and science and religion. He has given many public and professional talks and published numerous articles and three critically well-received books on these subjects: *Not By Design, Physics and Psychics,* and *The Unconscious Quantum.* His most recent effort, *Timeless Reality,* published in October 2000, moves him closer to the philosophical arena and deals with the nature of time.

33

SKEPTICISM ABOUT RELIGION

ANTONY FLEW

Although the only subjects of religious belief with which CSICOP is directly concerned are the evidence or lack of the evidence for the occurrence of miracles and for human survival of bodily death, the present volume would be seriously deficient if it did not include at least one somewhat more comprehensive treatment of skepticism about religion.

During the first three-quarters of the twentieth century the skeptical writings of Bertrand Russell about religion were surely both more widely read and more influential than any others. These were collected and edited by Paul Edwards as *Why I Am Not a Christian and Other Essays on Religion and Related Subjects*. The title essay itself was first delivered as a lecture to the National Secular Society in March 1927 and shortly thereafter published as a pamphlet by the Rationalist Press Association. The whole collection was published in London by George Allen and Unwin in 1957.

There are two main ways in which the arguments presented in those essays fail to address what have during the fourth-quarter of the twentieth century become the religious claims most requiring skeptical attention. One is that there is now a fresh argument for the existence of God to be considered. *Why I Am Not a Christian* included a discussion between Bertrand Russell and the Jesuit Father F. C. Copleston on "The Existence of God." This discussion was originally broadcast in 1948 on the *Third Programme* of the British Broadcasting Corporation (BBC). In conclusion, Copleston summed up his position in a single sentence. He was arguing, he said, "First, that the existence of God can be philosophically proved by a metaphysical argument; secondly, that it is only the existence of God that will make sense of man's moral experience and of religious experience" (p. 166).

Metaphysical arguments for the existence of God—arguments such as the Five Ways presented by Thomas Aquinas—all belong to a period when there was no good scientific reason for believing that the universe had a beginning. They were therefore intended to demonstrate the existence and activities of God as a sustaining rather than an initiating cause of the universe and of everything that is in it. They also employed some of Aristotle's pre-Newtonian scientific ideas of the need for supernatural support for the operation of the order of nature.

The relevance of this to us is that it seems that in the years since that Russell-Copleston debate was broadcast a consensus has emerged among cosmologists on the correctness of the big bang theory. So now, for instance, in the debates organized by the Campus Crusade for Christ such spokespersons for theism as Dr. William Lane Craig challenge opponents to choose between admitting that the big bang was caused by God and maintaining that everything "popped into existence without a cause."

The second way in which the arguments presented in *Why I Am Not a Christian* fail to address the religious claims which most require skeptical attention today is in their exclusive concentration upon Christianity. For today the claims of Islam—which in terms of the total numbers of its supposed adherents is still only the second largest of the world's religions—demand even in the West an at least equal share of skeptical attention.

This necessity arises ultimately from the fact that Islam has never had a Reformation or enjoyed an Enlightenment. It is a long-term consequence of these two great social and political movements that the countries of what would once have been described as Christendom but is now more usually termed the West have been progressively secularized, and have in general become tolerant both of other religions and of the lack of religion.

But the same, to put it very mildly, is not equally true of all or even any of the Islamic countries. The intolerance in these countries impacts upon the West in two ways. In the first place there has been a substantial and still continuing emigration from Islamic countries into all the major countries of the European Union. This might not be a matter of any relevant concern were it not for the widespread abandonment—in favor of a multiculturalist insistence upon the supposed equal validity of all cultures—of the older ideal of assimilating immigrants into the cultures of their host countries.[1]

The second way in which intolerance in the Islamic countries impacts upon the West is through the social movements in and from those of these countries which are usually described as fundamentalist. That is a very inept description. For every Muslim is as such committed to believing that every word in the Koran was uttered by God speaking through some angelic intermediary—in, of course, the original Arabic—to the Prophet in a series of visionary and auditory experiences extending over a period of several years. This makes every Muslim more totally and unequivocally fundamentalist than any of those Christians who take every word of the King James Bible to be the word of God. For everything in that book has been translated from an original in some language other than English, while only a tiny proportion of all its sentences are directly attributed to the Deity as their utterer.

These so-called Muslim fundamentalists would be better characterized as Muslim extremists or Muslim fanatics or Muslim enthusiasts.[2] Muslims of this kind, because of their determination to attain state power and by that means to impose Islam in its most extreme and intolerant form upon their own peoples, are in the first instance a danger to those peoples. But, by forming terrorist organizations to operate alternatively or additionally in countries other than their own, they become a danger also to parts if not to the whole of the rest of the world.

A second long-term consequence of the fact that Islam has never benefited and/or suffered from either a Reformation or enjoyed an Enlightenment is that its fundamental documents, unlike those of Christianity, have never been subjected to a thorough and well-publicized historico-critical examination. Taken together these two long-term consequences provide us with the strongest of reasons for maintaining that of all the achievements during the last twenty-five years of Prometheus Books, and of the various organizations loosely associated with that firm, by far the most valuable has been the sponsoring and publication of Ibn Warraq's *Why I Am Not a Muslim* (1995) and of the series of books on Islam, including *The Origins of the Koran* (1998) and *The Quest for the Historical Muhammad* (2000). I hope that in the next twenty-five years that firm and those organizations will continue to do whatever they can to promote skepticism about the doctrines of Islam.

* * *

To the challenge to choose between accepting that the big bang was caused by God and accepting that the universe just "popped into existence without a cause" the immediate response ought to be to ask why these two options are supposed to be not only mutually exclusive, as they obviously are, but also together exhaustive, as they certainly are not. For one obvious third option is to suggest that the big bang might or must have had a physical cause, albeit one which human physicists, whose researches are necessarily confined within the (or perhaps it is only our) universe, may never be able to discover.

The great merit of this option is that it is what is most unequivocally suggested by everything we know about operations in and of the universe subsequent to the big bang. For, so far as we know, the most complicated kind of objects, and the kind with the greatest potentialities, is our own species: and that kind, like every other kind, seems in the end to be a product of exclusively physical causes.

Some lines from *Uncle Tom's Cabin* are more revealing here than perhaps the author herself recognized. For, unlike the Yankee Miss Ophelia, poor country girl Topsy had never been theologically indoctrinated by either parent or preacher. Yet she had had abundant opportunity to learn from rural observation what in my young day urban fathers used to reveal to schoolbound sons as "the facts of life." So it is Topsy who answers for unprejudiced common sense and common experience.

> "Do you know who made you?" "Nobody, as far as I knows on," said the child with a short laugh. The idea appeared to amuse her considerably; for her eyes twinkled, and she added "I s'pect I grow'd. Don't thin' nobody ever made me."[3]

* * *

For all of us who were raised among what Islam calls "the peoples of the Book" it is extremely difficult to approach the question whether the big bang was produced by God free from the prejudices of those theistic or post-theistic cultures. It is, I contend, significant that almost everyone who has ever given sustained attention to the question of the existence of God has been a product of one or other of those theistic cultures. So we have all of us seen this concept of God as one referring to the logically presupposed source of some putative self-revelation of and by that God. For accounts of these putative self-revelations have been handed down and made familiar to us by and through generations of parents and pedagogues, of priests and rabbis, of imams and ayatollahs.

If therefore we want to approach the question of the existence of God without prejudice we need to try to see it as it would look to people who, having been raised in a totally secular culture, met it for the first time after they had become adults. I confess that I myself came fully to appreciate this need only as a result of conversations with my very able graduate student "minder" during a visit to the Institute of Foreign Philosophy at the University of Peking, Beijing.[4]

So let us begin by citing what I hope will to anyone raised in the cultures of either Judaism or Christianity or Islam be an acceptable definition of the word "God" and then try to look at this definition in that entirely unprejudiced way. Richard Swinburne, in the first of his three major contributions to the field of natural theology, has provided a definition: It runs:

> A person without a body (i.e., a spirit), present everywhere the creator and sustainer of the universe, able to do everything (i.e., omnipotent), knowing

all things, perfectly good, a source of moral obligation, immutable, eternal, a necessary being, holy, and worthy of worship.[5]

By no means all of the defining characteristics listed here are necessarily connected, and several should also provoke questions of interpretation. Crucially, if some Being created the universe "in the beginning" then that Being is not necessarily and by the same token its sustainer; even if sustaining is supposed to be required. Much less would such a Being be, also and necessarily, "perfectly good, a source of moral obligation, immutable, eternal, a necessary being, holy, and worthy of worship." Nor is it by any means obvious what it is to be either "a source of moral obligation" or "a necessary being" or "worthy of worship."

Even if and when it had been allowed that there must have been a cause for the big bang, and that a nonphysical cause, we would still be a very long way from securing an adequate justification for concluding that that cause must or even could have been "A person without a body (i.e., a spirit), present everywhere," and endowed with all the other characteristics embraced in Swinburne's definition.

For a start there is an enormous yet very rarely recognized difficulty with the very conception of "A person without a body (i.e., a spirit)." The idea that the universe was created and is sustained by a Superbeing of this kind originally became established among peoples who were convinced that the universe is full of such incorporeal personal spirits. And still today, throughout the whole world, a great many people believe that their own individual personal spirits could conceivably, and perhaps actually will, survive their own individual personal deaths.

Certainly the familiarity and the intelligibility of talk about minds and about souls does entitle us to infer that we possess both a concept of mind and a concept of soul. But these particular semantic possessions are most emphatically not what is needed if doctrines of the possible independent existence and perhaps the immortality of souls or of minds are to be cognitively meaningful.

The crux is that, in their everyday understandings, the words "minds" and "souls" are not words for what philosophers call substances. They are not, that is to say, words for entities which could significantly be said to survive the deaths and dissolutions of those flesh-and-blood persons whose minds or souls they were. For to construe the question whether she has a mind of her own, or the assertion that he is a mean-souled man, as a question, or an assertion, about hypothesized incorporeal substances is like taking the loss of the Red Queen's dog's temper as if this was on all fours with his loss of his bone, or like looking for the grin remaining after the Cheshire Cat itself has disappeared.[6]

*   *   *

The next question which must arise for anyone approaching the question of the existence of an omnipotent and omniscient Creator and sustainer of the universe freed from prejudices arising from an upbringing among "peoples of the Book" is "Why should such a Being be thought not only to have preferences as between different possible kinds of human conduct, and hence Himself to constitute a source of moral obligation"?

When I myself—in my sixteenth year during the late 1930s—first became an atheist it was because it seemed to me that the claim that the universe was created by a Being omniscient and omnipotent and yet at the same time in an ordinary understanding perfectly good is flatly incompatible with innumerable and manifest and undenied facts about the universe.

Given any ordinary, nonmetaphysical conception of goodness, it still does. It was only much later that I heard of the curious metaphysical equation between goodness and reality. This ultimately derives from Plato's identification, in *The Republic*, of the Form or Idea of the God with the Form or Idea of the Real. It was this and only this peculiar and to me wholly unacceptable semantic equation which enabled Leibniz, in his *Theodicy*, to demonstrate that a universe in which the majority of the human race is destined to unending extremes of torture is the Best of All Possible Worlds.

It is a remarkable indication of how much the traditional and surely crucial and fundamental Christian doctrine of hell has been—shall we say?—deemphasized in the teachings of the mainstream Protestant churches during the twentieth century that, although my father was a Methodist minister and I was at the time a pupil in a boarding school founded by John Wesley and effectively run by the Methodist Church, no one either at home or at school ever threatened me with hell as the consequence to be expected if I persisted, as it is now obvious that I did, in my atheist conviction.[7]

About the insistence that the putative omnipotent and omniscient Creator and sustainer of the universe is "a source of moral obligation" there are, waiving the question what exactly is meant by a "source of moral obligation," two things to be said here. The first is that it is only and precisely insofar as a Creator is believed to be in some way an actual or potential partisan within His universe that the question of the existence of that Creator becomes one of supreme human interest. Compare and contrast the gods of Epicurus who existed in "complete tranquillity, aloof and detached from our affairs . . . exempt from any need of us, indifferent to our merits and immune from anger."[8] (The God for whom in *A Brief History of Time* Stephen Hawking wondered whether he might find useful physical employment was, like the God of Aristotle, clearly of the same indifferent and nonpartisan kind.)

The second point about this definition is that had an omnipotent Creator wanted to produce creatures who would always act morally then He surely both could and would have made us creatures of such a kind that we always did. But if this conclusion does indeed follow, and given that the Gods of both Christianity and Islam intend to inflict for all eternity extremes of torture on many human beings as a punishment for what they have done or failed to do during their short lives under the Sun, then it must also follow with the same necessity those who are actually eventually damned were Divinely predestined to act and to fail to act in the ways which led to this damnation.

It is, it appears, widely believed that this appalling doctrine was among Christians peculiar to Calvin and the Reformers. Certainly it is today vehemently repudiated by many, perhaps most, sincerely professing Christians, not only Reformed but also even Roman Catholic. C. S. Lewis, for instance, who was unquestionably the most widely read of Christian apologists throughout the whole of the second half of the twentieth century, used to try to block any such implication by insisting that God had endowed us all with freewill.[9] But in arguing in this way Lewis ignored Locke's warning that "*the question is not proper, whether the Will be free, but whether a Man be free.*"[10] He thus misled himself and others to believe that God or Nature had done something different from merely making human beings members of a kind of creatures who can (and therefore cannot but) make choices between the possible courses of action which are open to us; of which some are made freely and others are made under various forms of constraint.

The relation of God the Father in Christianity to his earthly children is thus altogether different from the relations between human fathers and their grown-up children. God the Father is all the time in total control of all the behavior of all his human children. Human fathers, as many of us have occasion ruefully to protest, are not. That God is thus always and entirely in control of all his creatures is clearly and most categorically stated by Aquinas in chapter 67 of his *Summa Contra Gentiles*:

> Just as God not only gave being to things when they first began, but is also—as the conserving cause of being—the cause of their being as long as they last . . . so He also not only gave things their operative powers when they were first created, but is also the cause of these in things. Hence, if this divine influence stopped every operation would stop. Every operation, therefore, of anything is traced back to Him as its cause.

This is spelt out more fully in chapters 88 and 89:

> God alone can move the will in the fashion of an agent, without doing violence to it. . . . Some people . . . not understanding how God can cause a movement of our will, have tried to explain . . . authoritative texts wrongly; that is, they would say that God "works in us, to wish and to accomplish" means that He causes in us the power of willing, but not in such a way that He makes us will this or that. . . . These people are, of course, opposed

quite plainly by authoritative texts of Holy Writ. For it says in Isaiah (xxxvi, 2) "Lord, you have worked all your work in us." Hence we receive from God not only the power of willing but its employment also.

*   *   *

When in 1879 Walter Bagehot, editor of the *Economist* (London), maintained that "Great and terrible systems of divinity and philosophy lie about us which, if true, might drive a wise man mad" he must have been thinking primarily if not exclusively of Christianity.[11] However, as has been said already, mainstream Protestant churches have throughout the twentieth century been progressively de-emphasizing the terrible, appalling, nightmare doctrine of hell. And as a no doubt unintended effect of the Second Vatican Council, the Roman Catholic Church has it would seem been taking its first tentative steps along the same road. It is a road which appears ultimately self-destructive. For since we sinners are as such more or less strongly inclined to the committing of our sins, the promise of salvation from them can for most of us be only the weakest of incentives unless it is backed by some formidable perceived threat to those who would persist in their sinning.

The truth of this suggestion tends to be in a rather striking way confirmed by the fact that *The Mystery of Salvation*,[12] a report of the Doctrine Commission of the Church of England, was published at the midpoint of a Decade of Evangelism, the effect of which, if any, did not amount to any discernible check on the continuing decline in the number of active members of that organization. For this Report did not merely de-emphasize but categorically repudiated the doctrine of hell: "It is incompatible with the essential Christian affirmation that God is love to say that God brings millions into the world to damn them" (p. 180).

But in Islam there never has been and scarcely could be any de-emphasis upon, much less categorical repudiation of the doctrine of hell. For while every Surah (chapter) of the Koran[13] begins "In the name of God, the Merciful, the Compassionate," the first proceeds forthwith, as sooner or later do most of the rest, inconsistently to indicate that there is to be a Day of Doom on which the mercy and the compassion of "The All-Merciful, the All-Compassionate" will be revealed to be very strictly and very narrowly restricted:

> Praise belongs to God, the Lord of all Being
> the All-merciful, the All-compassionate,
> the Master of the Day of Doom.
> Thee only we serve; of Thee alone we pray for succour.
> Guide us in the straight path,
> the path of those whom Thou hast blessed,
> not of those against whom Thou art wrathful
> nor of those who are astray.[14]

The central, fundamental, continually, and emphatically repeated message of the Koran combines a promise with a threat. The promise is to "Those who believe, and do deeds of righteousness—theirs shall be forgiveness and generous provision"[15]; a generous provision including among other attractions not only "Gardens of Delight" but also (for men only) "wide-eyed houris as the likeness of hidden pearls."[16] The threat is to unbelievers "those who strive against Our signs to avoid them—they shall be inhabitants of hell"[17]; a habitation in "which garments of fire shall be cut for the unbelievers" and where "for them await hooked iron rods as often as they desire in their anguish to come forth from the eternal fire."[18]

Since no attempt is ever made to reconcile these threats of eternal torture for too belatedly repentant unbelievers with the endlessly reiterated assertion that Allah is "the All-Merciful, the All-Compassionate" it becomes appropriate to recall a very characteristic observation made by Thomas Hobbes in chapter 31 of his *Leviathan*:

> . . . in the attributes which we give to God we are not to consider the signification of philosophical truth, but the signification of pious intention, to do him the greatest honour we are able.

The Koran calls above all and all the time for obedience. It is clearly calculated to inspire fear, indeed abject terror, rather than love. So it is altogether appropriate that the apologetic argument since attributed to and named for Pascal was employed centuries earlier by the famous Sufi theologian Al-Ghazzali, who died in A.D. 1111.[19]

In the Koran God ("Allah" is Arabic for "God") is, notwithstanding "the attributes . . . of pious intention," actually presented—or, supposedly, presents Himself—as a cosmic oriental despot who penalizes perceived disobedience and crushes perceived opposition by eternally extended exercises of uninhibited and total power.

The qualification "perceived" has to go in since actually to oppose or to disobey we should need to believe in the existence and orders of the despot, while any who actually knew that opposition or disobedience was to be rewarded by eternal torture and yet chose to disobey or to oppose would, simply by engaging in such egregiously and inordinately insane behavior, show themselves not to be fit and proper subjects of punishment.

The sentences which Allah is to hand down on the Day of Doom are alleged to be just, despite the inordinate disparity between finite offenses and infinite penalties, because "every soul earns only its own account; no soul laden bears the load of another."[20]

By the hypothesis that is no doubt correct, but only so long as "the load of another" is construed as the load of another human being. Yet the Koran contains an abundance of passages, paralleling those notorious hard sayings of Saint Paul which insist that God, conceived not only as the omnipotent initiating and sustaining cause of the entire universe and of everything in it, but also as punishing some of its creatures, must therefore be recognized to be punishing all the creatures whom he punishes for conduct for which, by the hypothesis, He alone bears the ultimate sole responsibility.[21] All such divine discriminations have therefore to be seen as, ultimately, arbitrary exercises of total power. This is an implication which the Koran makes clear at the very beginning, and it is later reiterated many times:

> As for the unbelievers, alike it is to them,
> whether thou has warned them or hast not warned them,
> they do not believe.
> God has set a seal on their hearts and on their hearing,
> and on the eyes is a covering,
> and there awaits them a mighty chastisement.[22]

* * *

Let us, finally, turn to chapter 46 of *Leviathan* in order to discover the Hobbist way of justifying the ways of God to man. In doing this we have to remember that the Book of Job was written well before the Maccabean persecutions, and the consequent adoption of what were in the time of Jesus the distinctively pharisaical doctrines of life after death. In the time of the Book of Job all Jews were in this respect "like the Sadducees, which say there is no resurrection."[23]

> When God afflicted Job, he did object no sin unto him, but justified his afflicting of him by telling him of his power. . . . "Hast thou," said God, "an arm like mine? . . . Where were thou when I laid the foundations of the earth?" . . . Power irresistible justifies all actions, really and properly, in whomsoever it be found; less power does not. . . .

This Ockhamist principle—that absolute, total, irresistible power constitutes its own justification—provides the only possible way of justifying the treatment of His human creatures by the God of either Islam or traditional Christianity.[24] It is made much clearer in the Koran than it is in the Bible that in both these religions God is to be conceived and obeyed as an oriental despot—an omnipotent and immortal Saddam Hussein. Given that the words "god" and "real" are to be taken to be metaphysically synonymous in the definition of the word "God," then it can only be this principle that absolute, total, irresistible power constitutes its own justification which makes this God "worthy of worship."[25]

NOTES

1. When, for instance, Dr. Kalam Siddiqui, director of the (UK) Muslim Institute incited a crowd of his coreligionists in London both, in general, to disobey any British laws incompatible with the prescriptions of the Sharia and, in particular—in obedience to the notorious Fatwa of the Iranian Ayatollah Khomeini—to promote the murdering of Salman Rushdie, the British authorities took no action whatsoever against Siddiqui himself. Apparently it was considered that, although it was going to be necessary for many years to provide Rushdie with round-the-clock protection against possible Muslim killers, that by itself was a sufficient domestic response to murderous Muslim intolerance. For a brief treatment of this affair and its implications see chapter 17 of Ibn Warraq, *Why I Am Not a Muslim* (Amherst, N.Y.: Prometheus Books, 1995). The most thorough treatment of the whole question of Islam and the secular modern world is provided by Mervyn Hiskett, *Some to Mecca Turn to Pray: Islamic Values and the Modern World* (London: Claridge, 1993).

2. Those Englishmen who in the eighteenth century caused their obituary inscriptions to describe them as having been "religious but without enthusiasm" were, of course, intending thereby to repudiate any such extremist fanaticism in their Christian commitment rather than to indicate that that commitment was itself reluctant and halfhearted.

3. Harriet Beecher Stowe, *Uncle Tom's Cabin* (New York: Books Inc., n.d.), p. 97.

4. See chapters 1 and 2 of my *Atheistic Humanism* (Amherst, N.Y.: Prometheus Books, 1993). I am happy to report that that "minder" now holds a tenured position in the department of philosophy of a U.S. university.

5. Richard Swinburne, *The Coherence of Theism* (Oxford: Clarendon, 1977), p. 2.

6. For a much fuller discussion of the possibility of incorporeal personal spirits and of their surviving the deaths of the flesh-and-blood people whose spirits they were, see my *The Logic of Mortality* (Oxford: Blackwell, 1987). This book, furnished with a fresh introduction, was reissued by Prometheus Books in the fall of 2000 under the title *Merely Mortal? Could You Survive Your Own Death?*

7. It was in fact only earlier in this present year—after a TV argument in Charlottesville, North Carolina, about the historicity of the Resurrection—that anyone ever urged me to make in prudence Pascal's Wager on the truth of Christianity.

8. Lucretius *On the Nature of Things* 2.646–51.

9. See, for instance, his first and many times reprinted apologetic work *The Problem of Pain* (London: Bles, 1940). Critical readers of those works will be glad to learn of John Beversluis, *C. S. Lewis and the Search for Rational Religion* (Grand Rapids, Mich.: Eerdmans, 1985).

10. John Locke, *An Essay concerning Human Understanding*, II (xxi) 21, p. 244 in the Clarendon edition.

11. Earlier John Stuart Mill had described "The recognition . . . of the object of the highest worship in a being who could make a Hell; and who could create countless generations of human beings with the certain foreknowledge that he was creating them for this fate: as a "dreadful idealisation of wickedness." See his *Three Essays on Religion* (London: Longmans Green, 1874).

12. London: Church House Publishing, 1995.

13. All my quotations from this work follow A. J. A. Arberry's rendering, in the Oxford University Press World's Classic paperback edition of 1985, giving the number of the Surah in roman and the number of the page in arabic numerals.

14. I, p. 1.

15. XXII, p. 339. Nowhere do we find any suggestion that unbelievers who "do deeds of righteousness" might be excused resurrection and hence damnation.

16. LVI, p. 560.

17. XXII, p. 339.

18. XXII, p. 335.

19. See "Is Pascal's Wager the Only Safe Bet?" chapter 5 in my *God, Freedom and Immortality* (Amherst, N.Y.: Prometheus Books, 1984).

20. VI, p. 142.

21. Thus in the Epistle to the Romans 9:18–21, we read:

Therefore hath he mercy upon whom he will have mercy and whom he will he hardeneth. Thou wilt say then unto me, "Why doth he yet find fault? For who hath resisted his will?" Nay but, O man, who art thou that replies against God? Shall the thing formed say to him that formed it, "Why has thou made me thus?" Hath not the potter power over the clay, of the same lump to make one vessel unto honour, and another unto dishonour?

22. II, p. 2. Compare VI, pp. 123, 125, 134, and 136; VII, pp. 161 and 166; LX, p. 194; XVI, p. 269; XXIV, p. 357; XXXIX, p. 474; and LXXXI, pp. 632–33.

23. Mark 12:18. This must surely raise the Sadducees in our estimation.

24. This principle is named for William of Ockham (c. 1285–1348), an English Franciscan philosopher who taught at Oxford until called to Avignon to answer charges of heresy.

25. In fairness to Hobbes it should perhaps be added that although he was prepared both to say in chapter 31 of *Leviathan* that "the power of God without other helps is sufficient justification for anything which he doth" and in chapter 46 that "Power irresistible justifies all actions, really and properly, in whomsoever it is found,

ANTONY FLEW is professor emeritus of philosophy at the University of Reading and a Fellow of CSICOP. He is the author of many books and articles, including *How to Think Straight: An Introduction to Critical Reasoning; Philosophy: An Introduction; God, Freedom, and Immortality: A Critical Analysis;* and *Atheistic Humanism.*

less power does not," and although he had in chapter 31 also said that "in the attributes which we give to God we are not to consider the signification of philosophical truth, but the signification of pious intention to do him the greatest honour we are able," nevertheless, and very reasonably, Hobbes was himself disquieted. He proceeded to seek an alternative, less appalling interpretation of the relevant Gospel texts.

34

BEYOND THE BIBLE CODE
Hidden Messages Everywhere!

DAVID E. THOMAS

We've long had religious apologetics. The old-time methods of the past (pieces of the True Cross, for example) have not entirely disappeared, as the Shroud of Turin shows us today. However, in recent times science has become so spectacularly successful that some believers covet its power to explain and prove things. For example, creation "scientists" often contend science supports a literal reading of the Bible.

In recent decades, there has been a significant increase in the use of advanced methods from mathematics and computer science for various scientific-sounding "proofs" of the existence of the Judeo-Christian God, Allah, or various other deities. There are several hallmarks of such statistical apologetics:

- The proof of the existence of the Deity is said to depend on a hidden or secret Code or Message implanted by the Deity, usually in the sacred text for the religion.
- This Code or Message, once explained, is claimed to be obvious and compelling, even though it's been hidden and unknown all these years.
- The evidence for the Code or Message is claimed to be statistically overwhelming, and beyond chance.
- The Code or Message is claimed to be too complex to have been created by mere humans, and thus proves the existence of a Higher Power.

- The Code or Message is said not to exist in mundane, nonreligious works.
- Other Codes are dismissed as flawed, weak, or wrong. There can only be One True Code.
- Scientific or technical criticisms of the Codes are often dismissed by code apologists with personal attacks on the critic's integrity, or with accusations that the critic is mocking God (or Allah, or whoever).
- Presentations of Codes found in mundane texts are often dismissed as invalid for one reason or another.

The most famous recent example of mathematical apologetics is the "Bible Code." Several professional mathematicians have claimed that the Hebrew Torah contains a hidden code, verifiable with advanced statistical methods. Bible Code proponents point with pride to an article by Witztum, Rips, and Rosenberg entitled "Equidistant Letter Sequences in the Book of Genesis," published in the respected journal *Statistical Science* in 1994. The paper is said to provide compelling proof that details of modern rabbis and events are indeed encoded in the ancient symbols of the Torah.

The Bible Code is a few decades old, but didn't really attract serious attention until the 1994 paper. In June of 1997, a sensational book entitled *The Bible Code*, by journalist Michael Drosnin, brought the Bible Code into the mainstream.

I spent the summer of 1997 studying the Bible Code, and learned how to apply it to various texts. My analyses on the Code appeared in the November/December 1997 and March/April 1998 issues of the *Skeptical Inquirer*. I found that Bible Code puzzles can be found in *any* text, for *any* desired message. I found "Roswell" inside just one verse of the King James version of Genesis, accompanied by a "UFO." This particular find was outstanding because (a) the English text could not possibly contain the Hebrew Code, and (b) the step of just four letters for the Roswell match is *spectacular* by Bible Code standards.

Drosnin claimed that it was impossible to find linked pairs of words in mundane texts, and specifically claimed that one could not find "Hitler" and "Nazi" linked closely in Tolstoy's *War and Peace*. Yet I found a single 209-word-long passage in Tolstoy's book that held a stunning "Hitler/Nazi" Bible Code display. Perhaps my most elaborate puzzle to date was this one, also from *War and Peace*: "Guilty Lee Oswald shot Kennedy, Both Died."

Indeed, everyone who has put the word "generalization" to print has secretly encoded a Nazi: geNerAliZatIon. Watch what you write!

One of Drosnin's strongest claims in support of the Bible Code was that his code-based prediction of the assassination of Israeli prime minister Yitzhak Rabin was made a year before the event took place. So, almost two months before the 1998 NBA basketball playoffs, I searched for NBA teams in *War and Peace,* and found an excellent Bible Code message for CHICAGO, BULLS, and JORDAN. I rushed my prediction to several reporters and scientists, but didn't warn Karl "the Mailman" Malone of the Utah Jazz, preferring to let history run its course. Chicago almost lost it all, but Tolstoy's Bulls clung to their destiny. And on June 14, 1998, my prediction came to pass.

One of the chief arguments employed by proponents of the Bible Code has been the lack of a rebuttal to the original *Statistical Science* 1994 paper. But this argument too has collapsed with the publication of a devastating rebuttal by Brendan McKay, Dror Bar-Natan, Maya Bar-Hillel, and Gil Kalai, published in the May 1999 edition of *Statistical Science.* The paper, and many others, are available on the Web at McKay's excellent site (http://cs.anu.edu.au/~bdm/dilugim/torah.html).

THOMAS IN THE TORAH

Recently, a nice lady from Louisiana, "Dee," asked me if I had ever looked for my *own* name in the Torah. There's an idea, I thought. What she really wanted was for me to look for *her* name in the Torah, but that didn't come out till later. The fact that the Bible Code can be used to find *any* message (in *any* text) means that any John Doe can find himself in there. And if John Doe is a believer, the thought that even *he* is mentioned (secretly) by God in the Bible is appealing indeed.

I resurrected my trusty code programs, and learned how to spell "David Thomas" in Hebrew. I launched the search, and found several instances of my name encoded in the Torah itself. One of these was located entirely within the *first book,* Genesis; this appears below. Here, the Hebrew letters spelling "DAVID THOMAS" run from bottom to top.

Of course, I didn't stop with the Torah. I looked for myself in Charles Darwin's classic *Origin of Species,* and found my name in there too! When I told Dee about that, she replied, "Maybe that's just how Jesus says, 'Look, even here.' " I then told her about a Muslim who found coincidences with the number 19 in the Koran, and how he felt those proved that only the Koran is Divine. I told her I had found mysterious 19 coincidences, not in the Koran, but in Ted Kaczynski's *Unabomber Manifesto.* I asked her how she would respond to my Muslim correspondent if he dismissed the Unabomber's number-19 coincidences by simply claiming, "It's Allah's way of saying 'Look, even here.' " I don't think I heard from her again after that.

ש	מ	ה	פ	י	צ	מ	י	ה
א	מ	ל	כ	ס	ד	מ	ו	מ
ת	ע	ו	ל	מ	ו	ע	ר	ל
י	מ	ב	ל	ו	ט	ל	א	מ
ה	י	ב	ע	ת	ה	ה	ו	א
ו	א	ש	ר	ד	ב	ר	ל	י
ט	ו	ר	ה	ו	י	ת	נ	א
י	ל	א	י	ד	ע	ה	י	י
ל	מ	ל	ו	ז	ש	מ	ה	ע

THE MOSES CODE

I have received several e-mails about my Bible Code articles from people all around the world. Some of these people have developed their own Codes. In classic Mathematical Apologetics tradition, they agree with me that the Bible Code is bogus, but then challenge me to check out *their* compelling work.

In April of 2000 I received a letter from "Bill." Judging from Bill's e-mail address, his last name was Moses. Judging from Bill's wild statements, it's possible Bill thought he *was* Moses. He started out by saying that he enjoyed my article, and that he could see both sides of the Bible Code issue. He then got down to business, saying he would prove to me again and again that every written word from every source is secretly coded.

Here is Bill's Code in action. One hundred sixty-eight people died in a Barnum and Bailey Circus tent fire in 1944, and 168 people died in the Oklahoma City Bombing in 1995; 1944 + 1995 = 3939, which reduces to 12, 12 (3 + 9 = 12). Twelve is the foundational base number of Moses, because Moses lived 120 years, and "0" means nothing. The two fires saying 12, 12 means that there is a second Moses, who will arise in the "last days."

It got worse from there. Not only is Moses everywhere, he said, but O. J. Simpson is linked to the pyramids and to JFK's assassination, and on and on. I heard a lot about Moses and O. J. and Oklahoma City and JFK, but I never heard anything "supernatural." When Bill kept claiming that he had already proved the supernatural to me, I got a little exasperated, and finally asked him, "Where's the beef?"

Bill's reply was a letter with his Code applied to the message "WHERE'S THE BEEF." Each letter was assigned a number (its position in the A-to-Z sequence), and a running tally of the numbers was kept. Bill showed that "Where's the beef" summed to 129, which he claimed means that Moses (12) is Judge (9). "Beef" equals $2 + 5 + 5 + 6 = 2556 = 855$ (using $2 + 6 = 8$), and 855 is equivalent to 585, the "Main Sign of Moses." Bill said, in classic crank capitals, "NO MATTER [what] YOU SAY, YOU KEEP CALLING MOSES. THERE'S YOUR SUPERNATURAL BEEF."

Perhaps Bill initially sought me out because we both agreed that the Bible Code is bunk. But I certainly didn't provide the validation Bill wanted for his own code. I told him his code was simply a Moses filter, and that no matter what goes in, out comes Moses in 2025. Our correspondence did not end amicably. This was a pattern I would see again very soon.

SACRED SABBATHS OF ISRAEL

In June of 2000, I received a very brief e-mail message from one Eugene Faulstich of Spencer, Iowa. The message bore the title "Age of the Earth," and Faulstich simply asked me what I thought about the Web page at http://www.mashiach6000.org, and about the two scientists' comments.

I located the Web site Faulstich mentioned. His Web site was titled "Sacred Sabbaths of Israel, Scientific Proof of the Past, Key to the Future." It proclaimed "A NEW SCIENTIFIC BREAKTHROUGH IN RELI-GIOUS STUDIES" which "shows that the chronology in the Bible is scien-tifically provable through the exact science of astrophysics. This has the potential to 'prove' that G_d exists, and the One G_d of the universe is the One G_d of the Bible." Faulstich's site also claimed that "We have been given a divine mandate from G_d. What G_d reveals, He wants mankind to use for-ever (Dt. 29:29). He has revealed something new here (Isa. 48:6–7)."

Faulstich claims to have calculated exact astronomical-based dates for several key biblical events. Faulstich has two Web sites (a second at http://www.ncn.net/~chri), and most of the pages on both sites involve detailed calculations of these dates, based on both astronomical reckoning (timing of eclipses, for example) and biblical passages. Faulstich has also written numerous books about his chronologies, and markets them on his Web sites. I have checked with independent astronomy programs, and have confirmed that some of the dates for eclipses Faulstich cites are probably genuine. However, tying those particular eclipses to specific biblical events inevitably involves making some judgment calls.

Faulstich's "proof " of the God of the Bible involves curious patterns in the numbers of weeks between thirteen specially selected dates from the history of Israel. Each of the significant biblical dates has been assigned a specific day number, starting from the time of Adam. For example, Faulstich's first date in the list of thirteen, the day of the Burning Bush, is Adamic Day # 927,548, or October 9, 1462 B.C.E. It is a simple matter to calculate the difference in days between any two dates; just subtract one Adamic date from the other. Dividing the difference by seven yields the number of weeks between the two dates; Faulstich rounds these off to whole numbers.

When Faulstich calculates the differences in weeks between all thirteen special dates (13 things 2 at a time = 78 pairs), and examines the digits in this collection of 78 numbers, he finds a whopping 35 percent of them are *sevens*. One would expect only around 10 percent of the digits would be sevens, and likewise for any other digit, assuming random distributions of dates. Faulstich claims that this is scientific proof of Divine Intervention in Jewish history. Here are the thirteen dates Faulstich chose for his special Patterns Matrix:

THIRTEEN SPECIAL DATES IN THE HISTORY OF ISRAEL, PER E. FAULSTICH

Number	Date	Adamic Day	Event
1	Oct. 9, 1462 B.C.E.	927548	Burning Bush Exod. 3:1–4:17
2	Mar. 26, 1461 B.C.E.	927717	Exodus Passover Exod. 12:1–28
3	May 28, 1461 B.C.E.	927779	Ten Commandments Exod. 19–24
4	July 16, 1461 B.C.E.	927828	Golden Calf Exod. 32
5	Apr. 1, 1460 B.C.E.	928087	Tabernacle Dedication Exod. 40–Lev. 8FF
6	July 29, 1422 B.C.E.	942087	Aaron died Num. 33:38
7	Jan. 22, 1421 B.C.E.	942263	Law read Deut. 1:1–5:1
8	Apr. 6, 30 C.E.	1471938	Pesach Yeshua died
9	May 25, 30 C.E.	1471987	Shavuot Abodah Zara 8b, Gen. 49:9–12
10	Aug. 2, 70 C.E.	1486666	Temple destroyed 1 Kings 9: 1–9
11	Sept. 6, 70 C.E.	1486702	People sold to Egypt
12	Oct. 18, 1946	2171938	Ten Germans hung at Nuremberg
13	May 14, 1948	2172512	Israeli Declaration of Independence

And here is the corresponding matrix of weeks. Each entry is the differences between two of the dates, in weeks. For example, the number of weeks from Date #7, the Reading of the Law, and Date #11, the People sold to Egypt, is $(1486702—942263)/7 = 77777$ weeks.

SABBATH (7'S) PATTERN MATRIX FOR FAULSTICH'S SPECIAL SET OF THIRTEEN DATES FROM ISRAEL'S HISTORY

	1	2	3	4	5	6	7	8	9	10	11	12
1												
2	24											
3	33	9										
4	40	16	7									
5	77	53	44	37								
6	2077	2053	2044	2037	2000							
7	2102	2078	2069	2062	2025	25						
8	77770	77746	77737	77730	77693	75693	75668					
9	77777	77753	77744	77737	77700	75700	75675	7				
10	79874	79850	79841	79834	79797	77797	77772	2104	2097			
11	79879	79855	79846	79839	79802	77802	77777	2109	2102	5		
12	177770	177746	177737	177730	177693	175693	175668	100000	99993	97896	97891	
13	177852	177828	177819	177812	177775	175775	175750	100082	100075	97978	97973	82
#	1	2	3	4	5	6	7	8	9	10	11	12

There certainly are a lot of sevens in Faulstich's collection of numbers. A graph of the distribution of the digits 0–9 in this collection appears below.

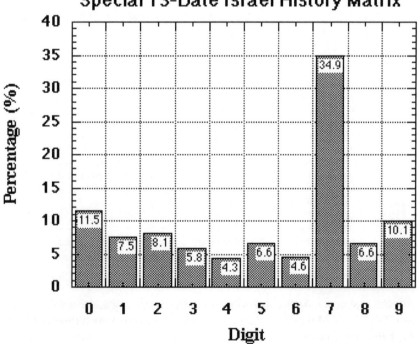

Percentages of Digits in Faulstich's Special 13-Date Israel History Matrix

Digit — Percentage (%):
0: 11.5, 1: 7.5, 2: 8.1, 3: 5.8, 4: 4.3, 5: 6.6, 6: 4.6, 7: 34.9, 8: 6.6, 9: 10.1

The large percentage of sevens is indeed highly improbable in a *random* collection of numbers. Of course, Faulstich's collection of dates is anything *but* random. However, his unusual result is far simpler to comprehend than the arcane Bible Code methods, and also truly surprising. A "chi-squared" calculation (a routine statistical test) performed by Faulstich's colleague Dr. Curt Wagner, a physicist, produced a huge value of 254 for chi-squared, and a corresponding infinitesimal probability of 6×10^{-66}—a number so small that 65 zeroes lie between the decimal point on the left, and the first significant digit (6) on the right.

Wagner also has done a binomial probability calculation for subsets of the collection of seventy-eight-week differences to have one, two, or more 7s. For example, Faulstich's matrix has fifty-five occurrences of one-or-more-sevens, with a probability of 8.9×10^{-8}.

I have confirmed these calculations, and the small probabilities are genuine (although the chi-squared estimates do look suspicious). Faulstich's collection of numbers indeed does possess anomalous properties. And that's why I became interested in the Sabbath Patterns. Were these anomalies only possible with dates from Israel, as derived by Faulstich, or could the patterns also be found in mundane histories?

I had a long and detailed letter exchange with Mr. Faulstich. With his permission, the entire exchange is posted at the Web site for New Mexicans for Science and Reason (http://www.nmsr.org/sabbaths.htm). It was a fascinating exchange. During this correspondence, Faulstich demonstrated every single one of the hallmarks of the Pseudoscientific Apologist.

From the first, I suspected that Faulstich's incredible results were due either to judicious selection of a few of many available dates, or to (perhaps unintentional) adjustments to the date calculations, changing certain events to better pattern-generating dates.

Accordingly, just three days into our correspondence I asked Faulstich the following:

(1) How were the thirteen "key events" on the "mileage chart" (Burning Bush, Exodus Passover, etc.) chosen? WHO DID THE CHOOSING OF THESE KEY EVENTS?
(2) How were the astronomical dates derived for the thirteen key events (and or others studied). WHO DID THE CALCULATIONS?
(3) Most importantly, who developed the matrix of weeks for the thirteen key events? Did this person have ANY SAY in what the key events and/or their assigned dates were?

Faulstich's answers to these questions were often confusing and evasive. At one point, Faulstich said that "we" had shown dates crucial to Jewish theology, and added that the loss of the second Temple and the modern Return of Israel events were selected *because they were found to fit the patterns.* Later, he would say that the key dates were derived *first,* with the help of colleagues Oliver Blosser, Ph.D., and programmer Mark Ness *before* looking for patterns with the computer, and that the dates were not changed one year. When I asked if he could say that the dates were not changed by one *day,* Faulstich referred to a discussion of the anomalous sevens, and simply said that, after looking at the data, what did I think? (In other words, he dodged the question.)

The answers to the question "Did the person developing the matrix also help choose the dates?" were particularly frustrating. At one point, Faulstich reacted to this direct query by acting as if it referred to the number of weeks differences in his special Matrix, and why he chose to display all seventy-eight entries, omitting none. Later, he stated bluntly that once the patterns were obvious, he felt compelled to study *all* of the important dates from Jewish history for their Sabbath Patterns.

I decided to accept Faulstich's dates at face value, and not assume that he was tweaking them in any way to achieve his spectacular patterns. I had neither the time nor inclination to delve into his detailed historical and astronomical analyses, other than to note that he admitted huge discrepancies between his and other chronologies, some over a century, which he dismissed as the result of a "cover-up" by the Great Sages for mysterious purposes.

Instead, I assumed the dates to be valid, and looked at the question of obtaining patterns by selecting carefully from a pool of valid dates. I told him it shouldn't be hard to find a set of dates from mundane American history that could match his compelling patterns. He answered "Sure," and then challenged me to find (1) a prediction that the chronology of a specific nation was controlled by God, and then (2) a set of testable dates that prove it. I replied that the first part, finding the prediction, was not what I had offered to do. Faulstich backed down on this part of the challenge to make it "easy" for me.

My attention turned to the problem of obtaining patterns of sevens in U.S. history. I took the THISDATE program written by New Mexican colleague Harry Murphy, which lists several key events for each day of the year, and selected about 315 key American history events for analysis. I developed a program that could evaluate the percentages of sevens in a weeks matrix for thirteen selected dates at the rate of 1,400 sets per second, or five million sets per hour. But at this rate, the analysis of the HUGE number of sequences of thirteen drawn from the pool of 315 dates would have taken hundreds of billions of years. I reduced the pool of dates by throwing out those that didn't produce any sevens with any other dates, leaving 138 dates to work with. But even that smaller number would have taken thirteen million years to analyze!

I didn't even have decades, as Faulstich and colleagues did when they performed their laborious studies. I wanted a solution in just days. So, I turned to evolutionary theory. Faulstich had been quoting several creationists in support of a young earth, and I thought it was fitting to turn genetic algorithms loose on his theories. An initial group of one thousand sets of thirteen dates was chosen randomly from the 138 dates. Those sets of thirteen having more sevens than others were allowed to "breed," and their progeny became the next generation; occasional mutations (a simple swapping of dates) were thrown in also. Each generation took less than a second to analyze. In just a few minutes, I had found sequences with over 34 percent sevens, about as good as Faulstich's matrix. Overnight, I achieved a stunning 39 percent of sevens.

Then came the fun part—cracking open the list of dates to see which significant dates from American history were responsible for my amazing patterns matrix. Here they are:

THIRTEEN SPECIAL DATES IN THE HISTORY OF THE UNITED STATES OF AMERICA, PER D. THOMAS

Number	Date	Julian Day	Event
1	Dec. 16, 1811	2382863	1st major New Madrid earthquake (Mag. 7.5)
2	Jan. 23, 1812	2382901	2nd major New Madrid earthquake (Mag. 7.3)
3	Feb. 7, 1812	2382916	3rd major New Madrid earthquake (Mag. 7.8)
4	June 18, 1812	2383048	U.S. declared war on Great Britain
5	Aug. 16, 1812	2383107	British captured Detroit
6	Sept. 10, 1813	2383497	The Battle of Lake Erie; Commodore Perry
7	Oct. 16, 1946	2432110	Nazi war criminals hanged in Nuremberg
8	May 1, 1960	2437056	Gary Powers, U-2 plane shot down over USSR
9	Jan. 3, 1961	2437303	U.S. breaks relations with Cuba
10	Apr. 12, 1961	2437402	Yuri Gargarin; first manned orbital flight
11	Apr. 17, 1961	2437407	The Bay of Pigs invasion of Cuba
12	May 5, 1961	2437425	Alan Shepard; first U.S. manned space flight
13	Oct. 1, 1962	2437939	James Meredith; 1st black student at U. of Miss.

(Note: Julian Day = Adamic day + 260174)

I was extremely pleased with the dates that turned up. They were all quite important events, and it was a stroke of luck to get all three New Madrid earthquakes included. When I presented these dates to Faulstich, I did not explain how I derived them, but rather presented them as being chosen for their significance, just as he presents his. Thus, I explained the inclusion of the New Madrid earthquakes as "perhaps embodying the hand of G_D himself moving across the land to awaken the new Nation to its destiny." I did this because I wanted Faulstich to focus on my statistics, and not on how I had obtained my dates. However, we both probably used similar methods in the end. While I analyzed thousands of sets at a time with the computer for a few hours, Faulstich probably analyzed one or a few sequences by hand (or with some computer assistance) over a period of *decades*. Either way, we both achieved the same result—a few dates that have a lot of sevens in the differences in weeks.

Here is my matrix of weeks with the amazing patterns of sevens. Each entry is the differences between two of the dates, in weeks. For example, the number of weeks from Date #7, Nuremberg hangings, and Date #11, the Bay of Pigs, is (2437407—2432110)/7 = 757 weeks.

SABBATH (7'S) PATTERN FOR THOMAS'S SPECIAL SET OF THIRTEEN DATES FROM U.S. HISTORY

	1	2	3	4	5	6	7	8	9	10	11	12
1												
2	5											
3	8	2										
4	26	21	19									
5	35	29	27	8								
6	91	85	83	64	56							
7	7035	7030	7028	7009	7000	6945						
8	7742	7736	7734	7715	7707	7651	707					
9	7777	7772	7770	7751	7742	7687	742	35				
10	7791	7786	7784	7765	7756	7701	756	49	14			
11	7792	7787	7784	7766	7757	7701	757	50	15	1		
12	7795	7789	7787	7768	7760	7704	759	53	17	3	3	
13	7868	7863	7860	7842	7833	7777	833	126	91	77	76	73
#	1	2	3	4	5	6	7	8	9	10	11	12

There certainly are a lot of sevens in my collection of numbers, too! A graph of the distribution of the digits 0–9 in this collection appears below.

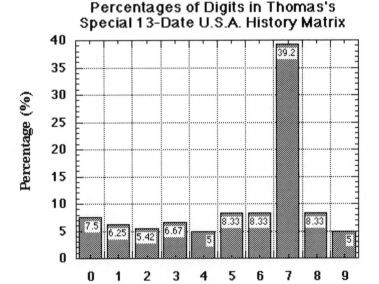

Percentages of Digits in Thomas's Special 13-Date U.S.A. History Matrix

By the only measure that can be shown visually, percentage of sevens, my mundane American history outperforms Faulstich's by 4 percent! My chi-squared calculation came out at 231, which is still huge by all standards, and has a correspondingly small probability (using Faulstich's methods) of 4×10^{-60}. My probability for the number of weeks with one or more sevens turned out larger than Faulstich's, but when I used a more reasonable estimate of the probabilities, by calculating the maximum week difference (instead of just assuming it to be 199999, as does Faulstich), then my probability for one or more sevens fell to 4×10^{-8}, less than half of Faulstich's corresponding value. Other statistics went both ways, but both sets contained very small probabilities!

After I sent him my matrix, Faulstich immediately dismissed my results, claiming that the *World Book Encyclopedia* listed 120 events, and only one of mine was included there. I responded that this was the first I heard the challenge was to be limited to dates from the *World Book Encyclopedia*.

His main challenge to my mundane matrix was that there was "no question" that my statistics did not match his. I eventually realized that Faulstich apparently doesn't comprehend small numbers. Instead of considering 10^{-60} and 10^{-66} as both being incredibly small numbers, for example, Faulstich only sees that one is slightly larger than the other, and therefore considers his smaller number to be "superior." I tried to explain that both of these numbers are really small—by comparison, the chances of winning the Powerball lottery with a single $1.00 ticket are vastly larger, at a level of around 10^{-8}. Faulstich never displayed appreciation of these considerations, and further, never acknowledged that my matrix has a higher percentage of sevens.

I asked Faulstich if he had other, larger matrices of dates with the Patterns. He never responded to this query, but his colleague Curt Wagner eventually did. Unlike Faulstich, Wagner did appear to understand my questions, and responded to them as best he could. Wagner supplied me with the statistics for patterns when Faulstich's thirteen original dates were combined with eleven new ones, listed below.

ELEVEN NEW SPECIAL DATES IN THE HISTORY OF ISRAEL, FOR TWENTY-FOUR-DATE MATRIX (PER FAULSTICH)

Number	Date	Adamic Day	Event
1	Oct. 6, 1460 B.C.E.	928276	Moses preps people/Day of Atonement
2	Nov. 24, 1460 B.C.E.	928325	12 leaders return from reconnoiter
3	Feb. 4, 1421 B.C.E.	942276	Moses dies
4	Mar. 24, 1421 B.C.E.	942325	Joshua sends 2 spies
5	July 5, 1950	2173294	Law of Return passed
6	June 7, 1967	2179475	Israeli army takes Old City/Temple Mount
7	Oct. 6, 1973	2181788	Yom Kippur War
8	Mar. 26, 1979	2183785	Peace treaty/Egypt
9	Sept. 13, 1993	2189070	PLO Declaration principles
10	May 4, 1994	2189303	Israeli/PLO peace accord
11	Oct. 26, 1994	2189478	Jordan Peace Treaty

Faulstich's twenty-four-date matrix (13 + 11) has a mere 23.66 percent sevens, but a very small chi-squared probability of 10^{-105}. While Wagner says the large twenty-four-date matrix still shows an overabundance of sevens, Faulstich contends the larger probabilities of some of the statistics show the modern peace treaties are not inspired by God.

I looked at larger matrices for American history, and developed another genetic algorithm, this time retaining my thirteen original dates, and selecting for fourteen new ones, for a matrix size of 27 (= 13 + 14). Here are the dates I found:

FOURTEEN NEW SPECIAL DATES IN THE HISTORY OF THE UNITED STATES, FOR TWENTY-SEVEN-DATE MATRIX (PER THOMAS)

Number	Date	Julian Day	Event
1	Dec. 21, 1620	2313108	Pilgrims land
2	Aug. 24, 1814	2383845	White House burns
3	Sept. 11, 1814	2383863	Battle of Lake Champlain
4	Sept. 13, 1814	2383865	Ft. McHenry; Star-Spangled Banner
5	Dec. 24, 1814	2383967	Treaty of Ghent, War of 1812 ends
6	Feb. 22, 1819	2385488	Florida purchase
7	Oct. 26, 1825	2387926	Erie Canal opens
8	Apr. 4, 1949	2433011	NATO formed
9	June 27, 1950	2433460	Truman orders U.S. to Korea
10	Oct. 31, 1952	2434317	1st H-bomb at Eniwetok Atoll
11	Dec. 1, 1955	2435443	Rosa Parks/bus ride/civil rights
12	June 12, 1963	2438193	Medgar Evers killed
13	Aug. 28, 1963	2438270	Martin Luther King Jr./"I have a dream"
14	Nov. 22, 1963	2438356	JFK assassinated

My twenty-seven-date matrix had 24.98 percent sevens, better even than Faulstich's twenty-four-date pattern; my chi-squared probability was a mere 10^{-86}, not quite as small as Faulstich's 10^{-105}, but very small all the same. For some statistics, such as one-or-more-sevens using real maximum week differences, I got results a billion times better than Faulstich's. At least he didn't respond by saying the Pilgrims' landing and the Kennedy assassination were not important events!

After I had sent him my mundane histories, Faulstich changed his demeanor considerably. No longer boastful that I would learn a lot from this, as would he, Faulstich instead broke off the entire discussion. After warning me not to mock God, and not to help God's enemies, he found a flimsy pretext for ending our correspondence—the fact that I couldn't find a Web page mentioned by Wagner (because the address Wagner provided was incorrect), and then later was able to find the page on my own. Faulstich said he could not deal with such silliness, and warned Wagner not to deal with fools and idiots. I tried to point out that I had met the conditions of the challenge, and had furthermore pointed out several errors in Faulstich's Web site. One error was that he missed the date for the hanging of war criminals at Nuremberg by two days, claiming it was on October 18, 1946, when in fact the date was October 16, 1946. Another error involved the omission of the binomial coefficients in some of the calculations, resulting in errors of several tens of orders of magnitude. Curt Wagner acknowledged this error, and showed me where it had been corrected. But Faulstich, abandoning his earlier confident attitude, cut off all communication.

After our two-month-long discussion ended in August of 2000, I came across a curious observation that should complete the job of assigning Sabbath Patterns to the junk heap of discarded apologetic methods. I had noted previously that Faulstich had mentioned several key dates in Israel's history that had somehow not made it into his special thirteen-date Pattern Matrix. I scoured his Web sites for such dates, and finally found a total of thirteen new dates—four from his twenty-four-date matrix, and nine others. These dates are all calculated by Faulstich, so he cannot argue about the chronology. Several of these dates are very significant, and were used by Faulstich to show patterns in days as well as weeks. Here are the additional dates I gathered to make a *new* matrix for Israel's history.

THIRTEEN NOT-SO-SPECIAL DATES IN THE HISTORY OF ISRAEL, PER E. FAULSTICH

Number	Adamic Day #	Event
1	605259	Noah's rainbow
2	770666	Jacob is born
3	770707	Rachel is purified
4	773377	Solar eclipse for Jacob at age 7
5	927777	Moses returned to Sinai
6	928276	Moses preps people/Day of Atonement
7	928325	12 leaders return from reconnoiter
8	942276	Moses dies
9	942325	Joshua sends 2 spies
10	942350	Joshua's long day
11	1246700	Temple is destroyed
12	1470666	Pilate comes to Jerusalem in C.E. 26
13	1470777	Spirit descends on Yeshua

I performed this last test just to check one more time on the compelling patterns of Sabbaths in biblical history. If these new dates performed as well as the other thirteen, I might have been at least a little impressed. But even I was shocked at how mundane the results turned out to be—a mere *11.3 percent of sevens*. The Patterns of Sevens had vanished *completely*! This experiment reinforced my view that the art of Sabbath Patterns is all in the selection of a few key dates from a fixed pool of moderate size (as small as a hundred or so).

As long as there are believers, and as long as science remains successful, there will be apologists who will be standing ready to misuse science in the defense of their faith. The accounts presented here are just some recent examples.

DAVE THOMAS is a physicist and mathematician employed at a small high-tech testing firm in Albuquerque, New Mexico. He is president of the science group New Mexicans for Science and Reason (http://www.nmsr.org/), and also is a Fellow of CSICOP. He has published several articles in the *Skeptical Inquirer* on the Roswell and Aztec UFO incidents, as well as the Bible Code. He wrote a cover article on nonreversing and other strange mirrors for the December 1980 *Scientific American*. Thomas has appeared on several local television shows, as well as national programs (*Fox News Tonight*) and internationally (*Good Morning Canada* and TV Asahi in Japan).

XII

FROM SKEPTICISM TO HUMANISM

35

IN RETROSPECT
From Skeptic to Humanist

ROBERT A. BAKER

Like other members of the human race I exist because of a set of concatenated and fortuitous natural circumstances over which I had no control. If one considers this fortunate I was also lucky in numerous other ways. First, though uneducated (no one in my great-grandparents' families was literate) my parents were both bright and liberal. They were also poor and were kind enough not to saddle me with any political, social, religious, or economic baggage. They encouraged me to read, think, and get an education. They also, inadvertently, started me on the skeptical path by taking me at an early age to the local First Baptist Church where the new minister—one Percy Walker—a kind, gentle, soft-spoken man turned into a fiery-faced, screaming maniac every time he took the pulpit. My parents and I would gape in awe at this amazing personality transformation. When I asked my father what was wrong with the reverend, he smiled and said, "Religion makes some people crazy."

My father also had a good friend who was a professional magician, Paul Stadleman, stage-named Sandow. Paul was not only a master of "close-up" magic but he was also a skilled ventroliquist. On one of his visits to our hometown a local reporter told Paul about an alleged "haunted cave" on the edge of town. Sandow and the reporter decided to investigate this haunt—supposedly of the notorious and ubiquitous Belle Witch—by spending several nights in this cavern from which passersby, on occasion, would hear unearthly moans and groans. Equipped with sleeping gear, lanterns, and the courage of curiosity, on the third evening of their vigil they were aroused in the middle of the night by a series of whistling howls from deep within the cavern. Chasing down the sound they found it was issuing from the cave's ceiling along with a stream of cold air. Tracing the airstream to the surface above, the two ghostbusters found a large boulder with a crack down its middle and a hole in the ground beneath. Whenever the wind blew from the northeast the naturally formed pipe organ whistled and moaned and groaned. Filling the crack with mud and leaves ended the reign of the town's Belle Witch forever.

This event convinced me there were no such things as ghosts, demons, and all their kin—only frightened and credulous people. Subsequent events, including a four-year overseas stint as an Army Air Force enlisted man serving in the African-Mediterranean-Europe campaign during WWII and reading hundreds of books from every possible genre—particularly philosophy and psychology—broadened and deepened my amazement at human behavior and human gullibility. Although I had completed two years of college before the war, I had never had a formal course in psychology. After reading an introductory text in the subject while stationed in Algiers, I resolved that the only thing that could save man from himself was a fully developed science of human behavior. Then and there I decided psychology was going to be my career.

At war's end I returned to Kentucky, finished a bachelor's and a master's degree, and went to Stanford for a Ph.D. in the field. I quickly learned just how little the psychological profession knew about major problems of human beings. I was also distressed to find that few psychologists were working on any human problem of great human significance. Endless petty theoretical arguments and thousands of meaningless minor research papers using rats, mice, dogs, cats, pigeons, and other nonhuman creatures filled the professional journals and cast little or no light whatsoever on human motives, drives, emotions, mental illnesses, aggressiveness, and evil. In 1962 Freeman and Marks published a psychological classic: "The Behavior of the Psychologist at a Choice Point" (*American Scientist* 50, no. 4 [December 1962]: 538–47). This paper revealed a perfect negative correlation between the size and importance of the problem to human welfare and the amount of psychological research devoted to such issues. Thirty-eight years later this correlation still holds.

Most of the famous men and psychological luminaries in the field during the fifties, sixties, and seventies had little or nothing to say about the most important problems facing modern humans. Antiscientific Freudian beliefs and radical behaviorist exaggerations dominated the scene. My disgust and disillusionment was such that I was ready to abandon the profession and choose another career field. Had it not been for Abe Maslow and his new "humanistic" psychology I would have long been gone. Maslow's philosophical stance seemed to me to offer an approach to a psychology that not only would study important human problems but also was deeply devoted to increasing human happiness and welfare.

Following completion of my academic training I worked for three years with the air force on air defense problems during the Cold War. Then I spent sixteen years doing military training research for the U.S. armor and infantry branches. During these twenty years, however, my interest in humanistic and anomalistic psychology never wavered and I managed to spend some of my spare time ghost busting, dehaunting houses, and working as an assistant in mental hospitals. On the anomalistic front one of my most memorable encounters was with a young matron in a small town near Fort Knox who was haunted by the ghost of a golden-haired three-year-old girl. After talking with her and her husband I quickly learned that she was the only one who ever saw or heard the child. Moreover, I learned that she and her spouse wanted children desperately but had no luck. I urged them both to consider adoption and as soon as they took these steps the three-year-old spirit disappeared forever.

While still at Fort Knox my research in human decision making led me to acquire and read Paul Kurtz's *Decision and the Condition of Man* (Dell, 1968) as well as his work in humanistic ethics and the *Humanist*. Kurtz's humanist principles, enunciated years ago, are still relevant and inspirational. Also my first encounter with "hypnosis" came while doing research on maximizing soldiers' alertness during guard duty. Having heard so much about its wonders, I brought in a hypnotic expert—Dr. Frank A. Pattie—to hypnotize the experimental soldier subjects and implant the suggestion they would find staying alert easy and guard duty exciting. When Pattie approached one of the soldiers he was so terrified that Pattie was helpless. Taking the GI aside and calming him down the soldier said his mother told him that "hypnosis" was the work of the devil and that while "hypnotized" the devil would steal his soul. I sent him back to the barracks with assurances that his soul was safe. Needless to say, the "hypnosis" suggestions failed to work on the soldiers but the experiment did arouse my curiosity about the "hypnosis" business.

Years later after I joined the University of Kentucky faculty and began teaching humanistic psychology I encountered "hypnosis" again. In the early seventies the American Psychological Association wrote a number of their members asking them to help fight the high levels of stress plaguing the American population. Agreeing with their stance and having read Jacobson's classic *You Must Relax* (University of Chicago, 1957) years before, I decided to teach Jacobson's technique to all the students in my humanistic classes. Each semester—two semesters a year—I taught two sections of eighty students each to systematically tense for fifteen to twenty seconds and then relax every one of the body's major muscle groups. Next, after all of the muscles were tensed simultaneously for twenty to twenty-five seconds they then let go and sank down onto the carpeted floor of the classroom. Once they were physically relaxed I then mentally relaxed them by taking them on a suggested fantasy trip to a sunny Florida beach. Without exception, each and every student participated fully in and were overjoyed by the experience. Many students, troubled by insomnia, were never troubled again after practicing and using this relaxation technique.

After doing this for a year or so it suddenly occurred to me that I was inadvertently *hypnotizing* all of these students. Could it be that that's all "hypnosis" is—nothing more than relaxation, suggestion, and the turning on of one's imagination? This insight led me to a systematic ten-year program of research into the ins and outs of so-called hypnosis. During this decade I looked at hypnosis and memory, past-lives regression, future-lives progression, the effects of emotion on hypnotic recall, the influence of suggestion on observation, accuracy of recall, and eyewitness testimony. This work culminated in the book *They Call It Hypnosis* (Prometheus Books, 1990) that was an attempt to demystify the hypnotic process and rid it of all the silly superstitions surrounding this natural human response to authoritarian requests, relaxation, and suggestion.

The most significant event in my skeptical career after moving to the University of Kentucky was my discovery that I was not alone in my interests in ghosts and the paranormal. At this time Joe Nickell was completing his doctoral work in the English department and we joined forces immediately. Along with mutual friends we formed the Kentucky Association of Science Educators and Skeptics (KASES) and did our best to improve rational thinking in our state during the 1990s. In 1992 Joe and I published *Missing Pieces* (Prometheus Books), which we hoped would serve as a do-it-yourself guidebook for would-be skeptical investigators.

My work with ghosts, hypnosis, memory, and suggestion quickly led to invitations to speak and lecture on these topics—especially on radio talk shows. On such audience call-in shows I was soon intrigued by the large number of individuals who reported waking in the middle of the night paralyzed; unable to move; seeing ghosts, demons, and dead people; and who were also convinced they were awake and not dreaming. Research in the medical library quickly led to my discovery of the universal phenomenon of "waking dreams." Such dreams are usually accompanied by hypnogogic and hypnopompic hallucinations and encounters with ghosts, demons, witches, and old hags as well as aliens and spaceships.

Recognition of the universality of these waking dreams as well as the vagaries and anomalies of human memory led to my publishing *Hidden Memories* (Prometheus Books) in 1992. Since many of my psychologist friends were clinicians and were struggling daily with the trials and tribulations of the emotionally disturbed and since I had had my own personal experiences working in Kentucky penal institutions as well as our state mental hospitals, I was very sympathetic with their professional aims and problems. Recognizing that, in most cases, the psychiatrists' ever-present pills only cover up, narcotize, and delay the patient's ultimate recovery and "cure" from his emotional trauma, I published *Mind Games* (Prometheus) in 1997 hoping it would serve as a "wake-up call" to the American public. Unfortunately, this alarm never went off, or if it did, it fell on unhearing and unheeding ears. Today the public is not only still asleep but snoring. The psychiatric roller coaster rolls merrily on and nothing has been done in the last few years to curb or attenuate the power and influence of the "therapeutic state"—a state which refuses to see and acknowledge that nearly all mental disorders are emotional, i.e., psychological disorders not biological or brain disorders. Pill popping is now the nation's most popular and pervasive pastime. Which is more dangerous and deadly to the public welfare— the street drugs, i.e., pot, ecstasy, or crack, or the prescribed drugs, i.e., Prozac, Ritalin, or Zoloft—is moot.

My work with memory and hypnosis also led to an agreement to compile and edit Prometheus's 1998 book *Child Sexual Abuse and False Memory Syndrome* and to contribute several papers to *The UFO Invasion* (Prometheus, 1999) and Gordon Stein's *The Encyclopedia of the Paranormal* (Prometheus, 1996). Over the past decade I have also had the pleasure of reviewing for the *Skeptical Inquirer* a large number of books—both good and bad—that are of interest to a skeptical audience. On the good side a few of the truly outstanding have been: Susan Blackmore's *In Search of the Light* (Prometheus, 1996); Nathan and Snedeker's *Satan's Silence* (Basic Books, 1995); Nicholas Spanos's *Multiple Identities and False Memories* (APA, 1996); Joe Nickell's *Entities* (Prometheus, 1995) and his edited volume *Psychic Sleuths* (Prometheus, 1994), to name but a few. I have also highly enjoyed contributing essays to *Skeptical Briefs* as well as contributing essays and columns to our newsletter, *KASES FILE*, which we have published bimonthly for the past fifteen years.

Reviewing this work leaves me with mixed emotions, i.e., sadness and joy. Sadness that my educational efforts have fallen so dismally short of my lofty aims and gladness that a few of my readers at least have had a few laughs and glimpses at what makes some of us human beings tick. Looked at objectively, like most so-called educators I find it hard to believe that my individual efforts have had any significant or lasting impact on the thoughts or actions of society at large. I can find only a little consolation in the fact that I was, after all, on "the right side."

As for my skeptical efforts I find myself in strong agreement with that noted anthropologist and skeptic Dr. James Lett who, agreeing with Paul Kurtz's discovery of "the transcendental temptation," noted:

> By their nature, human beings are meaning-seeking animals, but the sad conclusion of cross-cultural anthropological research is that most individual humans, and all human cultures, are content with the *illusion* of meaning.

For most people, it matters not, apparently, whether their explanations are true or false; it only matters that they are emotionally satisfying. For millions of Americans, paranormal beliefs fulfill that criterion ("The Persistent Popularity of the Paranormal," *Skeptical Inquirer* [Summer 1992]: 381–88). Lett also suggests that the only way to reduce the pervasiveness of paranormal beliefs is to reduce personal anxiety, revamp the media, reform education, and revise the culture's worldview. It is highly unlikely that we can succeed with any one of these—much less all four.

Though I sincerely agree with Lett, I am left with an itch unscratched: I want him to be wrong and I want skeptical humanism to win over the masses. Yes, the enormity of the task is paralyzing. As long as the human race is plagued by war, fear, religion, and religious intolerance, greed, hatred, cruelty, ignorance, and despair, we have no victories to proclaim and nothing to celebrate. As a species our history is apalling: it is a long sorry record of bloodshed, savagery, and stupidity and raises serious questions about the message our species would be able to deliver to other intelligent beings we may encounter if we are ever to leave this planet and venture to the stars. What have we to be proud of as a race of intelligent beings? What is the "best face" that human beings have to show an intelligent alien race? What do we have and what have we done that would instill in them admiration, respect, or (at the greatest stretch of imagination) love? How could and would we bridge that enormous chasm of estrangement and otherness? How should we best bridge all of the vast, complex, natural, physical, and mental evolutionary differences we would be certain to encounter?

Though some thought should be given to such speculative conundrums, much greater thought should be focused on specifically how we can make our own species into the kind of human and humane creatures that future generations can be proud to be a part of. Is a humanistically grounded, science-centered, public education sufficient to turn the tide, given a hundred years or so? How, when, and where will we begin to teach the basics of humanism, i.e., neighborly love, brotherhood, sympathy and empathy, succorance and nuturance, pity and caring? Who shall teach and where and to whom shall we teach *how to be a worthy, happy, and successful human being*? Who will teach courses at the high school and college level in *the introduction to human physical, mental, emotional, and moral needs*? Who will train and inspire the teachers who will teach such basic human skills? Is there any educational group on the planet today who even believes that such things are needed or who also believes they are teachable and learnable skills?

Over the years as a professional psychologist I have been dismayed at the psychological profession's neglect of human emotions. Whether we like it or not human beings are *emotional* not *rational* animals. Every act—everything we think, do, or say—is driven by our emotional nature. Affect and feeling color every aspect of human behavior. In fact, human emotions are the dynamos that drive human development motivation, cognition, and action. If and when something goes awry in the process of human growth and development, and we lose our ability to feel and emote, the result is a psychopath—an inhuman monster. When we lose our emotional balance and control, the result is mental illness and we turn to the psychiatrist's pills to numb, blunt, and tranquilize our emotional states—our feelings of loss, loneliness, despair, depression (sadness), and our aching feelings of hopelessness and worthlessness. Emotional traumas in childhood, i.e., mistreatment or lack of love, can warp, shape, and twist our personalities, outlooks, attitudes, and behavior for the remainder of our lives. Emotional wounds within families, i.e., conflict between mothers and fathers and their offspring and relatives, can spawn hate, violence, and tragedies beyond rational comprehension. There is great truth in the statement: God *Is* Love. And this is a human not a religious contention. Emotion lies behind and motivates all art, music, literature, dance, the theater, painting, and sculpture, and science as well. Though scientists pride themselves on their pure unemotional powers of intellect uncontaminated by base emotion, they fail to realize that their very intellect is itself driven by affect and feeling. Without an emotional core they would be little more than programmed automatons or robots. To be without affect is to be inhuman.

We also owe a debt of thanks to the brilliant ex-psychotherapist Dr. Jeffry Masson and his collaborator Susan McCarthy who in their sorely neglected masterpiece *When Elephants Weep* (Delacorte Press, 1995) have saddled us all with inescapable guilt by showing that the lower animals also are, like us, emotional creatures as well.

Those who lock themselves in a nonfeeling state of being for fear of suffering emotional upsets are depriving themselves of their very basic nature. It is the emotional highs and lows, raptures and despairs, ecstasies and aches that make human life and human existence worthwhile. To deny oneself of these basic human experiences is to never have been alive.

When and where shall we begin to teach elementary, secondary, and higher educational courses in the growth and development of human emotions? Courses such as An Introduction to Human Physical, Mental, and Emotional Needs; How to Be Happy and Healthy (Though Human); Basics of the Human Community; Basics of Human Welfare; Human Needs and Necessities in an Age of Challenge; Human Aggression and Its Attenuation and Elimination; Ego-Based Conspiracies and Anticommunity Movements; Principles of Passion and Commitment; Basics of Human Loyalty, Trust, and Love; Internationalism and the World Community; Basics of Environmental Stewardship; The Human Side of Animals; and Animal Preservation and Welfare are the sort of curriculum that should be a fundamental part of every human being's education, if we can ever hope to see a truly better and humane society. To have a better society we must have better people; to get better people we must educate and train them to value and respect human life and human welfare and to work for these aims and goals on a worldwide basis. The stated goal of every government and the aim of every political party should be: *To pacify, protect, preserve, and humanize the planet Earth.* Should we, as a sane and civilized species, ask for anything less? Utopian? Idealistic? Unattainable? While this is not presently possible, should we hope and strive for anything less than the humanization of the planet and the implementation and actualization of the newest *Humanist Manifesto 2000*? The total defeat of the forces of fear, superstition, unreason, as well as political and social oppression should in my judgment be—even if it now is not— our long-range goal.

HOPE AND A NEW BEGINNING?

In the early 1990s a small number of behavioral scientists began the work pointed to but left unfinished by Maslow's humanistic psychology and they began to develop what they now call "positive psychology." Their aim is to shift psychology from a "disease model" to a "health model," i.e., from a focus on curing the sick and deficient to a positive and preventive approach that keeps people well and healthy. Their work is centered on the kinds of human experiences that motivate, inspire, and fulfill people's needs and desires. They are examining the kinds of environments and social institutions that create and sustain the best qualities in human beings. They are asking the questions: What, exactly, *is* the good life? and How can we develop better people and build a better world?

In 1999 one of the leaders of this new movement, Martin E. P. Seligman, arranged a series of cross-disciplinary meetings with other social scientists— sociologists, economists, political scientists, anthropologists, and communications experts—and urged them to focus their efforts on human well-being and those social systems that foster it. From these meetings in Mexico and the Caymans, Seligman and his team urged the development of a "taxonomy of the good life" in its classical sense of social and civic well-being and one that would include the positive human traits of creativity, friendship, responsibility, community spirit, generosity, perseverance, courage, empathy, humor, and caring for others. Seligman has already shown that people can learn to be more courageous and optimistic by practicing cognitive skills that include disputing the internal negative messages people send themselves. People also "get better" from accepting difficult and challenging activities and struggling against them. The University of Michigan's Barbara Frederickson's recent work on the effects of positive emotions has shown that these emotions open and strengthen our minds and help us think in new ways. The

University of Maryland's Lisa Aspinwall, UCLA's Shelley Taylor, and Brown University's Joachim Krueger are currently doing research that clearly shows the health-enhancing quality of human optimism as well as the fundamental importance of emotion in our physical and mental health.

Fortunately, the developmental psychologists are now turning their attention to the importance of sound emotional development in the mental well-being of infants. Stanley Greenspan and his collaborator T. Berry Brazelton in their recent books *Building Healthy Minds* (Persus Books, 1999) and *The Irreducible Needs of Children* (Persus Books, 2000) have blazed a trail by pointing out in step-by-step detail what parents need to do to promote optimal emotional growth and development and a happy and healthy human adult.

These are but a few of the baby steps these psychologists are now taking in this new "positive outlook" that is stimulating a great deal of psychological thinking. We can only hope that more and more of the current and future crop of behavioral scientists will join them. It is most encouraging, indeed, to note that the new, so-called evolutionary psychology places a major emphasis on altruism. Human beings, they tell us, are naturally cooperative creatures and high levels of altruism are one of the distinguishing features of our species, shared only by a few others. Altruism, it notes, is a variable feature of human societies which can be promoted or discouraged by institutions, cultural norms, or even widely promulgated theories. This "new" psychology is not only scientifically valid, it is also morally sound, and it firmly discourages pessimism about human nature.

This new positive outlook is also one that skeptical humanists should adopt if we hope to make our calling as attractive and appealing to the millions of ordinary men and women as the major religious denominations have been over the centuries. We need to recognize and, somehow or other, "satisfy" the emotional and spiritual hungers that drive people to the temples, churches, and synagogues. We need to remember and replicate Carl Sagan's approach to making the wonders and glories of the cosmos and the mysteries of the universe awe-inspiring to every man, woman, and child. We need to emphasize the glory, joy, and beauty of human beings and human nature at its finest and most admirable. We need to bring forth and honor humankind's greatest achievements in every area of human endeavor. We need humanist myths, heroes, and fables—perhaps even a humanist bible, one more inspirational than those other enduring religious treatises. We need to emphasize—perhaps even romanticize—human dedication, human devotion, human sacrifice to the glorification and betterment of the human species. We need humanistic ritual, dance, music, art, fellowship, and communion with nature and with each other. We need to stress the fellowship of humankind and to promote the comfort and security that comes from belonging to and being a part of something larger and better than our own egos, i.e., the human community.

A "successful" naturalistic humanism must provide hope, sympathy, inspiration for action, loyalty, devotion, caring, and comfort for loss and bereavement as well as hope and promise for a better and more satisfying future. An emotionally satisfying naturalistic humanism must also entertain, energize, and enlighten, as well as educate the children of future generations—if we ever hope to win the battle against stupidity, superstition, and the transcendental temptation. Finally, it must never appear to be elitist or arrogant, and the humanist and humanitarian message and its parables must be simple and clear enough to be accepted and understood by the average person.

Does what we secular humanists know and advocate today provide such emotional benefits or even aim at such psychological targets and goals? Until it does, humanism cannot and will not ever attract legions of dedicated followers. We cannot blame the emotionally hungry masses for eating out of the garbage cans of creationism, evangelism, channeling, and fundamentalism, when we fail to offer them better and more nutritious fare. Can the promise of suffering, self-sacrifice without compensation or reward, ego-extinction, and eternal nothingness compete with religion's promise of immortality, spiritual wealth, unification, and everlasting glory? If we are ever to be more persuasive we must dip deeper into the wellsprings of human feeling and sympathetic understanding and communicate the beauty, uniqueness, and joy of human life and its place in the natural universe. This is a mission that science can help us fulfill, and it is a mighty, not an almighty, mission.

Many secular humanists believe science alone can save us. Others doubt it and have seriously questioned "hard science's" ability to do anything of further benefit to the human condition. Probing deeper and further into the nature of matter and the outreaches of space seems to offer little hope and comfort to suffering people. A science *of* and *for* human beings and for their health and happiness and contentment is certainly desirable and it is the kind of science that no one calling him- or herself human should ever reject or deny. It is perhaps our last and only hope and possibly the surest way for human evolution to be given a chance to fulfill its potential.

The prodigious challenge outlined by Gerald Edelman in *Bright Air, Brilliant Fire* (Basic Books, 1992) merits our closest attention:

> How would humankind be affected by beliefs in a brain-based view of how we perceive and are made aware? What would be the result of accepting the idea that each individual's "spirit" is truly embodied; that it is precious *because* it is mortal and unpredictable in its creativity; that we must take a skeptical view of how much we can know; that understanding the psychic development of the young is crucial; that imagination and tolerance are linked; that we are at least all brothers and sisters at the level of evolutionary values; that while moral problems are universal, individual instances are necessarily solved, if at all, only by taking local history into account?

Can a persuasive morality be established under mortal conditions? This is one of the largest challenges of our time. (pp. 171–72)

The future will most likely be a struggle between science and tribalism. Those of us on science's side can and will win if we make our scientific technology more emotionally satisfying and fulfilling. As the brightest and the best of our cosmologists say, the universe is empty, aimless, cold, and lonely. It does, however, contain one little planet—one pale blue dot—with intelligent beings who have purposes, warmth, and hope. Because of their rarity, if for no other reason, these human beings should be respected and protected, treasured and saved. They should also and always be loved. As the poet said a long time ago, "We must love each other, or die." This is a truth our species must recognize now and never forget if we hope to survive and evolve into a truly humanistic morality.

ROBERT A. BAKER, Ph.D., worked at the MIT Lincoln Lab (1950–1952), did training research for the U. S. Army (1953–1968), and taught at the University of Kentucky (1969–1988) where he was chairman of the psychology department until his retirement. He is a Fellow of the American Psychological Association and a Fellow of CSICOP.

Dr. Baker has published over one hundred professional journal articles, as well as fifteen books. His best-known psychological books include: *They Call It Hypnosis* (Prometheus Books, 1990), *Hidden Memories: Voices and Visions from Within* (Prometheus Books, 1992), *Mind Games* (Prometheus Books, 1996), and *Child Sexual Abuse and False Memory Syndrome* (Prometheus Books, 1998). He coauthored with Joe Nickell *Missing Pieces: How to Investigate Ghosts, UFOs, Psychics, and Other Mysteries* (Prometheus Books, 1992). Dr. Baker is a regular contributor to *Skeptical Inquirer* and *Skeptical Briefs*.

INDEX

417